If Eight Hours Seem Too Few

SUNY Series on Women and Work
Joan Smith, Editor

If Eight Hours Seem Too Few

Mobilization of Women Workers in the Italian Rice Fields

Elda Gentili Zappi

State University of New York Press

Published by
State University of New York Press, Albany

Cover illustration of Angelo Morbelli's *In the Rice Fields* courtesy of the
Spring Creek Art Foundation, Inc., West Palm Beach, Florida, and used by
their permission.

For information, address State University of New York
Press, State University Plaza, Albany, N.Y., 12246

Production by E. Moore
Marketing by Bernadette LaManna

Library of Congress Cataloging-in-Publication Data

Zappi, Elda Gentili,
    If eight hours seem too few: mobilization of women workers in the
  Italian rice fields/Elda Gentili Zappi.
        p. cm.-(SUNY series on women and work)
    Includes bibliographical references.
    ISBN 0-7914-0481-1 (alk. paper).-ISBN 0-7914-0482-X (pbk.:
  alk. paper)
    1. Women rice workers-Italy-History. 2. Women in trade-unions
-Italy-History. 3. Socialism-Italy-History. I. Title.

  HD6073.R482I89 1991
  331.4'83318'0945-dc20
                                                              90-9581
                                                              CIP

10 9 8 7 6 5 4 3 2 1

To the Memory of Concezione and Maria.
To Eduardo, Veronica, Victoria, Carla, and Julia.

Contents

Acknowledgments

I wish to thank many persons who have contributed their criticism and comments to help me bring this book to completion. Edward R. Tannenbaum and Mary Nolan from New York University provided me with encouragement, support, and guidance during the research process. I also owe my great appreciation to Marion Miller (University of Illinois at Chicago Circle), Mary Gibson (John Jay College of Criminal Justice, City University of New York), Patrizia Dogliani (Università degli Studi di Modena and New York University), and Margherita Repetto-Alaia (Columbia University), who read an earlier draft of the manuscript. They raised sharp questions, made many suggestions, and provided me with insightful criticism.

Several individuals and institutions in Italy offered me their invaluable cooperation. I should like to thank Maria Pia Rinaldi Mariani (Archivio Centrale dello Stato, Rome), Giovanni Silengo (Archivio dello Stato di Novara), Carmine Ziccardi (Archivio di Stato di Pavia), Rosaldo Ordano (Biblioteca Civica, Vercelli), Wanda Aiazza (Vercelli), Francesca Fontana (Vercelli), and Piera Gaia (Vercelli) for their knowledge, advice, and goodwill. My thanks are also due to the staff of the Biblioteca Nazionale Centrale of Florence and the Biblioteca Civica of Novara.

I am also grateful to Nancy Erber, whose care of the manuscript became a real collaboration, and to the staff of the New York Public Library and the Interlibrary Loans Service at the Library of Herbert H. Lehman College, City University of New York.

My final thank you is to the members of my family for enduring the whole pursuit.

Introduction

The history of rice field weeders in northern Italy sheds light on a neglected aspect of class conflict in a region of expanding agriculture. Rice was one of the costliest crops in the country. From the end of the eighteenth century on, rice cultivation in the western section of the Po valley grew at an accelerated pace, absorbing increasing amounts of capital and bringing about major economic and social changes.

For forty days at the end of each spring, squads of weeders gathered in the rice fields to do their strenuous job. On the eve of World War I the squads were almost a hundred thousand strong. Weeders residing in the rice belt comprised only about 60 percent of the work force, the rest having to move in from neighboring regions.

The temporary but nevertheless hazardous nature of this occupation, the composition of its work force, its low degree of education, its poverty, its submission to the authority of husbands, brothers, employers, the police, the army, the church, the local and central government, and judges, were all elements defining weeders' lives. Had they always abided by the prescriptions dictated by society, their history, if it was ever written, would have been a celebration of their resiliency, resignation, and sacrifice for the sake of the most profitable cereal in Italy. But weeders began to assert themselves in the last two decades of the nineteenth century, demanding their own terms at the work place, according to their female consciousness. This dictated to them certain notions about needs, such as shorter working hours and a concern for health, justice, and fairness. Because they demanded change, they left a historical record punctuated by strikes, petitions, marches, and protests.

This historical record has some exceptional traits. One is particular to labor in Italy. Here, contrary to what happened in other European countries, the mobilization of agricultural workers preceded that of industrial workers. Masses of rural day laborers began engag-

ing in collective action in the 1880s, a good decade and a half before
Italy's industrial takeoff in 1897. The weeders' case is also remarkable
because by 1901 socialist organizers, despite a traditional reluctance
to organize women, tried to mobilize the substantial segment of
women farm workers in the rice belt. The weeders' response to organization was singular in that these groups of women who labored
together for a period of about six weeks a year acquired a degree of
solidarity, class consciousness, combativeness, and political awareness difficult to image for such a loose and unstable work force.

Setting the stage for the mobilization of the weeders, which
started in 1901, demands a historical perspective that takes into account both the capitalistic transformation of agriculture in the Po
valley and its repercussions on the economy and society, and Italy's
uneven industrial development. Italy was unable to absorb large sectors of the population left unemployed or underemployed as capitalist agriculture advanced in the countryside. The formation of a
female proletariat, contributing to production for very competitive
national and international markets, was an integral part of these processes. Workers' families in the rice belt relied on women's wages
earned during the weeding season for their subsistence, but agriculturalists controlled the labor market. They could easily find a reserve of squads of migratory women workers from other sections of
the Po valley and leave rebellious local weeders unemployed, or willing to accept lower wages or a longer workday.

The main focus of this book is precisely on the conditions under
which the mobilization of weeders took place and the specific forms
that this took as a consequence of conditions prevailing in pre–World
War I Italy. It concentrates upon the weeders and their problems as
workers and as women, and traces the imprints that gender left on
the mobilization of this working class. It takes into consideration the
role of the government, the Socialist Party, workers' and employers'
organizations, and the interaction among these institutions.

At the turn of the century, the liberal political climate in Italy
favored labor organization in general. This golden age of liberal democracy—the Giolittian era—bears the name of Giovanni Giolitti, the
statesman who, with few intervals, dominated the Italian political
scene between 1901 and 1914, appearing as the guarantor of basic
democratic rights. In 1901 the reformist wing of the Socialist Party,
under the leadership of Filippo Turati, held the majority. Turati saw
Giolitti's policies as helping to advance Italy on a gradual course
toward socialism, a course based on mass support and on government action in legislation that would improve the lot of the workers.

In his strategy of relying on the masses, the attempt at mobilizing weeders into farm workers' leagues, as their unions were called, played an important part.

That same year, party organizers fanned out through the rice belt to mobilize weeders. Here they had to harness the impulsive energy of the weeders who in previous years had risen up, staging protests and strikes to redress injustices. Socialists tried to channel this tendency to what they considered spontaneous revolt into organized, disciplined actions that would reinforce the party's program of coherent gradual reforms. Agrarian employers, both landowners and big leaseholders, resisted; they were ready to organize themselves as an interest group and to counterattack, to annul any gains that workers might win. They too counted on government help—in the form of the military, police, and legislative powers of the state—to maintain centuries-old privileges.

Weeders' protests erupted around very concrete issues. This makes it necessary to investigate the circumstances leading to those very demands in previous decades. The time of Italy's unification is an appropriate date to start this investigation. It ends in May 1915 with Italy's entrance into World War I. The armed conflict curtailed the scope of the weeders' struggle. Weeders tried to resist this limitation, for it presaged a hiatus in labor organizational efforts that was much more than a lull. It was rather the end of an era in Italian working-class history.

The weeders' protests resulted from an awareness that individuals and institutions responsible for bad working conditions, low wages, and unemployment interfered with their duty to earn decent wages and meet their families' and communities' needs. Their form of collective action responded to the way this female proletariat originated, and the values, interests, concerns, and expectations it sustained during its mobilization. Women hoped to redress the situation created by increasingly bad working conditions, unemployment, low wages, soaring prices, and employer resistance. Traditional objectives—the care of the family and community—therefore, moved weeders to deploy their resources to stage mass strikes and defy a social, economic, and political order with which they felt more and more in conflict.

Relations between weeders and the Socialist Party and its labor organizations need special attention. Weeders shared with several other categories of women workers in Europe and the United States their willingness to go on strike, but also their unwillingness to obey party and organizational rules, to form leagues, or to go to union meetings. Pressure from male members of their families to remain at home, and their household obligations, might have discouraged weeders, but there was also the feeling that neither the Socialist Party and the leagues saw their concerns as legitimate, nor did they address problems specific to their gender roles, their double burden, and their actions against employers. According to the party and organizers' directives, the weeders had to understand the need for social legislation that would benefit their cause, had to heed calls for discipline during strike actions, to learn the value of negotiation, and to restrain themselves from outbursts of protest. However, these directives never completely eliminated the weeders' tendency to immediate direct action. Weeders never gave up their autonomy and their prerogative to go on strike whenever they considered it the proper step to take under given circumstances.

Over time, weeders broadened their perspective, so that when Italy entered World War I, they saw themselves as workers fighting for peace and for the betterment of the working class as a whole. This study attempts to asses to what degree the weeders' fight for what they viewed as their social rights and obligations also raised their consciousness as women, as workers, as members of a community, and as participants in political change.

The book has eight chapters. The first two deal with rice growing, its economic, political, and social impact, and the way it molded the lives of women workers before the twentieth century. Chapter 2 also treats of the first weeders' strikes in the province of Bologna. Chapters 3–5, covering the period 1901–1906, focus on the first year of successful mobilization, 1901, the weeders' defeats thereafter, and their unprecedented labor action in 1906. Chapters 6 and 7 deal with their ongoing mobilization in the face of enormous difficulties posed by the severe financial crisis of 1907, the years of recession, a colonial war, and the growing challenge from conservative and nationalist circles to Giolitti's liberal course. It ends with Giolitti's resignation in 1914 and the outbreak of World War I. The final chapter looks at the changes that mobilization produced in the lives of weeders and how Italy's political and economic developments, legislation, educational system, scientific schools, cultural currents, precepts on the role of women in the family and society, and feminist thought affected the way these changes took place.

The conclusion assesses the weeders' accomplishments, thanks to their solidarity, in trying to improve life in their communities, and in indicting a political, economic, social, and gender system that relegated them to the role of passive onlookers of political events.

The Formation of a Female Labor Force in the Rice Fields

The Italian Rice Belt

The basin of the Po River is the most extensive in Italy. It consists of a broad plain that occupies a large portion of the northern part of the country. The 405 mile-long river has its source in Monte Viso in the west and its mouth in the Adriatic coast in the east.

The establishment of rice farming in the Po valley transformed its economy and society.[1] The investment of huge amounts of capital in this crop revolutionized agriculture and led to the formation of a mass of landless agricultural workers. The changes brought about in the life of the Po valley were enormous, and the years from the introduction of rice growing in the second half of the fifteenth century to the end of the 1800s provide the background from which the workers in the rice fields mobilized in the twentieth century.

Around 1450, farmers in the present province of Milan became the first to sow rice in western Lombardy. Here many generations had worked to level the plain, drain swamps, and regulate the flow of water. Land reclamation started in pre-Roman and Roman times, decayed with the fall of the Roman empire, and was resumed in the later Middle Ages. However, in the fifteenth century vast surfaces still remained under stagnant water; these otherwise disregarded, mar-

ginal tracts of estates were good for planting rice.[2] Rice farming then
spread west from the Milan region (Milanese) across the Ticino River,
one of the many Po tributaries, to Lomellina, which is part of the
Lombard province of Pavia, and to the present Piedmontese provinces of Vercelli and Novara.[3] In the nineteenth century, Lomellina,
Vercelli (Vercellese), and Novara (Novarese) became, and are still today, the principal rice-growing regions in Italy. At the turn of the
century the economic supremacy of the Italian rice belt was unsur-
passed in Europe, outstripping even Valencia, the major rice-growing
province in Spain.

Originally, only a few peasants went to the marshes, sometimes
by boat, to sow and reap "the treasure of the swamps"—a popular
name for rice used by sixteenth-century writers—but they deserted
the area for the rest of the season.[4] Conditions had changed by the
end of the fifteenth century. The search for profit motivated farmers
to grow rice not only in swampy soil, but also in the best irrigated
fields of their holdings, and it displaced other popular grains like
wheat. By 1550 the largest surfaces under rice cultivation in the
Milanese were irrigated fields, not marshes.[5]

The expansion of rice growing went hand in hand with land
improvement, canal construction, and the capitalistic transformation
of agriculture in the western section of the Po valley. Since the early
1400s capital investment had been significant in the duchy of Milan as
investors from the duchy and elsewhere had begun to rent the farms
of impoverished landowners who lacked the necessary means to
work their own land, particularly those belonging to members of the
old nobility and the church. A new class of capitalist farmers (*affittuari;* sing. *affittuario*) promoted this change. Encouraged by high agricultural prices and the increasing demand for food by the swelling
population of the cities in the fifteenth and sixteenth centuries, they
were the main agents behind rice promotion and agriculture in general in the Po valley.[6] They helped to consolidate scattered tracts and
thus erased some vestiges of the feudal order and also drained more
fens, dug more waterways, and reclaimed more arable land.[7]

The same developments took place west of the Ticino (in Vercelli, Novara, and Lomellina) in the seventeenth century.[8] Though
the canal network expanded at a slower rate there than in the
Milanese, it occurred in a larger scale[9] as the crop prospered. Early
censuses, which were unreliable in many ways, showed a rapid rate
of expansion interrupted by the economic slump of the first half of the
seventeenth century. But the recession, which lasted until 1650,

brought about changes that molded rice farming into a modern capitalistic enterprise.[10]

Rice farming concentrated in a process that involved three factors: (1) many small landholders who had grown rice in a broader region, including western Piedmont, abandoned rice cultivation, sometimes because their lands were not suitable for it; (2) some cultivators went bankrupt in hard times; (3) some stopped sowing rice when governments began to restrict the surface under rice cultivation. Capitalist farmers preferred larger tracts over small and middle-sized holdings, because it was more difficult to implement complex crop rotation and utilize the complicated hydraulic methods that rice growing required on the smaller tracts.[11] The few peasants who still tilled their own small holdings owned land either in poor, infertile regions or in low areas vulnerable to flooding, where artificial irrigation was impractical.[12] Rice farming gradually became the most advanced form of capitalist farming in the peninsula. Capitalist agriculture made inroads in other rural areas in northern and central Italy after unification, but even then the Mezzogiorno, or southern part, remained untouched.[13]

Rice growing also began to spread eastward from the Milanese along the Po valley down to the Adriatic coast in the sixteenth century. However, in this, the eastern section of the valley, farmers made no investment in land reclamation and instead sowed rice only in marshy ground. They were attracted by the possibility of easy rewards from limited efforts.[14] For the history of the weeders who are central to this study, the events that took place in the province of Bologna from the Napoleonic period to the end of the nineteenth century were crucial. They will be examined in chapter 2, p. 58. Here I will focus instead on the rice belt—that is, the Vercellese, the Novarese, and Lomellina.

About 1760 the market price of rice caught up with the price of wheat and then surpassed that of all grains. It held this position until the end of the nineteenth century.[15] The rate of profit from rice growing became twice as high as that from other cereals and only in the Milanese did rice growing retreat by 1800 to give way to wet meadows (*marcite*). These were pasture lands where farmers using a complicated technique could grow winter grass and thus double the yearly pasture yield.[16] Then, the area east of the Ticino, the Milanese, lost first place in rice farming to an area west of the river, for its productivity was enhanced by the addition of new canals. Land on the west bank of the river offered greater possibilities for more concentrated,

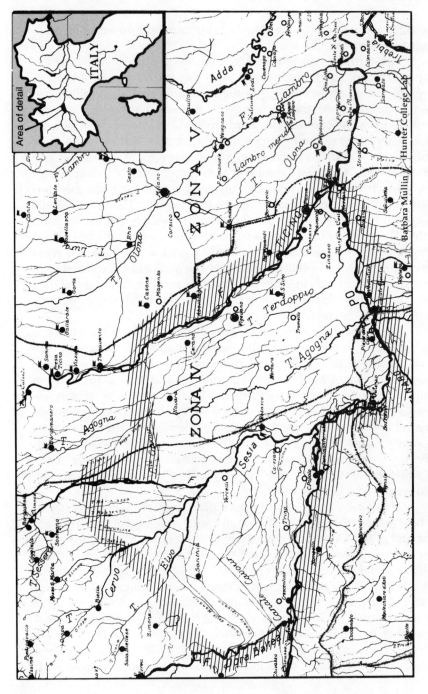

The Italian rice belt. (From the collections of the Geography and Map Division, Library of Congress.)

intensive farming.[17] This land produced higher yields so that after 1830 rice growing was firmly established in this almost monocultural region between the Ticino and the Dora Baltea rivers. The family of Camillo Cavour, the politician who brought about the unification of Italy in 1861, owned a rice farm at Leri (Vercellese), which stretched over neighboring communes also. When Camillo's father bought it in 1822, it counted 900 hectares. Because of new land purchases it grew to 1,248 hectares in 1835, just when Camillo became its enthusiastic manager (*il Cavour agricoltore*). His biography describes his instrumental role linking farming with the chemical and food processing industries, and with commercial and banking activities.[18]

At the time of Italy's unification, seven centuries of patient planning and digging had given rise to the largest irrigation system in Europe, which by 1861 watered half a million hectares in the Po valley.[19] A momentous event in the history of Italian agriculture took place in 1866: the Cavour canal opened. Laid upon solid foundations, it made almost a doubling of rice production possible.[20]

The canal had an enormous influence on Piedmontese and Lombard agriculture. An additional hundred thousand hectares in the heart of the rice belt benefited from artificial irrigation.[21] The irrigation complex grew to 1,493,330 kilometers with the digging of supplementary branches in successive years.[22] Thus the whole region underwent basic changes. The sediment brought in by the new streams connected to the network enhanced the fertility of the soil.[23] Swamps and occasionally flooded lands, which made up 30 percent of the rice grounds (21 percent located in the rice belt) in the early 1860s, were slowly abandoned[24] and then totally deserted toward the end of the century.[25] Meanwhile, trends evident before the unification of Italy were accelerated after 1866: higher rents, the concentration of property, and disappearance of peasants.[26] The average size of a farm was eighty hectares; a 200-hectare farm was considered big. Sometimes two or three capitalist farmers, with holdings of over a thousand hectares, cultivated almost a whole township.[27] The tillable surface in the rice belt amounted to 99 percent of the land.

The codification of regular agricultural statistics for Italy started only in 1910. Earlier figures on rice growing are unreliable. The crop was subject to restrictions, the reasons for which will be discussed later. Farmers frequently disregarded the limiting measures and concealed the real extent of their yield; hence the recorded data must be interpreted as conservative.[28] Comparative figures for 1860 and 1870 show not only an increase of rice-growing areas (85 percent), but also an increase of output per hectare: from 17.2 quintals per hectare in the years 1860–1864 to 20.7 quintals in the years 1870–1874 (1 quintal = 100 kilograms or 220.46 pounds). Novelli and Sampietro have presented the following figures for rice production in the whole kingdom:[29]

Years	Surface, Hectares	Production, Quintals	Output per Hectare, Quintals
1860–65	145,000	2,600,000	17.9
1870–74	232,000	4,810,900	20.7
1879–83	201,850	3,584,900	18.1
1890–94	182,450	3,046,400	16.7
1901–05	175,365	4,434,500	25.3
1910–14	144,998	4,878,700	33.8
1915–19	138,618	5,218,300	37.6
1920–24	121,400	4,698,800	39.5

The planting reached a maximum surface area between 1870 and 1874. Then there was a contraction.

Asian rice brought to European markets through the Suez canal put an end to the primacy of the Italian crop. A rice production crisis, characterized initially by a fall in the prices of both rice and land,[30] coincided with the general decline of European agricultural prices between 1873 and 1896 when huge cargoes of grain also began to arrive from America. But the 1873–96 agricultural crisis was worldwide.

In Italy, as elsewhere in Europe, the depression provoked campaigns for inquiries into the plight of agriculture, and, with the exception of some countries, also a change in official policies from free trade to protectionism.[31] An increased customs duty on foreign grain was first levied in Italy in 1878. It was so low that at first it did not affect the price of grains or bread. It rose significantly in 1887, 1888, and then twice in 1894. Rice import duties were as follows:[32]

Year	Import Duties, Lire per Quintal
1887	3.0
1888	5.0
1894 (Feb.)	7.0
1894 (Dec.)	7.5

Prompted by falling market prices, many farmers[33] followed the rule of minimum effort and thereby neglected the necessary rotation and tillage of their land. This impoverished the soil and provided the conditions for the reappearance of a destructive rice disease, *brusone*.[34] In 1884, the darkest year of the crisis, many farmers went bankrupt because of their failure to pay rent, which had skyrocketed during times of plenty.[35] In the long run, this catastrophe served to put rice farming on a sounder economic footing; the experts spoke of a "surgical operation" that cut out almost all the marginal land in marshes.[36] This recession continued from the end of the crisis in 1897 until 1910. It resulted in the elimination of less productive patches.[37] There are figures other than those of total surface under cultivation— such as the amount of rice harvested, yield per hectare, and market, land, and rent prices—that more accurately mirror the economic re- covery. In 1897, when the signs of a general revival of the economy were already perceptible, all these indices also showed a favorable upswing.[38]

Rice growing came out of the crisis improved by the hiring of a larger work force and the use of modern farming techniques using machinery. In the Novarese the investment in farming technology was higher than in any other part of Europe. In addition, the govern- ment distributed to farmers new Japanese rice seeds free of charge.[39] When the crisis ended, a centuries-old process was completed: a variety of landholdings gave way to big and middle-sized farms rented out to capitalist farmers by generally absentee landowners. Underlying all these changes was the investment of more capital, especially in the big farms. Large loans were available on better terms for big farms than for smaller ones.[40] Rice figured prominently among Italian exports and the conversion from extensive to intensive rice growing had taken place.[41] Even *brusone* disappeared by 1895.[42]

The Weeders

No other type of farming produced such a profound impact on the society of the Po valley. When it had taken hold in irrigated land, it introduced a new group of workers—wage earners.[43]

The employment of wage earners was not the only new thing about rice cultivation; there was also the presence of agents who recruited those who did the weeding (*monda* or *mondatura*).[44] The operation lasted about forty days beginning at the end of May, when the plants were two months old and numerous species of weeds threatened their normal growth. When the Milanese was a dependency of the Spanish crown (1535–1714), rice farmers were already using agents to recruit labor. Middlemen mistreated the work force (whose sex was not specified) in such a way that Spanish magistrates promulgated an edict as early as September 24, 1594, aimed at introducing a labor contract to discourage the most blatant abuses against workers. The edict, "a start in social legislation," sought to eliminate the middlemen who were notorious for the "barbaric cruelties" they used against the workers once they were lured "to the assigned place with promises and blandishments." These agents treated them "brutally, without either paying them or providing these wretched creatures with the bare necessities of life, making them work like slaves, with beatings and with more verbal abuse than is used with galley convicts." They also caused deaths among their victims. The edict ordered agents to stop recruiting and ordered landholders or their lessees to guide laborers to and from their work personally "as is the case in the fields and in the vineyards," and to humanize their relations with the weeders.[45] That the Spanish authorities kept on propounding similar measures again and again in the sixteenth and seventeenth centuries hints at their failure.[46]

In any case, the edict was an early response to the exceptional social phenomenon created as rice farming spread. There was the formation of a small but powerful group of rice growers and a great mass of landless agricultural workers, and also the need to hire a large number of migrants from the region or from more distant places. When investments in rice farming increased in the eighteenth century, the old peasant institutions (sharecropping, perpetual land lease) that allowed families to live and work together at the farms slowly fell apart. The paternalistic relations that had bound peasants and landowners when they had invested less significant amounts of money in their land disappeared.[47]

Beginning in 1792, the French revolutionary wars accelerated social disruption. The owners of many middle-sized and small holdings were hit by high taxes, the ravages of war, famine, and the high cost of living. They lost their properties to speculators during the economic depression caused by the hostilities.[48] When a temporary peace came in 1797, many independent peasants became landless victims of a "crisis of proletarization,"[49] and suffered from "physiological hunger"—in other words, starvation—as the price of grain rose while wages remained unchanged.[50] In Piedmont, emphyteusis—a perpetual lease of land to a peasant upon condition of tilling it—decayed and was officially abolished in 1837. Similarly the *mezzadria* or Italian sharecropping system, in use in Vercelli as early as 1107, withered away and almost disappeared at about the same time.[51]

In the 1830s, when more capitalist farmers stepped in as modern entrepreneurs, some fortunate sharecroppers (*mezzadri*) managed to rent land and come to be *affittuari*, but the majority of them lacked the capital necessary to grow rice. Once thrown off the land, they became mere wage earners, mostly rural. Only a few of them remained on a single farm all the year round with their families, with all members working for the same employer. The fact that they were called *schia-vandari* (slaves) in Piedmontese suggests the true nature of their sta-tus,[52] which was very similar to that of the permanent rice workers in Lombardy.[53]

As a result of these profound changes in the land tenure system, many uprooted peasants became temporary wage earners in the rice farms. This prompted one French Encyclopedist, observing the con-centration of such a large labor force paid with wages, to compare them to an immense manufactury.[54]

Economists and historians interested in these developments (Salvatore Pugliese, Giuseppe Prato, Luigi Bulferetti, Raimondo Luraghi, Luigi Faccini, Gabriella Facchinetti, Sergio Soave, Novello Novelli, and Giovanni Sampietro) do not estimate how many inhabi-tants of the rice belt became proletarianized in the process, nor do they specify the number of wage earners who worked in the rice fields. The weeders (*mondariso, mondine,* or *mondatrici*) were mostly women.[55] (*Mondariso* (sing. and pl.; fem.) and *mondine* (sing. *mondina*) are synonyms. The term *mondariso* is formal; it is used in official documents. *Mondina* is a popular term. Various sources refer to the size of this work force in vague terms, such as "thousands,"[56] "a great many" (*moltissime*),[57] or an "extraordinary quantity indeed" (*quantità veramente straordinaria*).[58] The population of the three rice districts (Vercelli, Novara, and Lomellina) increased from 178,931 in-habitants in 1774 to 541,681 in 1881,[59] but it is difficult to determine the total number active in agriculture. In the national census of 1881, in those three districts only, 73,608 persons over the age of fifteen declared themselves to be agricultural wage earners. Of these, 37,226 were women.[60] Still, the real number of women working in agri-culture was much higher, because the Italian censuses tended to list them under other categories, such as persons without profession, spinners, seamstresses, domestic servants,[61] which were all occupa-tions they undertook along with farming. Others may well appear as belonging to any of the other five categories of agricultural workers, besides wage earners, that the census adopted: small landowners, sharecroppers, tenant farmers, stewards, and permanent workers.

What is unquestionable is that the total of 37,226 women wage earners in 1881 is close to the figure of 39,921 local *mondariso* recorded in 1903 when the first inquiry on labor in the rice fields took place.[62] This total increased in subsequent surveys,[63] mainly because the study of 1903 did not take the small farms into account. To the 39,921 local weeders, almost the same number of migrants must be added— 36,224 or 46.57 percent—reaching a total of 76,145 weeders in 1903. One can speculate that each *mondatura*—excluding those of the crisis years—brought about a hundred thousand weeders to the rice belt from the inauguration of the Cavour canal until World War I. Eighty to 95 percent of the weeders were women;[64] the rest were men and children.

Several species of weeds grew in the rice fields with different degrees of stubbornness, depending on the circumstances, places, and times. If the rice field was "old" because the grower had sown the crop two or three times consecutively, undesirable plants would be reduced, but so would the amount of rice harvested.[65] Weeds would proliferate due to changes in the source of the irrigation water or to the kinds of seeds sown. In any event, the species of weeds tended to increase with the passage of time, sometimes spasmodically. Factors such as the opening of the Cavour canal, or the adoption of oriental seeds, while aiding rice farming, added to the unwelcome proliferation of new varieties of weeds.

In the nineteenth century, some farmers still relied on the cheap, though deficient, procedure of sliding a flat board over the growing rice plants to break the weed stems. These farmers saved money on wages by this method, but at the expense of a poor yield. A satisfactory method demanded a thorough *monda* by hand, and hence a huge capital outlay in wages. In Larizzate, Vercelli, the rate of expenditure on wages for the *mondatura* grew considerably in the course of 120 years. The figures for 1780, 1820, and 1900 indicate that, at the earliest date, only 1.3 percent (1.5 lira per hectare) of expenses went for the *monda;* at the second, 6.5 percent (8.25 lire); and at the last one, 28.2 percent (75 lire). In 1900 this percentage surpassed the cost of irrigation by almost one-third. It had previously been the most expensive operation: 50 percent of the total disbursement in 1780; 40 percent in 1820; and only 19 percent in 1900—but unchanged in absolute terms: 50 lire per hectare. Nevertheless, even an expensive weeding was a good investment. Profits doubled in these 120 years, as a result of the increase in the price of rice, the decrease in irrigation costs, and the improvement in agricultural techniques, including weeding.[66]

We do not know precisely when the weeding work force came into being and when men and women of the rural proletariat of the Po valley ceased to work together in the fields. But this separation by sex was common by the seventeenth century, when masses of women were doing most of the weeding.[67] There is a description of the whole female population and some children living in the vicinity of the fields congregating for the *mondatura* in the eighteenth century.[68] By the third decade of the nineteenth century most commercial rice growers had adopted weeding by hand.[69]

I may suggest reasons for the formation of a work force of women weeders and for the sexual division of labor. All ablebodied members of the workers' families in the rice-growing region had to earn their own subsistence. Budgets of workers' households during the eighteenth, nineteenth, and early twentieth centuries show that what the head of the family earned as a temporary or permanent farm worker served to pay for only his own food, garments, tools, and some basic common expenses, such as the house rent, lamp oil, firewood, and the purchase of home utensils and furniture. Pugliese points out that in order for the man of the house to meet these expenses, he had to be in good health, in his prime, and fully employed.[70] Given such a precarious household economy, employers expected the women and children from these families to sell their labor as well, and this is what actually happened.[71] A division of labor was established between the sexes, and as a result weeding became women's work. Male permanent farm workers performed other jobs at *monda* time.

Researchers on occupational sex segregation recognize this as universal, but underline the complexity of distinguishing the different tasks by gender. Cynthia Lloyd summarized anthropological findings in different farming systems: "Each society has a clear sexual division of labor . . . however . . . there is no common pattern of sex roles across society." In other words, each community has a different way of dividing the burden of work among the sexes, which its members will find quite "natural."[72]

Heidi Hartmann, while alluding to the disagreements among the different schools of anthropological thought on the division of labor, points to the control that men have traditionally exercised over the labor of women and children in the family. Moreover, she pays special attention to the anthropological school that studies changes in the social, political, and economic structure of different societies and their impact on the condition of women, including those stemming from the more recent emergence of the capitalist mode of production and the wage system. The results of these changes are the increasing complexity of these societies, their social stratification, and the decrease of the status and influence of women. She asserts that "in our society the sexual division of labor is hierarchical," enforcing the already existing domination of men over women. Women stay at home as unpaid family workers, or work outside the home in occupations labeled "unskilled" female jobs.[73]

More recent attempts at explaining the sexual division of labor reflect conflicting views. Some studies conclude that women's reproductive functions are the main determinants of their subordination in the family and then also in the labor market. Others tend to place greater emphasis on the role played by the capitalist mode of production and on women's productive activities in the establishment of a gender-ordered division of labor.[74]

Although sometimes working conditions seem to disclaim the existence of any labor segregation by sex, at close scrutiny the instances show a sort of sex-ordered division. Patricia Hilden, for example, found out that between 1880 and 1914 women textile workers in French Flanders performed most of the time the same factory tasks as men, together with them in the same workrooms. However, a hierarchical organization was clear when it came to wages: women earned only from one-half to two-thirds as much as men. Jane Lewis observed the same situation among weavers of both sexes in pre–World War II England.

The division by sex can also be merely formal, the arbitrary recognition of men's ability to perform certain operations that they monopolize in the work place, and a mental satisfaction or "gender pride" that does not substantiate better wages for the male work force.[75]

In the case of the Italian weeders, we may raise the question as to whether sex segregation simply perpetuated a tradition as old as the weeding itself or whether women became weeders because they were the only workers available at *monda* time, or whether male workers played a part in assigning the *monda* to women, or whether there actually was a certain inborn ability of women for the task, or whether employers elaborated such an argument to justify a sex segregation based on a mere economic consideration, such as profit. I will have to consider all these arguments to reach a satisfactory explanation.

The assumption that it was natural for women, constrained by their domestic duties, to look for jobs close to home such as the rice fields often within walking distance, merits scant consideration. Almost half the weeders, single or married, were migrants who stayed for forty days and sometimes more than a hundred miles away from their homes. Nor can it be argued that the occupation reflected home-based values that made it desirable to women because weeding bore no clear parallel to domestic labor. The idea that men were busy with other activities during the *monda* season applies only to years of full employment, but not to the frequent cases where men were out of work, even though they might have had recourse to temporary migration to urban centers or abroad. Furthermore, rice farmers, when in need of more *mondariso*, recruited migratory women. It is improbable that men workers, powerless and subordinated as they were in the social scale, might have had any influence in allotting the *monda* to women, at least in the period when this work force was formed.

Along with many other direct observers, rice growers had their own reasons to explain why women and children became weeders. One important factor was probably the cheaper wages women and children could be paid, but employers never said so outright. Instead, they presented what they considered to be rational statements, which were sometimes combined with more pragmatic arguments that leave the value of their rational convictions open to doubt. Some argued that only women displayed the patience needed for weeding, or that the bodies of women (and children) were appropriate for weeding because they were smaller and lighter than men's. They could move with more ease in the rice fields and, thus, cause less damage to the tender plants.[76] Even in 1903, Francesco Pezza, the public health officer of Mortara, upheld the notion that women and children had very flexible backbones and were therefore well adapted for this task.[77]

Antonio Aldini, an important rice farmer and statesman in Bologna during the Napoleonic era, gave two types of explanations in 1815. He said that "neither the experienced men nor the robust male youth" were employed in the weeding because "they were reserved for work requiring greater exertion," and also that "only women and children of eight to ten years are employed in this job, in which dexterity more than force is required."[78] Novelli and Sampietro, writing in 1925 the history of rice farming, also gave two sets of reasons. First, weeding, although tiresome, was suited to the physical capacity not only of women and children, but also of "those [men] who are already turning old"; in other words, "weak" persons. Second, that it was impossible to do without the female labor force at *monda* time

because a large concentration of workers was required in a brief period when other seasonal work, like the grain harvest, preoccupied the
male work force.[79]

These rational explanations thus point to the innate physiological and mental characteristics of women—agility and endurance—
that they curiously enough shared with children and middle-aged
men. These characteristics "naturally" predisposed them for the *mondatura*. Among other things, practical arguments stress that women's
light bodies inflicted less harm on the plants and that men were
needed for jobs that required more physical strength. But weeding
was an exhausting job. It was done at the time when fields were
flooded and the women, their bodies bent over, had to spend the
whole day standing in water up to their knees. This had grave consequences to their health. Besides, throughout the year weeders performed many other jobs requiring different degrees of physical exertion and qualities other than patience and endurance.

Therefore, there were no compelling physical or mental factors
to warrant defining weeding as a woman's job. No inherent quality
seems to determine their predisposition for weeding. Instead the observers, mainly employers, imposed certain physical and mental
traits on weeders, which were determined allegedly by their biological sex, but they were only their own social creation. We may use the
concept of gender here in reference to the socially constructed representation of women and men, based on biological determinism,
which assigned appropriate roles for both women and men, and prescribed relations between the sexes.[80]

We must ask ourselves, then, whether the socially constructed
gender traits that placed weeders in this specific task were not "a tool
of profit maximation"[81] on the part of farmers, who used gender
issues to assert economic interests. Weeding was the field operation
that required the largest labor force, cost the most in wages, and was
the one in which the employer would try to exert the greatest pressure. Harvesting and threshing were second and third. Hiring wom-
en for weeding was to the farmers' advantage in several ways. Special
wages, lower than men's, corresponded to a special unskilled wom-
en's job. There was a reduction or, sometimes, a slower rate of increase of men's wages in a labor market expanded by the presence of
women.[82] Finally, lower men's earnings forced the vast labor reserve
of women out of the home and into the work place, as happened in
the mid-1860s. This was perhaps a deliberate employers' maneuver to
expand production while keeping wages down.

In his study on rice farming in Vercelli, Pugliese follows the fluctuations of wages showing that a deterioration of men's wages can be partially attributed to women's employment. Besides being lower than men's, women's wages rose at a slower rate since 1700—when women were paid half of men's wages. Women's wages, however, made substantial progress in the years 1866–70 and after. The opening of the Cavour canal, the extension of rice growing, and the need to attract more weeders may well explain this upturn. In contrast, the rate of increase of men's wages, especially for harvesting, which had been very brisk since 1830, became slower than the rise of women's wages between 1866 and 1870 and between 1871 and 1875. Thereafter, men's wages actually contracted until the end of the economic crisis, while women's continued to climb until 1881–85, when they then plunged relatively faster than men's, but for a shorter period (1886–95). When the economy recovered, by 1896, women's wages also improved at a quicker rate than men's. "There is no reason to wonder at this," Pugliese concludes, "because it is well known how the rising demand for arms generally causes increase of the lowest wages, as those of women, who just then find jobs, while, if the demand slackens, they are the first to remain idle."[83] Therefore, the reduction of men's wages was caused by the increasing use of women's labor. We have to keep in mind that rice farms also included tracts of grain and pasture land, and that employers drew on the same local labor pool of men and women for various agricultural tasks.

The general assumption that women had fewer needs than men may have justified wage differences in the eyes of employers and of economists as well, who were far from considering that "fewer needs" might also mean eating less and worse, and therefore having poorer health than men. Pugliese's charts of workers' family incomes and expenditures show that only men's wages could cover key expenses, such as rent, and this calculation presupposes the dependence of women on men for their survival. There are no estimates based on circumstances when the head of the family or his income were lacking.

The relative value of weeding wages shows the progress of women's compensation—or the comparative stagnation of men's wages. In 1866–70 weeding wages were slightly less than two-thirds of those paid for the so-called special men's work, such as haying, reaping stubble, grain harvesting and threshing. Weeding was also "special" work, and thus paid more than the ordinary chores like haying and hoeing. Special chores were either harder, or took place at a time of great demand, or needed a longer workday, like rice and millet weeding, harvesting, and threshing, and turnip and hemp harvesting.[84] Rice weeding stood out because it employed the largest work force. By the turn of the century *mondariso* wages were more than two-thirds that of men's. The gap tended to narrow in the first years of the twentieth century, especially if we take into account the shortening of the woman's workday.[85] This last fact opened new opportunities for the weeders to do other things. Pugliese evaluates the new situation:

> Moreover, the woman, being less carried away by wasteful entertainments, in which the male sex more easily indulges, succeeds in employing with pecuniary advantage the many free hours left at her disposal from the shortened schedule, either gathering wood, greens, and gleaning in the fields, tilling a rented tract of orchard, catching frogs, breeding poultry, and the like.[86]

Be that as it may, it is difficult to assess the value of the weeders' wages, especially if we try to go beyond the unanimous understanding that they were very low. They were "a bit higher than those paid in the Far East," wrote the physician Gianverardo Zeviani, moved by the misery of the *mondariso* at the end of the eighteenth century.[87] Or they served only to pay for quinine to cure the malarial fevers contracted during weeding, if we follow another physician, Francesco Puccinotti, writing in 1843 about the health hazards posed by rice farming.[88]

Weeding wages changed from week to week. In 1878 they were low at the beginning of the season (about 1 lira a day) in a farm of Novara, increased in the following weeks (2 lire a day toward the end), and decreased to the initial level at the very end.[89] Local variations were the rule. A table of weeding wages for the period 1880–1910 shows the following figures:[90]

1880	1.65 lira
1903	1.79 lira
1905	1.95 lira
1910	3.00 lire

These statistics are of little help if we want to learn about the wage fluctuations during the depression that started in the 1880s and continued until the end of the century. Also, one has to keep in mind that after 1904 workers struggled primarily for the shortening of the workday and for full local employment. They considered wage increases a matter of secondary importance.

The problem is to try to evaluate the household needs that weeders intended to meet with their wages. These needs were always family needs and they changed according to whether the weeders were part of the household as daughters, wives, or mothers. One also had to consider in what kind of household the weeders lived, because this would determine how women coped with the problem of permanent scarcity.

Single *mondariso* were ruled by their parents.[91] As young children they were taken to weed (children numbered 4,904, or 6.44 percent of the labor force in 1903), probably because the number of household members exceeded the resources available to feed them. Other reasons were the lack of any type of child care while the mother was weeding, and the interest of employers in hiring mothers with children in order to increase the number of low-paid elements—elements considered "inferior," according to the inquiry of 1903—in work squads. Children were paid half the wages of adults.[92]

Daughters' obligations to contribute to the family economy often required them to move out of their homes to work as domestic servants. With their departure, they relieved their families of the burden of providing for their care while from then on they had to bear the combined burdens of supporting themselves, helping support their families, and accumulating their dowry. What about the dowry? The 1903 inquiry on weeding presents the case of a young woman servant who was allowed by her master to take leave to go to weed and save her wages for her dowry, and this had been stipulated at the time she entered service.[93] Surely hers was not an exceptional case.

These were possibly cases of single women who were part of households of wage earners whose family economy was basically a "family wage economy,"[94] that is to say, a family economy based on wages earned by its members. If the household was even partially a unit of production and not simply consumption, daughters assisted in this production. The life of Nanna, the protagonist of a novel entitled *In risaia* [In the rice fields], written in 1878, may have aspects in common with many other women's lives of the time and place under consideration.

In this novel the head of the family was a humble tenant in Novara, on whose farm no rice was grown. Nanna, his daughter, was a geeseherder until she was ten. Thereafter, she and Maddalena, her mother, took care of the kitchen garden and prepared baskets of

vegetables that Maddalena sold in local markets. This family arrangement suffered a crisis when Nanna turned seventeen, for at that age
young women began preparing for marriage. Marriage meant a dowry, and the accumulation of a dowry undoubtedly meant an economic burden to the family. Nanna's father could contribute only a
small amount to it.

One mainstay of a woman's dowry in the region was a mattress.
Nanna's was filled with the softest goose feathers, which Maddalena
had saved carefully since her daughter's birth. The other was a set of
silver hairpins, which indicated that a woman had reached the age of
marriage. No man would propose to Nanna unless she wore them.
The hairpins cost 72 lire, but Nanna's father, crushed by low prices
and high rent, had only 30 lire. So, to resolve this matter, all the
family members, including Pietro, Nanna's 15-year-old brother, met
and decided that Nanna should work in the rice fields. In this way,
she could earn enough to pay for her own dowry. Nanna and Pietro,
who volunteered to cooperate in the endeavor, went to work hoeing
rice fields prior to the weeding. This was an ordinary, lower-paid
operation that took place between April and May. At 75 centesimi a
day, they would earn 22.5 lire each. Finally, after buying her hairpins
and recovering from the malaria she contracted while hoeing, her
friends convinced her to go out to weed with them, hoping to amass
50 lire more for her trousseau[95] and, why not, be able to see a young
carter to whom she felt attracted. Very quickly she learned from her
comrades to earn a little extra money by letting water leeches bite her
legs. To cast the worms away was tantamount to "kicking fortune
out,"[96] because, once stuck to the skin, they could be caught and sold
in the town pharmacy on Sundays for 20 centesimi apiece. After
removing the leeches, the bleeding could be stopped by applying
cobwebs found on dry ground, the same ground that served as a bed
at night.

Other single women, if they lived in or near an important urban
center, alternated weeding with work in factories. We may look at
other women's lives. R.B., for example, born in Cappuccini, Vercelli,
in 1902, dropped out of school at the beginning of the second grade.
She never attended a whole school year because, being the oldest of
eight children, she had to remain at home taking care of her younger
brothers and sisters in the spring while her mother worked in the
fields. At nine, her aunt took her out to weed, but thereafter the
farmer did not hire her, in order to avoid penalties, which were instituted after 1907, for employing children under the age of fourteen.
At that age, she began to alternate work in the rice fields in the spring

and summer with work in the button factory in Vercelli. She preferred the ten-hour long night shift at the factory with its higher wages, although it was below what she earned as a *mondariso*.[97]

M.B., also from Cappuccini, was born in 1895. She was the fourth of eight children, and only finished the second grade, for she too had to watch over her younger siblings. She went to the market to sell silk yarn that she helped produce at her grandmother's house, reaped hemp and jute, and then put the bundles to steep in the Sesia River for several days, and carried them home to take the plants apart and gather the yarn. At twelve, she went to weed with her mother. Each time she wanted to straighten her aching back, her mother pinched her legs to keep her from being dismissed. She also worked in a brick kiln as her father's helper and in the button factory.

After marriage, women who had to quit one of their jobs stopped factory work, where their wages were lower than *monda* wages.[98] Wives and mothers also made a variety of contributions to the household economy. Maddalena, Nanna's mother, had weeded while she was single and continued to do so after her marriage and the birth of her children. Later on, she turned to productive activities on the farm—helped by her daughter when she became ten years old—and to selling produce at the local market.

The wives of the few permanent farm workers in the rice farms had to participate in different tasks, including the weeding, which was their best paid job in any year. By the mid-nineteenth century wives in this type of household earned "half of the bread necessary for the family" in a year.[99] In 1880 their earnings were calculated at 80 lire a year, if they managed to work for two hundred days, which was not always possible. This was more than one-fourth of the 360 lire earned by their husbands. We must keep in mind that growers took advantage of the women of the households of permanent workers. Because they were living on the farm, they were paid at a lower rate than women hired as temporary workers. The rights of gleaning and of being hired before the latter supposedly compensated permanent women workers for their lower wages.[100]

Additionally, the weeding wages of wives in households outside the farms contributed to the family economy. In some cases their households were structured within the family wage economy, with the head of the family working as the wage earner, as many rural day workers (*braccianti*) did. Other family heads gained a degree of independence, like poor fishermen, whose wives sold fish and frogs in the market before they went to weed.

The contribution of these women was sometimes defined as the payment of the yearly house rent.[101] In the early twentieth century, "after the big strikes," as one weeder explained, some could purchase a stove, which made their lives more comfortable and put an end to the old tradition of spending winter evenings in the stable.[102] The social aspects of gathering in the stables were not immediately obliterated by the change, because families with stoves used to invite their less fortunate neighbors to spend the evenings in their kitchens. By this time weeders' families began to buy wheat bread to replace homemade corn bread.[103] Some single women saved *monda* wages to buy flowered aprons and colored head kerchiefs, two luxury garments they wore to dances.[104] In general, women purchased "expensive and short-lasting dresses," men ate and drank more, but their housing remained as miserable as ever.[105] Silver hairpins apparently fell into disuse before the end of the nineteenth century. Thereafter, a wardrobe and a chest of drawers became the bride's typical dowry.[106]

While nursing their own offspring, weeders could often act as wet nurses for urban infants as well. In fact, many mothers weaned their babies early in order to work as wet nurses or in the rice fields.[107] Weeders breast-fed foundlings entrusted to them by charitable institutions or children of well-to-do families. In the city of Vercelli the percentage of "exposed" children in the foundling hospital (*ospizio*) went down from 9.26 percent in 1871 to 6.13 percent in 1911. Among "exposed" infants there were not only illegitimate but also legitimate children whom their families could not support. The proportion of illegitimate to legitimate children in the *ospizio* is unknown. Around one-tenth of these foundlings stayed in the institution; the rest were sent out to the families of wet nurses, paid by the *ospizi*, in the city or in the countryside. From 1880 to 1905 both groups amounted to about five hundred foundlings.[108]

In the fall and winter, many women were busy spinning linen and hemp in the stables. They also caught frogs and fish in the stagnant waters of the rice fields during the night. These were either to be eaten fresh or to be preserved with salt.[109] We also know that agents, with false promises, lured young women from Mede (Lomellina), and other localities of north and central Italy, to work at the Tobler chocolate works in Bern in the twentieth century. The contracts guaranteed good wages and living quarters, terms the employers never fulfilled once the women arrived in Switzerland. The factory system of wage deductions prevented Italian workers from saving the money that would have allowed them to flee the factory and pay for the trip back home.[110] Very rarely were women not engaged in some productive activity. M.B., a *mondariso* of Vercelli born in 1895, tells that her mother was an exceptional person because she had a passion for reading. Instead of going to reap grass or catch frogs after the weeding like all her co-workers, "she went to buy novels from a sort of news agent." This became "a sore point between her and her husband." M.B. adds that her mother was also a first-class storyteller, delighting women and children.[111]

This is an example of a group, M.B. and her audience, that endeavored to break the pattern that society imposed upon them by pursing interests other than the ones prescribed by the social order, socializing outside the usual context—the work place, the church, the neighborhood, the water fountain, or the stores—and resisting male opposition. Some migratory *mondariso* might have also taken to weeding not only for economic reasons, but out of the expectation that they would evade the boredom of the home and its surroundings for several days, see other places, be with friends, and meet new ones. We read that in the post–World War II period the *mondine* "live this experience as a break from family oppression, from their daily routine, and from the heavy control of the traditional milieu." They had probably imagined the same things when they had started their journey for weeding several decades earlier. The song *"L'amarezza delle mondine"* (The *mondine*'s bitterness) reminds us of what migratory workers expected when they returned home:

> When we arrive at Reggio Emilia
> The creditors will come toward us:
> *"Mondariso*, out with the money purse,
> We want to be paid."[112]

Given the prevailing economic conditions, family settings, and opportunities for women to allocate their own time, weeding became a significant and much sought-after source of income for both single and married women, the latter sometimes in association with their children.[113] Figures for 1904 show that, out of 65,209 local women engaged in weeding in the whole rice belt, 41,865 were over twenty-one years old, and 23,344 under that age, a distribution that may lead one to conclude that many of the *mondariso* were married.[114]

In *In risaia*, Nanna's birth in the spring forced her mother to miss a weeding season. At the beginning of the twentieth century, sanitary regulations prohibited women from reporting for the *monda* after the eighth month of pregnancy and during the first month after childbirth. Such prohibitions acknowledge the presence of married women in the rice fields. Another rule permitted women an extra break so that they could breast-feed their babies. Again it is evident that women who had recently given birth participated in the weeding season. All these regulations suggest that women could not afford to miss the *monda*, even under the most unfavorable circumstances, because it would cause a severe depletion in their family's budget.

Massimo Livi-Bacci shows in his study of Italian fertility that the proportion of married women was higher in the Po valley, and still higher in the rice belt than in the nation at large.[115] In the twentieth century, the marriage rate, as Novelli and Sampietro point out, tended to be higher in the rice regions than in the country as a whole. The authors give the following marriage rates (per 1000 citizens) in the rice districts:[116]

	1895–99	1902–6
District of Novara	7.51	8.34
District of Vercelli	7.18	7.91
District of Mortara	7.06	8.26
Kingdom	6.99	7.63

Stefano Jacini, the future director of the 1877 parliamentary inquiry (*Inchiesta Jacini*) on conditions in the Italian countryside, explains the reasons for a high marriage rate in the Lombard countryside in 1854 in terms that would have varied little if written after national unification:

> When he [the farm worker] reaches the age of twenty, he faces the most important steps of his life: military conscription and marriage. Every country girl is certain to find a husband, as every young man is certain to find a wife, even when nature has not spared him some physical imperfection. This does not mean indifference in the choice, for in that class the art of appealing is very well known. But in the end, the girl of marriageable age does not want to condemn herself to a long wait. She brings always some dowry, usually the bed and a lot of goodwill, to work and procreate many offspring.[117]

A high marriage rate accompanied marriage at an early age. According to the *Inchiesta Jacini*, women in agricultural families married "very young," between the ages of eighteen and twenty-four.[118]

The investigators considered this an early age: in general, Italian women married later in life. The mean age at first marriage in the rice belt was lower than the national age of twenty-four. Carlo Cipolla states that this marriage age did not show changes between 1880 and 1951.[119] Inheritance patterns did not postpone or forestall early marriage among landless workers,[120] nor did the emigration of young men affect the general trend, for many of those who left were replaced by immigrants from the surrounding mountains.[121] The author of *In risaia* explains that, according to custom, after their seventeenth birthday women could find suitors during Carnival and marry by Easter. Nanna's mother had given birth to her first child at the age of twenty-two.[122]

In contrast to the marriage rate, the birthrate in the rice belt, including all categories of the population, which was overwhelmingly rural, had been below the national rate for centuries, and its decline after 1880 was faster than the general fall in the kingdom. The birthrates were (live births per 1,000 inhabitants):[123]

	1895–99	1902–6
District of Novara	32.61	31.27
District of Vercelli	31.56	27.16
District of Mortara	29.19	26.99
Kingdom	33.55	33.11

This situation, I suggest, indicates the practice of birth control. According to Ugo Giusti, rural Italy was not characterized, as one might expect, by a high birthrate. A low rate seems to have been the case in the rice belt. The average family size in Vercelli at the turn of the century was 4.5 persons.[124] Voluntary birth control like the common practice of prolonged breast-feeding—between twelve and eighteen months, with many exceptions above the upper limit—delayed the resumption of ovulation and spaced births. Perhaps some other precautions also prevailed as means to avoid pregnancy.[125]

If our story were projected into the third decade of the twentieth century, weeders would desert the marriage bed as often as possible to go frog hunting in the fields as a ruse to avoid pregnancy. If they became pregnant, these women helped abort one another using time-honored techniques.[126]

Weeders Under Scrutiny

During the Enlightenment and the century that followed, many observers became interested in the weeders: in their lives, their working conditions, and their role in society. The lives of the weeders came under the scrutiny of various specialists, who followed their own personal bent in viewing their subjects and in describing their living conditions. These observations were part of a discussion that embraced all aspects of the workers' lives and involved politicians, agronomists, physicians, economists, and philanthropists who contributed polemical writings to it. They were moved to investigate the *mondariso* because they were surprised and stirred by the unexpected changes due to rice growing. The reason for this interest was the changes it caused in traditional social structures, and the need for a huge number of laborers, and the unforeseen implications these developments had for the well-being of the population. Their writings are a rich source of details on the conditions of rice workers. They appeared when Italian agriculturalists were rapidly expanding rice cultivation and causing a radical economic and social transformation in the Po valley, and continued to appear in the 1880s, when the long depression was affecing rice growing and its labor force.

Writers from the period revealed two distinct attitudes toward women's labor in the fields. First, there were those who saw only economic benefits in women's work. They focused on women's contribution to the prosperity of rice farming, and ignored humanitarian considerations of the arduous nature of the work and the hazardous working conditions of the marshy, malaria-infested fields.

Giovan Battista Spolverini was a renowned eighteenth-century agriculturalist from Verona. He is remembered for his didactic poem written in free verse, *La coltivazione del riso* [The cultivation of rice].[127] Spolverini divided his poem into four books. The third book is instructive for our purposes, for it tells us about weeding. He celebrates women's assistance in rice growing. The poet summoned young women and children from nearby villages and settlements to destroy the threatening weeds in order to save the crop. Like a general on the eve of a great battle, he exhorted weeders to attack the weeds in a warlike manner. He emphasized that the task was from from light; it required skill and alertness to avoid pulling out rice plants along with weeds, or overlooking them altogether. He cautioned that neither the spirit of youth, nor laughter, jokes, or songs should distract them. The narrator enumerates twenty-six varieties of weeds, and adds hy-

L A
COLTIVAZIONE
D E L R I S O
DEL MARCHESE
GIAN BATTISTA SPOLVERINI
AL CATTOLICO RE
FILIPPO QUINTO
SECONDA EDIZIONE.

Fran: Lorenzi Ver. di.

Dome: Cunego inc. Verona.

IN VERONA;
CIƆIƆCCLXIII.

Per Agoſtino Carattoni Stampator del Seminario Veſcovile.
CON LICENZA DE' SUPERIORI.

Title page of Giovan Battista Spolverini's poem *La coltivazione del riso*, Verona, 1763. (Spencer Collection, The New York Public Library, Astor, Lenox and Tilden Foundations.)

perbolically that there were "thousands and thousands" more. Thus, weeders need to be experienced and attentive.

After admonishing the *mondariso,* the speaker addressed their leader who would urge the members of his squad to keep the same pace and to keep together, with the help of a long switch. In addition, he recommends that the leader open the fist of a weeder once in a while:

> . . . and curiously observe
> Whether in the bunch she grasps, any is hidden
> Thread of the noble sprout, and, at once, order,
> With soft clamor, to plant it again.[128]

The list is long, tedious, and minute. The squad leader should also watch the way the *mondine* stepped: with long, light steps, on tiptoe, without straying from the assigned route: "like a swift and orderly army," the group should follow the signals the leader gives with his whistling. But Spolverini's poem also suggests that work in the fields should not be an entirely solemn experience. The natural rights of youth cannot be denied. A brief rest, straightening the backbone, a short conversation, or a chance to look around should not be chastised. The overseer had to control his fits of anger and restrain himself from using his rod on the weeder's "gentle" bodies on these occasions. Courteous and pleasant manners were the best motivators, the third book postulates.[129]

Weeding had to be done two or three times between the end of May and the beginning of July, the *Coltivazione del riso* notes. The narrator also urged the young women to participate in the *monda* before they assumed "the sweet cares of women and mothers." They should battle the weeds quickly and merrily, without fear of spoiling their beauty by spending the whole day with their feet in water, or hurting their hands on rough-edged weeds "before swollen breasts and bulging wombs"[130] prevented them from bending and crouching. Neither the contorted positions of their bodies nor leeches and snakes in the water should distract this band of graceful workers.

Arthur Young, the peripatetic eighteenth-century Englishman and admirer of capitalist farming in the Po valley, left us a much more prosaic account of the rice-growing cycle. His description is devoid of Spolverini's sentimentality and idyllic flights of fancy:

> The rice grounds receive but one ploughing, which is given in the middle of March, and the seed sown at the end of the same

DELLA
COLTIVAZIONE
DEL RISO
LIBRO III.

Ià de gli aſtri Ledei ſcorſa gran parte
Verſo il Cancro s' avvia rapido il Sole :
E già appeſa il Villan la lunga falce
Tolta dianzi a ſegar gli erboſi prati,
L' altra più breve a le ricolte impugna.   5
Prima che dunque a cotal opra cento
Da più contrade mietitori e cento

Spi-

First page of Book Three of Giovan Battista Spolverini's poem *La coltivazione del riso*. This section of the poem describes the weeding of the rice field. (Spencer Collection, The New York Public Library, Astor, Lenox and Tilden Foundations.)

month, in water to the seedman's knees, which is left on the ground till the beginning of June, when the crop is weeded by hand, by women half naked, with their petticoats tucked to their waists wading in the water; and they make so drole a figure, that parties in pleasantry, at that season, view the rice grounds. When the weeding is finished, the water is drawn off for eight days, and it is again drawn off when the ear begins to form, till formed; after which, it is let in again till the rice is nearly ripe, which is about the end of August, when it is reaped, or in the beginning of September; and by the end of that month, all is finished.[131]

Antonio Aldini, a farmer from Bologna and the secretary of state of the kingdom of Italy between 1805 and 1814, shared Spolverini's and Young's perspective. He was the most prominent of the "new men" who promoted and profited from what came to be known as the "golden age of rice farming" in the province of Bologna during the Napoleonic period (1796–1815). After Napoleon's fall, Aldini wanted to prevent restrictions on rice growing by the government of the Restoration. Therefore, in 1815, he defended rice farming in the name of progress against those who had attacked it in an anonymous pamphlet published that year. Aldini rejected the pamphlet's assertions that rice farming had negative effects on society and health, and stressed instead how suitable women's (and children's) skills were for the *mondatura*.[132]

Oreste Bordiga was a well-known professor of agronomy at Novara and the author of the Novarese section of the *Inchiesta Jacini*. He was also a fervent champion of capitalist farming. He brooked no criticism when it came to the *monda* and dismissed as utter nonsense questions raised about the hardship of weeders' lives, in spite of descriptive evidence supporting this view in his own studies of rice farming.[133]

In contrast, another group of observers deplored the living and working conditions of the *monda* proletariat. Physicians such as Gianverardo Zeviani and Luigi Angeli, who were sensitive to the plight of the working poor and distressed by the effect of economic changes on society, have left us much information about the lives of the poorer classes. Not all physicians criticized the economic transformations that seemed to be at the root of ill health. However, many of them did connect cause and effect and, starting in the second half of the nineteenth century, they began to apply the principles of social medicine to combat disease and better the living conditions of the population.[134] Prompted by simple pity for the suffering of the *mondariso*, Zeviani wrote in 1796:

> It moves one to compassion to see platoons of young women put together in the rice fields, on the longest and most burning days of the year, the whole day under the sun, half of their legs buried in the swamp, their bodies bent and crooked, under the whip and constant rebukes of a reckless leader, alert to select with the eye, to extricate with the hand the numerous weeds suffocating the rice; or in the hands and in the feet cut by canes, to see bites and wounds of snakes and leeches, for an earning a bit better than the one paid in the Far East.[135]

The pamphleteer who had aroused Aldini's wrath was probably Luigi Angeli, a physician. He ascribed the deterioration of health and morality in Bologna to the mingling of workers of both sexes during the weeding. Migratory weeders were the target of this criticism and, according to an anonymous author, they were responsible for "enormous excesses of dissoluteness and licentiousness," especially in "the darkness of the night." (Such promiscuity may also have increased the birth rate.) According to a priest whom the author quoted, "they say and do things that cannot be repeated without offense to honesty, of which one cannot even think without horror." And, no less scandalous, weeders did not attend Mass, because they had to work on Sundays.[136] But the author who described the weeders' loose morality had something else in mind; he was attacking not only the new social order but also the economic changes provoked by the *risomania* (rice mania) during the Napoleonic period. Instead, he evoked the ideal life of a precapitalist era in a critique written in the spirit of the Restoration.[137] This particular point of view had its origins in the Restoration but outlived it by almost a century.

In the late 1870s, the *Inchiesta Jacini* endowed Italy with a collection of agricultural data unmatched by any other European inquiry on the subject, as Raimondo Luraghi notes. It also described the "moral traits" of women in the rice fields. Some investigators referred to young migrant *mondine* returning home physically injured by fevers, the harshness of their squad leaders, and the strains of heavy labor, who were also damaged "in their most delicate feelings as a consequence of the promiscuity of the lodgings, and by the loose morals that are its results."[138]

The *Inchiesta* offered a stricter judgment on women who alternated weeding in the countryside with domestic service in the cities.

These "find themselves increasing the number of fallen women, and when rendered worn-out by vice, see themselves as outcasts, and even become thieves." This was the fate of single women who migrated to Italian cities, according to middle- and upper-class commentators. If not actually prostitutes, they were potential ones, or were otherwise part of the dangerous classes because, as social historian Mary Gibson asserts, "they did not fit into any of the traditional female categories: daughter, mother, wife, or perhaps, nun." Left without the protection of family and friends, maid servants were at the mercy of strangers at a time when the same economic crisis that had caused single women to leave their families was giving domestic service an uncertain future, too.[139]

Francesco Coletti brought up the morals issue in his 1911 work on emigration when he stated that migrant weeders were drawn to work:

> . . .by force . . .by habit, as well as by some not strictly economic reason, such as the wish to evade, even for a few days, domestic dependence, and the scrutinizing and gossipy tyranny of everyday surroundings, to break the oppressive monotony of the whole year and have some distraction, that sometimes becomes somewhat sinful (of the young *mondariso*, who are quite enthusiastic about these migrations, it is currently said that they depart alone and return double—namely, pregnant).[140]

But Coletti's analysis is simply impressionistic; he does not support it with statistics, as he does all the other arguments in his book.[141] On the other hand, Novelli and Sampietro thought that "if the [weeders'] pay was not worth the sacrifice, this remained a neglected factor when the need sprang from misery."[142]

The third and most frequent approach stressed the dangerous effects weeding had on weeders' health. Commentators pointed out diseases that were common to men working in the rice fields. Malaria, bronchial infections, intestinal disorders, typhoid fever, anemia, and rheumatic fever, to name only a few, were endemic to the rice belt and in some areas the population had an average lifespan of only eighteen to nineteen years in the first half of the nineteenth century. These writers also underscored the ailments the *mondatura* inflicted on women, like ulcers of the legs and especially abnormalities in reproductive functions, which, consequently, affected their children's physical development.

Girolamo Alghisi, of Pavia, writing in 1794, advised that weeders' children, starting when they were one year old, undergo a treatment of cold baths and rubbing to stimulate their blood circulation. This was intended to inure them to the cold and humidity they would encounter as adults in the rice fields. Alghisi believed this treatment was particularly useful for girls because it would forestall the harm that cold, wet feet caused during menstruation when weeders stood for long hours in the water.[143]

In 1863 Giacomo Besozzi, a physician in the Piedmontese army, defended rice farming, but tried to enlighten the public about the effects of amenorrhea among weeders, "with its sad consequences identical to those of the washerwomen," at the same time. This was a reference to women's infertility, because ovulation did not take place under these conditions.[144] Members of the medical community in Ravenna expressed the same fears in 1870.[145] In 1871 the distinguished Tuscan physician Carlo Livi pointed to disorders in uterine functions as one of the many reasons why rice farming should be outlawed.[146]

What worried most observers was that all these ailments held ominous consequences for weeders' offspring. Agostino Bertani, a radical deputy member of the *estrema* (parliamentary left) and a physician, headed a government inquiry on the sanitary conditions of rural workers. Bertani found that weeders who were weakened by malaria produced children who aged prematurely, inherited the disabilities of their parents, and had few natural defenses against malaria. Ten percent of pregnant women with malaria had miscarriages or premature births. These mothers could hardly nurse their infants due to agalactia, deficient milk secretion.[147] Sometimes this condition was aggravated by breast infections.

A study of social medicine sponsored by the chamber of commerce of Pavia in 1880 (*La pellagra in Italia*) called attention to mastitis, inflammation of the breast, which was caused by congestion of the milk and the pressure of the corsets worn by lactating *mondariso* while weeding. This, too, harmed mothers and impeded breast-feeding.[148] Substitutes for breast-feeding were often inadequate and proved fatal to many infants. Mothers concocted a rather unhealthy flour pap[149] or, if they had a little milk, boiled it mixed with bread crumbs.[150] According to the Pavia study, these procedures accounted for the high infant mortality rate. Only the strongest children survived this process of "natural selection"[151] and even the survivors could expect to suffer from rickets, scurvy, and tuberculosis.[152]

What motivated these commentators to make their opinions public? No doubt the physical and mental health of present and future generations of rural workers concerned them. How could this situation be remedied, according to them? They based their hopes for change on private or government intervention. Bertani assigned to the state the duty of protecting the health of the poor. He recommended preventive measures and saw his inquiry as a first step toward the formulation of a new sanitary code that would stop the abuses of workers, limit the size of the rice fields, or prohibit the crop altogether. The feasibility of organized action on the part of workers to improve their own situation was unthinkable for almost all these sympathetic physicians.

In risaia contained some particularly revealing observations. The Marchesa Colombi, an upper-class woman, described the life and folklore of the lower classes. Though no Zola or Verga, she nonetheless succeeds in evoking a typical peasant household, with sympathy and understanding for her characters and their plight.

Colombi never denounces the victimizers of the lower classes. Instead, she accepts the social relations that capitalist farming introduced in the rice belt without any nostalgia for an idyllic, patriarchal, precapitalist social order in the countryside. It is possible that the very early destruction of that order in the rice belt might have led her not to consider a return to the past, but she neither mentions the causes of the families' problems or the possibility of change in their living and working conditions, nor does she propose solutions to their dilemma.

A sense of immobility is conveyed in the novel. Soon the attitude of acceptance represented by Colombi's novel would start to change, partly because of the agrarian crisis of the last decades of the century, when humility would cede its place to disobedience and protest. If the marchesa's pessimistic description of a static society reflects certain upper-class biases, nevertheless her story enlightened the reading public of her time about this tremendous social problem. There is no doubt that this sentimental Racconto di Natale [Christmas tale], as she subtitled her novel, served to alert the ruling classes to the gravity of the situation. This can be seen in Bordiga's reaction to the novel. A highly respected authority on rice farming, he warned the novel's readers not to believe in the hyperbolic depictions of social conditions in the rice belt.[153]

Thus, capitalist rice farming in the Po valley greatly transformed the life of that region. It created a large rural proletariat. It brought women out of the home to weed the fields. During the *monda* an observer could see the bent backs of the women in the rice fields. Their meager pay went to supplement the barely adequate income of other members of their families, while their intensive labor contributed to the prosperity of the rice farmers.

Weeders' Lives

Weeders' Working Conditions

Although all nineteenth-century workers had a hard lot, rice workers' hardships seem to have been especially tied to the nature of the work itself. Novello Novelli and Giovanni Sampietro stressed:

> Misery was common to the whole rural proletariat, and was not directly attributable to the nature of ordinary farm work. The case of rice farming was different. The general public was struck by accounts of the unhealthy and demanding labor of rice field workers; general feelings of sympathy and compassion were aroused. The conditions of rice growing itself were seen as determining that misery.[1]

Even a staunch supporter of capitalist farming like Jacini pondered the coexistence of profitable production and an impoverished labor force.[2]

Many women traveled far from home to work as weeders. They found themselves at a disadvantage compared to the *mondariso* who lived within walking distance of the fields. Once they started on the journey to the rice farms, and for the duration of their work, these women depended entirely on their contractors for any contingency. Nevertheless, in spite of these differences, migratory and local weeders had much in common, especially in their experiences at work. For example, many farms provided no potable water. If there were water wells, they were inadequate and permeable, so that water spoiled in the middle of the summer because of the heat, or because of seepage from polluted irrigation canals full of human refuse, rotten plants, and dead animals.[3] Where there were no wells, the *mondariso* drank ditch water. Many physicians, including municipal doctors and professors, recommended that weeders drink wine instead of water;[4] others, that they "purify" the water with a concoction of wine, vinegar, lemon juice, anisette, or aqua vitae, this last heavily consumed in northern Italy in the second half of the nineteenth century.[5]

The meals were as bad as the water. In his study of the Italian diet, Stefano Somogyi writes that in the period 1850–1914 food accounted for about three-quarters of the expenditures in a working-class budget and in general was meager and unhealthy.[6] Local weeders brought their own food to the fields. Because wheat was a luxury, they baked bread from millet, corn, or rye, but fuel was scarce and the bread seldom reached the right baking temperature, either in the baker's or a home oven. For the same reason, bread was baked only once a week or once every two weeks. Therefore bread "in the summer becomes moldy on the second day,"[7] and hard and indigestible after the fifth or sixth day.[8] Even polenta seldom reached its proper cooking point.[9] Rye contained impurities like darnel, and rice was acidic; drinks were distasteful. Peddlers came to the fields with discarded fruit they had gotten in the towns.[10]

Meals were slightly more tolerable for permanent than for day workers. Besides bread, rice, and corn, the diet was based on beans and vegetables, which were all of the lowest quality, and on a small amount of dairy products. On Sundays, men drank wine of poor quality in the taverns.[11] Nevertheless, the agronomist Oreste Bordiga argued in 1880 that this diet should not be considered miserable, because it included some pork, cheese, and cheap coffee as well.[12] The *Inchiesta Jacini* investigators agreed that there were some improvements in the rice workers' diet after unification in 1861. Yet such a diet did not prevent the weeders from "contending often with hunger." This was more severe in the winter, when farm workers incurred debts with millers and bakers who charged high interest. Eating little and badly, farm workers continued to suffer from a lack of adequate nourishment. *Mondariso* were also cheated by millers who ground their corn, when they gave adulterated flour in exchange for good-quality grain.[13]

Migratory weeders had their meals provided by the squad recruiters (*capi, caporali,* or *capisquadre*) in a system that had "the ap-

pearance of a speculation made at the expense of poor devils," because of the bad quality of the food.[14] Nanna, the protagonist of the
Marchesa Colombi's novel *In the Rice Fields*, had a daily portion of
slightly over half a pound of corn bread. A friend recommended that
she bring something extra from home to eat with her bread (*com-
panatico*), especially on Fridays and Saturdays when the bread was
already stale, because "with some cheese you won't taste the acid."[15]

At lunch and dinner hours, recruiters served a soup of rice,
beans, and bacon of such bad quality that it even provoked the
weeders' complaints and recriminations,[16] in a rare instance of labor
protest in the nineteenth century. In 1902, at a lunch break, a squad of
three hundred *mondine*, coordinated by the weeder who acted as
cook, threw bread into the water and remained standing on the bank
of the rice field with their arms crossed. Then they smeared the walls
of the farm with the polenta that had been prepared with moldy flour.
Thereafter, the quality of the food changed for the better.[17] In another
farm, complaints were about the beans that spoiled the soup. As late
as the 1903 inquiry on weeding, one investigator saw "more than
once plates and bowls flying in the air because of the impossibility of
eating such bad food," where meals were prepared from cheap and
often rotten foodstuffs in dirty copper pots without the proper tin
lining, and with polluted water.[18]

The majority of the *mondariso* who came from far away spent the
night in the open air, or, at most, in the shelter offered by a porch or
stable. Weeders who came from the households of the few permanent
laborers bound by contract to live and work all year round in the rice
fields had to weed and perform other tasks for the farmers.[19] Of
course their lodgings had all the earmarks of the peasant huts of the
time: filth, lack of space, the proximity of cattle and dung. Hence the
inhabitants of these dwellings were highly susceptible to tuberculosis
and other diseases. And, once again, the environment in rice-growing regions only aggravated the situation.

The only trees that grew in the surrounding areas were spindly
because the water from the fields weakened their roots. Fruit trees
and other nutritional plants also rotted.[20] Giovanni Momo, a Vercellese jurist, wrote in 1838 that as wet rice farming spread, it took
over land used for grazing and growing grain. The flooding of the
land deprived these regions of a fresh local supply of grain, vegetables, eggs, milk, cheese, butter, beef, and pork.[21] Wood, the fuel that
could have kept shelter and clothing dry, was scarce and inadequate,
though common elsewhere in the Italian countryside. The record
shows that descriptions of these huts varied little, be they Alghisi's in

1794,[22] or Jacini's in 1854,[23] or that produced by the commission of inquiry in 1903.[24] Neither landowners nor capitalist farmers who rented the estates in the nineteenth and twentieth centuries did anything to renovate old buildings or build new shelters for permanent workers.[25] Rice growers felt this was a worthless expenditure that would only cut into their profits.[26]

The workers did not have the type of clothing that would protect their bodies against the rigor of the environment. They found it difficult to stay dry with only one set of clothes. Bordiga did not find it "proper to give the workers the advice to wear wool or flannel, when they can barely afford cotton or hemp cloth."[27]

In view of the workers' miserable living conditions, the investigators of the *Inchiesta Jacini* did not hesitate to blame poverty and hunger in the winter on the improvidence and insobriety of the workers.[28] They did not consider that population growth, changes in the land tenure system, and an economic depression were causing the number of job seekers in the labor market to swell and keeping wages low and unemployment high.[29] These factors explain the exodus of young women from the countryside to urban centers to work as maids[30] and men's migration too in search of temporary employment away from home. In this case, their families had some relief from the economic crisis thanks to the remittances of family members far away. Novelli and Sampietro state that rice workers lived in acute misery until the turn of the twentieth century.[31] Maternity, hard work, and poor food caused women to age very rapidly: "at thirty they look mature, at forty old, at fifty, decrepit," with bent backs and ghastly faces. When they could not work any more and lacked the help of their husbands, the almshouse was their last resort.[32]

In cases of great poverty, destitute mothers who could not breast-feed their infants qualified for a subsidy for the purchase of milk from charitable institutions or hospitals. For example, in the 1880s the Main Hospital (*Ospedale Maggiore*) of Novara dispensed several grants, worth 4 lire a month, but only for mothers with four children or more. All in all, this was not sufficient for a region where many infants, for a variety of reasons, depended upon charity for survival.[33] When mothers were away from home, they left their babies in the care of an older child, or of a woman who was unable to work,[34] or even alone, "in the mud of the courtyards."[35]

From the *Inchiesta*'s bourgeois-liberal perspective, the inhabitants of the rice belt, and especially the women, were superstitious, because they believed in the evil eye, ghosts, witches, and miracles, and feared hell.[36] They believed in witch doctors, whose collective prayers and thaumaturgical ceremonies were associated by the sick with official religious dogma.[37] Highlanders were allegedly more intelligent, because they were less indigent, but signs of change were evident to the investigators. In the districts of Novara and Vercelli, religious feelings mixed with superstitious beliefs were strong among farm workers, but less firm among the young.[38]

This decline in religious sensibility could mean an openness to newer, more modern ideas about organizing the weeders. The attitude toward authority also gradually changed. Cavour described his paternalistic relations with permanent workers on his land in the 1840s, where he supervised "private life and behavior at work, morals and demeanor of his 'subjects' with an intransigence that easily explains his reputation of being 'a little bit of a dog' (un po' cane)."[39] Cavour wrote in 1846 that "in an estate like this, a strict subordination is the first requisite for good administration" and this rule applied to everybody, including his secretary and the priest and doctor living on the farm, as well as the young people who had to obey the count's authority even in marital arrangements. Cavour did not spare young women; in an 1849 letter he stated that he had promised them that "Sunday I shall make them dance."[40]

Around 1880 the *Inchiesta* inquirer noticed that the peasants of Lomellina had become fond of arguing with landowners, priests, and authorities in general. They neglected their duties, and day workers especially were distrustful, false, vicious, and not at all devoted to their employers or country. They were obstinate, showed a spirit of independence, and even disregarded religious teachings. The report stated:

> The causes of this worsening are due, in great part, I believe, to the absolute lack of moral instruction. Once upon a time our peasants went to church to hear the word of the priest, like the duties of every good Christian, like the obligation to respect property and persons.[41]

Weeders reaped few benefits from the public school system and few advances were made in rural education after unification. The population in the rice belt followed the usual pattern and there were more illiterate women than men. This disparity increased over time. In 1871 in the districts of Novara and Vercelli, 55.7 percent and 55.1 percent, respectively, of the illiterate were women; ten years later, the figures were 56.3 and 56.7 percent, respectively.[42] The Coppino law of July 1877 made education free and compulsory for children between the ages of six and nine, but the apathy of the local authorities, and the families' need for their children's earnings, hindered the enforcement of the law in most rural areas. A teacher reported that children under the age of nine left school during the weeding season in Lomellina at the turn of the century. The article in the socialist newspaper *La Plebe*, published in Pavia, noted:

> On the part of the parents it is misery and ignorance, always combined, that lead to the infringement of this enlightened law; on the part of the muncipalities that were supposed to provide the funds, it is in great part the antagonism, open or secret, of the authorities toward popular education that makes them close their eyes to violations.

The teachers talked "to the benches" for six or seven weeks, pupils returned exhausted or feverish for their exams and, as expected, they failed.[43] The girls who did learn how to read and write lost these skills by the time they turned twenty for lack of practice.[44]

The investigators found that both permanent and day workers were convinced that they were paid less than they deserved, and therefore they tried to work as little as possible.[45] They regarded the farmer as "an enemy whom one must serve." An increase in the incidents of rural theft was another sign of the decline of patriarchal authority, and one that was noted before this period. There was less respect for property; farm workers saw co-workers stealing and did not report them or even participated in the theft, because there was a general consensus that stealing when hungry was a human right and that there was no harm in it. Again, the day workers were worse than the permanent ones: "the real rural thieves come from this category," the investigators proclaimed, reiterating an accusation already common in Cavour's time.[46] In 1847 evidence of frequent thefts of firewood provoked a heated debate in the Piedmontese Agrarian Association. Interestingly enough, some members, mostly aristocrats, recognized that theft was the only resort left for impoverished peasants, and they argued that landowners should be blamed for not providing enough firewood. As expected, only a minority shared this view; the rest called for severe punishments for thievery.[47]

One can argue that rural theft is an individual spontaneous act of social protest. For instance, rice workers stole to meet their basic needs, with the conviction that this act was not a common crime, but rather an assertion of a fundamental right to justice. Workers had an alternative value system, which clashed with the one sanctioned by the official laws defending property. Like thievery, irreverence toward "superiors" was a gesture of independence, indicating workers' opposition, legitimate in their eyes, to persons and institutions they considered responsible for their pauperization.

The *Inchiesta Jacini* presented a series of reasons for these social ills. One of the explanations, supplied by the workers themselves, was that they resorted to theft because they were being paid less than they deserved. The investigators also insisted on the lack of ethical education among wage earners and stated that stealing was not condemned by workers because the amount stolen did not regularly exceed the needs the workers intended to meet with the transgression. The investigators attributed to these workers a morality "characterized by a practical socialism," in other words, not in keeping with bourgeois morality and the Italian penal code.[48]

This particular set of values shared by rural workers produced its own code of honor. The scholar Francesco Coletti, writing in 1925, explained that the rural population distinguished the common thief, who stole to sell, from the one who believed in the natural right to steal to survive. This was considered fair. Coletti mentions the old rights of common use, which had admitted the gathering of goods necessary to keep a person alive, as the tradition at the heart of the indulgent attitude that workers had toward theft.[49] These values persisted into the twentieth century.

M.B., a weeder born in 1895, declared during an interview in the late 1970s that after having taken care of her children and home, she would return to the fields during the night to take from her employer what he had stolen from her during the day. She offered this justification: employers had become rich exploiting the poor, like her. She said that, therefore, she had always participated in the workers' struggle, but had also stolen to give her children something to eat. She considered this "neither sin nor crime." What did she steal? A sack of millet each night, because "after taking off the leaves, separating the grain, grinding it, paying the miller in kind, just what was necessary was left."[50]

M.B.'s conduct was not uncommon. In fact, women and children were in charge of the excursions[51] to gather firewood, sticks, acorns, pasture grass, fruits, and other edible plants growing in the fields. In contrast, a woman who stole linen would be ostracized, according to Coletti.[52] The *Inchiesta Jacini* conveys a sense of despair over this "moral economy of labor." With such experiences and teachings from their parents, children would never learn correct principles. Employers called for a corps of rural guards composed of ex-soldiers from other regions to deal with the problem.[53]

In fact, the presence of more rural guards would have aggravated the severity of the punishment embodied in the criminal code of 1859, which was already very rigorous against violators of rural property. Guido Neppi Modona points to the class character of this code, as well as of the laws of public security of 1889. The first piece of legislation contains a minute description of aggravating circumstances that showed the government's intention to control the rural lower classes with extreme severity. In 1890, out of 131,162 offenders sentenced to prison, 73,662 were agricultural workers and 24,292 industrial workers and craftsmen. On the other end of the social scale, there were 763 professionals. The laws of public security of 1889 further elaborated the repressive system by naming a specific category of "dangerous classes" of society. When the 1889 laws were enforced, the number of Italians sentenced to prison went up. In 1906 there were 145,163 jailed, among them 77,021 agricultural workers and 30,368 industrial workers and craftsmen. The number of professionals declined to 538.[54]

In a polemical study, Raimondo Luraghi compares the conditions of wage labor in the rice belt with those of slave labor in the United States. In 1861 the new kingdom, where landowners were very influential, embraced the abolitionist cause in the United States and referred with horror to the institution of slavery and to the working conditions of the slaves. Given the extremely low income of agricultural workers in Italy, Luraghi asks the question:

> Was not the Italian ruling class, by spreading "information" about the miserable status of the American slaves, trying to conceal the bare fact that the average Italian field laborer, even if exploited by a "highly advanced" kind of capitalistic agriculture, was faring worse than the black slave in the United States?[55]

According to Luraghi, Afro-American slavery was a monstrous institution. But it does not follow that slaves lived under the worst conditions. Quite to the contrary, they had a better standard of living. The *Inchiesta Jacini* showed an absolute lack of human relations between capital and labor in the rice belt. Among the wage laborers there was no community like the one that existed on slave plantations. This conclusion may be debatable, but the comparative analysis of income, meals, mortality rates, health care, housing, and clothing of both groups reveals that slaves seemed materially better off than rice workers, who were subject to heavy indirect taxes, haunted by the fear of unemployment,[56] and, it may be added, having to pay rent and permanent, pressing debts.

The Migratory Weeders

Migratory weeders made up almost half the work force at *monda* time. The recruitment of migrant weeders followed well-established rules, which assured the middleman (*capisquadra, capo,* or *caporale*) absolute dominance over a squad of about fifty members. In contrast, local squads, of around eighty *mondine* each, were hired directly by entrepreneurs. The *capisquadre* were notorious for the poor food they supplied and for the long workday they imposed, longer than that of the local *mondariso,* for the low wages they paid, lower than the one locals earned, and for ignoring their squads' need for shelter. They justified the longer workday by saying that the migrants had nowhere to go and nothing to do in the evening, unlike the local *mondine;* their singing and joking while working, and their occasional dancing after dinner, showed that the *monda* schedule was far from exhausting. Nanna's squad in *In the Rice Fields* worked from four in the morning until four in the afternoon, when the reflection of the sun in the water was blinding and made weeding impossible. Some squads had an extra shift until dusk; others worked for fourteen and a half hours.[57]

Nanna's *caporale* made a lot of money with his squad. To begin with, it was customary for Nanna's father to pay a deposit of 20 centesimi a day to close the "contract." The employer paid the *capo* wages for fifty *mondariso* at 2 lire a day, plus 40 centesimi a day for meals, but the *capo* hired only forty weeders instead of fifty, gave them a daily wage of 1.80 lira and spent less than 40 centesimi on food. This was a common policy.

The *capisquadre* usually concluded their strictly verbal agreements in December and January. Some had powerful organizations, lived in anonymity, and operated their network through subcontractors. The major *capi* would also pay all the wages to the squads and be reimbursed by the entrepreneurs at the end of the harvest. If they were food dealers, which was often the case, they were able to get rid of old and deteriorated food by supplying it to the weeders. Many local grocers were *capi* who coerced the weeders, whose families were indebted to them, into accepting lower wages for the *monda.* Other middlemen worked on a more modest basis, and among them there were also women called *cape* (sing. *capa*). The *capisquadre* were dishonest in other ways, too, such as when they extorted a longer work schedule than the one agreed upon by finding accomplices who would turn the town clock back so that weeders would be tricked into staying longer in the fields. This was not surprising, for the squads often had fewer weeders than necessary for the job. Or *capi* took "bonuses" from rice growers if they managed to make squads work more days than agreed on without extra pay.[58] Sometimes *capi* even failed to pay the promised wages. In the novel, Nanna's *caposquadra* used another ploy: he ran away at the end of the *mondatura* with wages and down payments of the forty weeders.[59]

Migratory squads came from a variety of places, ranging from neighboring villages to sites over two hundred kilometers away, such as Reggio Emilia, and Modena, in Emilia. Squads from Piacenza, also in Emilia, and Lodi, in Lombardy, traveled about a hundred kilometers to get to the fields. Besides these workers from the east, squads from the surrounding mountains, from the Novarese Highland (Alto Novarese), the Biellese, Ivrea, Valsesia, Pallanza (in Lake Maggiore), Ossola, Voghera, Bobbio, Monferrato, and Tortonese came from fifteen to seventy kilometers away.[60] One may assume that railroad lines allowed for this mobility. Main lines that passed through vital points of the rice belt were built in Piedmont in the 1850s, and in the following decades new branches connected these centers with remoter areas of the Po valley.[61]

Despite their shared interests and problems, migrants and local weeders did not socialize. Local weeders were called *avventizie* (day workers), sometimes also *di piazza*, because they reported to the public square (*piazza*) of the nearest center to be hired for six days at a time. No middleman intervened in the negotiations; the employers paid the wages agreed upon at the end of the week, and those *mondariso* who lived within walking distance carried their own meals to the fields.

Sanitary Problems and the Debate over Rice Cultivation

Given their diet, housing, clothing, environment, and working conditions, the *mondariso* were susceptible to disease. Some of these are difficult to identify today based on the descriptions left by pathologists of the time. Malaria had been known in the Italian peninsula since ancient times and was believed to be caused by miasmas rising from the swamps. It was the first of many diseases to be connected with rice farming. Malarial fevers were widespread in the Po valley before the introduction of rice, but, as it expanded, cultivators began to frequent formerly uninhabited places where they ran the risk of being bitten by anopheles mosquitoes, which carried the disease. This was already the case at the time when rice was "the treasure of the swamps." As rice cultivation spread, more and more surface area was flooded, artificially creating larger mosquito breeding grounds.

Many inhabitants of the nearby countryside, villages, or cities became vulnerable to the contagion. The *mondariso*, and after them the harvesters, were the most affected, because they worked during the most dangerous months, when the anopheles carried and transmitted the parasite. The easiest victims were migratory weeders who, besides being less immune than locals to the infection, had to spend the night in the open air. Once they returned to their homes, they could spread the disease and thus affect local health conditions. Therefore the problem far transcended the boundaries of the low-lying fields. For one reason or another, a broader segment of the population was threatened with malaria, which occasionally crossed class lines.

The inhabitants of the Po valley grasped the connection between rice fields and malaria very early. By 1523 epidemics in relation with the new crop had reached alarming proportions.[62] This caused local rulers to act as mediators between rice growers and the public. They established the distances to be kept by law between fields and populated places, and even main roads. Legislation restricting rice farming started in 1576 and continued until this century. As a general rule, rice farmers did not obey these laws, in spite of severe punishments, like fines or destruction of fields. Corruption and opportunism accounted both for lax supervision and a failure to enforce penalties.[63]

During the Napoleonic period the contrast between theory and practice became clearer than ever before. In spite of rigid regulations that reflected a general concern for the health and welfare of the people,[64] more rice fields were established in prohibited, as well as in legal, areas. Rice farming spread rapidly; it was a measure of the drive of the enterprising bourgeoisie of the time. Influential farmers of the province of Bologna suffered from *risomania* and many of them bought land from the church. Rice cultivation yielded a profit two and a half times higher than that of any other cereal; the area under cultivation grew from fifteen hundred to eight thousand hectares.[65] In Vercelli a prefect of the French administration complained in 1802 that "one cannot see without indignation, on all roads that lead to Vercelli, written on top of high milestones 'end of rice farming,' while on this side of them one views rice fields for the extent of hundreds of *trabucchi*" (a *trabucco* equals 3.36 yards).[66] An admirer of the old Savoyard regulations, he wanted to see them enforced, but it was not an easy task. In the long contest between conscientious officials and rice growers with influence in administrative and political circles, the latter ended victorious.

During the Restoration, conservatives raised humanitarian arguments against rice farming, but only to disguise their defense of traditional social relations in the countryside, like those established between landowners and sharecroppers, probably the ones they maintained on their own estates. They feared the imbalance that the uprooted masses could provoke in the political and public order, and also the threat that capitalist farming posed to their economic stability. But the pleas for a return to the past were too weak to change the official leniency toward those who ignored the laws.

Medical congresses on the subject of rice farming also considered its relation to the spread of malaria. The first congresses took place in Florence in 1841, in Padua in 1842, and in Lucca in 1843. The discussions were far from impartial or dispassionate. The majority of physicians declared in each of the meetings that rice fields, especially the artificially irrigated ones, impaired human health and had to be prohibited. Despite this, an articulate minority ready to defend the rights of growers was able to impose its views in the general conclusion of the congress of Genoa of 1852:

> Therefore, the grave evils attributed to the rice fields by the common opinion in great part have been exaggerated, and in part are not peculiar to cultivation, but dependent upon the particular circumstances accompanying it.[67]

This ambiguous and incongruous declaration was tantamount to the defeat of the "abolitionist thesis," which had prevailed in the earlier congresses, calling for the prohibition of rice farming. The harm the crop caused, though too obvious to be ignored, could be remedied by providing health care to laborers and by implementing sanitary regulations in the countryside, according to the new premise. We must keep in mind that the medical debate was no more than an academic discussion. On the basis of centuries-old experience, any victory by "abolitionists" would surely have been annulled by growers, who customarily ignored official regulations. In any case, there was no move to introduce the health measures proposed at the Genoa convention.

Giuseppe Giardina's study, "Malaria in the Rice Fields" (*Malaria in risaia*), published in 1925, still used many of the old arguments, which were often contradictory. The author says that many doctors, moved by their philanthropic spirit, were drawn to "exaggerate the real range of the evil, not to let it be clouded and overpowered by the concomitant economic interests, which naturally found easier support." Governments, too, according to Giardina, passed restrictive legislation in response to exaggerated medical evaluations of unsanitary conditions. He severely condemns such claims, yet he declares that it is not possible to compare the seriousness of past infection with its mildness in his own time. Furthermore, if it was difficult in his own day to measure the severity of malarial infection in a region, it was impossible to infer anything about malaria in the past.[68]

Discussions about malaria were often biased and involved contradictory interpretations of the effects of a number of agents on human health. Authorities were therefore reluctant to take measures or intervene among the contending parties. Impartial observers refused to consider any kind of mitigating circumstances. They condemned the unhealthy working conditions in the rice fields. Supporters of rice growing, like Bordiga and Jacini, were always ready to exonerate rice growers and their labor practices. Bordiga insisted on the mild character of the contagion in the rice belt. He reasoned that, after all, it caused death very seldom. He also blamed the weeders:

> [They] become sick either of malaria or of extreme exertion, and more of this last cause, because wanting to earn much and spend little, they make longer workdays than usual and economize as much as they can on food.[69]

Jacini was ready to recognize that rice farming was hazardous to human health but viewed the situation in the early 1880s confidently; the risk had been greater earlier because of the uncontrolled expansion of rice cultivation. But as a result of the agricultural crisis, rice growing was restricted to land suitable for it and other crop rotation, and rational farming methods were being introduced. The senator hoped to see these innovations adopted throughout the Italian countryside, to check the spread of fever. For example, better drainage helped keep the air less moist and protected water wells more effectively from pollution.[70] The permanent cultivation of rice in marshes was still going on, and marshes were more dangerous than rice fields;

therefore he recommended that rice should be sown in a swampy patch only if it was unsuited for other plants or for reclamation. To him, fumes were not the cause of the worst cases of fever. Instead, filth, humid and miserable houses, poor wells, and pitiable food were. They were all evils that progressive legislation could eliminate.[71]

The radical deputy Bertani found that benign malaria, widespread in the north, was, unlike the pernicious malaria typical of the south, milder in individuals who had built up a certain resistance. However, it could quickly destroy the bodies of those coming from nonmalarial regions, like the migratory weeders who were worn down by poverty and fatigue. The sick almost never lived to old age. According to the census of 1881, the majority of the Italians who had lived to be over seventy-five were from the six provinces, out of forty, that were free from malaria. The mortality rate in the Piedmont and Lombardy districts without rice fields was somewhat lower than in those areas where the crop was grown. Here the population showed a lower resistance to all diseases. Laborers of the province of Novara, except for those of higher lands, were particularly victimized; in Vercelli they looked wretched, had yellow skin, and suffered from splenic tumors—all symptoms of grave malarial infection. An enlarged spleen and also an enlarged liver could become permanent because of hyperplasia, and this led to disturbances in blood circulation and to swelling of the stomach. The heart, muscles, kidney, and brain could also be damaged.[72]

The graphed curves representing the numbers of those stricken by malaria and treated in the hospitals of Novara and Vercelli in the second half of the nineteenth century might help explain what happened at least among hospitalized patients, who were a minority. But the curves specify neither the sex nor the occupation of the sick. They show three stages of intense recrudescence, culminating in 1855–58, 1867–69, and 1881–84, respectively. The peak of 1867–69 was attributed to the many swampy areas created during the digging of the Cavour canal. The outbreak of 1881–84, which was much more severe than the preceding one, was of "pandemic" nature. In 1884 the hospital of Novara admitted about thirty-one hundred malaria-infected patients. In "normal" periods, the curves do not indicate any reduction in the number of patients, from 500 to 800 per year. In the hospital of Novara they constitute 31 percent of the patients in 1884, a critical year, and 6 to 11 percent in "normal" years until 1903. By then factors such as a more generalized use of quinine contributed to the drop of malaria victims.

The only favorable sign in the whole period is a decrease in the malaria mortality rate, though not in the number of cases. Malarial patients generally died from complications that malaria had predisposed them to. Therefore, mortality rates do not indicate malaria as the cause of death. In a table showing mortality rates caused by twenty-six different diseases in Mortara between the years 1882 and 1898, malaria appears only in the twenty-first place, with a rate of 0.94 per thousand inhabitants. The five highest death rates are those of lung infection (28.83 per thousand), gastroenteritis (24.1 per thousand), pneumonia and croup (15.54 per thousand), and cardiopathy (12.8 per thousand).[73]

In fact, rice was one of the most unpopular crops among the population at large, and not only because of the social dislocations and threats to health and the environment that it caused, but also because it was grown exclusively for export, and was therefore of little use in alleviating the hunger of the poor. This explains why in 1816, in the middle of a severe famine in the province of Bologna, the exasperated rural masses staged protests and marched to the rice fields in order to destroy them.[74] Quinine could have aided the sick. In fact, the Italians were acquainted with the therapeutic qualities of the drug, but its high price restricted its use to the well-to-do.

There were other diseases in the rice belt as well, such as scurvy and typhoid fever. Typhoid, sometimes complicated by malaria, had reached epidemic proportions in the Po valley during the last decades of the eighteenth century[75] and recurred later on. The typhoid organism thrives in contaminated water and the *mondariso* ran a high risk of contagion in the flooded rice fields.

Again we find divergent opinions about these illnesses. Bordiga denied the existence of cases of typhoid fever; patients with phthisis, rickets, and scrofula (tuberculosis of the lymph glands, especially in the neck), he wrote, were fewer in the rice belt than in other parts of the peninsula, although he found that scrofula was very common in the rice belt, chiefly among women.[76] Bordiga, trying to dispel any fears of the environment, attested to the fact that there were only a few cholera victims in Novara during the epidemics of 1866–67.[77] Like most studies of the time, Bordiga's does not include figures to corroborate his argument.

An 1880 study on health conditions in the province of Pavia (*La pellagra in Italia*) focused on illnesses among the rice workers of Lomellina. The most frequent and deadliest was lung disease. Workers had few defenses against it, the authors explain, because of their habit of staying in stables in the winter and then going outdoors without clothing. Enteritis came second in frequency, followed by intermittent fevers, ophthalmia, gastritis, "phlegm," pellagra, and accidents. Ophthalmia had many victims among weeders; it was caused by the reflection of light on water. Pellagra was central to the study. Although not very widespread in Pavia, it severely attacked those who lived on irrigated land, mainly in Lomellina. The study concluded that pellagra was due to conditions created by the land tenure and cultivation systems of the large rice-growing estates. Day laborers, particularly weeders, were easy prey, because they worked under bad conditions. Disease rates in the nonirrigated parts of the valley were in direct contrast to those in Lomellina. Property was divided into smaller tracts. Wheat and dairy products were produced, and pellagra seldom appeared.[78]

Sanitary conditions were also bad in the province of Novara, especially in irrigated areas. If health was poor in the winter and spring, it was worse in the summer and fall, when malaria reached the uplands, carried by women workers returning home. Many day laborers, who inhabited the most unhealthy places, died between the ages of fifty and fifty-five.

In *In risaia*, Nanna fell sick for the second time when she went to weed. The other *mondariso* sang a slow, moaning song, but she could not utter a word, found the smell of the water nauseating, and felt as if the sun were burning her brains. She was dizzy and her head throbbed for days afterward. To make things worse, her companions decided that she suffered from "cephalitis" and covered her head with a black hen cut in half. She actually had typhus and had to stay in the hospital for six months. She slowly recovered her health, but never her hair, which she lost because of the infection caused by the hen stuck to her scalp, so she had to live with her head covered with a kerchief.[79]

Legislation on Rice Farming

Legislation on rice farming and its labor force in the second half of the nineteenth century remained very limited in scope and was even more restricted in its application. The burning question of the damage that rice farming caused to humans and the environment spurred some parliamentary deputies of the kingdom of Piedmont-Sardinia to action. In November 1848 the chamber discussed a projected law to lift all restrictions on rice farming in Vercelli, but the country was at war with Austria and the plan was dropped.[80] Another debate in 1851 ended with the approval of a provisional rice law, which would be in effect until a definitive law could be prepared the following year. However, the definitive law never materialized. The immediate purpose of the 1851 act was to eliminate all the illegal fields planted after 1849.[81]

In both 1848 and 1851 the Piedmontese champions of rice cultivation rehearsed the usual arguments. They insisted that the prohibition of rice growing was an attack against property rights. Besides, far from causing misery, the crop brought prosperity to the regions involved. Moreover, its export increased the flow of foreign currency into the whole kingdom. And, after all, the harm was exaggerated, they said; statistics did not show an increase in the death rates of the rice-growing regions. Still, there was room for improvement, such as the construction of taller houses to lodge workers on the second floor, away from dampness. The apologists also argued that the riches produced by rice brought good health and that restrictions on rice would result in losses. They would conspicuously decrease job opportunities for seasonal workers, increase the competition among them, and lower their wages. Last but not least, working conditions in the rice fields were not worse than those prevailing in mines and factories, which nobody would think of closing.[82]

During the 1848 parliamentary debate, Giovanni Lanza, a physician and future prime minister, observed that where rice thrived, the environment was unsafe for laborers. During the height of the weeding season, he argued, hospitals did not have enough beds for the victims of malaria and other diseases caused by the humid summer days:

> It is not [so] for the big proprietors, because they collect the product of these rice fields, and then go to eat it here and there, in healthy and salubrious places, because they furnish themselves with everything necessary, advantageous, and comfortable to preserve their own health.[83]

Lanza's observations reflected not only his professional knowledge as a medical doctor, but also his concern for the plight of the lower classes when he still sat on the left in the Piedmontese parliament. He demanded that rice farming be limited to land that was absolutely useless for any other agricultural use because it lacked adequate drainage. Yet only after unification were laws finally passed.

On June 9, 1862, the minister of agriculture, Gioacchino

Napoleone Pepoli, an enlightened conservative and a nephew of Napoleon III, presented a measure that, in his own words, permitted "unrestricted rice farming, subject solely to some hygienic rules."[84] Urbano Ratazzi, the prime minister, decided to table his proposal and used the numerous bills that awaited discussion during that parliamentary session as a justification. The real reason for postponement was the criticism that Pepoli's scheme had drawn from influential circles. It left to the central government to determine regulation of the distances that had to be kept between fields and inhabited places. For the rice growers who were members of the Agricultural Association (*Comizio Agrario*) of Milan this was to "enter into certain detail that would easily give rise to an oppressive surveillance or else to an often arbitrary, more often incorrect, application. . . . All these general provisions, moreover, hurt the eminently local character which, in our opinion, any law or regulation on rice cultivation must have."

These same farmers put forth an alternative proposal, which was hastily approved on June 12, 1866, after the minister of the interior requested that it be treated with all possible urgency. It gave local authorities the power to regulate distances.[85] According to article 1 of the bill, each province was to make its own regulations after hearing testimony from the municipal and sanitary councils of the rice districts; these were then to be approved by royal decree, after the vote of the superior sanitary council and the council of state. The provincial regulations became known as the Cantelli regulations. The topographic and atmospheric conditions of each area would thus determine the limitations and, according to article 4, offenders were to be fined up to 200 lire for each hectare cultivated in forbidden areas. All the old norms and rules (article 7) would expire once the provincial regulations had been passed. The provincial councils were also in charge of passing various measures to improve housing for workers and the quality of water.[86]

Yet many rice growers and interested persons criticized even these lenient provincial regulations as rigorous, unjust, and an abuse of private initiative.[87] In fact, the regulations had almost no teeth when they were applied—a situation that disappointed many public spirited individuals and institutions. The Pavia chamber of commerce study on health conditions in the province found the farmers' unregulated actions absolutely unjustifiable:

> It would be enough if only the prescriptions of the written law, which are scattered in the multiform provincial regulations of the rice fields, were enforced both uniformly and strictly, or, if

the government proclaimed by law the minimal conditions imposed on those who want to cultivate rice, arrogating to itself the supervision, to see that these conditions are respected.

These complaints about the total neglect of the legislation of 1866 are not surprising in view of the nature of its enforcement mechanism. The Cantelli regulations entrusted inspections to the mayors (*sindaci*) and municipal councils, but "mayors and councilors are all proprietors and capitalist farmers, or persons who depend on them and who have an interest in violating the regulations rather than in seeing that they are observed."[88] The few appointed provincial inspectors did very little besides close their eyes to abuse. It was useless to ask the central government to intervene, for agriculturalists were very influential there too. One very important, albeit little mentioned, point in the regulations was the one banning weeding during the hours when the risk of contracting malaria was regarded as most probable. These were the first hour after sunrise and the hour before sunset, when "contaminated" fog hung over the fields. The regulations also prescribed that the pulled weeds be taken to a dry place to prevent their rotting in the water.

The weeders lacked charitable aid, just as they lacked methods of collective self-defense, reform programs, or a political ideology that might have helped them overcome their poverty.

Luraghi searched in vain for signs of collective action in Vercelli by the mid-nineteenth century. Having found none, he explained that the monopoly exercised in the kingdom by men like Cavour through the Agrarian Association had made such actions impossible. The association's policy was to suppress any talk of a minimum wage, or of a reduction of work hours in the *risaie*. In other words, they advocated the same liberal economic policies that its most prominent member, Cavour, implemented for the kingdom and they deemed this to be the most effective way to combat any state interference in private enterprise.[89] Only the generous and paternalistic capitalist farmer who acted out of his own convictions could change things for the better. Therefore the influence of the association served to impede the workers' organizing for several decades.[90]

Jacini, writing in Lombardy on the conditions of the lower classes, situated himself ideologically close to the Piedmontese moderates; he regarded socialist and conservative programs alike as retrogressive. Instead he backed a "reformist" course of action, which was also in substance the practice of liberal economics. He proposed changes to be carried out by individual initiative, which, however, no farmer was willing to put into effect.[91]

Here and there weeders showed signs of "disrespect," in the form of complaints, displays of stubbornness, a spirit of independence, or violations of private property. The attitude of workers may well have been due to the relative prosperity of Italian agriculture during the 1860s, when some workers left the countryside for the towns to work in prospering new industries. Some of those who remained on the land may have become dimly conscious of the deprivation they lived under as the lot of town dwellers improved. But if weeders complained and hoped for improvements, their aspirations were ill defined. The investigators of the *Inchiesta Jacini* were surprised to find that, in general, weeders and other rice workers, despite their wretchedness, quietly endured their lot.[92] They had no organization and made no claims for better treatment. This was a situation that the parties in power after unification, the *Destra* (right) and, after 1876, the *Sinistra* (left), considered eminently suitable for Italy's economic, political, and social structure. The political groups that could have helped weeders frame their demands were just beginning to organize and were unable to make inroads in the rice belt.

The Social Question

In the late 1870s, at the beginning of the long economic recession, fears of social upheaval, fed by the memories of the 1789, 1830, and 1848 revolutions, and the 1871 Paris Commune, as well as concern for the lot of the lower classes, awakened public opinion in general to the need for improving workers' conditions. The investigators of the *Inchiesta Jacini* had this point of view, and advanced their own practical prescriptions along with those proposed to them by local notables, especially magistrates, or bodies such as agrarian societies (*Comizi Agrari*), to remedy the situation of rice field workers.[93] Since the *Risorgimento*, philosophers, politicians, churchmen, economists, sociologists, activists, and intellectuals, among them Carlo Pisacane, Camillo Cavour, Giuseppe Mazzini, Giuseppe Ferrari, Osvaldo Gnocchi-Viani, and their followers, had understood that the social question was a fundamental political question, which, if not addressed, would provide serious challenges to society as a whole. The spread of brigandage in southern Italy during the 1860s, the Paris Commune, peasant uprisings, and the foundation of the Italian anarchist federation in 1872 disturbed the ruling classes. But it was during the economic depression that the full implications of the social question began to concern rulers and broader sectors of the bourgeoisie, and spur investigations and searches for remedies.[94] The government instituted two official inquiries about that time, one on the conditions of agriculture (*Inchiesta Jacini*), and the other on industrial strikes.

The spirit of Cavour still pervaded many of the responses of the investigators of the *Inchiesta Jacini*, who aimed to preserve the established order. Francesco Meardi, a lawyer and parliamentary deputy, even recalled Cavour's exhortations to landowners. They were not only to look after the land, but also to care for the minds of the tillers by giving them positive principles, examples, and teachings in order to consolidate a social hierarchy built on more just and stable foundations than those destroyed during the era of the French Revolution. For Meardi, Russian nihilism, Fenianism, the Spanish Black Hand, the spirit of the Commune, German socialism, and internationalism presented new threats to the social order. What was to be done? Meardi and his colleagues gave a broad range of suggestions to the government, entrusting it with the tutelage and guidance of workers.[95] The mutual aid and worker societies could help the rulers attain this goal. There were some mutual aid societies (*società di mutuo soccorso*) in urban centers of the rice belt. In many mutual aid and worker societies, workers often met under the auspices of honorary members such as politicians, local authorities, professors, army officers, churchmen, and landowners, who often contributed financially to their support. One had been founded in Stroppiana (Vercellese) in 1853, another called Work-Temperance-Union (*Lavoro-Temperanza-Unione*) in Lignana in 1867.[96] In Lomellina the Mortarese Workers' Society was formed in 1850. Many others were founded in the region.[97] Workers, mostly craftsmen, received sickness and old age benefits as well as funeral expenses in exchange for small dues.

From 1860 on, Mazzini's followers struggled, with success, to wrestle many of the worker societies from moderate leaders, whose liberal views prevailed from 1853 to 1859. They clashed with the Mazzinians on the issue of whether the societies should enter politics. Mazzini wanted these to be political bodies where workers could challenge the sway of the church over the Italian people, and affirm their republican faith and their repudiation of privilege, while discussing ideas about national unity and class harmony. But Meardi, writing in the early 1880s, regretted that day workers, especially the women weeders, did not belong to these societies, and therefore proposed that the rice growers create and direct new ones that would attract the rural proletariat.

Other proposals intended to guide farm workers in affirming their allegiance to the social order included the abolition of, or decrease in, taxes on foodstuffs, especially salt, the creation of more savings institutions, cooperative societies, and communal ovens sponsored by provincial governments. Several bourgeois reformers also urged the reorganization of charitable associations and the improvement of education, "the great redeemer of the people." New day and evening schools, libraries, and lecture series should impart moral and, above all, political education to farm workers, acquainting them with the rights and duties of citizens and with the organization of the state. These would expedite "wise" discussion of the social question, "to refute the most fantastic and noxious theories that circulate among the people."[98] Some magistrates recommended that the investigators of the *Inchiesta Jacini* introduce laws to help administer justice promptly and free of charge, while punishing rural theft with greater severity. The Agrarian Society (*Comizio Agrario*) of Vercelli offered immediate practical recommendations to improve the rural workers' lot. It called for the appointment of municipal doctors in all rural communes, to be nominated by sanitary commissions, not by the municipalities. Other magistrates stressed the need to protect labor against capital and to intervene with the strength of the law to regulate farm workers' wages.

"Of these proposals," Meardi readily comments, "the first is of a very general character, to deserve due consideration. The other, impossible to apply, is opposed to the principle of liberty to which the laws of the state conform and to the more elementary one of political economy."

Two proposals touched on children's and working mothers' issues, such as the need of preschool care centers, and of a law on child and woman labor. Another opinion supported women's education "because women will always exercise great influence within all social classes."[99] Jacini, the investigator of Lomellina, agreed that social equality was impossible, that nature itself had stamped and sifted distinctions for the sake of order, but he lamented "that the difference be such . . . that farm workers . . . should be treated as things and not as human beings," which was "incomprehensible and unjust." He insisted that the farm worker should be rescued from servitude and become a human being—that is, a strict observer of duties and virtues—and not a prey and supporter of the castes that "have a sword of Damocles permanently suspended above the head of society." For Jacini "in Italy the social question is especially agrarian . . . and may flare up terrifyingly between today and tomorrow."[100] But for Jacini, all these ethical considerations apart, the key to solving the social and technical problems of the countryside was the promotion of agricultural prosperity by private initiative, which, of course would count on the generous assistance of the government, in the form of tax exemptions, loans, reforestation, and land reclamation works.[101]

In any case, the recommendations of the inquiries followed the fate of the fifteen volumes of the *Inchiesta*, which were shelved and forgotten after their publication. Neither the state nor the ruling classes fulfilled the redemptive role that the investigators expected of them. With few exceptions, women weeders made use of methods, institutions, and ideas other than those advanced in the *Inchiesta* to change their situation.

The Agrarian Question

Nevertheless, Jacini and his collaborators were correct in perceiving the social question as an agrarian problem. Italy began its industrialization only after 1869, and long thereafter the proportion of the economically active population in agriculture remained very high— almost 56 percent in 1921.[102] Especially noteworthy in Italy was the early formation of a large agricultural proletariat, concentrated mainly in the Po valley, as a consequence of high capital investments in the region. These farm workers had no illusions about cultivating their own land in the future; consequently they were ready, when the occasion arose, to challenge the power of the state, the church, or the landowning class, and fight for better wages, a shorter workday, or the eradication of unemployment and oppressive taxes.[103]

One such occasion did arise in 1868–69 when the Po valley became the main site of bloody uprisings against the introduction of a grist tax (*macinato*), which was bitterly opposed by the poor. The grist tax set the masses of the poor against the nation state that oppressed them with unbearable burdens. The riots, which aimed at destroying what their participants—men, women, and children—viewed as the instruments of state power, were severely repressed.[104] The *macinato* uprisings were particularly violent in Emilia, but they affected the rice belt too. Renato Zangheri, focusing on the province of Bologna, rules out the influence of socialist ideas on the protests, and sees in them a

valuable experience for the rebels, whose solidarity and combativeness would very soon be fueling the socialist struggle in the region.[105]

In effect, widespread violent protests continued in response to
the effects of the severe economic depression of 1873–96, to the rapid
changes caused by capitalist agriculture, and to new, more oppressive
taxes on the working population. A new electoral law in 1882, which
extended the franchise to some skilled workers, had little effect on
these protests. As they spread across Italy, leftist political groups
sought to direct workers' actions according to their own prescriptions
for the social problems that the process of national unification had left
unresolved. The republican and radical followers of Mazzini stressed
class collaboration. Like their leader, the ardent revolutionary who
had to spend most of his mature years in exile, they rejected class
conflict and collectivism. Mazzini envisioned a republic where the
bourgeoisie and the workers would be educated in the principles of
justice, duty, and responsibility. In the new free society, entrepreneurs would share ownership and profits with the workers, and exploitation and class struggle would have no place. Socialists and anarchists emphasized class conflict. Anarchism particularly, with its call
for social revolution and the abolition of private property and the
state, found fertile soil in Italy as it strove for the social justice and
equality that the liberal state was denying to the majority of Italians.

In Rimini in 1872 the Italian Federation of the First International
was founded under the influence of the Russian anarchist Mikhail
Bakunin, who believed that the Italian rural population was endowed
with revolutionary spirit and had, therefore, an innate propensity
toward staging spontaneous insurrections. Anarchist associations
flourished in the 1870s to the detriment of Mazzinian organizations.
Many members found it more and more difficult to live up to
Mazzini's ideals on class relations, given the inequalities present in
Italian society. The anarchists staged two unsuccessful insurrections
in Bologna (1874) and Benevento (1877); by 1880 their revolutionary
activities were firmly put down by the central government[106] while
the anarchist-dominated Italian Federation languished.

But anarchists continued their insurrectionary propaganda despite the fact that in the 1880s workers became more receptive to
socialist ideas. They were to remain embedded in a labor movement
that would use what came to be called "resistance" (*resistenza*) as a
method to direct its struggle. But the political vocabulary of the time
made a clear-cut distinction between anarchists and socialists difficult, because the former not only called themselves anarchic so-

cialists, but also usually applied the term "socialist" to almost every-thing that concerned them. One significant event in the growing distinction between the two currents would be the founding congress of the Italian Socialist Party in 1892, during which anarchist and so-cialist delegates split conclusively. The anarchists, who were in de-cline, continued their antiauthoritarian insurrectionary action. Never-theless, some anarchic traits would remain in the Socialist Party and would come to the surface at the beginning of the century.[107]

In the 1880s a series of massive strikes erupted in the Po valley, organized by mutual aid and cooperative societies, day workers asso-ciations, and new local unions called resistance leagues (*leghe di re-sistenza*). Members were mainly day laborers (*braccianti*) of both sexes,[108] exasperated by scarcity, high prices, low wages, and unem-ployment. The focal points of the strikes were Polesine, Parma, Reg-gio, Modena, and Ravenna. They culminated in 1885 with the strike at Mantua, where organizers of progressive political groups, from radicals and republicans to anarchists and revolutionary socialists, set up *braccianti* unions. Troops sent in by Prime Minister Agostino De-pretis routed the leagues.[109]

These struggles made a lasting impression on the people at large. Weeders were the main participants in rural conflicts in the provinces of Milan and Bologna. In the 1880s rice farmers in Bologna were expanding the area under rice cultivation, which had been so popular during the Napoleonic period. The fields reached an extent of twenty thousand hectares (about a tenth of the total area under rice in the kingdom) at the end of the century.[110] The labor force consisted mainly of women wage earners who, in some communes of the province of Bologna, like Molinella, became protagonists of cou-rageous strikes starting in 1883. By then socialist propaganda had penetrated the region. Zangheri states that in the following years "Molinella will become the center of a profound political and human transformation,"[111] and it may be added that Molinella's weeders became vital agents in this transformation. In 1886 fifteen hundred weeders went on strike and succeeded in having wages increased from 0.70 to 1 lira.[112] In 1887, a year of severe unemployment, the *mondine*, who wanted higher pay, stopped working. They got their raise. In all cases, weeders of the neighboring communes also went on strike and shared in the Molinella victories.[113] A young woman from one of these communes, Medicina, exclaimed to the subprefect who had arrived to persuade the workers to resume work: "Ah! You say that a 1.30 lira wage is too much! Come here with us for one day, bent, with your buttocks facing the sun for ten consecutive hours, and in the evening you will be able to tell us if twenty-six soldi [1 soldo = 5 centesimi] is too much pay!"[114]

In 1890 the socialist organizer Giuseppe Massarenti began his activities in Molinella, fighting unemployment and setting up leagues, cooperatives, and placement offices, mediating in labor conflicts, and suffering persecution and exile. Elected mayor in 1906, he managed to convert the commune into a "proletarian republic" until it fell victim to the fascist violence of the 1920s.[115] The protests reached a wider scope under Massarenti's leadership. A strike in 1893, involving seventeen communes, ended in defeat. A strike in 1897, instead, lasted more than forty days and was finally victorious. The police flaunted terror, beating and arresting forty-three weeders, who were all sentenced to imprisonment, some of them for more than three months. The work stoppages of 1900 began during the weeding and continued at harvest time, when over six thousand strikers were completely defeated after thirty days of abstention from work. Rice farmers used soldiers and immigrant workers to replace the strikers. In the following year, they suffered another defeat, which was the more tragic because the police killed one laborer and wounded several others.[116]

At the turn of the century, women workers in the Bolognese had to face a different situation. Employers decided to quell the weeders' militancy by drastically reducing the size of the rice fields (by 50 percent between 1901 and 1905) and by cultivating labor-saving crops instead,[117] thus contributing to the slow disappearance of rice workers from the province. Weeders would take up other kinds of work and continue their epic struggles, but women in Novara, Vercelli, and Lomellina continued weeding.

Many of the socialist organizers of the first protests in the Po valley became deputies. The first was Andrea Costa, and like him, the ones who followed remained committed to the cause of the field laborers whose problems they had learned about through direct contact with many sectors of the Po valley society.[118] They were to put this early experience in the battles of the rural proletariat to good use when they later strove to ally agricultural and industrial workers in a common cause.[119]

But the militancy of farm workers in the lower Po valley left the rice belt apparently untouched. Given its proximity to the theater of events, one may surmise that news of the protests reached weeders and made them aware of the similarity between their problems and those of the mobilized workers. But it was a mistake to see the *mondariso* of the rice belt as a completely harmless group. The investigators of the *Inchiesta Jacini,* who were gathering information on the rice belt in the late 1870s, had the feeling that workers could become a dangerous class. An alarmed investigator asked:

> Where will we end up if this already hostile element would be infiltrated by socialist theories whose spread has been surreptitiously upheld for some time? If they are told that the landowners had been thieves, because the land belongs to the community and cannot be alienated?[120]

3

The Early Stages of Mobilization: Protest Actions, Socialist Propaganda, and the Weeders' Response in 1901

In the 1880s the Italian ruling classes propounded vague solutions to meet the needs of the majority of the rural population. Their formulas for social betterment failed either to produce results or to generate a mass response. Also in the 1880s weeders in the rice belt staged group protests and demonstrations that were a far cry from the day laborers' epic battles fought in other areas of the Po valley. At the beginning of the twentieth century, the *mondine* mobilized for collective action and became a visible group in Italian society, molding a common program and striving to implement it against enormous obstacles. The socialist program for the weeders' mobilization took root in the wake of the strikes in Polesine, Parma, Reggio, Modena, Ravenna, Mantua, and Bologna, and of the propaganda and organizing activities by anarchists and members of the Italian Workers' Party.

The city of Vercelli had an eventful political life, to which farm workers may not have remained completely indifferent. New currents were suffusing fresh blood into the conservative district capital. The Vercelli anarchist Luigi Galleani (1861–1931) was active in the city, as well as in Turin, during the 1880s. In his youth he abandoned the republican cause to fight for anarchist principles not only in Italy, often from jail, but also in several other European countries and in the United States, in the state of Vermont. He was a dazzling orator and an outstanding labor organizer, agitator, writer, and journalist. In 1883 he wrote for the city democratic newspaper *L'Operaio* [The worker]. In one of his articles he severely criticized an order given by military officers to their troops to disband a peaceful demonstration of men and women workers at Vercelli. As a consequence, he fought several duels with the insulted officers, who left him largely unharmed. He founded the newspaper *La Boje!* (1885), where he published his invectives against the bourgeois order. He delivered revolutionary speeches in several locations of Piedmont, and organized workers' associations and protests.[1] In Vercelli in 1887 he founded the socialist circle *Difesa del lavoro* (defense of labor) and the *Lega dei lavoratori* (workers' league).

His program was to unify these associations with the Italian Workers' Party (*Partito Operaio Italiano* or POI), whose stronghold was in Milan, with the purpose of infusing it with the anarchist idea of revolutionary struggle. He failed; the majority of the POI became part of the new Italian Socialist Party in 1892, ready to follow a nonrevolutionary (*legalitario*) path. Galleani had no place in it. In fact, as a delegate to the party's founding congress, he was literally left outside it, along with all his fellow anarchists.[2] He also disappeared from the Vercelli political scene.

In 1886 the Italian Workers' Party attempted to organize weeders. The POI had been founded in Milan in 1882 when the new electoral law allowed a limited participation of male workers in elections.[3] It was called "the party of the calloused hands" because it accepted only workers in its ranks, with the exception of its founder, Osvaldo Gnocchi-Viani. Working-class leaders, among them Giusseppe Croce, a glover, and Alfredo Casati, a brass-smith, were highly educated artisans or workers.

One of the distinctive traits of the POI was its interest in organizing both urban and rural workers and in removing them from the influence of radical bourgeois politicians, such as the Mazzinians, the republicans, and the radicals. It engaged almost exclusively in economic battles, and was not so keen about participating in political ones. Committed to class struggle, it endorsed the formation of trade unions and resistance leagues, along with the use of strikes and protest actions.

At the peak of its agitation in 1885 in the Po valley, the restlessness of both urban and rural workers radicalized the POI and drew it into revolutionary positions. Its most resolute leaders decided to do what some anarchists of the Italian Federation of the International were also attempting—to give direction to spontaneous forms of traditional, antiauthoritarian protests, which often flared up when the masses resented the excessive hardship of what they viewed as unjust political, social, or economic measures. (A famous example of such rebellions were the 1869 riots against the grist tax.) Under POI leadership, work stoppages, tumultuous demonstrations, and riots sometimes ended in attacks on landowners' residences, the burning of registers with records of tenants' debts, or the invasion of farm stewards' houses. This party activity lasted, with ups and downs, from 1885 to 1890.

In 1886 members of the POI led by Alfredo Casati, the party's candidate for the chamber of deputies in Vercelli, organized the first resistance leagues among weeders. Employers denounced them as "strike instigators," and pressured police to put Casati and his comrades in jail, thereby ending this short-lived experiment.[4] Government, judicial, and police harassment seriously weakened the POI, to the relief of the bourgeois political groups whose influence it was trying to supplant in the rice fields.[5] The government had already ordered its dissolution in 1886. A year later, the reconstituted POI lost its unity of purpose: while one group strove to maintain its proletarian character, the other, the so-called socialist branch, showed its readiness to follow the leadership of upper middle-class socialist intellectuals like Filippo Turati.

Socialist Propaganda in the Rice Belt

In 1889 Turati founded the Socialist League in Milan. It attracted a broad range of socialist sympathizers, mainly middle-class intellectuals and manual workers. Turati considered these two elements essential in shaping a national socialist party aimed at the conquest of public power through political struggle. That is why he excluded intransigent members of the Italian Workers' Party opposed to labor participation in electoral contests, as well as anarchists and bourgeois radicals. During the founding congress of the Socialist Party at Genoa in 1892, the moderate delegates of the POI followed Turati to form the new party, while intransigents, like Casati, along with anarchists, remained a weak and isolated revolutionary minority. Yet, although weakened and seemingly cut off from the masses, the hard-liners' call for revolution found echoes in many sectors of the urban and rural proletariat. In the 1890s the forces fighting for democracy since the

Risorgimento were unable to bring their program into being. The government continued to ignore the afflictions of the lower classes, using repression to quell their protests.

These same political circumstances prevented the new Socialist Party from organizing the weeders during the 1890s. On October 22, 1894, Prime Minister Francesco Crispi ordered the suppression of the party and of all groups associated with it in the wake of the repression of the uprisings of farm workers that took place in Sicily in 1893–94, the Sicilian Fasci (*Fasci siciliani*). The socialists did not regain their freedom of action until March 1896 when Crispi fell after Italy suffered a humiliating military defeat at Adua, Ethiopia. The socialists lost out again after the May Events (*Fatti di Maggio*) of 1898 in Milan, where widespread riots to protest the high price of bread were crushed with mass arrests and the massacre of eighty demonstrators.[6] Prime Minister Antonio Di Rudini's declaration of martial law after this bloody event once again crippled the socialists and all democratic organizations; only in 1900 did they recover in a more propitious political climate.

Nevertheless, during the 1890s Socialist organizations did try to penetrate the rice belt. In mid-1893, for example, a socialist circle was founded in the city of Novara, a "conservative fortress" in socialist opinion. There it presented, unsuccessfully, its own candidates for the local July elections. It slowly extended its influence and founded other branches in the Novarese. In June 1896 it established the Socialist Provincial Federation of Novara.[7] Its press organ was the weekly *Novarese Worker* (*Lavoratore novarese*). But the hopes of this federation for carrying on electoral campaigns and discussing the labor problems of rice weeding fell short of expectations, due to intensified police intervention at meetings and other forms of harassment in 1897.[8]

In July 1893 there was also socialist activity in the Vercellese. Farm workers of both sexes crowded the premises of their cooperative in San Germano Vercellese to hear for the first time a speech of Giacinto Menotti Serrati, the future leader of the Italian Socialist Party. The enthusiastic audience, following Serrati's exhortations to unite in order to end their victimization, joined the Socialist Party. These were promising beginnings, but only in appearance; Crispi's repressive measures broke up the organization. Two years later, recruitment had to start again, this time leading to the creation of a socialist electoral circle in Vercelli. It too, another victim of political reaction, was very precarious, and was made still more uncertain by the presence of bourgeois elements, which, according to the socialist weekly *Lotta di Classe* [class struggle], "assassinated the organization" from within. The same weekly announced the constitution, in March 1896, of a "real" section of the Socialist Party in that "impregnable fortress of bourgeois domination and lackeyism" (*del borghesismo e del pecorismo*), and circles in other communes: Tronzano, Bianzè, Santhià, and Crova.[9]

The case of Bianzè deserves special attention. In December 1894 a young physician, Fabrizio Maffi (1868–1955), a graduate of the University of Pavia, was appointed one of its municipal doctors. As a student, he had joined the socialist circle of Pavia and participated in its propaganda campaigns. Tommaso Detti, in his biography of Maffi, writes that Bianzè, like many other Vercellese communes, had so far been cut off from any political or cultural influence from the district capital, excepting that exercised by conservative and Catholic groups. No winds of renewal could have come from a place that, compared to Pavia, lacked any strong class organization in the 1890s.

According to Detti, Maffi introduced the Vercellese socialist movement, which indicates the inability of other democratic and socialist institutions to play a leadership role for the masses of land workers. As a physician who blended his professional care with words about social justice, as an unforgettable friend, and as a socialist organizer, he succeeded in his mission among the poor agricultural workers. There were obstacles in Maffi's way besides the problem of adapting to, in his own words, "an ugly place, all rice fields and water meadows,"[10] and to the constant sight of human suffering. Municipal doctors were appointed for only three years and thereafter they had to be ratified. He suspected that the city would deny him this confirmation for political reasons, as did happen. The mayor was Carlo Marcone, the richest capitalist farmer in the region. Maffi, as the founder of several socialist circles, as the candidate for the parliamentary seat of the electoral district of Crescentino (Vercellese) in the 1895 elections, and as one of the main organizers of a 2-month-long strike, the first in Bianzè, in 1896, became a threat to powerful farmers and political rulers. The strike settlement was favorable to the workers, who won better pay. Maffi left Bianzè at the end of that year, but he still had to appear at three or four trials, accused of being part of an "association that incites class hatred."[11] On February 18, 1897, Modesto Cugnolio, the future socialist leader of Vercelli, defended Maffi.[12] Cugnolio's defense of socialist activists like Maffi and of poor strikers probably played a role in his conversion to socialism during the *Fatti di Maggio* in 1898.[13] After being sentenced to three months imprisonment and the payment of 100 lire for his participation in the 1896 Bianzè strike, Maffi decided to escape to Switzerland in June 1898.[14] He was able to return to Italy a year later under an amnesty.

In 1897 the prefects began a nationwide shutdown of socialist circles. In February it was Santhià, and in March all the others in the province of Novara. With this kind of harassment, the resolution of the second congress of the Socialist Provincial Federation of Novara of June 6 to discuss a minimum agrarian program never got beyond the stage of a simple declaration.[15]

Socialist efforts in Lomellina followed a similar pattern; there the party made its first attempts to organize the migration of weeders of Lomellina. It went down in defeat. In 1893, however, the rice growers reached an agreement with the farm workers' associations of Emilia on wages for the migratory weeders from that region. But as the *mondatura* approached, employers spread the rumor that they had no need for weeders and hired unorganized migrants as weeders instead, through the traditional *capisquadre*[16] for lower pay.

In 1894 socialist party sections sprang up in many communes of Lomellina. Why in Lomellina and not in the Vercellese? It was the result of the work of the socialist students of the University of Pavia, Maffi among them, who "went to the people" in 1893–94, visiting rural communes and setting up circles.[17] Socialist votes even removed the Sannazzaro and Mede mutual aid societies from bourgeois hands.

In May 1894 the reaction was brutal. The socialists likened it to the repression in Sicily against the *Fasci* uprisings of 1893–94, because the government sent three military companies to Mortara, one to Mede, and another to Ottobiano. They closed the socialist circles and prohibited conferences and other party activities. Employers fired militant workers, sometimes accusing them of stealing. Soldiers searched the houses of socialist leaders and the socialist circle of Ottobiano as well. The subprefect then removed from the electoral list the names of those who appeared in the circle's membership roll, to preclude their participation in elections. Considering these measures inadequate, the prefect also ordered the closing of the tavern in Ottobiano, reputed to be a center of socialist discussion.[18]

Despite the influence of the doctrine of German Social Democracy that interpreted class struggle mainly as a struggle between the bourgeoisie and the industrial proletariat, many Italian socialists acknowledged the magnitude of the so-called agrarian question and the need to organize agricultural workers. They saw the importance of the mobilization of farm workers in the Po valley in the 1880s, as well as that of the Sicilian *Fasci* in 1893–94. The socialist students of Pavia recognized this and "went to the people" in the early 1890s. Nevertheless, unfavorable circumstances after 1894 hindered any significant approach by socialists to weeders.[19] The main obstacles were, first, repression itself, and second, the fact that socialists, under duress, gave priority to the defense of badly trampled basic civil rights, and to the increase of its strength among the electorate, which remained overwhelmingly urban.

One promising sign was that the farm workers' organization of Bianzè did not collapse after Maffi's departure.[20] When we think that in 1901 local socialists had to dedicate enormous efforts to set up new institutions, such as leagues and chambers of labor, in order to launch their mobilizing campaign in the rice belt, it will be easier to understand the inadequacy of the party's attempts during the 1890s. But we also have to keep in mind that many sectors of the Socialist Party did not acknowledge the urgency of the matter. Procacci makes reference to "that mistrust toward the farm workers' world that is a distinctive feature of a great part of Italian socialism at the beginning of the century."[21]

In Vercelli, too, after the Italian Workers' Party failed to organize the rice workers in 1886, they were left to their own devices. Impelled by growing dissatisfaction in June 1888, the weeders of San Germano Vercellese had threatened "disorders and arrogant manifestations against employers," to the point that a police officer had to appear on the scene. A year later they staged the same type of "riot"[22] because the entrepreneurs had hired migratory squads instead of local weeders. This time a police officer and five carabinieri intervened.

By July 1893 the weeders of Vercelli were resorting to other tactics in response to efforts of the Savioli brothers, the owners of a large farm, to pay less than the established wage. The Saviolis offered 1.70 lira, while the weeders wanted at least 1.90 lira. There was no agreement, and the women left the farm and marched to neighboring ones to ask the weeders to stop working, thereby causing a general strike in the commune of Vercelli. A commission was sent to negotiate with the subprefect, Facciolati. He entered into negotiations with the Savioli brothers, but failing to convince them to pay the extra 0.20 lira, he paid the difference out of his own pocket in order to put an end to the strike. The bourgeois press reported that Facciolati behaved like a "real gentleman," and the weeders remained immensely grateful to him for this gesture. Actually, he felt partly responsible for the strike, for the established wage had been arranged under his authority.[23]

Some common tactics employed by the weeders during the 1890s were: (1) rallying in the city center to petition the authorities; (2) marching with tall rods and asking weeders at work to strike; (3) sometimes splashing their rods in the water-covered fields to douse those who did not respond to their words. During the strikes of 1893 they reported to the subprefect with their rods, and some used rags as banners tied to sticks. In Caresana they resorted to a shower of stones to "convince" outsiders to go home. Witnesses observed that, although some of the weeders were men, women were the real instigators of the acts of protest.

In 1898, the rice belt, as in other parts of Italy, had its share of upheavals. The high price of bread was one of the main causes of nationwide protests. On Sunday, May 29, the weeders of Trino initiated protests, including acts of vandalism and plunder; this led authorities to call in the militia. The disorders started early in the morning when weeders in the *piazza* saw that the wage posted for the first *monda* week had been fixed at 80 centesimi. At seven o'clock a crowd of women and children began shouting that the *signori* wanted to starve them (*far morire di fame*). Infuriated, they went to the mayor's house; more workers and children with sticks and "banners" joined the marchers. They removed the gratings of the building, entered the mayor's office on the ground floor, turned everything upside-down, tore up all the papers and scattered them on the street. They took away registers and tried to set them afire. Then they threw stones at the Workers' Society (*Società Operaia*) nearby, breaking windows and the pictures hanging in its hall. The crowd poured back to the square and plundered the house of one of the local elites. The parish priest faced the mob and tried in vain to placate it; only the arrival of troops restored peace to the city. The municipal government of Trino then brought the employers together and asked them to fix the wages at 1.25 lira. The weeders reported to work the following day. Fifty-eight demonstrators, including ten weeders, were arrested and taken in carts to the city of Vercelli. At the sight of the jail, the women raised moans and cries, but, together with twenty men, they were acquitted two days later. Similar events occurred in at least eight other communes. In Villata, for example, the ferment subsided when the mayor negotiated a wage increase combined with a decrease in the price of bread.[24]

These acts of rebellion in 1898 caused great uneasiness among the authorities and members of the middle class. Apparently, no specific political or religious goals guided these protests, but the deep-seated belief in what was right and wrong, and the aspiration to obtain justice in an unbalanced society. Weeders and their followers attacked what they saw as the basis of their discontent. When they plundered the house of a rich proprietor, they fought the employer who paid low wages and caused unemployment. The stoning of migratory workers was meant to stop competition and the lowering of wages. The attack on the Workers' Society probably signified their dissatisfaction with the management of workers' problems, probably by members of the ruling classes, many of them presidents of mutual aid societies that advocated social peace. Destroyed records documented their oppression. Angry appeals to authorities were an accusation of their failure to do justice and provide inexpensive bread for the poor.

The weeders' forms of protest blended traditional and modern traits. Women had learned how to strike effectively. Strike techniques, I suggest, came through word-of-mouth descriptions of farm workers in other parts of the Po valley who struck successfully for their demands. Migratory workers might have brought news about these protests. To be added to this were the activities of the Italian Workers' Party in 1886 and the influence that some short-lived episodes in socialist organizing, such as those in San Germano Vercellese (1893), Lomellina (1893), or Bianzè (1896), might have had upon weeders' protests. The weeders must have also followed the example of urban strikes in the 1880s and 1890s. City workers' actions might have had a direct impact and served as a useful model. In the cities, anarchist, POI, and socialist propaganda was effective in undermining the worker societies' ideal of achieving democratic rights while preserving social stability.

In 1887 the anarchist Galleani founded a socialist circle and a workers' league in Vercelli, and in July and August 1888 he gave direction to strikes conducted by textile and button factory workers.[25] Italy was an agricultural country, but it was exceptional because its people were remarkably urban, and many agricultural workers lived in towns. There was no clear-cut separation between urban and rural society. Sometimes farm and industrial workers were members of the same family, demonstrating weeders marched to the cities, and workers who joined them there perhaps were not exclusively farm workers. Work stoppages and demonstrations by men and women in Vercelli may well have exposed the weeders to insurrectionary anarchist, POI, and socialist propaganda and instructed them in methods of social protest.

The Attitude of the Socialist Party Toward Women

In the 1890s, the Socialist Party, committed to the emancipation of working-class women, developed a program to address the woman question and the problem of women workers' participation in socialist activities and organizations. The debate on the woman question, like the one on the social question, stemmed from new conditions that rapid economic, political and social transformations were creating in the nineteenth century in European society. The debate centered on issues such as women's subordinate status in society and the family. In Italy, women contributed to the struggle for national unification; and their role in agricultural and industrial production, and in education was more than ever in the public eye. Changing patterns in birth rate, and women's involvement in working-class agitation heightened the challenge of new political groups to Italy's economic, and social order. Although political repression limited socialist activity among weeders in the last decade of the nineteenth century, it was then that the party set the theoretical background for the organizational drive that began at the turn of the century.

Italian socialists reproduced in the 1890s the shortcomings and contradictions of other European socialists' thoughts on women and the socialist movement. Many male socialists had conflicting feelings toward women's emancipation, an attitude that further accentuated the theoretical limitations of the socialist approach to the woman question and hindered the development of a party strategy to fight for women's rights.[26] Some were antifeminists and still thought that the proper place for women, even for those of the working class, was in the home,[27] or shared the same hostility of many nonsocialist male workers toward female labor on the grounds that it lowered wages.[28]

The historian Patricia Hilden refers to the "confusion" over these issues besetting the French party and "muddying the waters of such a difficult issue as that concerning working women's place in the socialist project."[29] Italian socialists asserted, following German Social Democratic theories, that only in a socialist society, after the elimination of private property that determined the inferior status of women in society and the family, could women emancipate themselves and become equal to men. Thus, they subordinated the woman question to the social question without addressing the social division of labor within the family, and least of all the role of women in the reproductive process.[30]

Many male members of the Italian Socialist Party shared this ambivalence regarding the woman question. Antifeminist prejudice was stronger in the upper echelons of the working class, which were ready to strike to prevent the hiring of women.[31] It was little wonder, then, that any hope for the furthering of the cause of women's emancipation stood beyond the socialist vision for reform.

We find in Italy women's analyses of what was at the root of women's oppression and the means to redress the situation without having to wait for a social revolution. We shall deal with some aspects of the history of women's emancipation in Italy in chapter 8. Many women in autonomous associations or in the ranks of political parties agitated for the improvement of the conditions of abused, poor, illiterate, unemployed, and working women, legitimate and illegitimate mothers, and prostitutes. Here, a brief reference to the ideas of two of the major exponents of the Italian emancipationist movement, Anna Maria Mozzoni (1837–1920) and Anna Kuliscioff (1854–1925), will show the tradition that the founding congress of the Italian Socialist Party inherited only to partially obliterate in 1892.

Mozzoni, an upper-class Milanese, was a Mazzinian in the 1860s and a radical close to Agostino Bertani in the 1880s. Thereafter she became a sympathizer and agitator for the Italian Workers' party (POI) and a co-founder of the Socialist League of Milan (1889) with Turati, Kuliscioff, and Costantino Lazzari. In 1889 Mozzoni became associated with the *Rivista critica del socialismo*, edited by the anarchist Francesco Saverio Merlino. A reader of Charles Fourier and Charles Leroux, but also of August Comte and Pierre Proudhon, she wrote *La donna e i suoi rapporti sociali* [The woman and her social relations][32], the first important work on the condition of women in Italy in 1864, and translated into Italian John Stuart Mill's *The Subjection of Women*, published in 1869.

Mozzoni was a champion of what in Italy in the 1860s came to be called women's "emancipation." This term evoked the struggle for the emancipation of slaves in the United States and connoted also the parallel that some emancipationists drew between slave labor in the American south and women's status. In Italy the "emancipationist" struggle was for educational rights for women equal to men's, for civil rights, and for the emancipation of the working class. This last goal explains Mozzoni's active role in the Italian Workers' Party and in the Milanese Socialist League; society had to change, and women and

workers should be the agents of that change. In the last decades of
the nineteenth century women comprised around 60 percent of industrial labor, and a high proportion of the field labor. The capitalist
system was uncovering the abuses women and children were subject
to, abuses that had been less evident to the public in preindustrial
times.[33]

It was against this backdrop that Mozzoni developed her own
ideas. In her earliest writings she rejected outright the notion that
woman was the supreme guardian of the family hearth. "Do not call
work," she advised, "the insignificant management of a house or the
labors of Arachne [whom Athena changed into a spider] . . . which
will never make woman into a useful being for society."[34] She claimed
instead that a woman reached her true proportions with the disappearance of the social stereotype, the woman of the house (*la casa-
linga*).[35] The home oppressed women no less than did the factory,
without even providing mothers with a free and happy motherhood.
This was the case because bearing children, although necessary to
perpetuate humankind, was passive from the economic point of
view, passive to the point that "the economic world is utterly disposed to let the saintly woman, as mother and wife, starve with her
children." Mozzoni disapproved of the family because it sanctioned
the dependence of women. She postulated instead the creation by
women of new collective bodies centered in the work place, around
which they could better organize their lives.[36]

Mozzoni charged that the solution to the woman question proposed by the Socialist Party, which was to work for a socialist revolution to abolish the inequalities between the sexes, amounted to total
indifference. In a speech at a women's mutual aid society in 1892, she
indicted male socialist writers for the unscientific, smug, and compla-
cent style with which they referred to women's emancipation:

> Still for them the problem of women's emancipation lies . . . in
> that women are *by nature* . . . equal to man: the future is full of
> promises for them; but if they [the men] condescend . . . to
> write directly on the subject . . . they do it always in the flowery
> style of priests, reformers, philosophers, democrats, who each
> from their perspective, called on women to work, to sacrifice
> themselves, because they will reap certain and huge benefits in
> the future; but when it comes to the present, they preach that
> women's interests do not have to be addressed now. Improve-
> ment will come naturally—it is of necessity implicit in the gener-
> al doctrine. . . . But I say to you . . . that if we let ourselves be

swindled and put to sleep another time with this eternal lullaby, we will become as stupid as tunas, who go through the same motions every day—getting caught in the nets that fishermen lay every morning for the catch. If we allow ourselves to be caught once more in these arguments, we deserve our lot.

If women remained passive, they would find themselves the day after the revolution "pupils, disabled, excluded, subordinated, accessory, more or less as today."

Mozzoni also criticized the way women yielded to men's decisions in public assemblies. She urged them to demand equal treatment for all members:

I know of associations where the women's sections are treated like wards, and in which the male members—fathers, brothers, and husbands—consider themselves members of the women's sections and take decisions in the name of their daughters, sisters, and wives, and women acquiesce in this treatment, affirming that what the men of the family say is in their best interest— and this happens, maybe out of indolence, or out of passivity, or out of the usual holy love for peace and quiet in the home, all factors that contribute to the fortune of the overwhelming men.

If women tried to assert their claims against male participants, the men "call off the game like spoiled children, and appeal to the quality of fathers, brothers, and husbands, demanding that, given their status, women members should always surrender and give in to them."[37]

Mozzoni opposed the socialist reformist course, especially the draft of a bill that the party proposed in 1897 on women's and children's work. The draft, prepared by Kuliscioff, became law, after lengthy modifications on June 12, 1902. Mozzoni spurned the policy of reform from above, insisting that women workers should rely on their own awareness and strength to win better conditions at work. She had witnessed and participated in successful strikes and protests by women factory workers and in the farm workers' strike in Polesine, Mantua, and Bologna, an experience that the new Socialist Party ignored and even slighted. Women participating in direct action, she concluded, would put an end to the competition of cheap women's labor. Protective legislation regulating working hours and the type of work women can do, she feared, would dampen women's militancy in opposing capitalists. The "protection" under which women lived within the family would be extended to the work place. Such "protectionist" laws, she felt, would make male labor more attractive to employers, thereby either excluding women from more decent and higher-paying jobs or driving them back to the home. Such a development would bring joy to the hearts of some socialists, she thought, and condemn "mothers to die healthy because they do not have to fall ill working."[38] Her stand widened the gap that separated her from the main proponent of the bill, Anna Kuliscioff,[39] and from the Socialist Party. The division between the two women grew after the foundation of the party, when Kuliscioff stressed the need to struggle along class lines, and saw the struggle of women against men as defeating party aims.

In 1880 Kuliscioff, in collaboration with Andrea Costa, wrote the "Programma" for the *Rivista Internazionale del Socialismo*, stressing the need for women's participation in the socialist work of renewal

> if we wish that not only the exterior and apparent conditions of life be transformed, but also the personal and familial relationships, and that socialism insinuate itself into everyday life and change for the better the habits, the customs—in short the whole human being.[40]

Kuliscioff, like Mozzoni, recognized the legitimacy of the woman question and the duty of socialists to address it simultaneously with the social question, given the inferior status of women of all classes in society. Ten years after the publication of the "Programma," Kuliscioff elaborated its basic ideas. In her lecture "Il Monopolio dell'uomo" [The monopoly of man] she incorporated the premises of the "Programma" with concepts expressed in August Bebel's book *Women under Socialism*. She welcomed the opportunities that modern industry offered women to become workers. These would make poor women equal to men and liberate them from their dependence on men, thus ending the long martyrdom of women at home. For Kuliscioff, work outside the home was the core of the woman question.[41] Many industries employed more women than men, but women workers did not use their numbers to organize. The working woman who does not unite in a common front against the employer "is doubly a slave: on the one hand of the husband, on the other of capital."

Kuliscioff's compassion for the mother—"the woman," she said, "who, being mother and manager of the house, ought to have one of the most rewarding occupations, ends up being considered by the husband as the laziest person in this world"—made her reflect on changes in family relations:

> Certainly all this will undergo profound modifications, which cannot yet be precisely defined, when the evolution of the family, after dissolving the former domestic relationships based on male domination and on the isolated home . . . will have prepared a more elevated form of the family founded upon spontaneity and equality. It is possible then that a greater part of the guardianship of the offspring might devolve on the community and, hence, this might give rise to a clearer distinction between the role of the mother and that of the community as educator of the child, as befits a modern society.

She also took the occasion to deny any scientific value to the theories of physiologists and psychologists who, in line with the theories of social Darwinism, used data on skull size to prove female inferiority. But Kuliscioff concluded her address on a moderate tone: "I wish, for the triumph of the cause of my sex, only a little less intolerance from men and a little more solidarity among women."[42] Overall, her challenge to the institution of the family and the "monopoly" of the male remained unchanged. Nevertheless, after the foundation of the Socialist Party in 1892, she modified her feminist polemical tone. She came into line with the party program, which united workers of both sexes in an undifferentiated struggle against the capitalist class, while Mozzoni refused to join the new party because of its lack of commitment to the cause of women workers. Kuliscioff even cut the edge off the "Monopolio" speech in the party biweekly *Critica Sociale*, when she recommended that any debate about the family be postponed to a better time:

> Certainly the *Critica Sociale* could and should concern itself with all these questions related to the emancipation of the woman and changes within the family but, unfortunately, battles in their beginning can only be partial.
> Honest people . . . are already alarmed . . . and believe, among other things, that the class struggle was invented by this journal. Imagine therefore . . . if, to provocation to the hatred between the classes, the destruction of the family were also added![43]

Still in 1893 the Russian-born socialist did say:

> The woman, even with the advent of an economic revolution,
> will be considered by the majority of men as an ignorant, a straw
> brain, just as the bourgeoisie did with the working class who,
> after all the revolutions made with the blood of workers . . . left
> the worker to starve and put his equality in Paradise. . . . The
> emancipation of the proletariat will only come about by the
> efforts of the workers of both sexes. But the emancipation of
> the woman will only come about by the efforts of the woman
> herself.[44]

Nevertheless, as Claire LaVigna asserts, Kuliscioff "was always a socialist first and a feminist only secondarily."[45]

Despite the negative attitude toward women that Mozzoni and Kuliscioff, among others, denounced in male socialists, many of these men did try to organize women farm workers. Male leaders in the rice belt invited them to organize by "breaking shortly with all the superstitious conventions of bourgeois life, and so offering a good example of solidarity . . . and a warning to their friends, who still think that they must not occupy themselves with such questions and ought only to knit (*attendere soltanto alla calzetta*)."[46] This socialist message was extended to urban women, too. An article in October 1892 in *Lotta de Classe*, the Milan socialist newspaper, signed by "A Woman," welcomed the membership of an organization of dressmakers to the party and fully confirmed its official stand regarding women. Impelled by necessity, women not only work on competition with men, but are also exploited twice as much as men; women's wages are always lower, and the employers' use of women as competitors against men put them outside the progressive proletarian movement. Corroborating male socialist prejudice against feminist ideas of sexual equality, the author rejected "the old romantic propaganda for women's rights," seeking emancipation from men as a triumph for rich women but of no help at all in rescuing a woman worker from economic dependence: "Her struggle is not therefore the struggle against the man, but is instead the common struggle, the class struggle." The only solution would be the complete change of a social system that creates class slavery and sex slavery, through the action of the Socialist Party, the only one that has "hoisted the banner of equal rights of the two sexes." These basic themes recurred again and again in written and spoken appeals as the party strove to enlist women in the socialist cause.[47]

At the turn of the century, socialist appeals were directed specifically to women weeders. In *La Risaia* [The rice field], the Vercelli newspaper founded in December 1900, we read that weeders were "martyrs" working like men at their jobs, and then at home in their multiple obligations. One such appeal condemned "cheap moralists who argued that women must remain at home to take care of the children and knit." Others tried to give the weeders convincing reasons to organize. One organizer, for example, disregarded what "the grand and irresponsible bourgeoisie" said, namely "that the woman worker does not need a high wage, because she has other means to earn a living." This was a justification to pay women wages that were less than men's. These low wages placed women in competition with men in the labor market, and very often women were hired first. This left men unemployed. Therefore *La Risaia* told the weeders:

> As your men fight, you must fight too. Besides, any attempt made by men workers to improve would be only a mistake. On the contrary, it would only aggravate the precarious conditions and add new chains, because in time you will finish up by completely replacing men at work.[48]

Women's low wages served to keep men's wages low too, insisted one writer of *La Risaia*, reasoning that women with higher wages and shorter workdays would be able to run their homes with more dignity, provide better care, food, and health for all, and, most important, a better future for their children.

If the drive to organize agrarian workers was unprecedented among European socialists, more unusual still was the Italian socialists' readiness to organize women farm workers despite their antifeminist prejudice and reluctance to unionize women workers. The reason for this male organizer's attitude may have been simple acceptance of the masses of women wage earners in the Po valley as an accomplished fact, as the product of a long and irreversible historical process, the introduction of capitalist farming. The socialist attitude toward organizing women corresponded to the singularity of Italian economic developments characterized by the huge amount of capital invested in agriculture and the early formation of a massive agricultural proletariat of both sexes with no hope for a return to a household economy. The organizers attempted to cope with social, economic, and political aspects of the changes: the increase in the number of landless workers, which grew even more during the agricultural depression; the swelling, especially with the economic recovery starting in 1896, of the wave of seasonal internal migration from and to the different regions of what Procacci calls "that 'west' of the poor that used to be the Po valley at the beginning of our century,"[49] and the need of daughters', wives', and mothers' wages for subsistence.

Regular farm chores performed year round occupied different groups of workers, but the level of wages for one group's work often set the wage rate of the other. High weeding wages were therefore vital to maintain all other wages at an acceptable level and thus avoid the peril of men's unemployment, because farmers would prefer to keep wages low by hiring only women. The new situation did away with the traditional peasant attitude of waiting for better weather, a more abundant harvest, or better prices, to compensate for a bad year, as well as traditional family hierarchies and degrees of specialization within the peasant world. Slow industrial development ruled out opportunities for work in the cities that would alleviate the scourge of rural unemployment. The new circumstances required a new tool, organization, to which the socialists were dedicating their energies. Based on solidarity, their aim was to achieve higher wages and basic rights, like the right to work or to improved working conditions.[50]

Also, the increasing militancy of women gave momentum to protests and strikes under the auspices of other parties, like the POI in the Po valley, which staged protests and acts of rebellion in the rice belt before the founding of the Socialist Party. These actions showed that women's organization might lead not only to their improvement, but also the betterment of the whole social group. Many male socialists even thought that economic betterment could, in the future, return women to the home to fulfill exclusively their domestic duties. The effort to channel women's protests into a disciplined movement took place under the aegis of the reformist wing of the Socialist Party.

The Socialist Party and Weeders' Organization in the Twentieth Century

In 1900, when socialist organizers started their work among the weeders, a six-year period of political turmoil, colonial defeat, widespread popular revolt, and government repression seemed to be coming to an end. During those difficult years, the suppression of constitutional liberties unleashed a wave of prosecution that restrained the activities of left-wing parties, hobbled labor organizations or caused them to disband, and also posed a threat to the workings of parliament.

The unpopularity of these repressive policies became clear in the elections of June 1900, when the socialists increased their representation in the chamber of deputies from 16 to 32 seats, while the representatives of the extreme left increased from 67 to 95. General Luigi Pelloux, the prime minister responsible for the antidemocratic order of the previous two years, resigned.

Hopes for the resumption of a liberal course arose when his successor, Giuseppe Saracco, led a transitional government until the king turned to the leader of the left-center liberals, Giuseppe Zanardelli, who was prime minister from February 1901 to October 1903. His influential minister of the interior, Giovanni Giolitti, became his successor in November 1903, and held power, with brief interruptions, until March 1914. Giolitti tried to put into practice his conviction that it was possible to counter reaction and begin a dialogue with left-wing politicians.

Those were years of Italian economic expansion and industrial development, and of the formation of a modern working class. Giolitti saw the legitimation and integration of the Socialist Party and of the socialist working-class movement into the framework of the constitutional monarchy as a key step to strengthen liberal institutions, because this would allow for the introduction of progressive legislation calling for economic and social reforms, and for the preservation of social peace. To offer party and labor associations the conditions for their existence, the government would remain neutral in labor conflicts as long as the demands were economic and not revolutionary. A large sector of the population, the working class, would thus contribute to the stability of society. Besides, workers' higher wages would stimulate internal demand.

In September 1900 the Socialist Party held its sixth national congress in Rome, the first after four years of government prosecution. After the electoral victories in June, the mood was optimistic, but not to the point of dispelling some members' suspicions that the new government would abolish political and civil liberties again and return to the policies of the previous years. There were revolutionary and moderate or reformist socialists among the delegates, and the congress succeeded in temporarily bridging the gap between them by the proclamation of a maximum and a minimum program. The maximum program reiterated, to the satisfaction of the revolutionaries, the program of 1892, declaring the revolutionary aims of seizing power, and expropriating and socializing the means of production

through proletarian struggle. In contrast, the minimum program ca-
tered to those who stood for evolution and peaceful reform. Positivist
philosophy and its underlying ideas of social, material, and moral
progress influenced the thought of many Italian socialists, mostly
reformists.

The report to the congress, which defined the minimum program as the means to ends listed in the maximum program, disguised
the fact that these were not complementary programs, but rather two
disconnected ones, expressing two conceptions of socialism. The
minimum program, drawn up by Turati in 1895, opened the possibility of cooperation with bourgeois parties in order to ensure
the viability of a liberal government, the framework within which the
socialists could gain democratic reforms. The appointment of the
Zanardelli-Giolitti government in February 1901 gave the moderate
(*legalitari*) or reformist socialists the opportunity to implement this
program, a move they envisioned as equivalent to working for socialism. They saw that with the Zanardelli-Giolitti government the
modern bourgeoisie was coming to power. The proletariat had to ally
itself with it in order to strengthen its ranks and bolster industrial
development. It considered industrial progress indispensable to prevent a return to reaction and ensure political freedom, which would
guarantee the growth of a vigorous labor movement, eliminate the
power and political influence of conservative landowners,[51] and set
up the political and economic foundations for major reforms.

Reformist socialists found out that there were coincidences between Giolitti's program of reforms and the minimum program. Thus
they thought that under Giolitti they would be able to implement its
basic points: social legislation, labor's right to work, to associate, and
to strike, the rights of labor cooperatives to bid on public works,
nationalization of transportation and mining, and universal male suffrage. Government neutrality in labor conflicts and a peaceful foreign
policy were basic preconditions for the fulfillment of these goals.

In the following years, many of the points of the minimum
program were subjected to long and bitter debates that pitted the
reformist against the revolutionary socialists, who supported a policy
of intransigence toward the government. During the socialist congress of Rome, those resolutions encouraging the formation and guidance of new associations of land workers—proposed by labor leader
Ettore Reina—and of more rural cooperatives and mutual aid societies—by delegate Quirino Nofri—had a very stimulating effect in
the Po valley. At that point, the slow organization of rice-belt workers
began to take shape.

Members of the Italian Socialist Party took on the effort to attract a mass of farm workers, unequalled in Europe in concentration and militancy, to widen its social base, and become a major force able to lessen the influence other parties or groups had over field laborers, groups such as the anarchists, the sympathizers of the POI, Catholics, or middle-class radicals. They had to further solidarity among rural and urban workers too. In the freer political atmosphere after 1900, the party under its reformist leader, Filippo Turati, accepted Giolitti's mediating role among field workers to reach objectives like the improvement of labor conditions, electoral gains, promotion of labor legislation, and the gradual democratization of the country.

Agricultural workers greeted the political change of 1901 with an outburst of labor activity heretofore unprecedented in the rural sector. In the new political climate, many labor associations that had been victims of repression breathed new life. Others, suppressed at their birth during the 1890s, flourished again, and many new ones appeared. This phenomenon took many contemporaries by surprise.[52] "So far it does not find its parallel in any other place," wrote the republican Napoleone Colajanni.[53] Observers such as Alessandro Schiavi and Colajanni ascribed this impetus to the work of dedicated socialist organizers.

The socialists of Lomellina took the first hesitant steps to organize weeders during the fifth socialist provincial congress in Pavia, February 1900. While the majority of the delegates recognized the need for the "economic" organization of weeders (as the party activities to organize labor were called), delegate Bertoldo insisted that the role of the party should be restricted to "forming socialist consciousness," and that any special action in favor of weeders should be postponed until the following year. Angiolo Cabrini, the president, shared the idea of postponing the "arduous question" to a more propitious time.[54]

After the congress, in *La Plebe*, the socialist weekly of Pavia, Bertoldo alluded to the conflict resulting from the employment of migratory weeders, hired in regions far away from Lomellina:

Some of [them] are already *infested* with socialist propaganda while others are completely unconscious, as, for example, *our* electoral college of Bobbio, worthy, in this respect, of being located in the center of Abyssinia. This recruitment of workers is made with an anarchic method. The capitalist farmers go to the *piazza* on Sundays and enlist weeders or have at their service a mediator without scruples. . . . In any case, *our* weeders are always *more demanding* than the others, even than those who, like the Emilians, are already attracted to the orbit of the socialist party. From here, hates, struggle, unrestrained competition, fights, always strained relations.[55]

Therefore, the main task of socialists should be to preach peace and quiet in order to avoid unpleasant scenes for which the party would be held responsible. Even a plan for appointing a simple secretariat to register local weeders and fix their wages would be difficult to carry out, for there were too few organizers and socialist rural workers. With the exception of Mortara, San Giorgio Lomellina, and Ottobiano, "the other communes, politically speaking, are as they were before 1848." The *mondariso* of these three communes could easily form a league of four hundred or five hundred women. Then two things might occur: if the weeders of the other communes did not join, the entrepreneurs would hire them and boycott the league, whose members would remain jobless; if the others actually formed a league without the guidance or supervision of the socialists, this would be a source of competition.

In the long run, the only move the socialist section of Mortara attempted in 1900 was to intensify economic propaganda and expand its influence also "in barbarous and semibarbarous places," a reference to villages untouched by socialist indoctrination, for one year.

Other articles of *La Plebe* exposed some of the hardships the weeders had to contend with, like the practices of the middlemen or *capi* who recruited migratory squads:

> The *capo* will give them a certain amount for the whole season, will pay for the trip (in the cattle cars) and the food (boiled rice with a bit of rancid bacon); at the end he maybe will make a present . . . and together with the present will probably come the fever, too. If the fever would come earlier, during the working season, the *capo* will pay for the treatment (and what a treatment!), and, if it were the case, will send workers back to their home town, still deducting the expenditure of the cure and the return trip from what the laborer has already earned.[56]

The average *capo* easily earned from 300 to 500 lire a season with a squad; considering that it took him only forty days to earn that amount, it was a good sum. A *mondariso* had to work the whole year round, usually to earn less than 200 lire. The anonymous writer in *La*

Plebe proposed eliminating the *capisquadre* through the formation of workers' associations in the rice belt to which groups in distant regions could apply for work. There had been some short-lived attempts by agricultural workers to set up placement offices in some areas of the Po valley in the 1890s, but they had met with fierce resistance from employers.[57] Socialist friends of migrant weeders would instruct them on the procedure for getting the discount tickets that the railroads granted to groups of migratory workers, which involved paying a deposit in advance at the railroad station.[58]

Socialist educators deplored the habit of the *mondariso* of taking their children to the weeding, in violation of the July 15, 1877, law that made education compulsory for two years. One teacher advanced timid solutions—the only ones possible, given the lack of an effective law limiting child work—like forming children's squads with local and migratory children, who would attend school in the afternoon after working half a day. (The 1885 law on child labor imposed few restrictions.) Another alternative, still more difficult, but more humane, was a program of subsidies to poor families whose children could then be kept at school.[59] The Socialist Party gave priority to the problem of workers' education. It tried in general to induce parents of working children to make the sacrifice of sending them to school.

The socialists in Novara also decided that the time had come to deal with the same set of problems. The third socialist provincial congress of Novara met in December 1900. One of its aims was to revive the dying Socialist Provincial Federation. Giulio Casalini and Modesto Cugnolio dealt with the matter of labor organization. Casalini urged all the socialists in the province to revive, federate, and transform the old-style mutual aid and cooperative societies, founded mainly by the urban trades, into modern unions. He envisioned the creation of three chambers of labor in the province to direct and supervise the leagues. Cugnolio limited his report to the rice workers, whose organization he soon expected to see accomplished:

> Those workers have already expressed, enumerated their wishes, their needs. Following these *desiderata* we will have in our grasp the safest weapon of economic propaganda. . . . Only the Socialist Party did and will do something for their relief.[60]

In Vercelli a sign of the new times was the foundation, on December 1, 1900, of the newspaper *La Risaia* by Cugnolio, who was also its political director. He saw his weekly as a vehicle both for socialist propaganda and for achieving the organization of rural workers. At least the literate farm workers would read *La Risaia* and, by word of mouth, instruct others about its content.[61]

In December 1900 there was a general strike in Genoa that had a profound impact on Italian labor, set an example of the fruits of organization and militancy, and encouraged labor to close its ranks and adopt a militant position. On December 18, 1900, the prefect ordered the closing of the city chamber of labor, which the workers had just reopened. Two days later six thousand dock workers started a strike, which soon spread to other sectors of the city and prompted sympathy strikes in other parts of the country. From eighteen thousand to twenty thousand workers struck in Genoa alone. "The government . . . digs an abyss between itself and the new Italy," noted an editorial of *La Plebe*.[62] On December 23 the Saracco government, which was to fall two months later, ordered the reopening of the chamber of labor. According to Renato Brocchi, in *L'Organizzazione di Resistenza in Italia*, this lesson of solidarity at a time of political renewal gave farm workers "energy and courage the more they came to realize that, by then, they had nothing to fear from the government."[63]

The institutions around which the socialists intended to organize the workers were the rural leagues and the chamber of labor. They adopted the term "league" as a synonym for union or *sindacato*. The leagues (sing. *lega;* pl. *leghe*) organizers used as models were the militant associations formed among the agricultural workers in Mantua and along the lower course of the Po valley during the 1880s. These so-called resistance leagues had been in the vanguard of agrarian agitation from 1883 on, and had survived into the 1890s despite the wave of reaction and prosecutions, including the trial of their leaders at Mantua in 1885 and 1886. The Mantua leagues were revived early in 1900 and, as in Vercelli, their constitution, with few or no variations, was adopted by all the other *leghe* that were mushrooming in the Po valley. The leagues were considered the most appropriate body to fight against employer resistance. That is why they excluded, or controlled, other associations, such as mutual aid societies or cooperatives, which did not stick strictly to the principles of class struggle, or called for mediators other than agricultural laborers.[64]

The term "resistance league" (*lega di resistenza*) was current in 1900, although at the end of that year the word "improvement" was added to, or began to replace,[65] the word "resistance," which soon disappeared from the titles of these organizations. Elaborating on the change, Angelo Bertolini, author of a report on agricultural strikes in Italy for the French Agricultural Society, linked the change in terminology to a difference in farm workers' political behavior, which after 1898 moved from spontaneous outbursts of protest to conscious, deliberated, disciplined action. He observed their tendency "to carry out the struggle on a calmer and more practical ground," and if a strike broke out, "this is the fruit of the past."[66] Perhaps the linguistic change also responded to the interests of the socialist leadership, which wanted to sever its ties with the revolutionary past. "Resistance" was a word that evoked that past. The resistance leagues had blossomed under the aegis of various political groups: radical, anarchist, Italian Workers' Party, revolutionary socialists. The majority of these were characterized by their extremism, intransigence, and resistance to agreements or negotiations, either with the state or with employers. In May 1901 one organizer explained in *La Plebe*:

> Almost everywhere, movements similar to ours have had from the beginning a tough, rough form of violent fight, with painful sequels of hate and retaliation. Then, little by little, the edges have begun to blunt, the *resistance leagues* changed into *improvement leagues*, arbitration took the place of strikes.[67]

"Improvement" was a word adapted to a new political style, and applied by and large to the policy that Turati had been championing since the socialist congress in Rome.

The reformist socialists strove to meet workers' needs precisely at the moment when Giolitti was trying to implement a democratic regime favoring a reformist political course. He thought that this political course would favor the expansion of Italian industrialization while avoiding the social conflicts that arose from a process of rapid economic change and the growth of the working class. Giolitti's reformism rested upon the assumption that rural and industrial entrepreneurs on the one hand, and workers' organizations on the other, would subscribe to the same course: the former would offer some wage increases and the latter would agree on a program of gradual reforms. So, in spite of the fact that the socialists of the Novarese and Lomellina had a revolutionary leadership, the reformist wing of the party held the upper hand, organizationally speaking. Representatives of other tendencies within the party challenged it and implemented their own particular tactics, but these were always infused with reformist labor policies. Still, the party's reformist tendencies did not prevent individual masses of workers, like the weeders, from following their own path at times. At crucial moments, the weeders used their own discretion and self-taught strategy of rebellion, which were the fruits of experience.

If we take a look at the figures representing the number of day laborers in the total rural population over nine years old in the different districts of the Po valley, we see that in Vercelli and Mortara (Lomellina) the figures were 65,187 and 64,264 for the total population, and 36,957 and 35,108 for the day workers—more than 50 percent of the whole rural population. In Novara, instead, less than one-third, 31,309 inhabitants, out of a total rural population of 95,113, were day workers. In Mantua the proportion was similar to that of Vercelli and Mortara: 94,884 inhabitants with 45,174 day workers or *braccianti*. In the rice belt we have to add the numbers of migrants working several months a year at the times for weeding, harvesting, and threshing the rice fields. These numbers may partly explain why the league organizations acquired much more strength in the Vercellese and Lomellina—and Mantua, the "lead" province, where the rural proletarian struggle preceded the others—than in Novara.[68] We may say, following Giuliano Procacci's analysis of the formation of the Italian working class, that in the Vercellese and Lomellina, and in Mantua, of course, the countryside conquered and left its mark on the city,[69] while in Novara, it may be suggested, the leagues lacked the force to do so.

The leagues, in turn, formed district federations, which were represented, along with the industrial workers' federations, in the chambers of labor. The chambers of labor (*camere del lavoro*) were modeled on the French *Bourses du Travail* (labor exchanges), the oldest one being the Paris *Bourse du Travail* founded in 1887. The first in Italy was the Milan chamber of labor set up in 1891. Other Italian cities followed this example, and by 1901 there were fifty-seven chambers providing geographic coordination and a centralized leadership to all the working-class organizations in a given community, district, or province. The *Bourse du Travail*, as organized by the French syndicalists, rejected, at least in theory, any involvement with electoral politics or religious discussions, and acted only as an employment agency and center for trade union activities.

In early 1901, the socialists in Novara and Vercelli were busy organizing chambers of labor. They described the work of these bodies as strictly limited to labor problems and, adopting the same precepts as their French counterparts,[70] declared political and religious matters extraneous to the chambers' purpose.[71] The chambers' official program included the mediation of strikes and the preparation of labor contracts advantageous to workers, as well as the promotion of labor legislation, the dissemination of propaganda, education, medical and legal aid, and the gathering and dissemination of information on local, national, and foreign labor markets. Sometimes the chambers provided cooperative and mutual aid.[72]

The *camere del lavoro* of Vercelli and Novara, founded in March 1901, called on farm workers to participate in the movement by organizing local agricultural improvement leagues in each commune, combining these leagues into district federations, and sending delegates to their respective chambers of labor. These, along with the delegates of all the federations of the district, made up the general council of the chambers of labor, which set the program to be carried out by an executive commission elected by all the members of the chamber. There was a national federation of *camere del lavoro*.

The most striking characteristic of the chambers of labor was their potential to bring together under one roof rural and urban unskilled workers, thereby fostering a unity of purpose between them. For unskilled workers, out of place in trade federations, the chambers of labor were refuges where workers found assistance, companionship, and guidance in work and personal problems.

There was no *camera del lavoro* in Lomellina, however. Its leagues in theory joined the one in Pavia, but in practice they enjoyed complete autonomy from it. *Il Lavoratore*, the socialist weekly of Novara, greeted the new *camera* (March 3, 1901) as the "embryo from which the world of the future will spring." Its founding marked the beginning of the era of "new rights" (*il nuovo diritto*) for both employer and employed, and because of its role as peacekeeper, it was a source of satisfaction for the proletariat and also for "intelligent and civilized capitalists." It removed from the struggle the impetuosity and brutality that would have resulted if the unorganized worker confronted the "violent" entrepreneur. According to the proponents of this idea, sensible social legislation would develop from the balance of these two forces.[73] The proletariat of Vercelli was admonished that the chamber would recognize only the salutary force of persuasion, brotherhood, and solidarity in the proletariat.[74]

Like the French and other Italian chambers of labor, the *camera* of Novara requested subsidies from municipal councils, chambers of commerce, provincial officials, banks, and other institutions. The chamber of Vercelli asked the city for both subsidies and a building.[75] According to the socialist leader Claudio Treves, a refusal of aid would eliminate a moderating body because the chambers were advising their members to avoid tumultuous protests and strikes.[76] The chambers of labor prided themselves on their role as mediators in labor disputes; work stoppages or other signs of labor unrest could be construed as a failure on their part. But the *camere* paid only lip service to their avowed purpose of preventing strikes and their federations went out on strike again and again, regardless of the *camere*'s official antistrike policies.

The workers themselves belonged to the chamber of labor only indirectly, through their membership in the leagues' federations. Therefore, it was the "tint" of the federations, and the strength of the local political forces, that gave the different *camere del lavoro* their real character. In the rice belt, as well as in many other places, they had trouble complying with the principle of political neutrality. Many of their leaders and members in the rice belt were socialist sympathizers.[77] In Mantua and Ferrara the leagues rejected all connections with the chambers of labor, in Mantua because it had a mixed leadership of democrats, ex-members of the Italian Workers' Party, and anticlericals, and in Ferrara because the league federation considered that the chamber, by requesting municipal and provincial subsidies, was too closely tied to bourgeois capitalism.[78]

The chamber of labor in Novara, for example, had the same revolutionary leadership as its party section. In Vercelli Cugnolio was the *camera*'s legal adviser. Outside the rice belt, some chambers of labor changed their leadership; the chamber of Milan, reformist at the turn of the century, was in revolutionary hands between 1904 and 1906. Therefore, notwithstanding the chambers' declaration of political neutrality, they served, according to Procacci, as "organs of popular self-government" because they served the aspirations not only of labor unions but also of local democratic groups, eager to continue the battle that had started with the Risorgimento to achieve a true democracy. The *camere* were "the promoters and protagonists of that particular form of citywide struggle that was the 'general strike,'" such as the already mentioned general strike of Genoa in 1900.[79] We shall see in chapter 5 an example of this phenomenon in the rice belt.

In their periodicals, the socialists also tried to clarify their party's goals and describe methods of defense and conscientization among workers.[80] The final aim of socialism was, as they explained, the socialization of land, machines, and all instruments of labor for the betterment of humankind.[81] Addresses to farm workers took the form of declarations in the second person or series of questions and answers called land workers' "catechisms," and still more frequently didactic dialogues: between peasant and employer, a member of the league and a Catholic priest, two land workers.[82]

The socialist leaders of the weeders' leagues (none of whom were women) also stressed civil liberties—a new concept for most workers. They told them that Italian law, according to the laws of public security of 1889, granted everybody the right to assemble, associate, work, and even strike, if there was no violence.[83] To clarify these concepts, they presented the example of the agricultural workers of Forlì, Reggio, Modena, Ravenna, Mantua, and Cremona who, thanks to the intensive socialist campaign of speeches and pamphlets, now enjoyed the advantage of association.[84] Worthy of imitation also were French and British workers who were loyal to their powerful unions. In its first issues, *La Risaia* (December 1900 and the early months of 1901) gave much publicity to the rice workers' four-point program, which asked employers for changes in some of the old labor practices. It was the first time in history that they made such demands as an organized group. The resident weeders claimed their right to be hired before *mondine* who came from far away. They insisted on this point because, when the supply of labor exceeded demand, growers hired only outsiders and cut wages to a minimum. The three other requests were: (1) to do away with the mediator who recruited migratory weeders, giving equal pay to all members of the squads; (2) to pay for part of the time spent walking to the field; (3) to fix on Sundays the wages for the "major works" (*grandi lavori*), as the most important operations like weeding and harvesting were called, for the rest of the week.[85]

The socialist organizers' efforts to form leagues were hampered by variations in the degree of workers' receptivity to propaganda as well as in their customs and work schedules. These differed greatly in places that were only some miles apart. There was absolutely no hope that the idea could reach key areas before the 1901 weeding.[86] If some groups were more responsive than others, it may be attributed to past experience in protests during the 1880s and 1890s, to the dedication of their organizers, or to other circumstances such as the less successful preaching of the church against socialist interference in labor relations.

Who were these mainly anonymous organizers who visited the small communes on Sundays, traveling by bicycle, train, or the interurban tramway that ran around Vercelli? They were mostly city dwellers. Only a few of them can be identified as agrarian workers (*contadini*), like Gigetto, who wrote for *La Risaia*, or Rocco Guida, of Mortara. There were two main groups of leaders. One comprised deputies or aspiring deputies of the Socialist Party, who occasionally or fully cooperated in organizational work, like Luigi Montemartini,

Fabrizio Maffi, Modesto Cugnolio, Egidio Cagnoni, and Umberto Savio; for the most part they belonged to bourgeois, sometimes well-to-do, families, and were, except Cagnoni, who never graduated from law school, members of liberal professions: physicians, professors, and lawyers. The other group of organizers were city workers: teachers, journalists, and even municipal employees. Romolo Funes, a Novara watchmaker, was a political and labor leader of his district until 1904. Some of them may probably have had family ties to rice workers.

The organizers used the examples of Albano Vercelli and Asigliano as evidence that more mobilizing efforts were needed. In the commune of Albano Vercelli, the *mondariso* worked ten and a half hours a day instead of nine, as in all the other communes, and for less money than anywhere else. They were so miserable that mothers took their 10-year-old, and even 8-year-old, children to the fields. They woke up at 2 o'clock in the morning and the children "even fall down asleep in the road" while walking to work. Asigliano, another commune where "the improvement league . . . has not yet entered into the heads" of the rural workers, urgently needed visits and talks from the comrades of Vercelli to convince them to establish a league.[87]

Conditions in some of the places of origin of the migratory *mondariso* such as Monferrato and Piacenza were no less discouraging.[88] In those places with chambers of labor, reports to the *camera* of Vercelli indicated that women of their regions had been recruited for payments unheard-of in the past, namely 50 or 60 lire for the weeding season.[89] Such low wages threatened the weeders of Vercelli with unemployment or wage reductions, for they expected to work fewer hours and for more pay—75 to 80 lire.

Under those conditions, the socialist organizers thought that demands for the 1901 season should be limited to slight wage increases. To crown this effort with a degree of success, they had to curb and discipline the workers' propensity toward what they called "spontaneous" protests. The word went out that women had to avoid "impulsive strikes, strikes without preparation." If the weeders could not control themselves, the organizers told them to stay home and send a delegation to the mayor (*sindaco*) instead, for through his good offices negotiations could begin with employers. Otherwise, other weeders, mostly migratory, would come to replace the local women who would lose work and income. But if these weeders heeded the organizers' advice, negotiations would lead to small increases in pay, thereby settling any strike quickly without threatening their jobs and wages. Another piece of advice was to refrain from threatening and disturbing women who came to replace them, because according to the law, that was a crime against the right to work, for which they would be prosecuted.[90]

There was another recommendation against the "third" (terzo) during the monda—namely, the practice of weeding for three more hours for one-third the wages. This, it was insisted, was detrimental to the health and interests of the weeders. By accelerating work, employers were saving money, because in the following week they would have had to pay a higher wage. The monda wages followed an upward trend from the first to the fourth and fifth weeks, and then a downward course during the sixth and seventh weeks. Most of the time, the wage was fixed at the beginning of each week. Weeders were hired on a weekly basis and reported to the piazza every Monday to find a new farmer. By accepting the terzo, the mondariso ran the risk of being left without work for the following week, just when they would have received better pay.[91]

In May 1901 socialist leaders organized the weeders of Vercelli into an improvement league and they lost no time in making known their demands for the coming monda. On May 11 they presented a courteous memorandum to the subprefect, calling for a meeting with him and the employers to discuss the conditions under which weeders would work during the approaching monda season. The leagues asked for equal pay during the weeding season: 0.30 lira per hour, nine hours a day. An equal pay scale, they thought, would compensate for the long hours and backbreaking labor, especially since the employers traditionally decreased wages during the last weeks of the monda even though these were "the hardest, because the heat is the most intense, the rice the tallest, and the work the most wearisome." They also wanted to extend the payment of hourly wages rather than pay by the day for work other than weeding.[92] This would have been a breakthrough, because in Italy wages were seldom calculated by the hour.

But before the weeders presented their May memorandum, other episodes had caused alarm among employers. Early in the spring, there had been signs of agitation among permanent and day laborers. There was even a one-day strike among the farm workers in Tronzano, besides other work stoppages, which were prevented by last-minute negotiations.[93] On April 30, 1901, the rice growers of Vercelli found it necessary to form the Association of Agriculturalists of the Vercellese (Associazione fra gli Agricoltori del Vercellese), a move that landowners and leaseholders were also taking in many provinces and districts of the Po valley, including Novara and Lomellina. It was ready to combat the leagues.[94] Its members did not even acknowledge their existence.[95] They decided that they would continue to set wages each week, based loosely on the rate established by the municipal labor bureau that the moderate city government of Vercelli founded at the request of the *agricoltori*.[96]

Another labor bureau was set up in Novara, run, as in Vercelli, by city councilors. They performed some of the mediating roles usually associated with the *camere del lavoro*, in an attempt to make them superfluous. In Vercelli the guiding spirit of the municipal labor bureau was the conservative deputy Piero Lucca. The socialist press denounced these labor bureaus for their partiality toward the rice growers and for their neglect of the most essential tasks of the chambers, mainly the organization of workers and improvement of their conditions. Their efficacy was equated with that of a cataplasm on a wooden leg.[97]

In Vercelli the wages fixed by the municipal labor bureau were: first week, 1.30 lira a day; second week, 1.70 lira; third week, 2.05 lire; fourth week, 2.30 lire; fifth week, 2.30 lire; sixth week, 2.05 lire; and seventh week, 1.60 lira. These rates, according to deputy Lucca, were not binding, but a maximum, and therefore employers were free to fix wages according to their custom. The socialists called them a "joke."[98]

All these activities raised workers' expectations, but they also served to reinforce the employers' siege mentality. The farmers resolved not to concede one iota of their traditional privileges. They were determined to counter attacks either from the mobilization of weeders or from the government's new political course, which gave impetus to labor militancy. A test of strength came less than a month after the Vercelli association of agriculturalists was founded.

The first troubles were reported when the weeders of the commune of Albano Vercelli requested, through the subprefect, a wage increase and the shortening of the workday from ten and a half to nine hours. Employers agreed to pay the raise but would not accept the new work schedule. The women struck on May 20. Things became complicated because thirty *mondariso*, members of the families of permanent workers, were obliged by contract to weed. When this other group approached the work place, some acts of violence took place. The mayor, Dionigi di Gattinara, his brother, the municipal councilor Count Carlo, both powerful landowners, and six carabinieri arrived on the scene. The mayor told the press that the crowd of strikers attempted to stop the arriving weeders, that a fight took place, and two strikers were arrested. The strikers explained that the arriving women refused to work too and decided to leave, but then the employers and the stewards began to drag them back by the arms. When the strikers tried to free them, the arrests occurred. Then Modesto Cugnolio, the legal adviser of the chamber of labor, arrived and counseled the workers to be calm; he said later that "under the circumstances," it was the only thing he could do. Because the employers refused to shorten the workday (which was one of the weeders' demands), the strike continued for nine days. It ended in complete success, but at a rather high price; out of one hundred fifty women and fifty men who struck, fifteen were sentenced to jail terms of fifteen to forty days.[99]

In the communes of Formigliana[100] and Stroppiana[101] the weeders also suspended work on May 28, 1901, in order to obtain wage increases. Their demands were granted, and everybody went back to work the next day. On May 28 there was a very important strike in Crescentino, with the participation of a thousand women and fifty men. They requested that their wages be increased from 1.60 lira to the rate stipulated by the municipal labor bureau. But when the employers refused, the defeated weeders returned to work. There were scenes of violence, and strikers were denounced for violating the right to work as they tried to persuade two squads of weeders to stop working and join their ranks. They convinced one of the squads but failed with the other. Fourteen strikers were sentenced to twenty-five days in prison.[102] What determined the favorable outcome of the Formigliana and Stroppiana strikes seems to have been the solidarity of the whole work force, something the Crescentino women failed to achieve.

These were cases of actual suspension of work, but not all of them appeared in the statistics for agricultural strikes, which are much more incomplete than those for industrial strikes. Thus the official figures are an imperfect guide for estimating the extent of the confrontations that were taking place.[103] Also, cases in which a threat to strike sufficed to obtain the desired gains were, of course, never included.

Besides strikes, there were other types of incidents. Some originated in the discrepancy between wages paid and those proposed by the municipal labor bureau: the application of a wage scale sometimes meant an improvement for weeders. In Bianzè the employers refused to adopt the labor bureau proposal, because the wages they traditionally paid were lower. In Tronzano the mayor, in connivance with the employers, neglected to post the municipal rates (which was his duty) because they were higher than the local rates. Only after the local league wired the subprefect, asking for them to be published, did the mayor post the rates. But all protest was to no avail; wages did not improve. In Ronsecco the situation was just the opposite. The *mondariso* were being paid 2 lire, but the employers adjusted the pay to 1.70 lira in accordance with the official daily wage. The authorities did not mediate in this case and, confronted with the employers' obstinacy over wages, town officials could hide behind the bureaucratic explanation that higher wages were, after all, not obligatory.[104]

In Crova all the farmers dismissed their local *mondariso* on Saturday, June 30, 1901, on the pretext that the weeding was over. But when the women were to receive their weekly pay on the following day, the farmers proposed that, if they still wanted to weed, they would be given only 1.75 lira a day instead of 2.05 lire, the "municipal" wage the farmers had promised to pay.[105]

The migratory squads, even if organized, were not informed of working conditions beforehand. Once they arrived somewhere and saw that they would have to work twelve hours a day instead of nine, they could not break the contract without running two dangers— either being left without food, because they came with no cash to buy it, or being handed over to the police as persons without means of support. In that case, they would be sent in a column to the nearest railway station, packed into cattle cars, and returned to their hometowns.[106] Once their dependence on their male "protector," the *caposquadra*, ceased, these strikers became jobless and homeless women in a strange place. They could come under scrutiny of the police and were therefore subject to repatriation. Coincidentally, protesters also met all the criteria police used to identify lower-class women as prostitutes and, as such, were threatened by the prostitution laws ("whose tentacles touched the lives of prostitutes and nonprostitutes alike") with possible forced repatriation.[107]

The Cremona newspaper *Eco del Popolo* launched an appeal to the socialist papers of Modena, Mantua, Piacenza, Parma, Pavia, and Lodi, all places of origin of migratory weeders, imploring that measures be taken to avoid traditional abuses, like long working hours and the so-called *calca*, extra hours on several Sundays to make up for the time lost by bad weather, or to supplement the earnings of the squad leader or his cook.[108]

The availability of a replacement squad of migratory weeders, hired for a low wage, enabled owners to dismiss their local workers. This happened in Trino (May 20), in Tronzano (May 21), and in Balocco (May 28), where the most serious confrontation between strikers and carabinieri took place. The Balocco weeders went on strike on

May 27. In the morning of May 28, three hundred farm workers of both sexes, armed with sticks and sickles, stopped the march of a migratory squad escorted by a brigadier and four carabinieri. The women were more boisterous than the men. When this escort proved insufficient to break their resistance, a company of carabinieri appeared in the afternoon and subdued the defiant strikers after arresting seventeen of them.[109] Some sources record sixteen strikes in the commune of Vercelli in 1901, eight of them during weeding time.[110]

In the district of Novara, the statistics show ten strikes between May 10 and May 25, with the participation of 1,767 men and 583 women (the numbers in Vercelli were 400 men and 583 women).[111] The majority of the striking men of Novara were not weeders but other types of agrarian workers, who jointly struck with the women in job actions. These strikes usually lasted from one to five days. (Only one lasted thirteen days.) The most common demand was for wage increases. This was granted in nine cases. But another commonly voiced demand, for a shorter workday, usually met with total resistance. The workday remained as it always had been, ten or eleven hours long. It was much longer than the workday in Vercelli. In six cases the carabinieri intervened. Sixty-one workers were denounced for preventing others from working, and twenty were convicted and jailed for eight to ten days. In Vercelli, too, the interference with the right to work was the only offense that resulted in thirty-four detentions and convictions, with one-month jail sentences.

In Lomellina the farm workers around Mortara formed their leagues in March 1901, and spurred all the agrarian workers of the district to unite in a federation. The guidelines the socialist organizers had to follow in forming the leagues were published in *La Plebe* of March 22. Their function "had to be not only that of the engine driver who propels and guides the machine, or that of the stoker who feeds it, but also, in due time, that of a *brakeman*." They had to leave all rhetoric aside and dispel the illusion that the league could prevent all disasters and misfortunes. The Lomellina leagues formed a federation coordinated by a central committee at Mortara.[112] In April *La Plebe* began to publish a monthly supplement, *La lega dei contadini*, to cover the organizational activities in Lomellina.

In preparation for the weeding, the central committee of the leagues asked the *comizio agrario* to agree in advance on a uniform wage for the whole district. The members of the *comizio* blatantly ignored the existence of the leagues and announced that they would continue with the old practice of "free contract" between farmers and

their workers. Meanwhile, the committee of the leagues only expected to make inquiries in the different districts to coordinate action
for the future.[113]

Despite the socialist policy of moderation, a wave of strikes
swept Lomellina before weeding time. The government even sent
troops to the region because of the growing agitation. The weeding
thus started in a tense atmosphere. Some city officials showed goodwill in fulfilling their traditional role of mediators with some equa-
nimity, but the mayor of Vellezzo Lomellina threatened to jail those
workers who struck or even read their newspapers in public. The
mayor of Ferrera Erbognone put five women in jail for several days
because, along with their fellow weeders, they had struck and asked
for a raise in their wages of 0.60 lira a day.[114]

In San Giorgio Lomellina, where employers hired only migratory weeders for very low wages, two hundred local women and children arrived at the rice fields and began to weed without permission
from the employer. He called the rural guards, who threw the women
out, verbally abusing them. The women, whose husbands were unemployed, reported to another farm, only to be dismissed again by
the owner. They shouted, "We want to work too, we also have the
right to live!" The farmer threatened them with a stick and they
decided to leave. The most serious threat to the weeders of San
Giorgio were the weeders of Piacenza and Bobbio, hired by a certain
Enrico, "a merchant of human flesh," who engaged the women by
advancing them sacks of grain during the winter and then deducting
the cost from their wages for weeding.

Something similar occurred in Ottobiano on Monday, June 23,
when the farmers, "out of hatred for our leagues," according to the
weeders, did not report to the *piazza* to hire them. The women proceeded to several farms and started to work along with the migrants.
On the following day, they saw a "great display of carabinieri" and
other officials, who had been called by the rice growers to expel the
women weeders. The authorities were unable to convince the employers to hire them until two days later. Then they hired only a few
of the Ottobiano weeders.[115]

In June 1901 the central committee of the Lomellina leagues
initiated a policy of establishing friendly relations with the migratory
weeders. It gave a special welcome to the migrant workers, distributed leaflets bearing a message of solidarity, and set a meeting at
Mortara on Sunday, June 2. There, twenty-five hundred farm laborers, among them many enthusiastic migratory weeders from Emilia, met to hear Luigi Montemartini, a socialist deputy from Pavia

since 1900, and Maria Incerti, a migrant weeder of Concordia, Reggio Emilia, and other orators. Incerti arrived at the meeting, bearing greetings of her companions in Emilia and their call for unity, having covered on foot the five kilometers that separated Mortara from the farm where she worked. Despite the employers' decision to make *mondine,* including Incerti, work that Sunday until midday (*calca*) to sabotage the meeting, many migratory *mondariso* rushed to it at the end of the workday.[116]

At the close of the *monda,* on Sunday, June 30, the central committee of the Lomellina leagues staged an imposing farewell rally for the returning squads. Representatives of the press, socialist party administrators, socialist deputies, and league leaders were present. Again, the farmers forced the women to weed on Sunday morning, but there were about six thousand persons at the afternoon rally, the women wearing red kerchiefs, the men red neckties, and those in charge of the organization red carnations. Incerti sat at the presidential table with five men, and her exhortations to fight for workers' rights brought clamorous applause and cheers of "long live socialism!"

The next speaker, Pompeo Ciotti, secretary of the chamber of labor of Pavia, recalled the killing of workers on June 10 at Berra Ferrarese. In spite of rousing public meetings, calls for unity, and faith in the progress of socialism, some workers in Vercelli, ignoring the fact that there was a strike in Berra (in the province of Ferrara) had hired themselves out to work there, thereby provoking a confrontation with local striking laborers. Three workers were shot down by the police; many others were injured. This episode stirred up public opinion. Unfortunately, the police shot other protesting workers in different parts of the country during the Giolittian era. Their deaths caused tensions to mount between the revolutionary and reformist socialists, the revolutionaries blaming the reformists for their cooperation with the government responsible for the killing of workers.

The Berra Ferrarese victims were commemorated by workers belonging to socialist organizations. But conditions remained unchanged, and persons in need of work went where they could find it. The migratory weeders posed a problem for the organizers, and the inroads of the party in the rice belt were uneven. In some areas they met with success; in others, failure. Yet the organizing effort went on. During the farewell assembly at Lomellina, deputy Alfredo Bertesi of Carpi pledged that no woman of Emilia was going to leave for the rice belt in the following year in the employ of a *caposquadra;* all workers henceforth would be guided by the leagues.[117]

In 1901 there were eight strikes by weeders in Lomellina. None was more than a day long and they ended, with few exceptions, in total defeat.[118] But the league federation of farm workers in Lomellina was growing, with five thousand members forming twenty-nine leagues in August; its leaders predicted continuing growth.[119]

In Lomellina in 1901, after being taken by surprise, the employers responded to the first signs of labor unrest in the weeding season by hiring only migratory squads wherever they anticipated trouble. It is difficult to determine whether the striking weeders were organized or not. What is evident is that in San Giorgio Lomellina, where there was a league and where many disturbances occurred, the workers did not have a chance to strike, because they were not even hired. After much struggle, they reached an agreement with the employers on June 9, 1901, stipulating a wage of 1.30 lira for local weeders, which was raised to 1.60 lira in the last week of the *monda*. (It had been 2.30 lire in 1900!)[120]

Several causes determined a strike's chances of success. At the beginning of the *mondatura*, the surprise element weighed heavily in obtaining results with work stoppages. Some factors were beyond anybody's control, such as a rich or a poor harvest, the amount of weeds, or the weather. Other circumstances, such as the weeders', farmers', or government's attitudes, could tilt the scale for or against strikers. These included the solidarity of unorganized local squads with striking weeders; the presence or absence of migratory squads; the intervention or not of the police to harass and arrest strikers. The carabinieri, the army, and the local police could hinder the protesters' efforts to convince nonstrikers, or migratory weeders, to go out on strike, while simultaneously defending the workers' right to work. Another factor was the nature of the strikers' demands. Employers were more ready to yield to requests of wage increases than to demands for a shorter workday.

Agriculturalists denied any cut in the length of the workday as a matter of principle. They claimed that such a curtailment infringed on their rights, among which they included the right to fix working hours. This, they emphasized, was necessary for the progress of agriculture and for the preservation of property, because fewer hours could damage both the crop and the land. In fact, they feared that yielding the prerogative of setting work hours was tantamount to losing their hold over the work force.

To what extent did weeders absorb modern reformist political ideas spread by the socialists from the towns, promising their betterment through organizations overlapping with their previous traditional social revolutionary background? The most that can be said is that the blending of both experiences allowed them to act simultaneously on their own initiative and for specific goals, disregarding the discipline the organizers wanted to impose on their ranks. Their strikes differed from the protests of the preceding period because there was now an organization presenting a comprehensive program of demands to both public officials and employers. The employers' refusal to recognize the weeders as a bargaining unit with a common program provoked a wave of strikes in 1901, the first time in history.

Whether or not the weeders were in accord with the program advanced by the rice-belt socialists or welcomed their initiative to set up organizations to further workers' demands and impress its mark upon them, they alone perceived, when they reported to work at dawn, whether the occasion warranted a strike. If they thought it was, then squads of women would act in unison, without the presence of their husbands, fathers, brothers, organizers, or party members.

4

The First Results
of Mobilization

Weeders' Versus Farmers' Organizations

I now will focus on the organizers' evaluation of the mobilization efforts of the weeders and their difficulties, on the employers' retaliation, and on the organizations' plans for the future in the three districts just surveyed.

The Vercellese socialists reflected on the campaign of 1901 with a note of pessimism. The entrepreneurs never accepted the wage rates proposed by the weeders' league of Vercelli. Striking weeders often had to go back to work without having improved labor conditions at all, not only because of the competition of the unorganized *mondariso* but, according to *LaRisaia*, "because not all the members registered in the league were principled, and the strike would not hold up."[1] Nevertheless, the newspaper's editor affirmed that the league was not dead and that it would be able to survive and grow.[2]

The whole experience showed the impact of the competition between local and migrant weeders, although the problems this caused were not resolved.[3] On the positive side, protest activity in some communities resulted in wages that were higher than in 1900. Wages fluctuated from 1.80 lira in Palestro to 2.70 lire in Asigliano during the last week of June. In Lamporo they were 1.75 lira, thirty centesimi less than the year before, because of the competition of the weeders from other communes "which do not yet have the league."[4]

In Novara frustrations and reversals upset short-lived gains too. In November, Romolo Funes, watchmaker, labor organizer, and secretary of the chamber of labor of Novara, described the experience at the first farm workers' congress of Bologna:

> What do employers do to hire a work force to break a strike? . . . First, they have to go to a village to hire laborers. But they assure these workers that they will work where there is no strike. They take up workers who after signing contracts are taken to the fields. When the workers arrive, they are going to a strike in progress; these newly recruited migratory workers have a stake in weeding despite the local strikes, since the employers exacted a deposit from them when they signed on, and hence they cannot refuse to carry out the terms of the contract. . . . I recall in fact that this spring . . . while we were fixing the rice weeding rates at the *comizio agrario,* the farmers sent agents to Piacentino and to the Emiliano to hire migrant weeders. We had hammered out an agreement at two in the morning . . . we were very happy because we thought we had won the most beautiful contract in our lives; wages went up from 1.50 to 2.50, with a shorter workday; our joy came abruptly to an end with the arrival of a telegram from the employers' agents, announcing the engagement of a huge labor force. The farmers told us now, if you do not accept what we have to offer you, you've no contract. . . . I was in contact with three or four mayors of neighboring communes, and had told them: don't allow anyone to leave unless we settle first with the employers. The next morning 5,000 Emilians arrived; their number destroyed us and our hope to reach agreement with the employers.

Funes acknowledged that the situation of the workers in Novara was "disastrous." The leagues almost disappeared. Out of 3,800 members, with 1,700 women, only 1,804 remained, 300 of them women. Nevertheless Funes remarked that they "do not lose heart."[5]

In Lomellina the employers tried to withstand the effects of the weeders' mobilization with means similar to those used in Vercelli and Novara. They ignored the leagues' role as negotiating parties for as long as possible; they requested the presence of troops in the countryside to intimidate farm workers, and they enlisted the help of mayors, carabinieri, and other public officials to deter workers' protests. Their use of migrant labor caused unemployment among the locals, and they eventually hired local women at wages far below the customary ones.

There were two entrepreneurial initiatives: the formation, on March 3, 1901, of the Federation of Agriculturalists of Lomellina (*Federazione fra gli agricoltori della Lomellina*),[6] and the organization of mixed leagues of farmers and workers, which would include the mayor and the parish priest. This began, not coincidentally, in San Giorgio Lomellina, where weeders' protests had been quelled during the *monda*. Workers were, of course, prohibited from joining other associations and from striking.[7] On July 20, *La Plebe* criticized the new Federation of Agriculturalists of Lomellina for its "false preconceptions of caste and superiority." And when the federation stipulated that farm workers applying for jobs would have to present work certificates and a work pass, *La Plebe* wrote that with this requirement the federation became the equivalent of the "Inquisition" for the workers.[8] In Lomellina, as well as in other parts of Italy, the agricultural employers were already organized into local *comizi agrari*, committees dealing with economic and technical matters. The new association and its counterparts in the Po valley were, in contrast, a militant farmers' organization and the agrarian capitalists' direct response to labor activism.

In the Vercellese, the weaknesses of the leagues contrasted with the resolve of the Association of Agriculturalists. On June 11, 1901, it prepared a memorandum to Prime Minister Zanardelli. In it, Marquis Vincenzo Ricci, the group's president, expressed his concern about the harmful effects the work stoppages had. Not only did they hurt rural production but they also depressed weeders' wages. This happened in spite of the association's efforts, in coordination with the municipal labor bureau, to keep them high. This statement might have taken many workers by surprise. Thus, the farmers tried to escape blame by the government for whatever future plan of action they developed. They pointed especially to the use of machines to substitute for human labor, if excessive demands for higher wages made traditional production no longer feasible.[9] In fact, machines could help in some operations. Thus, the agriculturalists' memorandum concluded, it was obvious that a battle fought by one group of rural workers would probably not only affect others, but might also lead to broad changes in planting and harvesting procedures.

At the first international rice congress, organized by the rice-growing interests in the city of Novara, October 17–19, 1901, one item in the farmers' agenda was "means to lower the cultivation expenses of rice and increase at the same time the quantity of the product."

Professor Vincenzo Sini of Vercelli proposed various methods, including sowing in rows instead of broadcast. He assumed that in this way weeds would be less widespread and that they would grow only between the rows; therefore only a small number of weeders would be needed to remove those weeds with shovels and hoes. Nevertheless, when put to the test, this rational way to reduce the ranks of what they regarded as troublemakers did not give the expected results.[10] The weeds grew as widely as before.

Aside from these tactics, the farmers did not attempt other measures, such as substituting other crops, or introducing farm machinery, which they had begun to do in the lower Po valley in the province of Bologna. Here, rice was too profitable to give up, and mechanized weeding was impossible to implement, which they deeply regretted.

But over the entire rice belt growers fortified their position early in 1902 by uniting in the Association of Agriculturalists in the Novarese, the Vercellese, and Lomellina on January 7. The association had eight hundred farmers. About two-thirds of these farmers were leaseholders (*affittuari*), and the rest, landowners. Rice fields covered almost sixty-five thousand hectares; an average rented unit was a little over one hundred hectares.[11] The association arbitrated disputes with workers and negotiated labor contracts for the whole region, although each entrepreneur was at the same time free to make individual agreements with his own workers, as long as they favored the employers. A good portion of the farmers' high membership fees went into a strike fund, which would compensate them for losses caused by work stoppages.[12]

There were historical circumstances behind the farmers' drastic reaction to labor unrest in the region. After 1890 industrial growth had challenged the dominant position of agrarians in the Italian economy and had hastened the transfer of political dominance away from the traditional landed elite to the new industrial groups of the north. Once the majority, the farmers' representatives in parliament became the opposition.

In 1901 the government instituted a policy contrary to farmers' interests. It declared its neutrality in labor conflicts and supported the ambitions of bourgeois industrial entrepreneurs, thereby seemingly producing a split in the alliance between agrarians and industrialists, which had formed the so-called agricultural-industrial bloc. "There is no doubt," wrote the socialist Giuseppe Emanuele Modigliani at the end of the 1890s, "the tree of modern capitalism has taken root in Italy and is growing. So finally—perhaps—the struggle between the two forms of capital, movable and landed, is going to start."[13] The reformist socialists thought that the new alignment of economic forces presaged political stability and industrial growth. "In Italy," Modigliani continued, "the development of modern capitalism is about to produce in the bourgeois social body the deadly disease of the capitalist system, consisting of rivalry and struggle between industrial and landed capital." This rivalry would leave the reformists space to implement their program.[14] But the agrarians never gave up their hopes of maintaining their ascendancy. We will see (chapter 7, p. 209) how the "bloc" came to life again in 1910.

The Federterra, National Federation of Farm Workers

The farm workers of the rice belt continued their efforts to form a united front, like the ones they were consolidating in other parts of the Po valley, starting in Mantua. On August 10, 1901, Modesto Cugnolio called the first regional congress of agricultural workers of Piedmont in Vercelli and founded the Piedmontese Regional Federation of Agricultural Workers (*Federazione Regionale Agricola Piemontese* or *FRAP*). *La Risaia* automatically became the FRAP press organ, too. Soon its subtitle, *Socialist Newspaper of Vercelli*, became *Organ of the Piedmontese Regional Federation of Agricultural Workers, of the Chamber of Labor of Vercelli, of the Socialist Circle of Vercelli, and of the Proletarian Institutions of the District*. Cugnolio participated in the life of all these organizations, besides being one of their founders and leaders. Following Procacci's analysis of the strength of the Socialist Party in relation to that exerted by the workers' organizations in the rice belt, we may say that in Vercelli, as well as in Lomellina, the leagues outdid the socialists, who remained relegated to a secondary position, and functioned mostly to meet the needs of the workers' federations.[15]

The federation of farm workers of Lomellina also announced its first congress, to be held at Mortara on October 27. A striking feature of this congress was the presence of women. The women called for the abolition of the *piazza* procedure, the establishment of one wage for the *mondatura* in the whole region, the elimination of squad leaders and their placement by the league, and a nine-hour workday.[16] The delegates of the permanent workers (labor hired yearly) proposed that the women of their household be paid the regular wage of the day weeders,[17] and not the smaller sum they usually got. Inasmuch as Mortara had no chamber of labor, the leagues would serve as the employment agency where the farmers could apply for weeders. The delegates also decided that a commission of representatives of all the leagues of the rice belt would meet at Novara on November 10 to make the final decision on pay rates and on the length of the workday, two things that local customs made it difficult to standardize.[18]

Despite the general enthusiasm, the federation recognized the weaknesses of the leagues, largely because of the little help and guidance they had received from the organizers and the absolute lack of coordination among them. The monthly *Lega dei contadini*,[19] a supplement of *La Plebe* of Pavia, was insufficient to remedy this and had to be replaced by a weekly published in Mortara. In addition, the federation needed to appoint a paid secretary in charge of propaganda.

Rocco Guida, a farm worker and organizer of Mortara, pondered the weeders' chances of success at the first national congress of the leagues assembled at Bologna on November 24, 1901:

> With regard to the employers, we expect to make an agreement with them, provided that the migrants from other regions stick to the goal of the leagues; otherwise we will gain nothing, neither for ourselves, nor for our competitors, the migratory weeders.[20]

The feverish yearlong activity of the field workers' organizations reached its culminating point in the November 1901 national congress of Bologna. Delegates to the congress represented the farm workers' district and provincial federations, which counted one hundred fifty thousand members, mainly from the Po valley. At the presidential table next to the socialist deputy Andrea Costa sat three farm workers, including the *mondariso* of Molinella Adalgisa Lipparini, a heroine of the bitter strikes the weeders of Bologna had carried out in the 1880s and 1890s. The delegates founded the National Federation of Farm Workers (*Federazione nazionale dei lavoratori della terra* or Federterra). The Federterra was exceptional on two accounts: first, no association comparable to it existed anywhere in Europe at that time; second, it preceded by almost five years the foundation of the General Confederation of Labor (*Confederazione generale del lavoro* or CGdL) on September 29, 1906, which included the majority of the national federation of industrial unions and the Federterra.

The day laborers, who refused to compromise with members of other agricultural classes, proved their strength at the congress when the delegates voted for a resolution approving the collectivization of private land as one of the main Federterra goals. This socialist affirmation of the Federterra not only surprised and alarmed national public opinion, especially in conservative circles,[21] but also caused some party leaders embarrassment. They objected that it was too radical and premature, beyond the scope of any measure the party was ready to endorse. Turati, like Claudio Treves, another party leader, would have preferred instead a neutral stand, acceptable to more moderate league delegates, among them radicals and republicans who withdrew, at least temporarily, from the Federterra.[22]

We may better understand the differences over the resolution on collectivization if we look at its antecedent, the polemic of the 1890s within the most important European socialist parties concerning the future of small rural property. The majority of the Italian party adhered to the notion that small property, often affected by the expansion of capitalist farming, was destined to disappear soon in Italy. It thereby alienated sizable elements not included in the category of day laborers, such as small landowners, tenant farmers, and sharecroppers, none of whom were ready to support any plan for socializing the land.

At the fifth national congress in Florence in 1895 the party had adopted an agrarian program and declared the small independent farmer an economic anachronism not worth its attention. This view did not affect the districts where big landownership prevailed, but it did apply to many other regions in the country, including those surrounding the rice belt, which were overlooked by socialist organizers even though they were the places of origin of many migratory weeders. But many of the day workers' federations, the Mantua one first of all, resolved to impress a socialist and classist character on the Federterra. This was crucial in adopting the resolution on socializing land.[23]

The next question, whether the leagues should continue to be part of the chambers of labor or remain independent, provoked much debate. The motion finally approved was the one proposed by Enrico Ferri, a revolutionary socialist at the time, although it was also signed by reformists such as Gerolamo Gatti, Egidio Bernaroli, and Ivanoe Bonomi. It read:

> The Congress, affirming . . . the necessity that the economic organization of the proletariat should be animated by genuine socialist spirit, and wishing that all chambers of labor assume such a character, advises the leagues of farm workers to join the chamber of labor, letting them free to hasten or delay that adhesion according to local conditions.[24]

This decision was in line with the declaration on the socialization of land because it corroborated the classist and socialist stance of the majority.[25] Not all chambers shared socialist and collectivist principles. Many were politically neutral or under the influence of other democratic political groups, one of the reasons why the leagues' federation of Mantua decided to stay out of the chamber of labor. In Novara and Vercelli, instead, the leagues' federations joined the *camere del lavoro*, under socialist control. The federations' concern with the problem of competition between local and migratory *mondariso* had been one of the factors underlying the meeting at Bologna and the foundation of the Federterra. This was the ideal body through which representatives of both groups of weeders could regulate employment. The delegates decided to study the national labor market in order to better organize internal migration.[26]

In Vercelli, Cugnolio continued his campaigns by other means, such as simply demanding the enforcement of existing legislation. On August 3, 1901, *La Risaia* published the long forgotten regulations of rice cultivation of the province of Novara of 1869, the so-called Cantelli regulations, which had always been a dead letter. Cugnolio revealed how the entrepreneurs had violated them in collaboration with the local government, thereby causing undue hardship for workers, especially in their living conditions. The farmers neither respected the distances to be kept free of rice between fields and houses, nor did they observe the sanitary standards mandated for workers' lodgings. As for conditions during the *mondatura*, they neither complied with statutes that called for moving weeds to a dry place, nor did they limit the workday (article 14) from one hour after sunrise to one hour before sunset, as stipulated.[27] The weeders had much to gain by the application of this last restriction, because it would have automatically kept the weeding schedule within certain limits, or in other words, shortened the workday. It also had the advantage of prohibiting the *mondariso* from working extra hours in the "third" (*terzo*).[28]

The Leagues Disband, 1902–3

The socialists organized only a few leagues of women (*leghe femminili*), three in the Vercellese in 1901. None of them sent women weeders to the meetings. More weeders' leagues appeared during times of strikes but disappeared when calm returned. Although men's leagues also tended to disband at the end of the season, this happened less frequently. We find the same trend among other categories of women workers, and in different places. Those immigrant women textile workers who staged the 1912 strike in Lawrence, Massachusetts, joined the Industrial Workers of the World (IWW) during the protest, to desert it soon after.[29] Among families of textile workers in France during the same period, men joined the Socialist Party only to represent an entire family of socialists. Even if women happened to be party members, they were hardly visible in party activities, especially formal ones.[30] Alice Kessler-Harris writes about "the discomfort many women felt about participating in meetings" in the United States at the turn of the century:

> Italian and Southern families disliked their daughters going out in the evenings. Married and self-supporting widows had household duties at which they spent after-work hours. Women who attended meetings often participated reluctantly. They found the long discussions dull and were often intimidated by the preponderance of men. Men, for their part, resented the indifference of the women and further excluded them from leadership roles, thereby discouraging more women from attending.

She gives the example of a union woman who had resisted joining the organization for a time because "church people disapproved of unions."[31]

In Italy representatives of the men's leagues took care of the affairs of the *leghe femminili*. What happened in the majority of the communes? The men—husbands, brothers, fathers—were delegates for the women of the family. Time-honored tradition confined women to the home; men took care of public affairs. The church was one deterrent to weeders' forming their own leagues. However, strong male opposition hindered them as well. They were living under the twofold pressure of wage work and housework, and under the stern eye of a husband, brother, or father who would disapprove of any activity beyond supplementing the family income and taking care of the home and children. Weeders, it can also be suggested, grew uneasy at discussions that did not address their problems and at the discrimination they were subject to, if they attended league meetings. During a 1903 inquiry on the *monda*, the commission asked weeders whether they belonged to a league. The proportion of organized weeders was surprisingly low—4.24 percent in Mortara; 6.53 percent in Vercelli; 0.98 percent in Novara; and among the migratory *mondariso*, 7.75 percent. But according to the investigators, these figures were abnormally low, because many weeders did not declare membership in the league out of fear of retaliation by their employers. Some women, the investigators observed, did not approve of nor deem it necessary to belong to these organizations because their husbands were already members and they, therefore, represented their wives. Of the local men, 33.52 percent declared their affiliation to a league. The figure for immigrant men was higher, 49.09 percent.[32]

In the early 1900s organized women textile workers in Biella (Piedmont) suffered discrimination not only from their families and the priest, but also from the community, which disapproved of their joining the Socialist Party and subscribing to its newspaper. During World War I they organized women's sections of the Socialist Party. In 1917 a group of them showed their indignation against those who called them "drunkards" because they were singing together (probably a protest song against the war.) One woman declared that she would refrain from participating in mixed demonstrations because in them she was being laughed at and bullied by male *compagni*. In the same year, a women's party meeting tried to cope with male hostility by concluding that no *compagno* had the right to mimic and thereby ridicule women's gestures.[33]

Although weeders seldom went to weeders' or farm workers' meetings, they could count on the presence of some migratory *mondariso*, especially from Emilia. The politicization of agrarian conflicts had started there in the 1880s and the presence of the great woman organizer, Argentina Altobelli, might have served as a model to many women. Perhaps also many migrant weeders had moved away from the authority of the men in their families and had become more self-assured, independent, and, in a desperate situation, prepared to fight by themselves. But in the rice belt relinquishing the weeders' power to men was complete, going well beyond the degree of submissiveness that Anna Maria Mozzoni condemned in the meetings when women acceded to men's decisions. In the rice belt women did not even attend the assemblies. Any attempt to change this behavior would no doubt have met with men's disapproval, for men saw little need to change. The church threw its support on the side of men; priests thundered from the pulpit against joining organizations that were a threat to the sanctity of the family and the church. Employers threatened women league members with reprisals. Though weeders were generally not represented by women from their ranks, one of the few exceptions was the first congress of Lomellina farm workers, when two *mondariso*, Gaetana Gallina and Teresa Vasori, represented the weeders, along with four men.

Flora, one of the few women contributors to *La Risaia*, refuted "the superstition that she must attend only to home and children." She called for advancing the cause of women through education:

> And you, men, what do you say: that women stay at home, that they learn how to cook, knit, mend the rags—that's their work. You are irresponsible and I swear that you are wrong thinking this way. . . . As long as women are considered serfs, slaves, we will attain nothing. Oh, men let your wives become educated, take them with you to the socialist circle, to the chamber of labor, take them to hear the beautiful and noble speeches of so many scholars . . . . Open the mind and the eyes of these poor women, especially in the villages, remove them from the ignorance that makes them victims of sly creatures . . . the priests, who, abusing their ingenuousness, attract them to the church, compel them to follow the priests' preaching.[34]

But this feminist outburst was altogether exceptional at the time. There must have been other reasons that made women's leagues so short-lived. Weeders' outbursts of protest in the past had not depended on leagues or organizers, and perhaps the women still preferred to rely on their own sense of the opportune moment to deal with employers. The repeated, and mostly unheeded, calls for moderation by socialist organizers lead one to conclude that the weeders, after having staged protests in the past, questioned the rationale of having their rebelliousness and independence disciplined and restrained. Subversive anarchist propaganda and POI proselytizing had stirred Vercelli labor into action. Against this background, the organizers' efforts to bridle the *mondine* must have seemed odd to them.

Despite their absence from official meetings, where they probably felt marginalized, weeders of the rice belt participated in all kinds of celebrations, which were frequently organized by the socialists in many communes of the Po valley. Women had more influence in these informal organizations than in the formal ones. They exercised their influence on a variety of occasions, as in the inauguration of a new league, or of a chamber of labor, or of a People's House (*Casa del Popolo*) that the socialists were setting up in urban centers, or in the dedication of the banner of a league, or in the visit of a famous speaker. These affairs had common traits, such as gatherings at railway stations to receive guests and delegations from other communes with their bands, big parades, gatherings at the People's House or a theater to hear speeches, an aperitif (vermouth *d'onore*) and banquet, sometimes followed by another rally in the open air and a big ball.[35]

Weeders' public involvement in these festive, public activities indicate an interest in political and collective practice. Their nonattendance at union meetings must not be taken as a sign of indifference to organizational matters affecting their lives. Apart from the festivities already mentioned where women workers participated in the life of the community, we have to add the daily household conversations, gatherings with neighbors in the stable in the winter and in the courtyard in the summer, church attendance, traditional celebrations, and dances, which were the most popular entertainment.

The political climate at the beginning of the twentieth century and the awareness of the weeders of their needs determined the progress of efforts to mobilize them. Thirty-eight Vercellese workers (twenty-seven women and eleven men), twenty of whom were over seventy, were interviewed during 1976–78. These older workers recalled that socialist propaganda found very fertile soil at the beginning of the century, and that at the time of the strikes everyone was "red," even without a party card. The interviewers concluded that "this idea molded the majority of the interviewees' life experience."[36] The German sociologist Robert Michels visited the league of Bianzè in 1904 and found that "admission to it was not allowed but to socialists; the members were two hundred four, all socialists, but no one of them had the party card."[37] They, as well as the majority of the day workers in the Po valley, made no distinctions between trade union and party activities.[38]

In the years 1902 and 1903, strike activity decreased considerably both on a local and national level (from 629 in 1901 in the whole country, to 221 in 1902, and 47 in 1903). When the weeders' protest actions encountered strong opposition, many leagues fell in disarray. The farmers, on the contrary, were more prepared to deal with contingencies such as surprise work stoppages. They firmly began the counteroffensive planned in the course of 1901: they ignored the weeders' leagues, refused to negotiate with them, and hired enough migratory squads to suppress local weeders' protests. Economic and political factors contributed to the weakening of the unions. An economic recession began in the winter of 1901 and continued through 1903. This was reflected in falling prices and was compounded by poor harvests. The threat of acute unemployment, added to the employers' resistance, further eroded the bargaining power of the leagues. According to Giampiero Carocci in his book about Giolitti, the economic decline led Giolitti, under pressure from conservatives who attributed the economy's downward turn to the strikes, to abandon his policy of neutrality in labor disputes in favor of a tougher stand against work stoppages.[39]

The few leagues still in existence and the unorganized workers who had staged many spontaneous strikes became more cautious. They tried to preserve whatever gains had been made in 1901. But the weakening of the league federations, the backbone of the Federterra, affected its vitality. Its decline accelerated in 1903, and on February 7, 1904, it was transformed into a simple secretariat. Yet even between 1902 and 1906, the secretariat still endeavored to coordinate the flow of migratory weeders to the rice belt. This was almost its only activity until the economic recovery that began in 1904, when a new burst of labor activity, albeit somewhat diminished in 1905, helped revive it in 1906.

On January 26, 1902, the Federterra called a meeting of the dispersed *mondariso* at Reggio Emilia. The secretary of the Federterra, Carlo Vezzani, spoke of fighting for a wage of 0.25 lira an hour and a nine-hour workday for the local women. Antonio Vergagnini, of the chamber of labor of Reggio Emilia, insisted that the migratory weeders ask for 0.25 lira without meals, for the meals could be provided more efficiently by the workers' cooperatives at the work place. He also called for clean and decent lodgings instead of "the present promiscuous bivouac, cause of immorality and nameless shame," and the exclusion of children from the rice fields. He asserted that "the financial problem should not prevail over those of health and morality."

Vergagnini's mention of immorality associated with the reputation of migratory women deserves some attention. I already made reference to the fact that women on their own—that is to say, outside the family or community environment—were easily identified with prostitutes. I think that Italian society had to overcome many prejudices in order to accept the grim reality that even girls of a tender age had no other alternative to starvation than leaving home.

Tens of thousands of Italian women of all ages, habitually subordinated to male authority in the home, traveled in many different directions to perform a great variety of jobs. Among them, the *monda* attracted one of the largest groups of migratory women. Other currents of temporary migration with conspicuous women's participation were those of grain and grape harvesters and olive pickers. In many regions parents hired out 7- or 8-year-old children to peasant families to work as goat- and cow-herders high in the mountains during the summer.

Maria Goletto, born in Cuneo in northern Italy in 1887, went to

France for the first time when she was eight years old to work as a nursemaid in Nice for the summer. Then, on the way back, she joined a party of three Cuneo women who had been employed in the picking of jasmine and orange flowers on their way home, and they walked for three days over the Alps to save ten lire, the railroad fare. In the fall Goletto left for Provence with her mother and brother to pick olives. She continued to alternate olive picking in the fall with work on a farm in the summer for some years. Her father took her to the town square of Barcelonnette in France, where she joined a hundred other Cuneo children who waited to be hired for the season.

Lucia Abello, born in 1892, also from Cuneo, first left for France when she was sixteen. For three consecutive years she, with many other Italian women her age, picked violets and made bouquets from October to February in Hyères, near Toulon, and then worked in the gardens and orchards until June, when they returned home. I may suggest that the dictates of economic necessity in a society undergoing deep structural changes prevailed over preconceptions of women's place to bring about working-class husbands', brothers', and fathers' sanction of women's migration.[40]

The Federterra tried hard to organize as many migrant *mondariso* as possible, thereby avoiding the manipulation of migrant weeders' squads and their use as strikebreakers by farmers and *capsiquadre*. But it had little success, because few migrant weeders belonged to leagues and the majority of the migrant women still resorted to the old recruitment system set up by the *capisquadre*.

An inquiry made at Reggio Emilia showed that out of twenty-six thousand migratory weeders (including children) from Lombardy, Veneto, and Emilia, only three or four thousand were organized.[41] Because of this, the Federterra had to take a position on whether the organized migratory weeders should be able to refuse to sign contracts that did not stipulate the same conditions asked for by local weeders. The decision was that they should sign:

> Refusing now to sign the contract, they would run the risk of becoming victims of the competition of the disorganized and hence of losing the miserable earning of the season.[42]

Both migratory and local weeders were correct in taking a cautious view of their possibilities in 1902.

In Novara the local Federation of Farm Workers tried to reorganize its ranks at the time of its second meeting, on February 2, 1902, when it was made up of twenty-four leagues and four thousand workers. But soon the leagues began to disband. One of the delegates to the meeting reported that at the commune of Casalvolone the employers, threatening to hire outside workers, not only exacted the usual deposit before the *monda* from the local women who wanted to weed that year, but they also added an extra hour to the work schedule of the preceding year. To add insult to injury, they refused to pay the agreed wage of 0.25 lira an hour. Other entrepreneurs also ignored the Novara agreement of November 10 and were ready to sign only individual contracts.[43]

In 1902 the lot of the *mondariso* of the Vercellese was sealed even before weeding time. In March the day laborers (*braccianti*) of the district asked the subprefect to arrange a meeting with employers to discuss the general pay rates agreed upon at Novara on November 10. The farmers refused to attend, and the *braccianti* declared a general strike, determined not to negotiate individually with their employers.[44] Some permanent workers joined the day laborers in solidarity. But on the eleventh day, all the strikers had to give up. They were compelled, therefore, to sign separate contracts in each commune. The two main reasons for the defeat were the lack of strike funds to compensate for the loss of earnings, and the employers' threat to evict permanent workers. The illusion of having respected a general wage for weeding vanished with this early defeat; the farmers flooded the fields with migratory *mondariso* to cause local unemployment.[45]

In early June, 1902, two hundred fifty weeders in Asigliano were denied work by the rice growers who claimed that "the weeding is late and the weeds do not abound." The growers then hired migrant groups. Local women who were employed had their wages cut considerably. In Vercelli workers were promised by deputy Lucca that, at least, they were going to have the wage scale fixed by the municipal labor bureau the preceding year. At the time, according to a weeder, the employers declared, "There are no weeds . . . but if instead of 2.30, you go for 1.70, you'll have as many weeds as you want." Many workers were idle for several months, up to two-thirds of them in Vercelli by mid-June.[46]

Trying to avert a similar disaster in 1903, the secretary of the Piedmontese Regional Federation of Agricultural Workers wrote to the Association of Agriculturalists of Vercelli announcing that his association was prepared to provide local and migratory squads for the year. He said that this would be easy to arrange because sister chambers of labor and federations would be assisting in the matter. The agreement would assure a strike-free weeding and, no less important, provide the moral satisfaction of seeing the squad leaders eliminated.[47] The arguments did not convince the employers, who rejected the proposal. Things looked bleak for 1903.

The events of 1902 in Lomellina had some similarities with those occurring in Vercelli. In March the farmers in San Giorgio Lomellina failed to appear at a meeting called by representatives of the farm workers who wanted to propose wages and conditions established at Novara. The workers declared a general strike, but they were luckier than their comrades in Vercelli, because their concerted action forced their employers to negotiate conditions for all operations. The wage stipulated for weeding was 1.70 lira for ten hours of work. The strikers saw this as a success, considering that they were struggling under very adverse conditions.[48] But theirs was a temporary victory; in June local weeders were paid much lower wages.

The concrete effects of the defeat in Vercelli and the victory in Lomellina in March were indistinguishable from each other. The leagues' representative protested to the authorities who, after listening to the employers, declared the league leaders guilty of breaking the contract because "they [the leaders] do not know how to direct them [the weeders]." On top of this, the employers mocked the women by saying, "See what you have won with your leagues."[49]

The weeders, not disheartened in spite of their setbacks, held their first national meeting of weeders on November 9 at Guastalla, Reggio Emilia, with 188 delegates representing the Federterra (organizer of the meeting), leagues, federations, chambers of labor, and other institutions. Reports do not specify the number of women delegates. As usual, men represented the women of the rice belt. But the leagues of migratory weeders from Mantua and some places from Emilia did send women, who spoke out about their personal experiences and the strategy "for the next rice-field campaign."[50] Weeders from Emilia complained of many cases in which they had been lured by attractive contracts to work ten and a half to eleven hours, and were then forced to stay in the fields for thirteen or more hours. Shelter and food were "awful" and many squads were obliged to return home sick and penniless before the end of the season.

The delegates at Guastalla voted on two resolutions. One proposed methods to eliminate the "parasitism of the middlemen" in the contract procedures by creating a central placement office, assisted by local bodies, such as chambers of labor, leagues, and federations. They considered the chamber of labor of Reggio Emilia the proper location for the placement office because of the city's central position in the region of origin of many migrant women. The other resolution advocated the abolition of the system of paying part of the wage in meals, another manifestation of alleged "parasitism." Meals could be supplied by local workers' cooperatives. The delegates also supported the enforcement of the most recent official sanitary and labor measures benefiting rice workers.[51]

Two rice belt congresses followed the Guastalla meeting. The Lomellina leagues sent representatives to Mortara on November 16, 1902, to discuss ways of improving the organization and of implementing the program mapped out at Guastalla. In January the second congress of the FRAP met at Vercelli. In both congresses, leaders tried to redefine the leagues' nature and their function. At their inception, the purpose of the leagues had been described as "economic" (battles for labor contracts, better working conditions, and so forth) with no political or religious overtones. But now the opportunity came to clarify terms.

After a report by Stefano Viglongo, "Economic Action of the Leagues," Egidio Cagnoni, representing the Federterra, presented another resolution called "political action of the leagues." Cagnoni, reiterating the principles he had defended at the Mortara congress in November, stated that political action should take precedence over purely economic goals, for political action would aim at "the integral emancipation of the working class through the conquest of public powers" and the transformation of the capitalist into a socialist system. Once having assumed a political and class character, the leagues would participate in the socialists' electoral struggles.[52] Since the weeders were denied the main weapon in this battle, the right to vote, what was left to them was the indirect use of this right, which consisted in encouraging enfranchised male relatives and friends to go to the polls to vote for socialist candidates.[53]

This statement on the socialist nature of the leagues took some members of the audience by surprise. One of them accused Cugnolio, who approved of Cagnoni's resolution, of "Jesuitical casuistry;" he should have stated his true position at the time the leagues were founded. Cugnolio justified his reticence by arguing that the need to appeal to all workers in the first stages of league formation made his presentation of the leagues as neutral the only logical one from a political point of view. Thereafter, when all workers understood that the only way left to them was to become socialist, it would no longer be necessary to be silent about political goals. The federations of Mantua and Ferrara also considered their leagues to be socialist. According to Procacci, this "did not imply that, as a consequence, their action had to be subordinated to that of the party, but sounded rather like the equivalent of the affirmation that there was no other socialism except that of the leagues." The leagues were denying the party its political function.[54] Cagnoni's and Cugnolio's declaration must have been a blow to members of democratic and anarchist groups, to those upholding the apolitical principles typical of the nineteenth-century Italian Workers' Party, or to socialists who believed that the party had to subordinate the labor movement to its political direction. It is not known how many farm workers opposed this disclosure, but it is certain that the leadership of Cagnoni and Cugnolio remained uncontested.

The reformist socialists' program and methods of mobilization prevailed in the rice belt, but their leadership did not go unchallenged. The reformist lawyer Modesto Cugnolio was the main political and workers' leader in the Vercellese, but he usually followed a personal, independent, practical political course, not always in step with Turati's policy,[55] an example of the autonomy local organizations enjoyed. Cugnolio's independent stance would make him the best-known socialist mediator between the proletariat and the employers in the entire rice belt. But other factors contributed to his ascendancy, such as his ability to carry out the struggle using imaginative and original tactics, and to raise the labor question in the rice belt from a local to a national cause.

But in 1903 Cugnolio's leadership came under attack in a dramatic way from Stefano Viglongo, a revolutionary socialist appointed secretary of propaganda of the Piedmontese Regional Federation of Farm Workers (FRAP), and very active in the Vercelli chamber of labor. The occasion for this tug-of-war was the ownership of the newspaper La Risaia, a struggle that lasted from May 1903 to October 1904, when Viglongo left Vercelli. During these months, Viglongo gained control of La Risaia and began disseminating his ideas in its pages. To counter this, Cugnolio published another newspaper, La Monda, to propagate his pragmatic views. He flatly denied that there was any difference between reformists and revolutionaries within socialism, because socialism was a movement that could eventually be accelerated by the revolutionary élan of the workers.[56] (When Viglongo left office, Cugnolio stopped publishing La Monda and resumed the direction of La Risaia.)

In this struggle, Viglongo represented the revolutionary wing of the party aimed at subordinating the leagues to its political leadership, and Cugnolio the force of the leagues that he wanted to keep independent from this political rule, to guide their activity toward what were called "economic goals," free from any political mediation other than his own. The leagues, Cugnolio understood, should not be subordinated to, but integrated with, the socialist circle.[57]

In Novara, Romolo Funes, a follower of the revolutionary socialist Enrico Ferri, defeated the reformist candidate in the 1902 elections of the local party section.[58] But the rice workers in the Novarese never had a leader entirely devoted to their cause, as the workers in the Vercellese and Lomellina had found. The party and the chamber of labor, instead, relegated the leagues' movement to a secondary position. The revolutionary line prevailed as well in Lomellina under the labor leader and politician Egisto Cagnoni. The chamber of labor was in Pavia, too far away to have any influence in Lomellina. The strategy for mobilization in the Novarese and Lomellina, therefore, should have conformed, to a certain extent, to the so-called intransigent, antireformist stand of the party's revolutionary wing. Their political and labor leaders opposed reformist socialists' policies such as support of the government (or *ministerialismo*), because it deprived the party of its class connotations. They also spurned labor legislation, at least in theory, considering it of little help in improving the lot of the workers within the capitalist system, and in waging the battle to overthrow the system. They also made frequent references to revolutionary aims, among them the need to expropriate private property. Cagnoni, elected secretary of the Lomellina Proletarian Federation (*Federazione Proletaria Lomellina*) in 1902, used its press organs, first *Il Contadino*, and then *Il Proletario*, to voice his revolutionary convictions.[59]

These differences, in fact, hardly had a direct impact on the labor organization in these three districts. In the Novarese, with the ascent of Funes in 1902, the leagues' combativeness slackened, because of his poor organizational skills.[60] Besides, Novara had the smallest number of weeders of the three sections of the rice belt. Therefore, the impact, if any, of the revolutionary hard line in the Novarese was felt, in the best of cases, only by a small number of *mondariso*. Instead, Lomellina had a strong proletarian organization, with revolutionaries at its head. Yet despite the leaders' emphasis on their revolutionary goals, their tactics seldom differed from those of Cugnolio in the Vercellese. Cugnolio, as we shall see, launched successful labor campaigns around specific issues, mostly related to questions of legislation. The Lomellina and Novarese organizers, their revolutionary stand notwithstanding, often followed his initiative. What is more to the point, however, is that when delegates from these three regions met in congresses, their common interests dictated common policies. Never did ideological differences become a source of conflict or overshadow harmony among them.

This commonality of interests favored a reformist line for several reasons. First of all, up to the 1912 congress of Reggio Emilia, the party had a reformist leadership, which dictated these kinds of policies. Second, the socialist parliamentary bloc in charge of promoting labor legislation was reformist, and consequently the measures it proposed or supported were reformist in nature. Third, the socialist representatives to the Superior Labor Council, instituted by Giolitti in June 1902, belonged to the reformist wing of the party. Finally, the organization that planned general policies for migratory workers was the Federterra, a bulwark of reformist socialists that continued to be so, even after the defeat of the party's reformist leadership in 1912.

The Catholic Church and the Weeders

The socialists faced an uphill battle when they went into the rice belt to organize. They had to contend with opposition from the agriculturalists, from entrenched political interests, from the police and the military. They had come into conflict with the Catholic Church as well. The church was squarely opposed to the policies of the liberal state, and because the pope retreated behind the Vatican walls after 1870, the church was in open competition with a reunited Italy for the loyalty of the Italian people. According to some observers, the influence of the church on the moral and political education of the rural population had already declined somewhat in the 1880s. However, its ideological sway, especially over women, continued to be strong at the turn of the century. This explains the continued efforts socialist organizers made to replace the church in the hearts and minds of the rural proletariat.

The masthead of La Risaia had a drawing of a squad of weeders bending down knee-deep in the rice paddy under the burning sun. They were observed from an adjacent mound by two supervisors under the protective shade of a tree. The two observers were the entrepreneur and the priest. This was an emblem of the dual struggle the socialists set for themselves against the two allies, the capitalists and the church.[61] The party asked workers to follow the Christian maxims of sharing, mutual aid, solidarity, and love outside the confines of the church, to thus think of socialism as a religious faith and Jesus Christ as a fighter for justice and equality.[62]

Masthead of *La Risaia*, Socialist weekly of Vercelli founded by Modesto Cugnolio in December, 1900.

The weeders' organizers found it difficult to challenge the Catholic opposition to the organization of women workers. When the chambers of labor of Vercelli and Novara were founded, their leaders called for the awakening of the proletariat,[63] to radiate "an immense moral light" in the countryside, especially among women. Women especially had to be taken away from the influence of priests, who up to that moment had shown little interest in fighting for the economic betterment of the disinherited. The clerical press countered with descriptions of the *camera* in an antireligious and antimonarchic light. All this, a collaborator to *Il Lavoratore* suggested, showed how effective the socialists were in their organizing efforts, and how backward the church was in setting up Catholic leagues to keep workers out of socialist organizations.[64] *Il Lavoratore* reported that threats of excommunication were directed from the pulpit to those who joined socialist leagues, especially women.[65]

Socialist organizers called upon women to scorn the church's admonition to pray for resignation in face of adversity, and to disdain the priests' condemnation of the Socialist Party and the leagues. They stressed, as we read in the rice-belt socialist weeklies, that the leagues had declared a position of neutrality on religious matters. Further they argued that the leagues could provide them with real help, while the church was unable to solve the daily problems of the faithful. The socialist press also appealed to women to stop discouraging their men from joining leagues and going to meetings. Such attitudes, it asserted, made them allies of the government and the farmers.[66] Still more significant, it rejected the priests' accusations that socialism attacked the family, an institution that the weeders did not wish to see destroyed. On the contrary, socialism fought to improve the quality of family life. A certain Celle argued in *La Risaia* on November 1, 1901, that labor unions would lead to better health by shortening work hours.[67]

Socialist organizers' repeated requests for weeders to stay away from the church or, at least to ignore some of its antisocialist pronouncements, seem to indicate that they were unwilling to abandon an institution that had traditionally been at the center of their social life. A similar situation existed among anarchist women of Andalusia, to whom, according to Temma Kaplan, the church provided "a sense of stability or dignity." According to Kaplan, the church was "a gathering place where women could reassert female community norms through gossip and commiseration," and "daily mass formed the core of poor women's society just as the local bar or café was the center of poor men's social life."[68] Anarchists did not offer women institutions able to meet their social needs. In Italy, too, the leagues were not yet an alternative to the church or a source of collective support for the majority of weeders.

The church apparently served as a deterrent to weeders forming leagues, but it did not have the same effect on women's striking and making economic demands on their employers. Hence, weeders had a margin of independence in their actions to redress wrongs, removed from both clerical and socialist influence. Why this contradiction? Declarations from old farm workers from Cuneo, another Piedmontese province, led the interviewer, Nuto Revelli, to conclude:

> Women farm workers were not much more than beasts of burden. Women required endless physical and moral stamina. Men could find refuge in taverns; they could drug themselves with wine. But women found refuge and escape in the church, the Mass, and vespers.[69]

It is difficult to tell whether this was a matter of social habit or belief. Yet the authoritarian Catholic Church, which also watched over women's behavior in the neighborhood, undoubtedly offered women workers consolation they could not find, as we shall see in chapter 8, p. 263, neither in the family nor in the Socialist Party.

Catholic priests and laymen began their own nationwide campaign to organize farm workers in 1901 and 1902, just in the middle of the wave of strikes. From 1903 on, the Catholic drive began to falter, but it was revived between 1907 and 1910. In 1910 there were 140 farm workers' leagues in Italy with a total membership of 37,148 workers, mainly in Lombardy and Veneto.

Catholic, or "white" leagues and nondenominational ones, attracted different categories of rural workers. In the Catholic leagues there were very few day laborers; most members were sharecroppers, small landowners, and permanent workers. Organized day laborers usually joined nonsectarian leagues instead. This was because they responded better to their plight, while the main reason why there were no "white" leagues in the rice belt was that the priests' attempt to set them up in the region met with failure, as we shall see.

This failure came as a result of the method the church used to cope with class antagonism in the rice belt. The Neo-Thomist social philosophy adopted by Popes Leo XIII (1878–1903) and Pius X (1903–14) was based on the theological concept of charity (*caritas*) as an instrument of social solidarity. The idea implied the defense of private property, which had to have a social function; owners had the duty of sharing the benefits of property with the poor. Out of this relation there derived, according to conservative church groups, a hierarchical ordering of society with two classes—superior, the property owners, and inferior, the propertyless, who remained under the tutelage of the rich. Such a stand angered Catholic activists, the young Christian Democrats, who proposed the formation of an independent militant labor movement organized in unions, a plan that socialist successes in labor organizing made more urgent than ever.

Church conservatives and activists also disagreed when they discussed the use of strikes in conflicts. The church ruled it out as a means of labor protest, because it did not fit in with the concept of social harmony, despite activists' opinion to the contrary. But in 1901 the church very reluctantly decided to accept strikes as a last resort, to be used as little as possible.

Another point of contention concerned the structure of unions. Conservatives emphasized the need for confessional but mixed unions, where workers and employers sat together, as ideal for keeping workers under paternalistic control. Activists preferred simple unions, which allowed workers to pursue their own interests and, most important, would be able to compete with socialist unions.[70]

The trade union model the church set up in the rice belt was the mixed one. In 1901 the priests organized a Catholic labor league (*Lega cattolica del lavoro*) in each parish of the rice belt. These recruited not only weeders and farm workers in general, but also persons from all walks of life, including employers, and avoided class divisions. The leaders were appointed by a committee composed of all the parish priests in the dioceses. The experiment was inauspicious and short-lived. In one case, the weeders struck and the priests did not dare report to the farms to negotiate with the employers, because their class identification with the latter interfered with their role as mediators. At that point, the abandoned weeders called on socialist organizers for help to settle the strike.[71]

Il Vessillo di S. Eusebio [The banner of St. Eusebius], a Vercelli Catholic weekly, launched its invitation to form the *lega cattolica* in late August 1901, when the strike wave was already abating. It used two statements, one for workers and the other for employers (*padroni*). They reminded the first of the practical and spiritual benefits the league would shower upon them, and the second of their obligations toward labor and society.

In early September, *Il Vessillo* announced that the league was already in existence and stressed its important role in preventing strikes, and in assembling members of different classes in one association. The experiment seemed to have come to a close at the end of 1901, because *Il Vessillo* stopped mentioning it in the following years, except for a short reference to it in 1903.[72]

In January 1902 the priest of Tromello (Lomellina) visited parish families gathering signatures for a manifesto against Prime Minister Giuseppe Zanardelli's proposal to introduce legislation about divorce, but he took the occasion also to register weeders for the next *monda*. The terms were 1.70 lira for an eleven-hour workday. He invited the women to church to form a Catholic league. During the meeting, the priest tried to chase out the men who joined the assembly, a gesture that provoked confusion. The chaos was compounded when a young man began to bang two saucepan lids together. Then everybody disbanded and the plan came to an end.[73]

The failure of the Catholic leagues must be attributed to both workers' and farmers' indifference for mixed groups. Workers preferred unions that defended labor interests only. Even the weeders, assiduous churchgoers, understood this and defected from the "white" leagues. Farmers chose to form their own associations based on principles other than charity toward workers.[74]

Government Action

Moving from the activities of labor to those of government, we find significant breakthroughs affecting farm workers. The discovery, at the turn of the twentieth century, that anopheles mosquitoes carried malaria parasites and transmitted the disease, and that quinine was the effective drug for its treatment, led the Italian government to develop protective measures for the victims of malaria. These steps to protect labor in the rice fields reassured the farmers on two accounts. No longer did employers have to fear that rice fields would be banned because of their deleterious effects on health. Also, because the government's program was making the fields "healthy," agriculturalists saw no reason to shorten the workday, as laborers had requested.

Rice growers had their own forum to defend their interests, the international rice congresses. Four more meetings followed the first international congress of 1901 before World War I (in 1903, 1906, 1912, and 1914). Only the last congress took place outside Italy, in Valencia, Spain. At the first international rice congress, the physician Luigi Del Bono, the director of the sanitary bureau of Novara,[75] addressed the issue of how to "reconcile the private interest with the more sacrosanct right of man, that is his health," thereby silencing "the war cry against the rice fields." The anopheles larvae could not be killed without destroying the plants. In reality, the rice fields could be "healthy" only as long as everyone with malaria took doses of quinine for a whole year to prevent recurrent fevers. The anopheles would continue to thrive as long as rice fields existed, and in the long run only the drastic reduction of infected persons, Del Bono thought, would stop the propagation of malaria. What was left came to be called "human prophylaxis" and "mechanical prophylaxis." The first would be achieved by the massive free distribution of quinine to workers (the state had put quinine under a monopoly by a law of December 23, 1901). The second, "mechanical," measure required rice farmers to pay for metal screens, to be installed on all windows and doors in workers' lodgings.[76] These were some of the provisions of the law on dispositions for the malarial zones existing in the kingdom, issued on November 2, 1901, and followed by its regulations on June 2, 1902.[77]

Either religious or nondenominational charitable institutions or, in their absence, communal administrations, had to provide quinine free of charge to migrant and local workers and their families in the declared malarial zones. Almost all the communes in the province of Novara were included in this category on September 11, 1902. In isolated areas, employers were obliged to store enough tablets for a three-day treatment for their work force. The government distributed the quinine at very low prices, which the farmers had to pay at the end of each year, proportional to the size of their farms.[78] The sick would be given enough tablets to cover the time of recurrent fevers. Even healthy workers could take the medicine as a preventive measure, and migratory workers had to start the treatment days before reporting to the rice belt to assure as complete a control of malaria as possible.[79]

The workers' organizers alerted their followers to the new legislation. In the second meeting of the FRAP on December 21, 1902, the physician Nicola Vaccino requested that the government declare some communes of Vercelli malarial, which had not yet been so designated. Cugnolio presented a motion requesting that the minister of the interior make local authorities observe the Cantelli regulations. He also urged socialist deputies to put pressure on the government so that protective health measures could be extended to areas with a high incidence of malaria.[80]

The new law on woman and child labor of June 12, 1902, did not affect weeders, because it did not apply to agricultural workers. The original draft was the work of Anna Kuliscioff in 1897. Kuliscioff was the target of feminist critics who suspected that any legislative reform undercut feminist militancy and led to the loss of better opportunities for women in the labor market. But in any case the bill, which finally passed, was a modified and much milder government project. The proposed age limits for working children and the protective measures for child and woman workers were much diluted.[81] It is also noteworthy that the government created a body of labor inspectors only as late as 1913.

The law on woman and child labor was promulgated almost at the same time a new official institution was founded on June 29, 1902. This was the central labor bureau (*ufficio centrale del lavoro*) and, attached to it, the superior labor council of the ministry of agriculture, industry, and commerce, which participated in its preparation.[82] The increasing number of votes on the extreme left in 1900 and the labor unrest that followed may well have encouraged the Zanardelli-Giolitti government to create this bureau to study workers' conditions and to draw up labor regulations. This was a key mediating function to implement the government's plan to bring opposing classes into harmony, a precondition for a durable liberal regime. In any case, the weeders were not the most immediate beneficiaries of the Central Labor Bureau.

In 1902 worker organizations suffered a series of setbacks and in 1903 they were unable to lead any actions at all. The weeders were completely unable to resist the conditions employers wanted to impose on them. Only in 1904, with the economic recovery and a spurt of organizational activity, did they regain their strength to stage protests and demonstrations that culminated in the widespread strike movement of 1906. The table below shows the sudden rise in the number of both agricultural and industrial strikes in 1901, its drop in the next two years, and its increase again in 1904:

STRIKES FROM 1900 TO 1904 (KINGDOM OF ITALY)

Year	Agriculture		Industry	
	Strikes	Strikers (1000s)	Strikes	Strikers (1000s)
1900	27	13	383	81
1901	629	223	1,042	198
1902	221	147	876	198
1903	47	23	546	110
1904	208	95	620	127

The Interaction Between Weeders and the Socialist Organizers

Those weeders who were exposed to organizers' propaganda and saw the possibility of fighting for material improvement, equality, and dignity, plunged massively into the resistance movement. A brighter, more hopeful economic and political picture made the situation favorable for the development of concerted action.

The reformist wing of the Socialist Party, the chambers of labor, the Federterra, and even the leagues' federations considered strikes a last resort. But the socialists and the weeders, as well as many tens of thousands of day laborers in the Po valley, were working at cross-purposes. The organizers recommended that they accept the slow formation of an organizational network before they initiated any labor action, but they themselves were unable to provide such a network. In any case, the weeders disregarded these voices of caution, and stood out from other strikers in the rice belt by their fervor and courage.

The women had already learned in the past to rebel, protest, and strike, urged on by hunger, unemployment, and injustice. At the turn of the century, they used these tactics under the guidance of party organizers, but exceeded the limits they set. The record shows that, in many instances, local weeders made few, if any, demands save that of being given first crack at weeding. This simple demand of being contracted first was enough to challenge the tradition of the employers' prerogative in hiring. To put these women, who dared speak up, in their place, employers resorted to the use of migratory labor, even though this type of labor often represented no monetary saving.

The reformist socialists insisted on the need for legislative action in favor of the weeders. But with the exception of the law on woman and child labor, which in any case did not protect rural labor, the measures to safeguard their health were passed without socialist or labor initiative or intervention.[83] But then socialist deputies and party and labor organizations became supporters of these laws and agitated for their enforcement.

The weeders' dynamism caught socialist organizers unprepared. On their own initiative, weeders went on strike, warded off the coming of strikebreakers, and pressed their demands. Sometimes organizers would then rush to a site to plead for calm, to sanction the formation of the league, and to help in negotiations. Other groups of working women in Europe and in the United States displayed a similar type of militancy. I shall present some examples of this militancy in chapter 5, p. 162.

By taking matters in their own hands the *mondine* may have forced the socialists to hasten the refining of organizational efforts in single districts and to coordinate actions in the entire rice belt and in areas of support elsewhere in the Po valley. The weeding was the first of the "big works" in the rice belt, employing the largest work force, both local and migrant. There were strikes during the harvest, which involved migrant labor also, but in a smaller proportion. That is why the impact of the protests at weeding time must have been decisive in the determination to search for new ways to put an end to the employers' hiring procedures. The memory of the weeders' strikes must have loomed large in the minds of the delegates assembled at Bologna in November 1901 to found the Federterra; the need to organize internal migration, mainly in the rice belt, emerged as a priority.

The weeders' confidence in their own strength to put forward solutions to age-old problems must also have forced socialist circles and organizations to increase their use of the party press to reach the rural proletariat through articles and directives. Thus they would help develop the weeders into disciplined workers who knew how to follow orders in labor actions. Labor organizers' and party members' caution might have derived first from their interest in giving precedence to league formation over strike action, although the leagues were volatile and often disappeared as quickly as they had appeared. Secondly, their hesitation may have been due to the fear of alarming public opinion to the point of imperiling the stability of a government that seemed to be consolidating democracy in Italy. Memories of the reaction of the 1890s haunted them. In Lomellina, for example, the *La Plebe* monthly supplement, *Lega dei contadini,* was turned into a weekly, *Il Contadino* [The peasant], in January 1902. As *La Risaia* in the Vercellese, it paraphrased the catechism and the credo to instruct field workers on the righteousness of their claims.

Yet the women's very impulsiveness, which the organizers found so hard to moderate, contributed in no small way to the rapid organizational drive. Job actions often preceded and even contributed to the visit of an organizer or a socialist orator. Once a socialist representative was on the spot, he simply sanctioned the formation of a league.[84]

Nevertheless, their organizational weakness did not diminish the women's advantage of just being there on the spot; in the absence of migratory squads, they could heighten the tension of the situation by simply withholding their labor, and by creating the havoc that the postponement of weeding would necessarily bring about. So the withholding of labor gave the women a sense of strength and unity they had not fully had before. As the weeders mobilized, it soon became evident that they had intricate ties with other rural workers' actions inside and outside the rice belt. As actions fanned out across the rice belt, the record shows that each local battle was but a skirmish in a general assault by the entire work force of the Po valley against the fortress of farmers' intransigence. Field workers needed new weapons and therefore created the leagues, the federations, and Federterra. And conversely, when the farmers retaliated against striking weeders, they declared war on the entire rural proletariat of the rice belt. In spite of initial failures and the shortcomings that became evident in 1901–3, the mobilization itself was a radical breakthrough in the lives of those who took part in labor actions.

Socialist propaganda spread, as did new views about the rights of the *mondariso*. A resignation toward the employers' will was something of the past. Suddenly women workers confronted newer, broader possibilities. They were quick to grasp the notion spread by the organizers that the time was ripe for action. They knew enough to spurn the appeals of the municipal labor bureau and the Catholic leagues for alternative solutions to their problems. They knew, we can infer, that these institutions did not represent workers' true interests. We can infer, too, that women began to understand their role as part of a labor movement. No less important, they began to realize that the rivalry between local and migratory weeders—mainly derived from severe unemployment in many zones of the Po valley—had to be transformed into understanding and solidarity.

Years of Progress,
Years of Action, 1903–6

Attorney Galbarini . . . claims . . . that there are no malarial fe-
vers, so that the monda *of the rice is the weeders' Carnival.*
June 27, 1903, session of the Pavia provincial council

A New Law on Rice Cultivation?

The year 1903 was the second of two years of economic recession and
unemployment. Employers were unyielding in the rice belt. Aided by
the economic recovery in 1904, weeders renewed their fight for what
they considered legitimate rights. Despite a slump in the economy in
1905, ongoing party and labor activities culminated in a momentous
labor action in 1906. During these years, the weeders' organizations
ceaselessly endeavored to solve deep-seated labor problems, lessen
the conflict between competing local and migrant weeders, and
search for a conciliation body to arbitrate labor disputes. Also, intent
on advancing the cause of the *mondariso*'s collective and personal
well-being, weeders and the labor organizations struggled for a shorter workday, for the enforcement of protective laws for rice workers,
and for the passage of new labor legislation.

The weeders' agitation in 1903 had caused the new supreme
labor council of the labor bureau instituted in 1902, an offshoot of the
ministry of agriculture, industry, and commerce, to write a new bill
destined to replace the law on rice cultivation of 1866, referred to as
the Cantelli regulations. However, agriculturalists tried to block this
legislative innovation, as well as the ones that followed, because they
were contrary to their interests. Yet they did not support the Cantelli
regulations either, which they found equally distasteful.

I shall analyze the struggles over new legislation between weeders and the agriculturalists, and the roles played in them by the government, the Socialist Party, and the scientific community. I shall also evaluate the results of these disputes and their impact on the events of 1906.

From 1903 on, the issue of social legislation was present in all discussions about cultivation and labor in the rice belt. Participants in these debates cited legislation in either of its two versions, the Cantelli regulations or the ones destined to replace them, to set forth their views, and to spur the government to action. Hence, workers and employers would mention, interpret, accept, reject, react to, try to change, or influence the laws, old and new, as a way of supporting their own positions. What workers feared most, and what farmers wanted most, was the abolition of any and all laws.

This, in short, highlights the actions taken by representatives of workers and rice growers in provincial councils, in the central government, and in labor organizations. Labor wanted protective legislation; employers tried to abolish the law of 1866 and to indefinitely quash any new ones, or at least mold any new legislation to serve their own interests. If a new law on rice cultivation was not passed until 1907, this was because the national government adopted dilatory tactics amounting to a policy of compromise with employers.

Modesto Cugnolio, socialist and labor leader of Vercelli, took the initiative in 1903. He demanded the enforcement of laws affecting the rice-belt labor force. His action was in keeping with the reformist socialist practice. Reformist socialists deemed the policy of social change through peaceful means to bring about socialist society viable only as long as the government lived up to its goals of sponsoring social legislation. Giolitti was shaping a political system that called for both bourgeois cooperation in reform and for respect for the law as a way of broadening national consent for the liberal state. Cugnolio, therefore, put the Giolittian system to the test.

The authorities failed to enforce the Cantelli regulations. The product of centuries-old experience, its article 14 forbade work in the rice fields in the first hour after sunrise and the last hour before sunset, when field workers could easily contract malaria. Article 14 had special weight because it embodied four major workers' goals: the shortening of the workday, full employment, higher wages, and malaria control. A 1903 inquiry by the Humanitarian Society attested to many violations by employers.

The Humanitarian Society (*Società Umanitaria*) or *Umanitaria*, as it was commonly called, had been established in Milan in 1893 with

funds bequeathed by the nineteenth-century Mazzinian phi-
lanthropist Prospero Moisè Loria. His dream was the creation of an
organization that would help lessen the evils of society by fighting
unemployment and the practice of begging in the streets. Loria entrusted the *Umanitaria* to the city of Milan as a guarantee that his will
would be properly executed. The Milan city council, which declared
the *Umanitaria* a public institution (*ente morale*), set up a special committee that recruited ten thousand members (*socii*), to periodically
elect a governing board. Reformist socialists were the majority on the
board and they gave a distinctive reformist stamp to *Umanitaria*,
which was considered one of the strongholds of Italian reformism.[1]

The *Umanitaria* was ordered to cease operations in 1898 by General Bava Beccaris in the wake of a general political reaction after the
May Events. Reopened in 1902, it set up a labor bureau (*ufficio del
lavoro*) whose main task was to find jobs for the unemployed by
studying the labor market and setting up a network of placement
offices (*uffici di collocamento*), which would mainly help migratory
workers, *mondariso* among them.[2]

In keeping with these aims, the labor bureau launched an investigation into the conditions of workers in the rice fields (*I lavoratori
delle risaie*) during the 1903 weeding season. According to the investigation, farmers did not maintain the proper distance between rice
fields and dwellings, and did not meet the housing requirements
stipulated by the law.[3] For their part, the authorities did not enforce
the 1901 law, which provided safeguards against malarial infection,
including the free distribution of quinine (*chinino di stato*) to the population of the malarial districts and to laborers migrating to these districts. Despite the law, malaria-stricken weeders had to purchase the
drug at their own expense, if they could afford it. Even communal
administrations sometimes lacked quinine. Investigators found many
sick weeders in the communes of the Vercellese that were not declared malarial and where therefore no free distribution of quinine
was required.

Some workers were still unaware of the fact that the law of 1901
provided for free treatment, and suffered from the disease without
even telling their employers. "If they catch the fever," explained one
of the investigators, "they stretch out in the sun, or they wrap themselves in rags, and lie down until the attack is over, and then they
resume work." Miscarriages, as well as gastric, eye, and skin ailments, were very frequent. From 30 to 50 percent of migratory
weeders who took the train back home had chapped and swollen

legs. The majority looked pale and emaciated, after having lost an average of five or six kilos.[4]

The Regional Federation of Agricultural Workers of Piedmont (FRAP) decided in February 1903 to ask socialist deputies to query the government why the regulations protecting labor in the rice fields remained a dead letter and to demand that they be enforced.[5]

On March 2, socialist deputy Angiolo Cabrini, a staunch advocate of social legislation, asked the minister of agriculture, in the chamber of deputies, "which means he intended to adopt . . . in defense of the workers of the rice fields, especially in relation to the laws on the work of women and children, and on malaria," and other problems "whose solution cannot be further postponed without betraying the interests of the proletariat and the decisions passed by the chamber."[6] He accused the government of blindness toward workers' conditions. He also castigated the farmers of northern Italy for their indifference toward the revolting situation of farm workers, which sharply contrasted with their own high profits. The socialist deputy looked back on the centuries-old polemic between the enemies of rice farming who wanted to see it eliminated to improve human health and the agriculturalists who clung to laissez-faire principles in order to enrich themselves. Cabrini rejected the arguments of both groups, advancing instead a third position, which he said was based on new developments in agriculture and hygiene. This new position, backed by organized labor, called for state mediation in the physical working and living conditions and the prevention of sickness and death among rice workers.

Cabrini stressed that the recent breakthrough in malaria research did not change the fact that the rice fields continued to be nests of anopheles larvae. Therefore it was the duty of the state to impose limitations on the age of the weeders and on the length of the workday, to inspect the food and shelter provided for migratory workers, and to distribute quinine regularly. "A series of facts reveal your impotence in applying the very laws passed in favor of the working classes," declared Cabrini. He pointed out that parliamentary laxity, compounded with the resistance of employers to the application of progressive legislation, amounted practically to its abrogation.

In reply, minister of agriculture Guido Baccelli gave his assurances that, in spite of a lack of inspectors, the government would guarantee the strict enforcement of the Cantelli regulations and of the 1901 law providing for free quinine distribution in the rice belt.

There was a lively debate between Cabrini and Baccelli about the interpretation of the June 12, 1902, law on woman and child labor, which still lacked the pertinent regulations. Cabrini recalled that it prohibited workers under fifteen in work places declared dangerous and unhealthy, in other cases workers under thirteen, if protected by special measures. Was a rice field considered an unhealthy place by the law? Its status appeared extremely ambiguous; the supreme sanitary council had not included it on its list of unhealthy work places, based on the criterion that if all hygienic measures were followed, the fields would not be insalubrious. Minister Baccelli, himself a doctor of medicine, disagreed with this decision, because he did not believe in ideal situations and knew that sanitary rules could be easily neglected in practice. But on the other hand, the same council cautioned that it would be preferable not to employ workers under fifteen years of age. Baccelli agreed to ask that prefects be instructed to enforce this principle in the provincial councils.[7]

Article 1 of the June 2, 1902, law on woman and child labor stated that the government could classify a work place as unhealthy and then impose safety and health measures. Scientific progress furnished the government with invaluable assistance, Cabrini thought, because new scientific knowledge allowed for a continuous reassessment of work sites and the extent of conditions hazardous to health.[8] Therefore, the socialist deputy concluded, the government should disregard the vote of the supreme sanitary council; recognizing the health hazards in the rice fields, it should make use of its prerogatives to take energetic measures to protect workers.

The ministers of the interior and of agriculture responded to Cabrini by sending a circular to the regional provincial councils requesting them not only to follow the Cantelli regulations but also to expand and update them in accordance with the latest scientific discoveries and social legislation. The circular's most important demands were: compliance with the workday limitations stipulated in article 14; construction of separate night shelters for men and women, equipped with protective screens to provide what was called "mechanical prophylaxis"; prohibition of work by children under thirteen; and use of foot and leg protection, such as boots, stockings, or bandages, to keep the skin from the irritating weeds that caused dermatitis.

While the Vercellese workers federation welcomed the ministerial circular as a triumph of Cugnolio's reformist strategy,[9] employers protested, objecting that "to the insubordination of the workers, provoked and maintained by propaganda, by the art of a few demagogues, now a new torture had been added: the law."[10] In

Novara and Vercelli, the association of agriculturalists and other agrarian organizations submitted their views of the new demands to the ministries and provincial councilors in charge of reforms.[11]

Farmers suggested that the screens required in the workers' shelters should be prescribed only for lodgings built from then on, not for any existing ones. In any case, it would have been impossible to fix screens onto the barns and other shabby hovels they used as dormitories. In fact, it was clear that the high cost of screens accounted for their unpopularity among the rice farmers who were required to provide them, to the point that Angelo Celli, a malaria researcher and republican deputy nicknamed the screens "a de luxe prophylaxis."[12] A conservative provincial councilor of Novara advanced the argument that screens were ineffective for they would keep mosquitoes inside the buildings and ready to bite.

But what employers opposed was the very need to build shelters for temporary workers. They argued in provincial councils that workers sometimes preferred to sleep outside in the summer in order to avoid not only the heat but also the mosquitoes inside their houses, and that in the open air the mosquitoes were carried away by the night breeze. Farmers did not say that they did not make periodical changes of the straw that served as beds. Lack of ventilation and filth, combined with insects and parasites, made existing shelters undesirable places to sleep. Would the migrant weeders also leave new dormitories during the night and make them superfluous? If not, the mosquitoes would enter the shelters each time their careless dwellers opened the doors, even if they had screens. And, no less important, constructing these lodgings would amount to an enormous expenditure that only a few farmers could afford.[13]

In the name of free enterprise, employers also demanded the suppression of article 14 of the Cantelli regulations, which shortened the workday to less than 10 hours, "something practically impossible and incompatible with cultivation." According to the rice growers, even the traditional working rhythm of the squads interfered with the application of article 14 because they wanted to start weeding as early as possible when the temperature was still bearable. Besides, health considerations were not enough to make article 14 worthwhile. The latest studies showed that weeding time did not coincide with the peak of the malaria season, which occurred in the second half of July and in August, when the *monda* was over and harvesting not yet begun. Only children under thirteen and women declared incapable of work by the local sanitary officers (those in the last month of pregnancy or who had given birth less than one month before weeding time) would be forbidden to work. After all, a few cases of malaria did not justify article 14, the employers concluded, and they enclosed medical reports to show that the malarial mortality rate was very low.

Agriculturalists also disregarded ministerial recommendations to provide protection for weeders' feet and legs, because rice-field workers, they argued, were always barefoot, and would find boots or stockings burdensome. Besides, cases of skin irritation were too rare to justify this protection. Farmers thought that it was enough to require local health officials to treat the cases of dermatitis that did develop. The Lomellina rice growers wanted to have the Cantelli regulations abolished by the Pavia provincial council. In the session of June 27, 1903, councilor Angelo Galbarini, president of the association of agriculturalists of Lomellina, called for its immediate abrogation, adducing that it was unconstitutional. He claimed that the Lomellina farm workers were in excellent condition (*benissimo*) and that "there are no malarial fevers, so that the *monda* of the rice is the weeders' Carnival." Therefore, the Cantelli regulations were unnecessary.[14]

The rice growers' guidelines did not remain unchallenged. *La Monda*, Cugnolio's newspaper that replaced *La Risaia* from May 30, 1903 to October 1, 1904, published a report prepared by a medical doctor who set forth the familiar conclusion that malaria caused few deaths in the rice belt because the victims died of complications to which malaria patients were predisposed. Furthermore, if there was any decrease in the mortality rate for malaria, this was not because the environment had become healthier but because in the preceding twenty years the price of quinine had gone down from 1.50 lira to 20 centesimi per gram and, as a result, the drug was more widely available to farm workers. Regarding article 14, the *La Monda* report affirmed that because there was "perfect accord between the modern scientific views and the old suppositions on the miasmas as the most dangerous hours to contract malaria," the regulation should remain unchanged.[15]

In any case, the members of the Novara provincial council decided in August to adjourn the debate on the new regulations until the end of that year. Most of the provincial councilors refused to discuss the adoption of new measures to protect labor because they ran counter to the interests of employers, whom they represented and defended. When the debate resumed on December 30, 1903, the councilors decided to abstain from discussing the issue once more, under the pretext that they were waiting to be informed about the draft of a proposed law on rice cultivation presented by Senator Carlo

Cerruti of the supreme labor council.[16] And several other proposed laws followed his until one was passed in 1907!

Many of the members of the scientific community whose opinions affected the legislative process recommended more or less rigorous hygienic measures. Their recommendations were based on personal interest or class allegiances, as we shall now see. The second international rice congress of Mortara, October 1–2, 1903, was one of the prestigious arenas where the highest authorities on labor-related issues in agriculture tried to influence future legislation. Amilcare Fracchia opened the debate by trying to discredit the groups that considered rice farming "with much exaggeration . . . as an unhealthy or at least far from healthy industry, and therefore recommended special legislative dispositions which, in any case, would no doubt increase agricultural expenses."[17]

Francesco Pezza, the public health officer in Mortara, proclaimed in his report to the congress, "Labor Diseases of Rice Farming," that thanks to modern pathology, "a breath of modernity could . . . reinvigorate the old refrain . . . about the relation between rice fields and malaria." To him this meant dispelling ancient fears about the dangers of rice cultivation. Pezza insisted that the rice fields were harmless for workers; that the night shelters in use were adequate if the straw used as bedding could be changed more often; that the meals of the migratory workers were nutritious enough, no worse than the regular food they ate the rest of the year, although admittedly there was the problem of the greed of the *capisquadre,* which led them to supply poor quality food. Pezza was opposed to a workday longer than nine or ten hours, but with a caveat that amounted to his capitulation as a public health officer: "I do not want to dwell upon this, because the limit of the workday has to be determined not only by sanitary considerations but also by financial and genuinely agrarian reasons, which transcend my study."

Weeding was light work, Pezza affirmed. It required little muscular strength and great flexibility of the spine, characteristic of the bodies of children and women, who were so well adapted to its performance. He dismissed the use of screens because "in general, farm workers do not seem to be fit to use so many precautions," without extending this observation to their capability to regularly take a daily dose of quinine, a treatment that aroused great enthusiasm among employers and their supporters.[18]

The physician Gian Battista Grassi, who, with his colleague Angelo Celli, was making important experiments on malaria, remarked that the rice fields were "the paradise of the anopheles." (Grassi made

his discoveries at the same time as Sir Ronald Ross, the British researcher of malaria, who received a Nobel prize in 1902.) But Grassi
had solutions to the anopheles threat: the use of both preventive
prophylaxis, quinine and screens. Therefore, he reasoned, the prohibition of work one hour after sunrise and one hour before sunset
were unjustifiable, "if not harmful." True, in these hours, the mosquitoes bit more often, but lacking protected shelters, the temporary
workers in particular would be better off remaining in the fields,
where the cool breeze blew mosquitoes away. Mosquitoes sought
refuge indoors, where the workers would be much more exposed to
the bites. Therefore, persons who were weeding were less likely to be
bitten than those who were not weeding.[19]

Grassi and Pezza did not propose any particular length of the
workday but did present recommendations to protect weeders'
health, all of which were approved by the majority of the assembly.
One proposal excluded women with infectious diseases or varicose
veins, those in the last month of pregnancy and first month after
childbirth, and those breast-feeding babies less than four months old.

Some members of the audience objected to these exceptions.
One participant, for example, exclaimed: "With these proposals it
seems to me that it is being established that the rice field is poisonous.
Regarding pregnant women we see that in so many industries where
work is more tiresome they are not excluded." And another, "But
with so many restrictions, plenty of the poor will be deprived of a
means of income, and one will not know where to find weeders who
do not have any such defects." In his report, the well-known agronomist Oreste Bordiga noted plaintively that labor was so expensive
that it was risky to burden rice farming with "excessive new regulations."[20]

Other recommendations intended only to instruct legislators
and others interested in labor issues in the rice fields included the
provision of rest periods for nursing women, one in the morning and
another in the afternoon; garments to cover feet and legs; a health
certificate for all migratory weeders; health inspections of the fields;
and a nutritional chart to guide the preparation of meals for migratory
workers. The final and most critical item was "reduction of the work
hours and their distribution in accordance with hygienic precepts."
This was also approved, with the majority agreeing to a ten-hour
workday and Angiolo Cabrini raising his voice in favor of nine hours.

Some participants argued that such an idea should not be discussed in the congress. They invoked either the liberal principle, that
there should be no special norms for more dangerous industries, or

scientific arguments. This last appeal led the socialist provincial councilor of Novara, Mario Casalini, to reply amid murmurs of protest: "I believe that the love of the agriculturalists for science manifested here is mere self-interest, because science makes them believe that they are right."[21]

Starting in 1903, we have to analyze the intervention of the Humanitarian Society, which mediated among the weeders, the farmers, and the government. The results of its 1903 inquiry, *Farm Workers of the Rice Fields*, would serve as a base both for the establishment of the placement office, with which the *Umanitaria* hoped to replace the *capisquadre*, and the enlightenment of legislators in the preparation of a new law on rice cultivation.[22] The investigators gathered many details on the work force in spite of an unfriendly welcome by many local authorities and farmers who suspected them of being tax investigators or subversive agents. Their findings corroborated the gloomy picture of the weeders drawn by prolabor elements.[23]

The places of origin of the migrant weeders remained the same as in the nineteenth century (see chapter 2, p. 43). The workers traveled by train with discount fares, if they formed a group, or in carts. The employers preferred migrants from the mountains of Bobbio and its surroundings, because they were "tenacious" and ready to obey, though not always very "capable." The weeders of Lodi, Piacenza, and Reggio Emilia were considered faster and abler, but quick to protest any violation, real or supposed, of their rights.

Weeders from the Bobbio region needed the earnings of the *monda* more than the others, who viewed them as a supplement to other sources of income. Such dependence may have contributed to the mountaineers' perseverance and submissiveness. Less submissive weeders from other areas had a history of experience in labor protest and organization that made them combative and insubordinate. The majority were farm workers and peasants, but there were also unemployed industrial workers, artisans, and maids who could earn more money in the rice fields than in workshops or domestic service.[24]

The inquiry's observations on food, health, and living conditions, published after the sessions of the second international rice congress, in no way corresponded to the optimistic reports presented to the assembly, and in fact showed little improvement from the conditions described at the time of the *Inchiesta Jacini* in the 1880s. The farmers did not comply with the recommendation to install screens, which they considered too expensive.

The section of the 1903 *Umanitaria* inquiry subtitled "Morality in

the Rice Fields" voiced the reporters' concern over the effect of co-
habitation among migratory weeders of both sexes and of the temporary liaisons that took place during the weeding, and speculated
about the moral health of women weeders, who sometimes bore illegitimate children. In addition, the inquiry found that many defenseless young women fell prey to the advances of the *caporali*, who
abused their power to "seduce" the objects of their sexual whims.[25]
These bourgeois observers were possibly disturbed by the presence
of "independent," "emancipated" women, because they were not
under the tutelage of a man as, according to prevailing opinion, all
respectable women should be.

While the inquiry of the *Umanitaria* was going to press, Senator
Carlo Cerruti, a member of the supreme council of labor, presented
his legislative proposal on rice cultivation (October 1903) to that body.
The major innovations of his proposal, which supposedly was to be
submitted soon to parliament, were the introduction of a written
contract between employers and weeders, and the prohibition of any
deductions from workers' wages to pay for the services of mediators,
whose earnings would be fixed by a different contract between them
and employers. It did not eliminate the *caporali*, to the dismay of farm
workers who wanted their federations, leagues, or chambers of labor
to act as recruiters of migratory workers.

Employers greeted the proposal with a storm of protest because
it stipulated a nine-hour workday, which Cerruti had adopted as a
compromise after learning about the recommendations made by the
supreme sanitary council in a memorable session on June 8, 1903.[26]
After considering that the weeders exerted themselves to the utmost
and worked under terrible conditions, the members of the council
concluded that the workday of the *mondariso* should not exceed eight
hours.[27]

The Weeders Unfold Their Own Strategy

Cabrini's speech in parliament on March 2, 1903, and the response to
it by public administrators, did not make employers more amenable
to negotiating with weeders' leagues over conditions for the next
weeding. Following the tactics of preceding years, the entrepreneurs
were "turning a deaf ear" to the leagues' offers. When by mid-May
the Vercellese leagues insisted on an agreement, the employers declared that it was too late to conclude one.[28] The farmers were con-

vinced that poor harvests that year would force the leagues to drop all their demands.

In 1903 the rice-belt organizers decided to press employers to apply all the rules that protected laborers and their health. They appealed directly to local authorities to enforce the laws, encouraged socialist parliamentary action, and organized labor protests. The employers soon found pretexts for disregarding the Cantelli regulations, particularly article 14, which limited the workday. They reasoned that more than thirty years of nonenforcement of this article was the best proof of its obsolescence. They wrote to local mayors that their workers "do not want to have anything at all to do with this regulation, because the old custom is more convenient."[29]

In the Vercellese, farmers deliberately intimidated weeders by offering special inducements to those who reported early to work and then pointing them out as workers who violated the legal limits. Some employers put their weeders in a bind—they could choose to start work at half past four in the morning or not. But if they started later, they should expect either to have their midday rest shortened by an hour, to work an extra hour in the afternoon, to report to work on holidays, or to have their wages cut. Of all these choices, the weeders preferred to start work earlier and this gave the employers an opportunity to tell the magistrates that "the formal will to violate the law came from the weeders."[30] Trying to make their plea more convincing, the farmers attempted to make the weeders sign a petition to the government requesting the abolition of article 14. They also induced their weeders to tell the carabinieri that it was the *mondariso* who preferred weeding early in the morning.[31]

All the organized farm workers in Italy gave high priority to the demand for a shorter workday. The *mondine* often went on strike for a shorter weeding day, but now they learned that they could use the Cantelli regulations as a justification for their collective action. The weeders saw many advantages in a shorter workday. One, it was beneficial to their health. Two, it allowed them to pursue other income-earning activities, such as selling fish and frogs in the local market before weeding. They might also till the land for another employer or work their own plots, if they happened to have them, or raise chickens, silkworms, geese, or pigs. Finally, a shorter workday allowed them "simply" to do their housework.

The weeders resented the fact that their employers never took into consideration the time required for them to walk back and forth from home to farm. This problem was on their minds when they insisted on a shorter workday. There were cases of weeders who walked three hours twice a day. Two friends were so sleepy that they took each other by the arms to sleep in turns while they walked; one day both fell asleep and fell down. In general, mothers complained about the difficulty of finding someone to look after their children before daybreak or of the big problem of having to leave their children unattended for several hours. The municipal day-care center of Vercelli (*asilo*) opened rather late in the day; fewer working hours for mothers would obviate this conflict. All the weeders thought that prohibiting work in the evening hours would result in the welcome abolition of the "third" (*terzo*), the extra hours added to their workday for one-third of their wages. It would also create less unemployment. Without being experts in political economy, they knew that the system contributed to increased joblessness and lower wages. The Socialist Party defended the eight-hour workday with an idealistic statement: workers needed eight hours to work, eight hours to rest, and eight hours for education and leisure.[32]

Until then, local *mondariso* had been accustomed to starting work at half past four and leaving the rice fields at three o'clock, to continue working at home or on another farm or doing the "third." The weeders were delighted to begin at six, as long as the farmers did not compel them to weed until four in the afternoon, as they were trying to do. They resisted this imposition because it seriously upset their daily schedule. For example, a group of *mondariso*, forced by a farmer to work from six o'clock until half past four, left in protest at three o'clock to bring their grievances to the mayor.[33] From three to four in the afternoon the intense heat and the reflection of the sun in the water made weeding particularly onerous.

Employers broke the law, reckoning on the passivity of prefects, subprefects, mayors, and carabinieri, who justified their partiality toward agriculturalists by saying they lacked instructions about how to proceed against violations of rice-farming regulations. A group of resolute farm workers faced the head of the constabulary in the commune of Confienza in Lomellina and insisted that he make public the ministerial circular that had been hidden in the town hall. It directed local authorities to follow the laws on rice farming.[34]

Violations pushed the weeders' organizations into coordinated action. On the local level the leagues denounced the infractions of article 14 to the carabinieri, who then had to report the violations to mayors and subprefects. At the same time the leagues of the Vercellese reported violations to the Regional Federation of Piedmontese Agricultural Workers (FRAP). *La Monda* published a sample of a denunciation. It showed the leagues' leaders how to present claims to the carabinieri against rice growers who intimidated weeders into working before the legal time. Their other choice was, as one employer put it, to "just remain quietly at home." Cugnolio, in his role as the FRAP legal adviser, bombarded the socialist deputies in Rome with telegrams charging local authorities with dereliction of duty. When deputy Cabrini interrogated Giolitti, who was also minister of the interior, he promised to order the local prefects and subprefects to enforce the regulations.[35]

The migratory squads were already in the fields and counting on the indifference of authorities. Employers and *capisquadre* could easily impose whatever work schedule they preferred. Local weeders had to agree to the same conditions if they did not want to "just remain quietly at home."

When the carabinieri reluctantly intervened on the farms, the rice growers were furious, saying "We just wonder at seeing that you lend yourselves to do these things wished for by the socialists." Farmers also threatened to resign all their posts as mayors, communal councilors, or administrators of charitable institutions (*opere pie*), although they never did.[36] If taken to court, they told the judges, according to one editor of *La Monda*, "I did not know, I did not say, I could not prevent the workers from doing as they wanted."

The same editor recalled how, in past years, when in desperation unemployed local weeders forced their way into the fields and began to weed with the migratory workers, employers did not hesitate to call on the carabinieri to drive the intruders out without pay. Now a new type of "intruder" (*mondariso* entering the rice farms very early and staying until late, violating the law) was not only paid regularly but was also allowed to stay, without recourse to the carabinieri.[37] The farmers' opportunistic approach to the law made the editor proclaim: "Here the farm workers can touch with their very own hands what the class struggle is all about." For *La Monda*, the workers were law-abiding citizens, and their employers the law-breakers. For *Il Contadino* the carabinieri applied the letter of the law only when they caught a poor field worker with 40 centesimi worth of firewood.

In one case, a judge not only acquitted all the employers charged with disregarding the limits on the workday, but also readily accepted the farmers' version of events and the statement of "three of four farm workers brought as witnesses." He declared the weeders guilty and liable for prosecution for reporting to work too early.[38] During the FRAP congress of August 22, the leagues' delegates viewed this as

a "judicial scandal." The leagues' delegates immediately decided to
send a petition with the workers' signatures to the interior and agriculture ministers, asking them to enforce the Cantelli regulations.[39]
They insisted that this would not mean the end of rice farming or its
profitability, because in the preceding years land rents in the region
had almost doubled, and the capitalist farmers had paid them in the
belief that rice would continue to be profitable.

In Lomellina the weeders also battled to work fewer hours, but
they made small gains.[40] All the organizations of the rice belt were
ready to recognize the almost complete failure of the 1903 action due
to the authorities' complete lack of support, their reluctance to mobilize troops "and [thereby] incur exceptional expenses, like those that
are met when one wants to repress the hungry farm workers." As a
result of violations of farming regulations and a longer workday, employers saved the equivalent of five or six weeding days' wages.
Nevertheless, weeders' representatives stated clearly that in the future they would resort to the same tactics,[41] with the thought that at
least the campaign served to direct attention of the government and
of the public at large to the situation in the rice belt.[42] In fact, the
members of the superior labor council in Rome even took the initiative of requesting local leagues to submit concrete guidelines for
the upcoming law. The leagues called assemblies to discuss the
recommendations.

Among other things, the leagues of Buronzo and Asigliano proposed shortening the nine-hour day of the Cerruti project by one
hour. They also proposed abolishing the "third" (terzo), work on Sunday, and the hated capisquadre. The league of Buronzo also requested
the use of the town hall's bell to mark the hours, and thus stop the
supervisors' usual cheating on the workday.[43]

All this helped to increase the alarm among employers. They
developed their own tactics to fend off or counteract the state's intervention in private enterprise. In case the new law sanctioned the
eight-hour day, they were determined to fix hourly pay rates instead
of daily wages for migratory squads. The FRAP immediately advised
the mondariso to multiply the proposed hourly pay by eight before
joining a squad, and to see that the total sum amounted to the equivalent of a nine-hour day in order to avoid decreases from the wage
level of the previous year, 1903.[44]

In January 1904 the supreme sanitary council named a special
commission to express its views on the length of the workday in the
rice fields, even though this council had already recommended an
eight-hour day on June 8, 1903. According to Cabrini, "a commission

of the Vendéen rice growers [Cabrini equated the diehard employers to the 1793 French counterrevolutionaries from the Vendée] dropped by in Rome and besieged ministers, ministries, and commissions in such a way that it was decided to consult three medical experts: Golgi of Pavia, Divestea of Pisa, and Maggiore of Modena." They were "misled . . . by the advocates of the exploiters of the rice fields ominously predicting the ruin of rice farming," Cabrini noted, and recommended a nine-hour workday. Their opinion was accepted by the special commission, and also by another special commission appointed by the labor bureau to study the new law.[45]

In the end, the special commission of the supreme sanitary council left unchanged the nine-hour workday proposed in the Cerruti project. But employers used their influence in the government to modify it, because they considered nine hours of weeding too short. They urged that time lost to bad weather should be made up on the following days, provided that the workday did not exceed eleven hours. The workers were indignant, because traditionally work schedules were fixed after allowing for days perhaps missed because of bad weather. Besides, this clause made any limit of the length of the workday unlikely.[46]

These developments prompted the National Federation of Farm Workers (Federterra) to hold rallies on February 28 in twelve communes to show their support for the rapid passage of a new law based on the Cerruti project. It was not that the institution of a nine-hour day made them happy at all, but the farm workers' federations preferred this to no law at all, or what was still worse, having rice farming regulated by provincial councils. Although it was not a decisive gain for local workers, the Cerruti project had significant advantages for migratory workers, who were accustomed at times to weed more than twelve hours a day. While supporting the Cerruti proposal, the farm workers' federation could plan further action to reduce the hours.[47]

The members of the federal council of the FRAP had more and more reason to suspect that the government was ready to abolish the Cantelli regulations,[48] and delay the approval of the new law. This would leave the workers without any protective legislation.[49] They remembered the ease with which magistrates dismissed almost all the charges against employers who tried to violate or suppress the Cantelli regulations.[50] The reformist socialists at Vercelli resented the staunch resistance that employers and the government put up when they tried to get reforms by legal means: by appealing to parliament and to public opinion. In their view, the middle classes were abandoning them and they foresaw that, without their cooperation, the reformist socialists would fail and become discredited. They would lose their majority in the party to the revolutionaries. This did indeed happen two months later at the Socialist Party national congress at Bologna (April 9–11, 1904).[51]

As the 1904 *monda* approached, the weeders were more determined than ever to fight for a shortened workday. In April *Il Contadino* announced that employers were fixing the following schedule: ten hours for the local, and eleven for the migratory *mondine*. A *La Monda* manifesto specified what to do after the eight hours of weeding: "Go home. What matters is to do so once or twice, and you will see that the boss will yield." Another one read: "What creates revolutionaries is the government with its improvidence, its disregard for the interest of workers. The rice field does not have a law anymore. *We accuse!*"[52]

On May 16 the weeders of San Germano Vercellese put words into action as soon as the employers stipulated the nine-hour workday. The women struck, followed by those of neighboring communes. In some of them, the permanent workers also joined the protesters and a total of four thousand workers were idled in the Vercellese. The federal council of the FRAP together with the league leaders moved into action. They decided to urge weeders outside the Vercellese not to go to the region as strikebreakers. In addition, they called on the mayor to promote negotiations between leagues and entrepreneurs, and decided to ask all the workers' organizations for subsidies for the strikers, and for the publication of a strike bulletin. The leaders also got assurances from employers who were ready to settle for an eight-hour day that they would hire the striking workers and not outsiders. Meanwhile, disregarding the mayors' warnings to abstain from such action, groups of strikers tried to persuade migratory weeders to leave the region.[53]

But the united front soon began to break down. Communication among the strikers' groups was insufficient, and this made solidarity and concerted action difficult to maintain. In the end, the strikers did not reach their chief goal, which was an eight-hour contract for the entire region. Employers agreed to it only on some farms.

There were violent episodes, when weeders tried to stop the work of the strikebreakers who were protected by troops. In Tronzano they even threw stones at a group that had just arrived by train. Seven of the assailants were sentenced to eight to twenty-five days in jail. Six women of Lignana were indicted "for abusing the mayor" and interfering with others' right to work. There were also

women detainees in Bianzè and Quinto Vercelli. The leagues mobilized to collect funds for the victims.[54]

Santhià underwent the longest conflict. The determination of its
eight hundred *mondariso* to forego all wages for the 1904 weeding
season before yielding, bore fruit; after a three-week work stoppage,
the majority of employers accepted the eight-hour workday. Perhaps
the *mondariso* were able to hold out because 1904 was a year of economic recovery after a two-year recession. Thus, other members of
strikers' families could possibly find jobs, and the entire family could
survive, even with the loss of the women's wages. Three of the four
recalcitrant employers had their farms "guarded by soldiers at the
commune's expense, although they are not running any risk."[55]

Around June 13, 1904, a second wave of protests started in
several communes because many local weeders were not given work.
In Formigliana, when employers decided to fix wages only at the end
of the first week of weeding, sixty *mondariso* refused to work until
they relented and announced the wages at the beginning of the
week.[56]

In Santhià there was a second stoppage on June 12 when one
farmer, after having hired about five hundred weeders for ten days,
dismissed them after the fifth day, and replaced them with the same
number of migratory weeders recruited by the association of agriculturalists of Vercelli. This happened despite the efforts of the mayor
of Santhià, who hoped to avoid conflicts by sending petitions to the
mayors of the neighboring communes asking them to discourage
weeders from coming.[57] While the masses of unemployed streamed
to other farms in Santhià to urge their weeders to stop work, the
cavalry came to the scene to guarantee the right to work, and amid
much turmoil five women were arrested for violating this right. The
mayor disowned any responsibility for the maintenance of public
order if the detainees were transported to Vercelli, but thanks to
"everybody's goodwill" the women were finally freed and the strikers
resumed work.[58]

The FRAP members lamented the lack of unanimity among the
strikers at the end of the protests, which in several cases led to uneven results and unnecessary acts of violence. Because of the limitations of communication in each commune, the protests followed separate courses. In some, the weeders returned to an eight-hour day; in
others, to nine; while in still others, the strikes continued.[59] They
were unable either to eliminate the competition of migratory squads
or to gain the support of public officials for their demands.

Some employers violated the law. In the chamber the socialist

deputy Leonida Bissolati raised the question of irregularities in Cas-
cine San Giacomo in the Vercellese. Not only did farmers there give
orders to weed before sunrise, but they also set the commune clock to
strike the signal to start work while it was still dark. Di Sant'Onofrio,
undersecretary of the interior, blamed the *mondine* for the offenses
because, according to him, it was in their interest to arrive at the rice
fields early. Even if this assertion were true, the argument did not
justify the mayor's disregard of article 14. But the undersecretary
excused him by saying that it was the population that wanted to be
awakened early. His argument that "it seems that these are persons
who like to sleep little" provoked lively comments in the chamber.[60] It
is surprising that even in these adverse circumstances the weeders of
Vercelli could win an eight-hour workday on several farms, as well as
wage increases.

In the Novarese there were strikes in 1904 in the communes of
Borgolavezzaro (eight days) and Vespolate (five days), which led to
the shortening of the previous year's workday by one hour, from ten
to nine hours.[61] Thanks to these successes the nine-hour day was
adopted throughout the Novarese, together with better wages.
Borgolavezzaro weeders had the cooperation of women from Emilia,
who stayed at home in support of the strikers.[62] In the wake of the
strike, Vespolate saw the formation of its first league.

The leagues' federations tried to conclude accords with all Emilian weeders stipulating an eight-hour day and a wage of 0.25 lira an
hour. This proved an impossible goal, but out of solidarity many
Emilian weeders did not migrate. The leagues thus had this advantage in pressing their demands, along with an extraordinary profu-
sion of weeds that season.[63]

On May 29 the leagues federation at Lomellina called an assembly and declared a strike for the following day. Its objectives were to
obtain not only the eight-hour day and a wage of 0.25 lira an hour, but
also pay increases for all other tasks of the rice fields besides weeding.
The weeders stopped working in twenty-six communes. In twelve,
they struck under extraordinary circumstances, for there had already
been a strike during the sowing season. At the time, workers and
farmers had settled not only the ongoing conflict, but also on conditions for the *monda*, which included a ten-hour workday almost everywhere. Following the old custom, the weeders involved had even
paid a deposit of 3 lire or more. In the commune of Gravellona the
agreement was to expire in December 1905, but solidarity with the
rest of the leagues and the prospects of better wages and a shorter

day meant more to those workers than breaking previous pacts, losing a deposit, or being called traitors by their employers.

Violent episodes took place in Olevano, Zeme, and Mortara. In Olevano an employer paid the local weeders 1.70 lira for ten and a half hours of weeding. He quickly raised the wages to 2 lire on May 30, the day of the strike, and promised 2.50 lire for the following week. The women struck all the same; they wanted a nine-hour day. When they went to a neighboring farm to stop migratory weeders from reporting to work, the mayor and twenty-two carabinieri with fixed bayonets blocked their way, and five women were injured. Fearful of further injuries, the mayor himself prohibited the use of migrants, and local weeders and farmers agreed to a nine-hour workday for 2 lire a day. For weeders, weeding for a shorter time meant more than a higher wage.

In Zeme the workers also struck on May 30 for a reduction of hours from nine to eight and for a 2 lire wage. Three employers, who badly needed weeders, agreed to the conditions immediately, but following the directives of the league of "either everybody or nobody," the women stayed away from the fields for a week, expecting that other rice growers would also yield. When the strikers tried to meet migratory weeders on June 6 to ask them to support the protest, the carabinieri stopped their march and pushed some women into a ditch. The strike ended that same day but the workday remained nine hours long.

In Mortara the May 30 strike aimed at reducing the ten-hour workday. Employers hastily gave in to a nine-hour day and a wage of 2.25 lire, "but afterward, because the *mondariso* boasted so much of their victory, on the following Monday, June 6, they reimposed the ten hours for 2 lire." The workers responded with another strike. After protracted negotiations, which established wages and conditions for the season's work, the weeders returned to work again for nine-hour days, at only 2 lire. The migratory weeders struck too and although "deprived of food, they are assisted by the federation of farm workers with bread, flour, and money collected by private citizens."[64]

In Sannazzaro farmers agreed to give their weeders the same wage rate as that in Mortara. They did so until they decided that they were paying too much and had to lower the wages. It took two weeks of work stoppages to force employers to pay the wages that had been originally agreed on.[65]

With few exceptions, if migrant weeders joined strikes, they ran

the risk of having to pay for their solidarity in a number of ways, such
as being deprived of food. In Zeme migratory weeders joined the
strikers without any trouble; in Valle they were threatened with being
sent back home if they struck, and were forced to return to the field.
In Lomello the surveillance of five hundred migrant weeders by the
carabinieri caused the local weeders' strike to fail, and the ten-hour
day continued. In Ottobiano migratory weeders asked to be sent
home, claiming that they suffered from malaria and ill treatment, but
in reality they did not want to interfere in the protests of their sister
mondine.[66]

The rice belt was the only rural region in Italy where strikes
resumed in 1904 after a lull in 1902–3. The struggle was fought with
different degrees of intensity and in forms so varied that they defy
generalization. As a result of the strikes, the majority of weeders,
both local and migrant, obtained wage increases and a shorter workday. The norm was 2 lire or more, while the average in the preceding
twenty-year period had been 1.35 lira for eleven hours. However, the
eight-hour day was won only in a few communes. This failure was
due partly to a lack of discipline and faulty channels of communication, for squads were ready to go back to work as soon as they were
offered better conditions in one place and often did not inform strikers on other farms. Solidarity among migratory squads was also deficient. Although they were sometimes willing to join the strikes, they
were not able to when working under military surveillance.[67]

The crucial problem for the local federations was how to stop the
movement of migratory squads, but in most cases they simply could
not do so. In some instances, rice-belt federations were able to inform
migratory workers in Emilia about local conditions and thereby discourage them from traveling to areas involved in labor conflicts. The
degree of organization in both the rice belt and some reservoirs of
migrant labor played a vital role. Otherwise, it would have been
almost impossible to resist the power of employers, who had the
prefects, subprefects, mayors, police, and troops on their side. The
sympathetic mayor of Santhià was one exception.

In any case, the slight gains in work hours and wages provoked
great alarm among the "dismayed" employers, who again predicted
the doom of the crop. The more daring ones resolved to continue
farming without *mondariso*, and experimented with mechanical
weeders, such as rollers drawn by horses, which broke the stems of
the weeds and killed them, while only temporarily bending the more
flexible rice plants. Another technique was to put filters at the mouths
of the canals to sift out the weed seeds and thereby keep them out of

the fields.[68] But these techniques in no way lived up to farmers' expectations.

An initiative intended to regulate at least the competition of migratory weeders came from the *Società Umanitaria*, whose efforts for full employment included regulating the flow of external and internal migration. It established a placement office (*ufficio di collocamento*) in Novara in order to dislodge the *capisquadre* from their key position in the hiring of migratory squads. A commission of five members ran the placement office, two of whom were appointed by the employers, two by the federation of farm workers of Novara, and one, the president, neither a farmer nor a worker, by the *Umanitaria*. The commission would meet the rice growers' demand for migratory workers but under conditions stipulated by a written contract. This was something completely new. The placement office could receive a deposit from both employers and workers to guarantee the fulfillment of the contract and to advance travel expenses to the squads, and it could act as an arbitrator in disputes over contract interpretations.[69]

Contrary to the expectations of the *Umanitaria*, the rice-belt labor federations disapproved of their action. They feared that in practice the placement office "would become a new and improved class instrument totally favoring the exploiters." Angry critics even attacked Loria, the founder of the *Umanitaria*, claiming that "during his lifetime he enriched only himself by shamelessly exploiting others' work and life". They criticized the *Umanitaria*, saying that it was completely controlled by the official labor bureau in Rome, which even named the five members of the commission. The federation of farm workers at Novara had not been asked to send representatives to the placement office although employers had named their two delegates.[70] Such a commission could hire an excessive number of migrant weeders, they feared, and negotiate for higher wages than those offered to local workers. Thus, instead of improvements in their working conditions, local weeders predicted unemployment, the loss of even small gains from past battles, and the ending of their organizations that resulted from decisions of the placement office, to the delight of farmers who "would see in the new institution the safeguard of social peace."[71] Also, with written contracts, migratory squads would find it more difficult to strike.

The second national meeting of rice workers on January 29, 1905, was held at Novara. The main purpose of the gathering was to debate the issue of legislation on rice farming, but the delegates also made clear their disapproval of how the placement office was constituted and asked the *Umanitaria* to incorporate genuine worker representation in it. In May league delegates met again in Bologna to try to reach agreements between migratory and local squads. They completely rejected the services of the placement office and condemned their contracts, which precluded the right to strike.[72]

In May 1903 Amilcare Toscano, ex-secretary of the farm workers' federation of Lomellina and one of the commission's "nonauthentic" workers' representatives, visited several communes of the Novarese on a propaganda tour, inviting weeders to make contracts through the placement office. The Novarese workers were willing to do so, but they strongly disapproved of Toscano's attacks on socialists who, in his words, "go around rousing farm workers, the ringleaders who go around preaching impractical ideas," an expression that made him the target of hoots of disapproval, and of even "more solid objects" from those present at his rallies.[73]

The real reason for the federation's rejection of the placement office was that it aimed at replacing that organization as the coordinator of migratory labor. The leagues' delegates knew that only labor organizations acting as placement offices, without employers' participation, would be able to hire the contingents of outside labor actually needed without causing unemployment or interfering with labor conflicts in the rice belt. The *Umanitaria* placement office, by its very structure and functions, did away with class solidarity. In fact in 1904 and 1905 local workers refused to use the services of the placement office, which fulfilled no practical functions at all.[74]

Another source of disappointment was the lack of government initiative in instituting labor tribunals (*collegi di probiviri*—from the Latin *probus vir*). The oldest of these bodies, the French *conseils de prud'hommes*, was establish in 1806. In Italy a parliamentary commission had proposed them as early as 1879. The law, finally passed in 1893, provided for *collegi* only for industrial workers, and there was no *collegio* in the rice belt. Farm and urban workers organized a rally in Vercelli to express their interest in the institution when the labor council in Rome seemed ready to take the first steps. The labor tribunals already operating in other industrial centers had half of their members appointed by employers, the other half by workers, and a president designated by the government. The farm workers of the Vercellese hoped that the tribunal with its two offices of arbitration and legal consultation would help to improve working conditions and reduce conflicts between capital and labor.[75] However, the proposal to establish a tribunal for farm workers remained only that.

A lack of government reforms did not mean an absence of new developments during these years. On the contrary, farmers redoubled their efforts to block the chamber from accepting the Cerruti proposal or any other project recommending a nine-hour workday; they preferred the rules approved by provincial councils, where a majority supported the growers' interests.

The political situation looked favorable for employers. Giolitti held elections on November 6, 1904, in the aftermath of a politically motivated general strike that had been called in September to protest the killing of several workers in the south. For four days life came to a standstill in almost the entire country. Giolitti refrained from using violent methods to repress the strike. Instead he called national elections for November. The prime minister assumed that the electorate would turn its back on the socialists, whom it would hold responsible for the strike. But this did not happen. On the contrary, there were three hundred twenty-six thousand votes cast (21.3 percent) for the socialists, double the number of votes the party got in 1900 (13 percent). Nevertheless, the socialists lost four of their thirty-three parliamentary seats. Giolitti felt reassured that what Ernesto Ragionieri calls "an antisocialist front"[76] was founded with an increase of "ministerial" deputies from 296 to 339. The parliament now had more conservative elements.

Employers did not waste time; in December the provincial council of Novara deliberated on the abolition of article 14 for the second time. This action prompted the FRAP to request deputies Cabrini and Bissolati to question the minister of agriculture again about delays in submitting the Cerruti law project to the chamber.[77] Instead, the government decided to drop this proposed legislation altogether.

The rice-belt socialists and farm workers' federations increasingly feared that the government's next move would be to revoke the Cantelli regulations. They hurriedly convened the second national meeting of rice workers at Novara on January 29, 1905. Cugnolio voiced the general alarm: "We must assume that the government, in compensation for the votes given to it by the agriculturalists in the last elections, has promised them to satisfy their wishes." Therefore, the scope of the meeting was precisely "to bring to the government the voice of the farm workers, so that it does not yield to capitalist pressures."[78]

On February 24, 1905, the conservative deputy Domenico Fracassi, who was also a rice farmer from Novara, presented his own legislative proposal to the chamber. It consisted of two articles. The first set a nine-hour day for the weeding. This could be prolonged to ten whenever necessary, to make up for time lost in bad weather. The second article stipulated that agreements for all other farm labor would be subject to no regulation at all. At the very last moment the government suspended the first parliamentary debate of the Fracassi law, which had been originally scheduled for March 2.[79] Perhaps this was due to pressure from rice growers. The suspension of the debate caused a great deal of anxiety among workers. They did not like Fracassi's plan, but preferred it to the provincial councils' regulations.

Hardly had the workers' tempers subsided when they learned of the existence of a third draft, presented on March 4. Its alleged author was Giolitti himself who, according to a *La Risaia* editor, put himself "against science and civilization." The writer continued: "We succeeded in getting a copy of that mysterious project that Giolitti took so much care to keep secret." The reason: "In it, everything that had been written in favor of the *mondariso . . .* has been lightheartedly trampled under foot." According to the scheme, women would be obliged to work up to twelve hours a day with no guarantee of a Sunday rest. The outcry from farm workers' federations and socialist deputies was so loud that the government withdrew this proposal too. According to the socialist deputy Leonida Bissolati, the bill had been prepared by deputies representing rice-farming interests. They had used the name of Giolitti, and had surreptitiously presented the bill to the chamber to take it by surprise.[80]

This incredible incident and its exposure did not stop the *agricoltori* from trying again. In December they submitted to the prime minister, the chamber, and the provincial councils a study of a new law, which followed in substance the blueprint of the plan that had been rejected.[81]

In February of the following year, the rumor that the chamber was going to grapple with a law instituting a nine-hour workday for weeding again frightened the rice growers. They immediately sent a telegram to the author of the bill, the minister of agriculture, emphasizing how "dangerous and harmful" this restriction would be for the crop. Instead, they proposed a minimum of ten hours for local weeders and eleven for migratory workers. The FRAP, no less alarmed, called for an eight-hour day. Considering this inadequate, FRAP members also collected signatures, as they had in 1903, which they sent to the minister.[82]

Another wave of anxiety overtook the employers in June 1906, when they learned that Prime Minister Sidney Sonnino had drafted a new law upholding the nine-hour workday.[83] Again, they made their traditional demands.

Aside from the question of the length of the workday, the question of health care, already mentioned, looms large in this story.

Workers in the rice fields began to understand health problems. Their organizers stated their view much more cogently and fully than did rice growers, many scientists, and, with few exceptions, members of the government, who used a much narrower approach to the issue of workers' health.

The many discussions, reports, and resolutions on the anti-malarial campaign show how the majority of the spokesmen for agriculture, as well as many influential representatives of the scientific community and the government, were interested in keeping workers fit for work with the minimum of effort, monetary investment, or concessions on their behalf. Thus, for them the massive distribution of quinine was the panacea for all labor problems.

Nothing could have been more distressing to these same interests than the recommendation of the supreme sanitary council on June 8, 1903, that the weeders' workday should not exceed eight hours. (It was changed seven months later!) Labor leaders and sympathizers often linked the issue of the eight-hour day to questions of workers' health. Cugnolio wondered "whether a wage increase leading to a general betterment of the standard of living would not be one of the best means to combat malaria."[84] The idea that the workers needed more than simply a cure for malaria was nothing new. In the past, members of progressive groups had demanded other remedies along with quinine to protect workers' health, but now this awareness was evident in the everyday vocabulary of workers themselves. It appeared in the leagues' campaigns, petitions, declarations, and congresses. Workers wanted a new law that would protect their well-being and to this end they testified to their own experiences in the fields.[85]

At the invitation of the supreme labor council, the leagues of Buronzo and Asigliano submitted their own guidelines for a new law. They contained not only the traditional appeals for an eight-hour day, rest on Sunday, and the elimination of the "third" or extra hours of weeding, but also a demand for two long breaks for eating and resting, because women who had weeded uninterruptedly in the preceding *monda* had fallen ill and spent all their earnings on medicine.[86] In the FRAP campaigns for a fairer law, it emphasized that the best defense against malaria was workers' improved physical resistance. This could be brought about by shorter work hours, better nourishment, higher pay, and full employment.[87]

In 1905 the deputies who represented employers' interests distributed to their colleagues copies of reports by Doctors Pezza and Grassi. These insisted on the uselessness of the Cantelli regulations as a contribution to better health. *La Risaia* called Grassi an "expert siding with the entrepreneurs" (*perito di parte padronale.*) It then stated its own interpretation of the regulations:

> Our opponents were smart enough to make us believe that the workday restriction in the rice fields was established to reduce malaria, but instead it is the very nature of the work that calls for limitations in the workday.[88]

A group of strikers articulated a variation on the same theme when they declared that their action was "the answer to those who affirm that one has to consider the anopheles mosquito when fixing the schedules" without considering "the greater suffering involved in the moist character of work in the rice fields compared with other work places."[89] This strike took place at the beginning of March, when the fields were free of mosquitoes.

An anonymous doctor commented on the significance of "the government's little pill" (*la pastiglietta governativa*), the quinine pill distributed by the state. "No burdensome work of reclamation, always fraught with economic sacrifices, but a cheap pinch of quinine— that's in its bare essence the principle to which the present campaign clings."[90]

The second international rice congress of 1903 at Pavia had entrusted Doctor Grassi with a research study to determine the effect of the environment of the rice fields on the health of the labor force. He concluded his work in 1904. *La Risaia* attacked Grassi's report because in it he stated that the Cantelli regulations were unnecessary, and also described weeding as light work. Grassi noted that some of the weeders' movements were so relaxing "that sometimes the young weeders fall asleep and tumble into the water."[91]

Labor organizations responded equally negatively to the conclusions of a commission in charge of preparing the regulations for the 1902 law on the prevention of malaria. This commission, consisting of Senator Camillo Golgi, a professor of medicine at the University of Pavia (he would be awarded the Nobel prize for his work on the structure of the nervous system in 1906), other scientists, and deputy Pozzo, authorized a workday for weeders lasting from *soon after* sunrise *until sunset* (italics in the original).[92] "One already knows that it is useless to expect the defense of our health from bourgeois hygienists," wrote a workers' leader in *La Risaia*, "hence it is our duty to impose the remedy—namely, never to work in the rice fields more than eight hours." An anonymous journalist echoed this advice: "Exert yourself less and eat better. Doctors, entrepreneurs, judges, and lawyers who live in the rice fields but eat well have no need to cram themselves with quinine to avoid catching the fever."[93]

The weeders found themselves with no support for the *monda* season of 1905 except that of their own resources. Their federations[94] called for tighter organization as the only means to cope with the old evils.[95] The prospect of fierce competition from migrant weeders loomed large in the region, especially in Lomellina. The farm workers' federations called a convention in Bologna on May 16, 1905, to smooth over the sharp differences between them and to assure the goodwill of organizations outside the rice belt. The federations of Bologna and Reggio Emilia guaranteed their cooperation, but could not predict how other Emilian groups would react.[96] Widespread unemployment in Emilia made the tide of migrant workers difficult to control, and more women than ever were ready to migrate. Many of them were not members of farm workers' organizations. Farmers sometimes offered the migrant squads very favorable working conditions to teach local leagues a lesson and put them to work in the communes with the strongest leagues. The position of the leagues of Mirandola (Modenese) was the most disappointing. Their leader, Sante Artioli, negotiated directly with the Lomellina farmers to find placement for migratory squads, and avoided the local labor federation altogether.

A second factor, a poor rice harvest in 1905, caused unemployment and the lowering of wages in the rice belt. Therefore, it is little wonder that violations of the Cantelli regulations occurred daily in the entire region.[97] In Castelnovetto, *Il Contadino* reported, a weeder decided to go home after complaining about the low wages to the farmer who employed her. The employer was a member of a charitable congregation and remarked: "Today you give up this pay and tomorrow you will come to the congregation to ask for a subsidy." The author of the article upbraided the farmer: "Do you pretend that all those subsidized by the congregation are obliged to come to weed your rice for free out of love for you?"[98]

Less adverse conditions in the Vercellese and the tight organization of some leagues accounted for several labor gains. Bianzè, Lamporo, and Tricerro set an example. There, women went home at three o'clock after having worked eight hours, and refused to weed at all if the employers ordered them to stay until four o'clock. The farmers knew that the work was unbearable between three and four in the afternoon and, by compelling the weeders to work another hour, they mistakenly hoped that the *mondariso* would finally disregard the Cantelli regulations and come to work at sunrise or earlier in order to be able to stop at three. There was also one successful strike in the Novarese, and four more in the Vercellese, which resulted in general wage increases. In Asigliano weeders decided to set weeding hours to the sound of the church bell.[99]

The weeders got moral support from the Russian-born socialist activist Angelica Balabanoff, who went through Lomellina on a campaign for the eight-hour day. She wrote in *La Risaia* about the harm that a workday exceeding eight hours caused to the health, the life, the family, the education, and the employment possibilities of weeders.[100]

The Vercelli General Strike of 1906

Once again in 1906 government paralysis and general public indifference left the weeders to their own devices. Work stoppages aimed at implementing the eight-hour day began on the first days of weeding in some farms of the Vercellese.[101] From there the strikes spread throughout the region. Never before did the rice fields witness the deployment of so many troops.

These labor conflicts had certain elements in common. Weeders were ready to return to work in the few communes where farmers agreed to an eight-hour day and wage raises. Some squads settled for a longer work schedule, but they struck over and over again until the employers granted the desired working conditions. They systematically rejected the very attractive wage offers with which the employers tried to entice them to work longer than eight hours. Later on, even those weeders who had won the eight-hour day often decided to strike for wage increases. Communes with weak organizations had their initiation in direct action and enjoyed their first successes.

Once a squad declared a strike, its members began marching from farm to farm urging the weeders to join them. The migratory weeders also followed the marchers, unless they were being monitored by cavalry squadrons[102] commandeered by the prefect after consultations with the minister of the interior. On one occasion, while the strikers were asking migrant weeders to stop working, cavalry soldiers rushed to the spot and entered the rice fields. The horses became frightened in the muddy water and lost their footing, thus trapping soldiers under their bodies. The cavalry were rescued thanks to the help of the women, who offered them first aid and cleaned them off with their red kerchiefs.[103]

The strikers marched from farm to farm carrying red and white banners, extolling the general strike, and singing the workers' anthem (*Inno dei lavoratori*), as well as a new song that was suddenly on the lips of all the weeders:[104]

> If eight hours seem few to you
> Try working
> And you'll see the difference
> Between work and giving orders.

> *Se otto ore vi sembran poche*
> *provate voi a lavorar*
> *e provarete la differenza*
> *di lavorare e di comandar.*

The increasing number of troops sent to the Vercellese did not intimidate the workers. More than once, the strikers tried to break the ranks of the cavalry soldiers who barred their way by thrusting themselves between the legs of the horses. Sometimes the soldiers achieved their greatest aim, which was to seize the strikers' banners and this wounded the marchers' pride.[105]

In Santhià the weeders wanted an eight-hour day and a daily wage of 2 lire. They struck and on Thursday, May 31, demonstrated in the square while their leaders negotiated in the town hall. All the workers of the town joined the rally after all the factories and stores closed their gates. But solidarity did not stop there. Suddenly soldiers with fixed bayonets marched into the square. When the demonstrators began shouting, "We are friends, we only ask for our rights; we are only defenseless workers; we do not want violence and think that tomorrow you also will ask for what we are asking for today," the captain ordered his troops to retreat amid noisy applause and cries of approval.[106]

But the most extraordinary events took place in the commune of Vercelli, where the situation was the most explosive. The metal workers, many of them members of weeders' families, were unemployed and in the middle of an 8-week-old lockout at the end of May 1906. The bakers were fighting for the abolition of night work.[107] Women working in the largest textile factory wanted a shorter day and a raise. The millers and gardeners asked for the same thing. Finally, the carters complained about unfair job conditions.

On Thursday, May 31, after marching through the farms, the weeders went to the railway station and decided to prevent a group

of migratory weeders from reporting to their jobs. Cavalry sur-
rounded the area and the travelers were locked inside the station for
two and a half hours before they were let out to the street through a
back gate. Strikers discovered the trick and ran after the newcomers,
aiming at the horses with their canes to fend off the cavalry charges.
Finally, the migrants joined the strikers and amid enthusiastic applause and cries of "Long live the general strike!" the two groups
returned to the station. But before going back they also demonstrated
in front of a nearby textile mill, and urged the textile workers to strike
for better conditions.[108]

Tension grew on the following day. At five o'clock in the morning the column of weeders began to stop all workers on their way to
work. Almost all the factories, workshops, schools, offices, stores,
and coffee houses of Vercelli were immediately closed. New strikers,
especially women, joined the crowd parading through the streets,
barring vehicles from entering the city and invading the public square
to interrupt operations in the market there. League organizers held a
rally and urged the workers to resist, but at the same time to get rid of
hotheads who were committing acts of vandalism. Meanwhile, the
troops tried unsuccessfully to rid the city of demonstrators, but they
remained in the streets until the labor leaders announced that the
employers had yielded to the weeders' demands.

The following day, Saturday, promised to be a quiet one, but
that was not the case. The textile workers were locked out of their
factory that morning and found it patrolled by troops. They then
walked to the Piazza Torino, where the main events of the day were
about to take place. Soon, all the other workers who had labor grievances reached the square, where they were supported by the weeders
who were not to return to work until the following week. On their
march they demanded that all the other employers dismiss their
workers for the day.

The greatest disturbances occurred when the cavalry attempted
to disperse the crowd in Piazza Torino. The demonstrators repelled
the charges, pushed the troops out of the square, destroyed a city
customs booth, and built barricades to block the cavalry from returning and strikebreakers from entering the city.[109] In the afternoon, it
was announced that the owners were conferring with workers' commissions and were ready to resolve all the pending labor disputes.
The clamor then subsided and the demonstrations at Vercelli came to
an end.[110]

No organization planned the general strike at Vercelli. The
weeders' strikes spurred on other dissatisfied workers, metal and

textile workers, bakers, millers, gardeners, carters among them, to stage a large-scale protest, which was crowned by great success. The weeders won the eight-hour workday; bakers, the abolition of night work; the others, a shorter workday and wage raises. Almost thirty demonstrators were arrested. Twenty-six defendants—eleven were women between seventeen and thirty-two years old—stood trial on July 26–28, 1906. They were charged with committing acts of vandalism, inciting to class hatred, hindering with violence and threats the freedom to work, using force against, and offending public officials, carabinieri, and the military with epithets such as "cowards, scoundrels, filthy, despicable" (*vigliacchi, mascalzoni, schifosi, morti di fame*). They also taunted them with "come on, we will skin you, we will pull you down from your horses." Two of the defendants were *mondariso*.

Maria Cagna, twenty-three years old, declared that she had participated in the three-day protests but disclaimed any responsibility for her activities, alleging that her friends had made her drink liquor and that the alcohol, as she put it, "excited my mind to the point . . . that I lost any awareness of what I was doing." With her *compagne*, she marched through Vercelli with a banner, singing the workers' anthem. When a carabiniere snatched her banner, Cagna, "blind with anger, cried the words: 'stupid, villain, rude.' " When the group stopped shouting, a marshal returned the banner to her. On the following day, "while my drunkenness still persisted," Cagna marched through the streets with other demonstrators, until the carabinieri stopped them. Infuriated again, she explained, "I lost my reason . . . therefore, I cannot say if I hit a carabiniere or if he hit me. Afterward, I was told by a person that I had made use of my clog, but despite my efforts to remember, I have not succeeded in recalling whether this is true or false."[111] Despite her description of extenuating circumstances, Cagna was given the maximum sentence of ten months in jail and fined 166 lire; the same sentence was also given to another woman and to five men. The mildest sentence was two months and a half in jail and a 50 lire fine. The victory was not so overwhelming in Lomellina. Its labor organizations regarded the Vercelli actions as an example for the whole proletariat.

The strike movement of 1906 reveals new and old tendencies. Years of political education and organizational life had taught the workers to resist employers by organizing leagues, and by sending league leaders (*capoleghe*) to negotiate with farmers or mediators in cases of strikes. They had also learned to be cautious when dealing with weeders who did not participate in the strikes. However, the weeders still resorted to some of their age-old tactics of protest that antedated socialist support; they decided on the right moment to strike with them. The weeders were in control of their own actions, made decisions on the spot, without asking advice from their leaders, and acted on their own initiative to the consternation of the organizers.

In June 1905 the secretary of the land workers' federation of Lomellina vowed that he would not mediate in strikes that had been declared without informing the central committee. Article 8 of the federation's statute stipulated that workers had to report in advance their decision to go on strike. Weeders at three Lomellina communes were staging unreported work stoppages at that time, one of them at Confienza. Perhaps the weeders were not members of the leagues, or had decided that there was no time for parleys. In 1906 the *mondine* of Confienza went on strike again and were one of the first to win the eight-hour day for a 2 lire wage. At the turn of the century, socialist organizers also reprimanded women textile workers at Biella in northern Italy for staging work stoppages not organized by the union, and they withheld support from the protests.[112]

The article on the Caresana strike in the 1890s in the Vercellese, which revealed that the real instigators of the conflict were women, comes to mind (chapter 3, p. 68). There are other examples in which women took the initiative in the protests. Luigi Preti states in his history of labor in the Po valley that during the weeding the *mondariso* of a given field constituted a unique community. This echoes the Encyclopedist's assertion that the rice fields resembled a large factory. It promoted close alliances among the women. Preti wrote that the weeders of the Bolognese "by temperament are more passionate than the men once they become part of a group: and this contributes a great deal to radicalize the environment of the *risaia*."[113]

At the beginning of the century in the Latium countryside, women frequently initiated and controlled labor actions to recover common lands that had been made private by law in the 1880s. Whole village populations led by women marched to the sounds of music and bell ringing to occupy the lost land.[114]

Turning to southern Italy, Frank M. Snowden found that in Apulia organized women farm workers "were regularly among the most militant participants in every strike and demonstration. . . . On many occasions the women lay down with their babies in front of the horses of the cavalry, or conspicuously took their place in the front line of crowds besieging town hall."

In 1908 the socialist newspaper *Avanti!* reported on a work stoppage in Foggia (Apulia):

> In the present strike those who stand out most for their enthusiasm and pride are the women. . . . They are genuine heroines! . . . Their activity is phenomenal: they dash wherever there is a danger of strikebreaking: they urge their husbands on and call out for resistance.[115]

The Biella women textile workers were in the vanguard of all strikes and protests in the district. During a 1912 strike, the organizers deplored the fact that they were dealing with a "mutinous army." They refused to give the women any direction, and left them to their own devices.[116]

Patrician Hilden refers to the militancy of textile women workers in France from a 1909 police report:

> In strikes, women generally distinguish themselves by their aggressive ardor with regard to the *patronat*, and encourage, by their attitude, their husbands to resistance. In important movements, in serious conflicts, one often sees them going down to the public streets to join the demonstrators. . . . In general they are animated by a spirit of struggle against capital, and show themselves very ardent in their demands.[117]

In the United States, "whether in mixed unions or segregated by sex, women often outdid men in militancy," writes Alice Kessler-Harris, and quotes the words of the president of the union of boot and shoe workers in Massachusetts in 1905: "It is harder to induce women to compromise; they are more likely to hold out to the bitter end . . . to obtain exactly what they want."[118] In January 1912, women operatives in a textile mill in Lawrence, Massachusetts, marched out of the factory when they discovered that their pay was short and stormed the city's largest mills. In a few days almost thirty thousand women and men workers had gone out on strike. The "bread and roses" strike, asserts Ardis Cameron, started upsetting the Industrial Workers of the World's plans for gradual and limited work stoppages. In their parades women carried the American and Italian flags.[119] Were some of the many Italian immigrants at Lawrence reenacting their past experience with direct action in their Italian hometowns? What reasons led all these groups of working women to exceed men's militancy when they resorted to collective action? Kessler-Harris explains that some militant could lean on family support in an emergency.[120] Hilden and Cameron stress the importance of the use of community ties, the "bonds of womanhood,"[121] to mobilize for collective action. Temma Kaplan writes about a female consciousness that "emerges from the division of labor by sex, which assigns women the responsibility of preserving life." Women may give to this a very broad interpretation.

Kaplan asserts that "women with female consciousness demand the rights that their obligations entail," and that "the collective drive to secure those rights . . . sometimes has revolutionary consequences insofar as it politicizes the networks of everyday life." Weeders' consciousness and that of other groups of women workers lead them to resort to collective action. Solidarity stems from the women's shared experiences of work and community. If authority, embodied in employers and the government, and supported by the police and the troops, hampered the handling of their responsibilities, they defended their rights to fulfill them with their actions.[122] Women workers' collective life at work and in community accounted for their notions of what was proper, and for their energy and decision when they applied their "pooled resources to common ends."[123]

In 1901 the women workers in one of the Biella mills were on strike and employers, hard pressed to deliver an order, made arrangements to have the work finished in another factory. However, the women there refused to finish it, saying, "We are sorry, but we cannot do it." The owner threatened them with dismissal, but the women insisted: "We deeply regret; but our heart and our consciousness do not allow us to do the work of our striking *compagne*," and they left the factory. Members of the congressional committee investigating the 1912 Lawrence strike "held to a conspiracy theory of the struggle; they repeatedly asked the workers who had told them to go out on a strike and seemed unable to understand when the strikers said 'the stomach' had told them to go, or that they had decided it 'all together.' "[124]

In the rice fields, older tactics were infused with new and overpowering force by the application of the principle of solidarity in a broader sense. Along with weeders' initiative, this gave labor actions their far-reaching scope and success. Several factors made the 1906 wave of strikes different from those of 1901. In 1901 the organization was still too new to coordinate a large-scale action; besides, it had little support from migratory squads, and the chamber of labor, founded in March of that year, was just beginning to organize all local workers into one body. A decisive element that made the 1906 protests so intense was the distressing situation of other groups of Vercelli workers ready to seize the opportunity offered by the weeders' city demonstrations to vent their own grievances in a general strike.

Important in this regard was the all-encompassing role played by the chamber of labor at Vercelli, which, like all the chambers of labor in Italy, grouped together the whole labor force of the city and its surroundings. Its structure allowed it to play a prominent role in general strikes. It fostered ideas of unity in all the categories of farm and urban workers, and therefore tightened the cohesiveness that the regular community networks provided and gave momentum to the protest. In similar fashion, anarchist farm and town workers of Andalusia struck together in 1902 and 1903 to press their demands.[125]

In all the work stoppages of the weeding season, weeders gained more with their protest actions than even organizers had expected. The leagues' leaders sometimes negotiated terms unacceptable to the weeders, who then continued the strike until what they considered a satisfactory agreement was reached. In many cases, wages and work conditions for all farm operations were also decided during strike negotiations to the advantage of groups of laborers other than weeders.[126] Here the countryside and the city forged links because weeders, members of their families, and their friends usually lived in towns, were engaged in both urban and agricultural work, and were equally exposed to socialist propaganda.

The socialist campaign both for the application of existing laws and the enactment of new legislation also contributed to the movement. Thanks to the party, the weeders learned facts about diseases at the work place, the right to health care, and the employers' disregard of these rights. This knowledge reinforced their will to resist abuses and to challenge the halfway solutions to weeders' health problems proposed by employers.

The weeders' sense of what was right explains their militancy, as well as the militancy of other working-class women. Weeders gave priority to their demand for an eight-hour day over the demand for higher wages. They had responsibilities as women, as breadwinners, and as part of the labor force. They knew that their duties in their households did not stop with wages earned in the rice fields. Shorter weeding hours meant more time to meet the other ordinary and extraordinary family needs that they faced as daughters, mothers, and wives.

If they rejected offers for better wages in exchange for a longer workday, weeders were not shirking more toil, because often they wanted more time to devote to other works. The scope of their protest transcended their own work-related issues. As part of the labor force, they were simply trying to impose their own idea of what was good for the whole labor movement. When they worked fewer hours, they battled to ensure full employment for all the weeders and a shorter workday for the entire local and migratory proletariat.

Finally, the weeders' strikes of 1906 moved the national government to prepare a new bill on rice cultivation after many delays. It was passed in 1907.

Between 1903 and 1906, weeders' organizations vainly sought the support of a government that was creating modern institutions and proclaiming the need for new labor legislation. However, all the weeders' attempts to improve their situation by legal means met with government indifference, which rice growers could influence for their own purposes. Organized labor regularly pressed its demands on socialist deputies, but their power was far from sufficient to offset the influence of employers.

Thus, the weeders resorted to direct action. By doing so, they were calling into question the basis upon which the Giolittian system rested.

6

Holding the Line, 1907–10

They say that in Vercelli such an uproar has never been seen before; the strikers—almost all of them women—spend half a day singing in the square and the other half praying in the church.
Spectator, L'Illustrazione italiana, *August 26, 1906*

Repercussions of the 1906 Strikes

The Vercellese workers' euphoria during the successful protests in May and June 1906 was clouded by two main concerns: one was the uncertain fate of those arrested during the strikes; and the other, worries about the employers' possible offensive after the weeders' triumph. The rice-belt work force participated in a variety of activities to collect money and assist the detainees and their families. The socialist section in Trino invited the whole town to a festival on July 15. Its main attractions were the launching of an aerostatic balloon carrying the inscription "Long live the eight-hour workday,"[1] and the playing of the song "We Want the Eight Hours!" The farm workers' league of Salasco invited its members and those of neighboring leagues to dances on July 29 and 30.[2] The FRAP (Regional Federation of Farm Workers of Piedmont) entrusted the chamber of labor with distributing donations of money and food to the families of arrested workers.[3]

Naturally the farmers were determined to avoid a repetition of the unprecedented weeders' strikes during the coming 1906 harvest. They thought that severe sentences for the agitators[4] were not enough to silence protest. They had to eliminate the piece of legislation around which the weeders had mounted their protests. They asked the senators and deputies of Novara and Pavia to approach

Giolitti at the beginning of August and persuade him to abrogate the Cantelli regulations. He did this by a decree of the council of state.[5]

The question remains: Why did Giolitti abandon his mediating tactics and yield so easily to the agriculturalists' demands? There is no answer except that his decision was in line with the political climate prevailing since the November 1904 parliamentary elections, held in the aftermath of the September general strike. Despite the increased number of socialist votes, the extreme left (*estrema sinistra*) was reduced to eighty-four members, having lost fourteen to Giolitti's parliamentary majority. From 1904 on, this majority had the support of many conservative deputies, some of them elected with the help of Catholic votes. This situation makes Giolitti's cooperative attitude toward the rice growers and the offensive tactics they adopted easier to understand.

After the abrogation of the Cantelli regulations, only the regulations issued in August by the provincial council of Novara and Pavia (which did not limit the workday) governed work in the fields.[6] Meanwhile, the Milan Congress of the Italian Agrarian Union (*Unione Agraria Italiana*) on June 4–5, 1906, had reiterated the need to rescind existing regulations and to put an end to labor unrest caused "by the existence and the interpretation of regulations for rice farming which no longer meet the dictates of hygiene."[7]

But in the summer of 1906 the farm workers continued their struggle. They protested against the repeal of the Cantelli regulations[8] and defended the eight-hour workday during the harvesting and threshing season by striking periodically throughout August and September. Both women harvesters and non-harvesters did lead a protest march with the leagues' banners in Motta dei Conti on August 14, and paraded with their children in the big demonstration on August 19 at Vercelli. There, the women, who had formed their own league at the beginning of August,[9] walked solemnly, as though they were in a religious procession. They wore festive garments, and were joined by many women sympathizers.[10]

In some communes employers even refused to sit at the negotiating table. Despite the deployment of police and army troops, they were afraid of the large crowds surrounding city halls during the long drawn-out discussions.[11] In San Germano Vercellese the entire labor force held a general strike in solidarity on August 20–24.[12] On August 21 the socialist newspapers spoke of thirty-five thousand who stayed out from work, as the permanent workers also went out on strike for a fairer contract. Spectator, a reporter for the monarchic weekly *L'Il-*

lustrazione italiana, describes the "predominantly illiterate" protesters:

> At the time of the rice harvest, the territories of Vercelli and Novara are being crossed by 36,000 strikers waving red flags, singing anthems of all inspirations, and going well beyond reformists, integralists, and syndicalists. . . . They say that in Vercelli such an uproar has never been seen before; the strikers— almost all of them women—spend half a day singing in the square and the other half praying in the church.[13]

All this made the league secretary in Balzola (Vercellese) conclude that if workers united in powerful organizations, "we will be able to dispense with the Cantelli regulations and with all the other laws in our favor, because nobody knows how to make them better than we."[14] The strike seemed to demonstrate that he was correct. Farmers had to yield to the three proletarian demands, symbolized by three numbers, 8–5–3: the eight-hour day, 5 lire a day for the men, and 3 for the women. The FRAP victory, guaranteed by its twenty-five thousand members,[15] spurred the leagues of Novara and Lomellina into action.

In Novara the Socialist Party and chamber of labor leaders suddenly showed their willingness to revive the farm workers' federation, which had been declared "dead of anemia"[16] since 1901, and to reconstitute the leagues. One explanation for the federations' death was the poor leadership of Romolo Funes, then in exile. The barber Edoardo Gemma,[17] a city councilor and organizer, called farm workers to a convention at the chamber of labor on September 2. Twenty-two revamped leagues sent delegates, who voted to prepare petitions, rallies, and strikes to win the 8–5–3 demand for Novara workers.

The farmers finally agreed on a pact on September 6, after four days of a general strike and demonstrations, punctuated by encounters with the police and cavalry charges against defenseless women and children. The leagues, although unable to impose their three-point program, won considerable improvements: an eight and a half hour day, 4.72 lire a day for the men, and 2.50 lire for the women. They also hoped that a strong farm workers' federation would be able to fight against the use of migratory workers, which labor organizers often cited as one of the reasons why many local workers migrated to America.[18] But the Novarese farm workers' federation was never able to match the strength of its counterparts in the Vercellese and

Lomellina. Harvesters and threshers also fought for the same three demands. The protests led to violent confrontations, as the troops defended the rights of migratory harvesters to work and replace strikers. But farmers had to capitulate and grant better conditions to the protesters.[19]

After Giolitti revoked the Cantelli regulations, the rice growers seized the moment to press for the passage of measures to neutralize the workers' gains and go back to the old, longer work schedule. Yet they soon realized that the revocation of the Cantelli regulations alone was ineffectual in lengthening the workday; they wanted, therefore, to reaffirm their ability to use the centers of power for their own ends. They used meetings, the sessions of the third international rice congress,[20] and propaganda to hit out against labor resistance and try to change the political climate that had allowed labor agitation to take place.

After a powerful labor demonstration against the revocation of the Cantelli regulations at Vercelli on August 19, employers staged their own protest rally in the market square; then they drew up an appeal to the government. In it they said that it was impossible for them to pay taxes when their crop was dwindling because of the strikes. They also charged that "the state and society had left farmers at the mercy of an irresponsible mob." They requested energetic action to guarantee the right to work. Another appeal solicited support from parliament and other agrarian associations, in view of the "acts of violence and threats of all kinds, with evident risks even to the personal safety of the rice growers and their own families" as well as to the impending harvest. The Vercellese association expected all the country's farmers to help, and called on "their devotion to the national economy and to the common fatherland."[21]

The farmers received prompt satisfaction. Deputy Lucca, the farmers' go-between, quickly persuaded a receptive Giolitti to form a three-member commission of inquiry on the strikes and to have it make recommendations for future legislation. In fact this commission was to replace another formed after the *monda* strikes, which had included the socialist deputy Luigi Montemartini, representing the superior labor council. It had already endorsed the nine-hour workday. The appointment of a new commission on August 28 foreshadowed a disaster for labor, for it had no representative from the superior labor council, but counted a police inspector and two pliant officers of the ministry of agriculture among its members, one of whom was from the Mezzogiorno and had never even seen a rice field.[22]

Both the abrogation of the Cantelli regulations and the appointment of the new commission shook the members of the labor bureau
who had supported Giolitti's scheme to bring the interests of capital
and labor closer together and integrate both into the democratic process. The labor bureau saw Giolitti's acquiescence to this aggressive
agrarian pressure as a definite sign of the failure and futility of the
reformist democratic notions that had nourished it since its inception.

While the dispirited delegates at the August 26 session of the
permanent committee of the superior labor council lamented all the
fruitless steps the labor bureau had taken to settle the problems of
workers in the rice fields, two days later the Association of the Agriculturalists of the Vercellese, together with representatives of the
Novarese agrarian association, celebrated Giolitti's intervention. They
saw it as a prelude to more energetic antilabor government actions.
As the president of the Vercellese association, Marquis Vincenzo Ricci
put it, "this is no longer the time for half measures, but for decisive
steps to prevent the ruin of rice farming." The assembly defined these
steps as nothing less than the reform of the *Statuto*, the Italian constitution, in order to bar workers' associational and protest activities.
In the meantime the assembly proposed that landowners and their
lessees, the capitalist farmers, protect their common interests, which
coincided with the interests of the nation and of the working class.[23]

The farmers presented some of their ideas to the government
commission upon its arrival at Vercelli. They labeled labor actions,
such as the disregard of previous contracts, as attempts against the
right to work. The request for a shorter day was unjustified, because
the work, they said, was neither unhealthy nor exacting. Thus demanding a shorter workday violated civil statutes.[24] The strikes black-
mailed employers into paying excessive wages and frightened away
migratory workers who either returned home or did not come at all,
because of insufficient military and police protection. As for public
order, they called for the dissolution of the leagues, a measure they
knew the government would oppose. They also asked for prosecution of the leagues' leaders because their teachings bred "real revolt,
despite the authorities' reports presenting them in a more favorable
light." As for legislative action, they wanted laws to regulate work
contracts, with sanctions against violators. The government steps
should be "energetic and immediate," to restore the balance between
capital and labor.[25]

One of the landowners' economic schemes to disable the labor
movement was to carry out their old threat to give up rice farming.
They had first formulated it when the leagues had begun to grow.

Would the lessees (almost 80 percent of the rice growers) go along with the landowners' strategy? Was there any ground for disagreements between landowners and leaseholders to come to the surface in the critical moments created by the strikes? What did the lessees think about abandoning rice farming and using the land, according to the landowners' ideas, not for wheat or diversified farming, but for grazing lands in order to provoke unemployment?[26]

The lessees objected. Vincenzo Tavallini voiced the opinion of many during the discussions of the third international rice congress (October 27–29, 1906). To substitute pasture for rice was not easy, he explained. The fields lacked haylofts and cattle shelters; besides, the price of milk was very low in Vercelli, and nobody was sure that the soil was suitable for forage. Angelo Galbarini, representing the agriculturalists from Lomellina, feared cattle infections, like hoof-and-mouth disease, which was common in the region.[27]

On December 13 the lessees rejected the incentives offered by the Vercellese landowners to induce them to give up rice farming— they were offered a 15 percent rent reduction if they turned half the land into meadows by 1907, and 30 percent if they converted a whole farm.[28] The leaseholders of the rice belt were not interested in the proposal, but apparently their refusal did not destroy their good relations with landowners. On the contrary, landowners and leaseholders found it more convenient to remain united.

At the same time, a commission that included representatives of both groups was drafting a statute "for the new, huge association," more effective than the existing one, whose object was the defense of rural industry and the care of "the members' interests," which were strictly associated with the "well-being of the workers." The association would register field workers in a new labor office, "assuring them [the registered ones] preference for any work," and would try to avoid strikes by reaching accords between the parties in conflict. The commission stipulated ordinary and extraordinary dues; the latter were of particular importance because they went to an insurance fund to assist members in case of strikes. The new association, founded on January 21, 1907,[29] followed by ten months the creation of a similar body grouping other agrarian leaders of the Po valley. This was the Interprovincial Agrarian Federation. This "institutional counterweight to the national Federterra . . . quickly became the most powerful and influential agricultural lobby in Italy."[30] From then on, common interests drew the two associations closer together until they merged, along with other agrarian groups, into a national confederation in 1910.

The 1907 Employers' Offensive

At Vercelli the FRAP began planning for the 1907 weeding in September 1906, but, predictably, the *Associazione degli Agricoltori* found its terms unacceptable.

The association was determined to impose a *monda* workday from dawn to sunset, with the sole exception of the local *mondariso*, who would work only nine hours. Both sides were too far apart to agree on a contract when they met on November 3.[31] On November 24, defending their freedom of action, or in other words a return to old practices, the farmers praised Fracassi, a landowner and deputy, for his words at an association meeting: "The liberal principle holds the right of one individual who wants to work sacrosanct and more revered than that of ten thousand strikers."[32]

FRAP decided to put off further negotiations until the convening of two farm workers' congresses: the national congress of rice workers of Pavia, called by the Federterra on December 16, and the regional congress of rice workers of Vercelli, Novara, Mortara, and Pavia, to be held at Vercelli on December 23. The national congress, claiming to represent 108 organizations with a hundred thousand workers, insisted on the need to regulate migratory labor by contracts made in agreement with the local organizations, and with the same terms for local and migrant workers. This would keep the number of migrants to a minimum.[33]

The congress also passed a motion to establish employment offices to replace *caporali*. The employment offices would be assisted by a special commission of five members, representing the Vercelli, Novara, and Mortara federations, the Federterra, and the General Confederation of Labor (*Confederazione Generale del Lavoro*, or CGdL, founded in Milan between September 29 and October 1, 1906). The Federterra and the CGdL were to disseminate information and educate the public in the regions from which strikebreakers traditionally came in order to restrain them in times of labor conflicts.[34]

By organizing migratory squads, the national congress wanted to avoid a repetition of the events of 1906 when the organized migratory *mondariso*, following their leagues' directives, remained "heroically" at home in the middle of the weeders' strikes, watching over the railroad stations in an effort to stop the strikebreakers.[35] The order that called on the organized migrants to stay at home had served only to favor the unorganized and the *caporali*. Out of over forty-five thousand migratory weeders, only five thousand were organized. The rest, who were hired by *caporali*, served as strikebreakers. The congress delegates thought that if the organized weeders migrated, they could at least help spread socialist ideas[36] and stage acts of solidarity with local strikers.

In the Vercelli regional congress on December 23, the delegates tried to find ways to put the Pavia resolution into effect. They decided to ask organized migratory weeders either to abstain from going to the rice belt in 1907 or to migrate only after being told that the rice belt was strike-free. And these migratory weeders would of course work with contracts identical to those in effect for local *mondariso*. The congress asked the CGdL, the Federterra, the socialist parliamentary group, the *Società Umanitaria*, and all socialist organizations to cooperate in informing the leagues about the resolution.[37]

The economic situation and the employers' maneuvers helped make 1907 a difficult year for weeders. Early in the year, even before an acute international financial crisis hit Italy in October, the cost of living went up, and many Italians remained jobless. Great numbers of unemployed workers from Emilia made their way to the rice belt and joined the already saturated labor pool.[38] The employers purposely cut down most of the routine winter jobs to keep up the paddies, and used their political influence in municipal governments to suspend winter public works in order to cause more unemployment and weaken the leagues. Demoralized, many unemployed male workers emigrated.[39] A member of the San Grisante (Vercellese) league complained in February in *La Risaia* that many discouraged men, anticipating a sluggish labor demand for the weeding, were looking for low-paid permanent jobs for their wives and daughters. What worried the San Grisante league member was that by doing this, husbands and fathers were withdrawing women from the weeders' organization and breaking its power to resist.[40] On the same day the Carisio (Vercellese) league workers protested against the influx of workers from neighboring communes.[41]

The farmers imposed such onerous working conditions for the March sowing[42] that the FRAP declared a general strike despite the prevailing negative conditions. It called for the eight-hour day for sowing, weeding, and harvesting, for full local employment, and fair wages. This occurred in the Vercellese on February 24 and embraced all the communes, where the number of labor marches, demonstrations, and exhortations to the undecided to stop working provoked numerous army and police countermarches, interventions, and arrests.[43]

The strikes ended more than a month later because the em-

ployers kept on postponing their reply to labor demands, most probably with the deliberate intent of exhausting the leagues' strength and
wanting more time to bring strikebreakers into the region. In Vercelli
the commissions of the FRAP and of the *Associazone degli Agricoltori*
met on March 20. The former demanded the eight-hour day for all the
rice-field workers and uniform wages throughout the region, but Ricci, the president of the association, replied not only that he did not
have the power to establish the length of the workday, but also that
the association preferred to fix wages commune by commune.[44] He
decided to cut off all negotiations on March 22.[45]

Between April 4 and 7, the little resistance that was left
crumbled. On April 4, strikebreakers arrived at the Vercelli station in
a special train and deputy Lucca, the intermediary between the farmers and the Catholic priests who organized the squads in Lodi and
Piacenza, welcomed them. Two carabinieri protected each cart taking
squads to the farms. Carabinieri also protected them as they worked
by prohibiting the approach of local workers and, in Lignana, even
keeping them inside their own houses. The strikers received the final
blow on April 7 when the FRAP proposal that called for an agreement
on an eight-hour day was definitively rejected. Ricci declared that the
proposal was not valid, because weeders would soon break the contracts and leave farmers "deceived and ridiculed." Some communes
made some very small gains from the strike, others none at all.[46]

The defeated strikers resumed work without even being allowed
to discuss conditions with their employers, who imposed a nine-hour
day for the sowing. More workers left for Turin, Switzerland, France,
and Germany, following a trend that continued for the rest of the year
and into 1908.[47]

At the end of February 1907 the Novarese leagues declared a
general strike, with the same demands as those of the Vercellese
workers. They suffered the same fate. According to *Il Lavoratore* of
March 9, Novara seemed to be in a "state of siege," with all "its
fundamental liberties suppressed." As in the Vercellese, the unprecedented number of troops sent to the region either precluded meetings
and rallies or disbanded them, arrested agitators, and guarded strikebreakers at work.[48]

After such a labor defeat, employers, with few exceptions, imposed the nine-hour day and weeders therefore went on strike. But
many could not hold out for long and had to resume work and accept
the nine-hour schedule. Others fought until migratory squads, escorted by troops, created an impossible situation.[49] Conditions were

made even less favorable for a successful strike by the 20 percent unemployment rate at the beginning of the *monda*. In Lomellina the invasion of squads from Bobbio and Piacenza, and the return to the region of many local emigrants, also aggravated the unemployment problem. Weeders went on strike in several communes.[50]

On June 7, more than two hundred *mondariso* from Mortara marched to the city hall to address the mayor about the abusive conditions the farmers imposed. To their indignation, he told them that they were too gossipy (*pettegole*) and demanding, that they paid too much attention to the bragging socialists, and that they had better return to reason and weed, as in the past, for ten, twelve, or sixteen hours a day. An officer who witnessed the scene "qualified the *mondariso* as persons lacking the will to work." The mayor dismissed the group until Sunday, to give him time to work on a settlement with the farmers.[51] In Mortara, as well as in Sannazzaro and San Giorgio, they won a modified victory. They worked for fewer hours than the farmers had asked for, but it was nevertheless more than an eight-hour day.

It must be kept in mind that the employers' obstinacy regarding the nine-hour day was not always a tactic to cut labor costs. In the Vercellese, for example, they paid 0.25 lira an hour no matter how long the workday was. Instead, it was an unmistakable ploy to hire fewer weeders. As an expression of solidarity with the strikers, many organized migratory *mondariso* refused to work. But that did little to mitigate the league's hardships; they were morally and materially strained, for their limited funds went to subsidize the strikers.[52] For example, because of the long-lasting effects of the setbacks in 1907, the Novarese were completely disorganized at the start of the 1908 weeding.[53]

Various factors accounted for the workers' failures in 1907. The leagues were debilitated by a long winter of resistance, by price increases, by unemployed farm labor coming to the rice belt from the Po valley, and by the return of temporary migrant workers from countries hit by economic crisis. In addition, employers had strengthened their associations in order to avoid a repetition of the 1906 strikes and they had succeeded in procuring a huge mobilization of both strikebreakers and troops. Weeders could hardly withstand the employers', the troops', and the strikebreakers' offensive. Behind this unprecedented deployment of forces we see a Giolitti unable once again either to stand up to the agriculturalists' demands or to mollify them with his concessions. He was therefore finding it increasing difficult to fulfill his role as arbiter between capital and labor.

Labor organizers such as Cugnolio and Gionino saw no other solution but emigration from some workers to combat the drop in wages, the hunger, and the repression. This would improve the bargaining position of the workers who remained.[54] But the emigration of some of the rice-belt population did not completely have that effect. From 1901 on, distressing living conditions in the surrounding highlands forced inhabitants to relocate to the plains, and thus partially replenish the farm workers' ranks.[55] In addition, we must stress that in the rice belt, as well as in other sections of the Po valley (like Ferrara),[56] late spring and summer unemployment were not always the result of an excess of farm workers. The events of 1907 showed the agriculturalists that by resorting to various expedients they were themselves creating unemployment and providing the conditions that forced workers to emigrate.

The 1907 Law on Rice Farming

The law on rice farming of June 16, 1907, was preceded by many debates and postponements. Employers had hoped that there would be no new law at all after Giolitti had abolished the Cantelli regulations in August 1906. At the third international rice congress of October 1906 the speakers endorsed the farmers' stand of minimizing the effect of hazardous environmental and working conditions on human health. These experts expected that their opinions would carry considerable weight with the senators who were preparing the new legislation.[57]

Senator Camillo Golgi, who had just been awarded the Nobel prize in physiology, spoke on the rice workers' health. He took his information from the works by Grassi and Pezza, both branded by Turati as "eminent professors of 'political' medicine who extolled the rice fields . . . as a genuine health paradise for the workers."[58] Basing his conclusions on statistics, Golgi confirmed that the workers' health was good, and that rice farming was no more dangerous than any other occupation. Therefore, he found no scientific grounds for giving rice-field labor a privileged status. He argued that more than nine hours of weeding actually resulted in better health, because the *monda* could then end before July, when the hotter weather made the transmission of malaria easier. On the other hand, with a long workday, fewer weeders would be needed, especially migrants more prone to the disease.

But Golgi blended science with a principle contained in the miscarried Giolitti law project of March 1905, which he quoted:

> So far, the Italian legislation has not yet introduced the principle of the limitation of the workday for all the employees of one industry either in agriculture or in the very manufacturing industries that lend themselves to restrictions even better than agriculture; and . . . for the same manufacturing industries the current law fixes a minimum duration of the workday only for women under twenty one and for children.

Following this, the only restriction he justified from the physiological point of view was a limited workday for 15-year-olds, or for older women who were not so strong.[59]

Very few delegates at the October 1906 congress dared to challenge the Nobel laureate's report. Nino Mazzoni, representing the *Umanitaria*, expressed the usual misgivings about the value of medical statistics that did not include the many sick persons who never reported to physicians. The socialist deputy Luigi Montemartini remarked that, despite Golgi's speech, observers of the journeys of migratory weeders knew that when these workers returned home, they looked ill and considerably thinner. Montemartini added that he wanted to have Golgi's opinion on the widespread view "that for women and minors nine hours of weeding are . . . harmful."[60]

The senator cited Grassi's observation that weeding was a question of habit, "that this work, after all, is not so dangerous as we are being induced to believe. . . . It is no worse than many others: it takes place in hygienic conditions less dangerous than in many other industries."[61]

Montemartini then cited the military corps of engineers' regulation setting the maximum work hours for soldiers working in the water at eight and stressed the desirability of applying this to weeders. "If the ministry of war is this solicitous about the most robust young men of the nation, I do not see why the legislator would not have the same consideration for children and women who are perhaps the mothers of future soldiers." He also asked Golgi about the 1903 report that bore his signature, issued by the superior sanitary council, which declared that the continual bending during weeding could be dangerous to a worker's health if done for more than eight hours a day. Golgi retorted that his observations and studies of the last few years had led him to change his opinions.[62] Golgi also disagreed with Roberto Rampoldi, a medical doctor, who said that the position of the body while weeding impeded regular blood circulation and caused not only the blurring of the weeders' sight, but also severe eye infections.[63]

The lawyer Angelo Galbarini, president of the federation of agriculturalists of Lomellina, who in 1903 had declared that the *monda* was the weeders' carnival, admitted that a ten-hour workday was the "physiological schedule." In other words, it was a moderate schedule that the *mondariso* could follow without exertion. Aside from that, he insisted, legislators should leave the responsibility for regulating labor in the rice fields to the provinces, to the initiative of the rice growers, and "to Italian common sense and to the proletariat's good sense," while also strictly observing the freedom to work. The congress approved a motion to this effect.[64]

Without any fanfare the government proposed a new law in February 1907, based on these guidelines. Thus started the last stage in the history of "one of the laws," according to Cabrini, "that gave rise to the most lively polemics and to the largest agitation because it affects both employers' and proletarians' interests walled within strong class organizations." The deputies supporting the *agricoltori* had a scheme: they would rush the draft through a commission on the following day, and then to the chamber for immediate approval. In doing so, the *agricoltori* and their allies in parliament counted on a cooperative commission and on widespread absenteeism among the deputies of the *estrema* (extreme left) to carry out their plan.

However, deputy Turati happened to be appointed to that very commission, and he sounded the alarm among socialist, republican, and radical deputies. This disrupted the scheme. Then Turati uncovered the parliamentary machination in the *Critica Sociale*: "Quietly (*piano piano*), without being noticeable, walking with smuggler's boots, Giolitti has proposed to the chamber on February 21 the new law on rice farming." The new draft legislation would have relaxed the prohibition on growing rice near populated areas and would have given rice growers the right to prolong the workday to ten and a half hours under special circumstances. For the *monda* contract, weeders would have had to put down a deposit of 20 percent of their earnings to assure employers that they would neither break contracts nor go out on strike. A local conciliation committee, described in very vague terms, would be the only mediator in the event of labor conflicts. Some regulations even violated the law on woman and child labor. Children, pregnant women, and women under the age of twenty-one

would not have needed the required medical certificates, and pregnant women would have had to return to work three weeks after
delivery instead of four, as specified by the law.[65]

Turati's denunciation of this "treacherous law" sparked a wave
of protests. During an extraordinary meeting at Bologna on March 3,
delegates of the Federterra and the CGdL planned a press campaign
and public rallies.[66] There was one at Vercelli on March 24. On April
7, workers held demonstrations in Milan, and on April 27 in Vercelli,
with Cabrini and Cugnolio as speakers, in Novara and Mortara with
Nino Mazzoni and Luigi Montemartini, in Bologna and in Molinella.[67] On May 19, the socialist section of Vercelli transformed the
inauguration ceremony of the People's House (*Casa de Popolo*) into a
protest against the proposed law; Enrico Ferri was the key speaker.[68]

By the time the law was debated in the chamber on May 22, it
"had lost the greatest part of its venom," according to Turati, thanks
to almost all the thirty-three amendments he tacked on to its text.[69]
Labor mobilization may have helped change the proposed law, but it
did not move the chamber majority either to accept the eight-hour
workday or the Turati-Montemartini proposal for a nine-hour workday for both local and migratory *mondariso*.[70] Instead, the new draft
fixed nine hours of *monda* a day for local weeders and ten for migratory groups. Even if local weeders were making up for time lost due to
bad weather, their day could not exceed ten hours; Sunday work was
strictly forbidden. The *terzo* ("one-third" or extra weeding hours) was
definitively abolished. Workers were neither obliged to accept as
binding the ruling of the conciliation committee nor to pay any deposit when they closed a labor contract. The obligatory contract itself was
a real innovation in labor legislation in Italy. In addition, employers
had to build adequate night shelters for migratory workers within
three years, and provide pure, fresh drinking water.[71] The age limit
for minor workers was increased from thirteen to fourteen. Pregnant
women and migrants would be permitted to work only with a medical certificate.[72] Mothers who were breast-feeding had half an hour
extra for nursing during their lunch break.

"The trap has been shattered," wrote Turati in *Critica Sociale*,
satisfied that this parliamentary episode had served to arouse public
opinion on the matter. "The devil had passed," he added, referring to
the principle of the limitation of the workday, which was introduced
in the law. Once restricted to children and women, it was now extended to men as well. This, he proclaimed, was a triumph of socialist
legislative work.[73] Turati also took the opportunity to criticize the
"sterile tactics" of the syndicalists: direct action and antiparliamen-

tarianism. Montemartini explained to the readers of *La Plebe* that the law, passed on June 12, "certainly does not give anything to you, yet it takes away nothing from you; it will neither harm you nor hinder you in fighting for the attainment of what you aspire to."[74] Perhaps Montemartini foresaw the continuation, with few essential changes, of the same struggle for the eight-hour day.

The law was in essence a step backward in some aspects compared with the Cantelli regulations, which had offered real protection to workers because the workday limitation applied to the total work force, local and migrant, and to those participating in all rice-field operations, not just weeding. That was the reason farmers had wanted the regulations abolished. Ironically, mistaken assumptions about the cause of malaria had been the force behind this protective legislation. Forty years later, the official interpretation of scientific findings opened the door to all kinds of abuses. The length of the workday was fixed only for weeders; for harvesters and threshers there was no such limitation. The stipulation of a longer day for migrant weeders was against all rational hygienic principles, but it was a victory for the *agricoltori*. However, it served to curb those who still demanded a weeding schedule of eleven or more hours. Employers would naturally persist in hiring more than the necessary number of migratory weeders, because they would work for ten hours a day.

Weeding under the New Law, 1908

The 1908 *monda* put the new law to the test. Was the enactment of the nine-hour workday for local weeders going to be as meaningless for the weeders' struggle as Montemartini thought? How was its strength going to be measured against other factors, such as labor resistance or the employers' enhanced means of crushing this resistance? Labor organizations would try to make use of the law in order to check the farmers' usual arbitrariness.

Sending local police, carabinieri, and army troops to the rice belt became more frequent in 1908, but this trend was unrelated to the new law. The farmers also made other inroads into the leagues' gains. In Vercelli on January 25, Cugnolio proposed the formation of mixed placement offices, which included representatives of employers and workers to the president of the *Associazione degli Agricoltori*, with the explicit goal of hiring local weeders. Ricci accepted the proposal, as long as the workers' representatives were not league delegates, but rather candidates selected by the association. As the FRAP surmised, this meant "the usual *capisquadre* and strikebreakers."[75] Three days later a group of employers formally invited four compliant workers to form squads, without the intervention of the leagues and for wages fixed by the *associazione*.[76] Again, in March, many disappointed male workers took trains to neighboring countries in search of better jobs. As in the previous year, this emigration had the backing of the local organizers.[77]

When the *monda* began in the week of May 25, there were work stoppages in places where the farmers wanted the nine-hour day. According to *La Risaia* of May 30, these strikes started suddenly and after little, if any, preparation; they spread to more than a dozen communes in Vercelli. The commissions of employers and weeders from the Vercelli league quickly defined their negotiating position, and the mayor mediated. The weeders demanded the eight-hour day, whereas the employers were willing only to discuss wages. While the weeders argued that they needed a shorter workday in order to be able to take care of their families, Ricci answered that "he could not leave aside" the law "made by scientists," which had established the nine-hour day, without infringing "a matter of principle" dear to employers. "The law must be observed," the mayor agreed, deploring the expenditure of ten thousand lire the commune had had to spend on maintaining public order the preceding year. Foreseeing the same costs for 1908, he remarked that it was the workers who paid. "Then don't spend it," was the league representative's answer as the conversation ended.[78]

In Formigliana and Casanova Elvo, permanent workers also went out on strike in support of the members of their families who were *mondariso*. After two weeks at a standstill, small agriculturalists afraid of losing the harvest began to call for squads to weed their fields for eight hours a day in defiance of their own *Associazione*.[79] The protesting weeders then transformed the strike into a boycott of the major employers who stood by to the *Associazione's* decisions.[80] Little by little, even the most adamant employers began to give in, in the Vercellese and in Lomellina.[81] By Sunday, June 14, the weeders claimed a total victory, settling not only for the eight hours, but also for a 3 lire wage instead of the 2.25 lire they were originally offered.[82]

There was a remarkable expression of solidarity in Casanova Elvo when twenty-nine weeders arrived from the Ferrarese. When they learned about the strike, they went directly to the local league instead of proceeding to the farms. The leaders of the Casanova Elvo league asked the subprefect to arrange the squad's return journey, but he disclaimed any responsibility. The league fed the migrants for

eight days and finally paid their railway fares with public donations.[83] A second squad of seventy-three weeders arrived with an
armed escort of three carabinieri and a cavalry platoon. It was destined for Crova, where five hundred strikers were blocking the way.
A cavalry charge dispersed the protesters, who threw stones at the
migrants until the police arrested three of them and broke up the
demonstration.[84] Several women were arrested, charged with attempting to deny the migrants the right to work; they were subse-
quently sentenced to several months in prison. According to *La
Risaia*, with these arrests the number of jailed farm workers of both
sexes in the Vercellese, between June 1906 and June 1908, increased to
140.[85] In Lomellina there was agitation for the eight-hour workday.
Farmers had to agree to that schedule in seventeen communes, and
the workers considered this a success.[86] In the rice fields of Bologna
and Mantua the eight-hour workday was an accomplished fact. *Il
Contadino* took great care to list the many farmers who were violating
the law with the complicity of the carabinieri.[87]

Developments in the rice belt during 1908 show that the new
law served to legitimize both the farmers' demand for a nine-hour
workday and the use of force by the government to implement the
law. Neither of these actions was new, but now the law served to
justify them. However, employers had a smaller migrant work force
with which to undermine protest actions. This was the result, on the
one hand, of the refusal by many potential migrants of the low wages
offered by employers, and, on the other, of new impediments to
temporary migration. Whole families from the surrounding hills used
to travel to the rice belt for the weeding season, but now that children
under fourteen were banned from the fields, fewer migrated. The
Lomellina labor federation claimed that the agitation for the eight-
hour day and for the application of the law helped to bolster the
leagues and even form twelve new ones, six of them women's
leagues.[88]

In May 1908, the Federterra appointed an inspector to the rice
belt for the first time. He was Doctor Ernesto Piemonte. To strengthen
the case for improved working conditions for local and migratory
squads, he gathered statistical data and registered complaints about
violations of the labor contracts and other regulations. He also attested to the absence of night shelters.[89] According to *Il Lavoratore* of
June 6, infractions were widespread in Novara, mainly because of the
leagues' disorganization. Many weeders were ignorant of the time
limitation established by the law, and of rules governing contracts and
child labor.

Another contract violation by employers involved the duration and distribution of breaks during the *monda*. Organized labor wanted to have the breaks specially written into rice-field regulations because they were always a matter of contention between employers and weeders. The weeders complained that employers robbed them of rest periods. According to the new law, breaks would have to be set by provincial councils, .following the advice of provincial sanitary councils made up of appointed, not elected, members.[90] Cugnolio presented the Novara provincial council with the results of a September 1908 investigation by the leagues. It emphasized their members' preferences. It was important to have the rest period at the same time and of the same length everywhere; this standardization would facilitate inspectors' duties. Weeders requested half an hour for breakfast, from eight o'clock to half past eight, and an hour and a half for lunch, from eleven o'clock to half past twelve if they worked eight hours, and two hours if they weeded nine. The employers wanted to shorten this by thirty minutes. Physicians from Vercelli and Novara, on the contrary, recommended a two-hour lunch break, stressing the beneficial effect on workers of a long rest period. These doctors also found that the thirty minutes the law allotted to mothers to nurse their infants was inadequate.[91] The majority in the provincial councils tried to shorten the breaks.[92] The superior labor council voted on June 16, 1909, for the institution of a lunch break an hour and a half long.[93]

The legal restriction on employment of weeders under fourteen elicited a surprising and unexpected resistance at Vercelli. Speaking for the weeders, Cugnolio called the law a "starver of the farm workers," because it affected entire families. As an example he cited a household with three children, one almost fourteen years old, and the other two, thirteen and twelve years old. None could weed, thus depriving the family of an additional 5.50 lire a day. The ideal situation would have been to have the youngsters at school until they were eighteen, the adults employed, and the elderly retired. Meanwhile, however, the children were left with nothing to eat. Besides, between the age of twelve and fourteen, these children and those placed in foster homes by the Vercelli foundling hospital remained on the streets, not under adult control.

Cugnolio went on to explain that the minimum age was not a socialist, but a bourgeois, proposal, intended to justify a nine-hour workday for the whole labor force. He spoke of reducing the workday to eight hours and of setting the age limit at thirteen, as recommended by the superior sanitary council on June 8, 1903, or even at twelve if a medical certificate attested to the child's good health.[94] In other words, he was coupling the goal of the eight-hour workday to that of reducing the legal age for working weeders. The FRAP organized a rally for a change in the law at Vercelli on June 28, 1908.[95] Faced with the alternative of starvation or child labor, Cugnolio preferred the latter, in the same way that he advised male adults to emigrate instead of starving. He indicted the government for paying only lip service to the protection of children: "Where you take away work, you must give relief." Instead, while increasing military spending, the government did nothing to help children stay in school for two more years, nor did it provide adequate school meals.[96] There was also the irrefutable fact that numerous violations of the law were committed by children with the complicity of their parents,[97] who even sent 9-year-old children to the fields,[98] and of the carabinieri.

The outcry against lowering the working age came from the socialist ranks. It sparked a debate. *Il Lavoratore* argued that the implementation of this "antihumanitarian and uncivilized" idea would lead to a larger potential labor force, leaving many adults unemployed or working for lower wages.[99] Deputy Cabrini, in the name of the socialist parliamentary bloc, and Maffi and other physicians, also objected to lowering the minimum age.[100] Only in the Vercellese did workers stand unanimously behind Cugnolio. Finally, at a big rally in Mortara on July 26, deputy Cabrini spoke in favor of fourteen as the minimum working age. He supported other measures to assist children, such as adding two more years of school with refectories to provide free lunch to children of working parents.

Cugnolio abandoned his position, satisfied to have called the public's attention to the shortcomings of the Italian educational system and to the need for creating new institutions to enforce progressive legislation.[101] He considered the socialist parliamentary uproar over the statutory age limit nothing but rank bourgeois sentimentalism, and a surrender to a law that sought "to hide the shame without thinking of remedying it." It was a law indifferent to the miserable conditions in the rice belt and ineffective in providing bread for hungry children. He also blamed socialist deputies for their poor record on social legislation, including their failure to press for the introduction of after-school centers and a maternity fund for new mothers to cover the two months in which they had to be, by law, out of work.[102]

Cugnolio's main target was deputy Cabrini, who was completely absorbed in the organization of cooperatives. Cugnolio distrusted cooperatives as a means of transforming capitalist into socialist society. He felt that this movement promoted the reformist policy of the CGdL and served to slow down the "strike mania" and the influence of the chambers of labor in guiding and coordinating protest actions in Vercelli and its surroundings. Cugnolio sarcastically remarked that for Cabrini the cooperatives were a good means to further the development and extension of more "responsible national trade federations," or, in other words, federations able to restrain strikes. According to Cugnolio, this was a policy of "universal castration."[103]

Cugnolio identified himself as a reformist socialist, but he set forth his own brand of reformism. He accepted direct action as an important weapon in the labor struggle, but only as a last resort. He was very pragmatic and dismissed party polemics between reformists and revolutionaries as a waste of energy, which took time that socialists could dedicate to workers. In this way, he endorsed the views of the integralist bloc formed within the socialist Party in 1904. The integralists described themselves as a compromise group between reformists and revolutionaries. The labor struggle in the rice belt had both reformist and revolutionary features, and Cugnolio was its most conspicuous interpreter and guide. But with this eclectic approach, he, and with him many other socialist leaders, precluded any serious debate about the issues that divided the Socialist Party and about the need for political reforms. Cugnolio thought that the betterment of the workers could be furthered by several methods.

In 1912 Cugnolio wrote in *Critica Sociale* that he believed in socialism without adjectives. Reflecting on the 1906 labor action, he described it as ultraconservative, endeavoring to reestablish the 30-year-old Cantelli regulations to shorten the workday to eight hours, and, at the same time, revolutionary, unafraid of barricades and cavalry charges. Cugnolio endorsed both extremes.[104] In 1908 he declared that as long as the bourgeoisie was in power, reform would never be wholly effective; the power of the military, too, obstructed the road to revolution. "There is nothing left but the weapon of the vote and the conquest of power, the most feared by the bourgeoisie and the easiest for us," he reasoned, concluding, "Are not the workers the majority?" If that was the way, increase in the socialist vote in the following years might have raised Cugnolio's expectations for a socialist conquest of power.[105]

Agitation for the amendment to the law on rice cultivation started in 1909. On April 3–5 the Federterra held a meeting at Bologna to launch a program to change the *monda* schedule from nine to eight hours for both local and migratory *mondine*. The FRAP of Vercelli called for an assembly at the People's House on April 12 and drew up a petition to be signed by *mondariso* throughout the region.[106] Representatives of the Lomellina leagues met on May 9. They set out the main proposals for change in several orders of the day. The first concerned the shortening of the workday. The next two dealt specifically with women. One attested to the need to enforce the legal limitations on work for pregnant women, and expand the benefits of the bill on maternity leave, then under discussion, to all women field workers, who had been excluded thus far. The third order of the day asked for a longer rest period for nursing mothers to breast-feed their infants during *monda* hours. In the area of labor mediation, the fourth proposal concerned the appointment of agricultural *probiviri*, who would act as conciliation officers in case of labor conflicts. The fifth declared the appointment of labor inspectors imperative. The sixth recommended the use of cloth leggings to prevent the skin lesions that often accompanied work in the rice fields. The final point dealt with the issue of the minimum age for weeding.[107]

Strike figures for the years 1904–8 reveal an increase in the number of work stoppages from 1904 on, after their decline in the 1902–3 period (there were only 47 agricultural strikes in 1903). The increase in protest activity in 1904 is due mainly to the strikes that took place in the rice belt. Thereafter intensification of strike activity reaches its maximum in the years 1906–8.

STRIKES FROM 1904 TO 1908 (KINGDOM OF ITALY)

		Agriculture		Industry
Year	Strikes	Strikers (1000s)	Strikes	Strikers (1000s)
1904	208	95	620	127
1905	87	44	640	104
1906	350	118	1,299	264
1907	377	254	1,891	327
1908	286	173	1,417	200

A Difficult Question: Relations Between Local and Migratory Weeders

With the expansion of capitalist agriculture, the shortage of workers at the time of labor-intensive farm operations became a generalized phenomenon. Rice weeding in the Po valley is an example of this. From the 1850s in Europe, and some decades later in America, the problem of seasonal labor shortages became increasingly crucial as cereal cultivation expanded. There are other cases in which temporary labor played, and still plays, a vital role, such as the harvesting of farm produce in California or sugar cane in the Caribbean. Like rice weeding in Italy, they have a long history of labor conflicts. Temporary migration tended to grow in size and scope as large numbers of agricultural workers sought work not only in neighboring regions, but also in other countries or even on another continent.

The internal migration of agricultural workers in Italy was the largest in Europe.[108] Zangheri calculates that eight hundred fifty-nine thousand farm workers (676,250 men and 182,750 women) sought work outside their places of residence in 1905. The 1910–13 figures reveal the increasing volume of some of the most important trends:[109]

Provinces	Immigrants			
	1910	1911	1912	1913
Novara and Pavia (weeding and harvesting)	63,790	67,020	73,660	75,258
Foggia (summer, fall, and winter work)	38,280	59,698	45,713	52,839
Potenza (summer and fall work)	12,074	13,937	11,346	10,367
Rome (summer, fall, and winter work)	43,997	82,199	83,665	78,953
Grossetto (summer, fall, and winter work)	4,571	9,303	9,160	7,756
Totals	162,712	232,157	223,544	225,173

The Federterra took two initiatives in favor of migratory weeders. One was the appointment, already mentioned, of an inspector for the rice belt during the 1908 weeding season. The other was the coordination of migratory squads of organized weeders by directly negotiating with the employer to place them. Federterra leaders were convinced that if they organized these squads, they would contribute to the disappearance of the *capisquadra* or *caporale* and, with him, of the most blatant abuses against migrant weeders. The local farm workers' federations, on the other hand, were struggling for the right to have all local weeders hired before migratory ones, whether they were organized or not. They fought for this goal until the outbreak of World War I. The best way to achieve it would be by giving

the federations the function of placement offices. The FRAP in Vercelli, for example, attempted to win that right by several means.

It took some time for the Federterra to realize that, despite its
good intentions, its organized migratory squads were also being used
as strikebreakers. In 1912 the Federterra finally understood this and
decided to demand equal payment and weeding hours for both local
and migrant squads, terms that the employers did not accept. From
then on, it stopped organizing migrants, but not before this caused
friction between the national and the local farm workers' federations.
At the meeting of rice workers on November 8, 1908, at Piacenza, for
example, the majority of the delegates represented the Federterra.
They overrode Cugnolio's opposition and endorsed a motion that
favored contracts between employers and migratory squads made
without consultation with local federations.

A second motion proposed that several inspectors be appointed
with the assistance of the *Società Umanitaria*. The work of the Federterra's single inspector, Piemonte, had reassured the weeders that their
complaints would not go unheeded, for the courts had convicted a
number of farmers. After approving these two motions, delegates
discussed the advantages workers could derive from the regulations
for shelters for migrant labor. According to the 1907 law, landowners
had to build not only separate screened dormitories for men and
women, of specific sizes according to the number of occupants, but
they also had to provide isolated shelters to house sick workers during their recovery or while they waited to be sent to a hospital. Delegates expected that landowners would be reluctant to spend money
on new construction and would thus decide to hire local weeders
who did not need this temporary housing.[110] Employers tried, in fact,
to evade the enforcement of the regulation as long as possible.

This encouraging perspective was not enough to bridge the differences between the Vercellese, Novarese, and Lomellina farm workers' federations and the Federterra. Despite all objections, the Federterra decided to negotiate a single contract between employers of the
rice belt and migratory squads. It did this at its January 17, 1909,
meeting at Modena. The majority were delegates of federations that
had migrant weeders among their membership, and they did not take
into consideration the effect on negotiations in progress between local
federations and employers. The Federterra stressed the moral value
of its strategy—this was a real blow to the *caporali* and was worth the
sacrifice of agreeing to a lower wage. The local federations were very
critical of the pact. Migratory weeders would earn 0.24 lira an hour,
whereas the year before the hourly rate had been 0.30 and even 0.40

lira.[111] They were also dismayed at the prospect that migrants sent by the Federterra would be protected like ordinary strikebreakers by carabinieri and local police.

The rice-belt labor leaders had a different approach. We read in *Il Contadino* that if there were fewer migrant weeders in Lomellina in 1908, this was because the new law had made the business of the *caporali* more difficult. Employers had to pay wages directly to the squads, not to the mediators. Furthermore, employers now had all legal responsibility. Therefore, with the ten-hour day, the *caporali* were less able to profit on squads that worked long hours. Since the cost of the trip and the meals for the squads remained the same, each weeder working ten hours instead of twelve came to cost the *caporali* one-sixth more. They could no longer hire children under fourteen for a pittance while charging employers the same rate as for adult weeders. As Egisto Cagnoni wrote:

> Those strikebreakers who once used to come down from the mountains in huge numbers chased here by the priests, by the mayors, and by the blood-sucker *caporali,* do not want now to come to the *risaia* any more because they cannot put to work children under fourteen, or pregnant women, or those who have just delivered a baby. Those unable to come with the whole family prefer to remain at home. . . . The *caporali* were before able to make a deal with the farmer for an average pay of 16–17– 18 centesimi an hour, because parents allowed an infamous exploitation of their children.

Considering that the migrant weeders who signed the Federterra contract were going to earn 60 lire for the season, Cagnoni commented:

> But the Federterra contract eliminates the *caporale* to the benefit of the employers and to the great damage of the migratory weeders, who will end up losing no less than twenty lire each. Out of discipline they are going to disregard better offers from the mediators, and thus contribute to lengthen the weeding hours and to bring down the pay already won by us.[113]

The Federterra held another meeting in Bologna on April 3–5. Cugnolio, for the Vercellese, and Cagnoni, representing Lomellina, tried to explain to the Federterra secretary, Argentina Altobelli, why the contract favored the employers, who boasted of the deal as a personal victory. But the only thing that they could achieve under the circumstances was the passage of a motion restricting the numbers of migratory squads in 1909 to the same level as in 1908 and the assurance of their solidarity in case of labor conflicts.

The Federterra's insistence on sending migratory squads to the rice belt had its own logic. It was firmly committed to doing away with the system of *caporali* and to the organization of migratory weeders. To this end it took some steps to coordinate a network of placement offices in the provinces of origin of migrant weeders, mainly Mantua, Modena, and Bologna. The league leaders in the hometowns of migratory weeders felt the pressure of their constituents to reduce chronic unemployment. They were not inclined to impose "too big a sacrifice to poor women, requesting them to resign to an earning which, according to custom, provides for the payment of the house rent."[114] Leaders feared defection and the weakening of the leagues if they could not allocate squads.

Many migrants came from Emilia, and the Federterra's headquarters were in Bologna, its largest city; these leaders tended to put Emilian problems ahead of the specific problems of the rice belt. They were unfamiliar with the ways in which local weeders were hired. At the Bologna congress not only Altobelli but also Cabrini, while approving of the Federterra collective contracts, requested that local weeders give up "the dangerous tactic of waiting until the beginning of the *monda* season to present demands." They recommended instead that the local weeders should make their pacts during the winter. But this was too early for leagues to bargain with rice farmers.[115] League leaders in Emilia also made use of the placement offices of the *Umanitaria*,[116] which worked closely with the Federterra. The local federations were critical of the *Umanitaria* placement offices because the one set up in Novara in 1903 had encouraged more weeders to migrate to the rice belt. These conflicts reveal how difficult it was for the Federterra to consolidate the conquests of the farm workers' leagues and implement an all-encompassing plan to organize internal migration in the Po valley.

Misunderstandings also arose from the form that the labor struggle took in Emilia. There, the nature of the work allowed strikes to be planned ahead of time. In contrast, weeders not only decided on a strike at very short notice, but they also did not coordinate them from one commune to another. The reason for this apparent lack of strategy was that the weeds in the higher lands grew before those in the lower lands, thus determining different starting times for the *monda* and for the strikes as well. The local federations found it was not worth the trouble to inform Bologna about the communes on strike, because the site of the strike would probably change the next day.[117]

The 1909 Strikes

In the Vercellese, negotiations for the 1909 *monda* proceeded from January 2 on, in the usual hostile atmosphere. On that day at city hall, the engineer Bertinetti, the agriculturalists' delegate, called for keeping "the old schedule, from sunrise to three o'clock" to compensate for the shortage of labor that had already been experienced in 1908. That shortage resulted from an expansion in the area under rice cultivation, the new restrictions on age and the workday, and the scarcity of migratory weeders who refused to work for very low wages. "It is natural that those who do not want to pay, remain without workers," said Cugnolio. Referring to the lack of workers for winter jobs, Bertinetti suggested closing the fertilizer factory. Cugnolio reminded him that when employers decided to cut winter work to starve the workers, this policy merely encouraged the federations to advise their members to emigrate.

But the discussions between the two representatives failed to resolve the issues, and new talks were set for January 17. According to Bertinetti, the workday he proposed would be eight and a half hours long, from sunrise to three o'clock, with the usual breaks. Workers' delegates argued that "sunrise" was too vague a term and could give rise to abuses, and that they preferred a five o'clock starting time. But they were ready to yield on the issue of the eight and a half hour day, if the employers agreed on a five A.M. to three P.M. workday. The employers, however, insisted on the word "sunrise" so as not to break what they called "the general rule" in the rice field.

Weeders greeted the mere mention of an eight and a half hour day with an uproar,[118] and, by January 24, labor delegates definitively rejected the employers proposal to start at "sunrise," in order not to "return to the anarchy of times past."[119] Undaunted, the *Associazione degli Agricoltori* announced its own terms on April 19: nine hours and a 3 lire wage.[120]

On May 20, the farm workers' federations of Vercelli and Lomellina were determined to defend the eight-hour day[121] and decided to go on strike.[122] The Lomellina federation complained about the fact that in many communes the migratory squads, including those sent by the Federterra, were acting as strikebreakers, to the farmers' delight. The struggle was particularly difficult because weeds were scarce, and the farmers declared that they would allow only those workers who agreed to weed nine hours.

As in 1906, the strike also convulsed the city of Vercelli. On May 26 many protesting weeders paraded in the city streets early in the morning. They had a dual purpose: to get town workers to abandon their work in six factories and to have as many migratory squads as possible join in the work stoppage.

The day before, in a great show of solidarity, six hundred migratory *mondariso* had already refused to go to the fields. After they spent their first night on the bare floor of the People's House, the municipal council decided to move them into a former convent, where at least they could sleep on straw and eat bread donated by Cugnolio and the newly appointed mayor.[123] On the following day, the local weeders went to the station. Numerous migratory squads were on a train, ready to leave for Santhià. The strikers, determined to stop their departure, resorted to a dramatic gesture. They laid down on the railroad tracks with their children, totally paralyzing railroad traffic until troops dragged them all off the rails. A second group, which was expected to weed in Cascina Strà, refused to go, while a third, destined for Buronzo, but which did not join the strike, had to remain hidden for two days in the station shed before it could leave.

In another incident in Vercelli on May 26, a group of women and children blockaded the streets to stop carts carrying fifty weeders from leaving the city. Soldiers and carabinieri had to charge the protesters before they could finally leave. The municipal council met in emergency session for the entire day. First, it drafted a proposal to end the strike; it appealed to the principle of freedom where the contending parties would agree on a schedule, and called on the farmers to pledge not to impose a nine-hour workday. Then it made public a proclamation urging conciliation and the restoration of peace.[124] But on the following day the demonstrations continued unabated. Along with the six factories, a number of shops remained closed. Protesters blocked the streets, disbanded at each cavalry charge, then reformed afterward. In the afternoon, the police arrested six protesters. At a meeting in the subprefect's office, the *agricoltori* granted an eight and a half hour day to a commission of weeders accompanied by Cugnolio, but they rejected the proposal and proceeded to an assembly in the People's House, where they declared a general strike for May 28.[125]

It was then that the marchers converged on the Piazza Roma in

Sciopero dei mondarisi nel Vercellese : come le risaiuole tentarono impedire il viaggio ai liberi lavoratori chiamati a sostituirle.
(Disegno di A. Beltrami)

Drawing by A. Beltrami for *La Domenica del Corriere* of June 6, 1909, depicting the May 26 strike in the Vercellese: how the weeders attempted to obstruct the departure of the strikebreakers.

front of the station to watch the departure of two hundred sympathetic *mondariso,* and later on the arrival of a squad en route to Pezzana. The cavalry had a hard time emptying the *piazza* and protecting the carts from hostile strikers as the migrants left Vercelli. The crowd then rushed to the city gate to intercept the vehicles, only to discover that they had taken another road.[126]

As a humanitarian gesture, the mayor and the municipal council, still in session, provided soup for the *mondariso* sheltered in the convent, but in exchange they requested that Cugnolio and Carlo Vezzani, representing the Federterra, act as mediators to put an end to the sympathy strike being waged by workers in the city's stores and factories. Both labor leaders appeared more than eager to take the council up on its offer.

That night, during a general assembly of the leagues at the People's House, Cugnolio and Vezzani, helped by two other local labor leaders, dissuaded protesters from the nonagricultural sector from continuing the general strike. The assembly passed a motion to this end. It dealt first with "the harm that further agitations would cause to industry, commerce, and the shopkeepers," and stressed that "the general strike would be an undeserved punishment for the city and would not help the movement." Then it declared that "the regular yearly outbreak of a general strike, a tool of difficult use and adapted to extreme cases, is not reasonable." Finally, the striking masses "who, without any deliberation wanted to give up work in support of the weeders," were asked to return to work and back the weeders morally and materially for the duration of their strike.[127] Thus, both the city government and the labor leaders put an end to the general strike.

The way the May 28 general strike in Vercelli came to an end was atypical. Perhaps the labor leaders were convinced that neither the urban workers nor the weeders would improve their lot by a general strike. The metal workers had been on strike since November 1908. By May 1909 the steel mill customers were sending orders outside Vercelli and letting the local industry wither away.[128] It can also be surmised that the reformist leadership was trying to discourage the use of the main syndicalist weapon—the general strike—to revolutionize society. Perhaps the memory of a big, protracted, and finally unsuccessful syndicalist strike in Parma in April 1908 was still lingering in everybody's mind.

On May 31 the weeders' protest in Vercelli and in neighboring communes ended in a compromise. The leagues may have lost part of their bargaining power without the support of the urban workers. The sight of trains arriving packed with migratory squads must have also influenced their decision to compromise. The *monda* would take five weeks and the workday would be eight and a half hours long.

The wages, which varied week by week, would average 3 lire a day. In exchange, the employers promised to hire local weeders to cut down on local unemployment. As for the following year's *monda*, both parties would be free to negotiate contracts around either an eight- or a nine-hour weeding day.[129]

In several Vercellese communes, the strike ended in late May. The leagues of Casanova Elvo, Pezzana, San Germano, and Pertengo reached settlements with an eight-hour day. In Santhià, Prarolo, and Costanzara, strikers accepted the same terms as those agreed upon in Vercelli. But overwhelmed by an invasion of migrant weeders, workers in Ronsecco, Tronzano, and Tricerro suffered severe unemployment.[130] In the Novarese, where the leagues were notoriously weak, migratory squads invaded the region to work for wages of 1.90 and 2 lire a day.[131] Local weeders won the eight-hour day in twenty-eight out of fifty communes in Lomellina after widespread strike activity. Their federation extolled the positive effect of the experience on the formation of new men's and women's leagues.[132]

In Vercelli the labor leaders' wish to normalize labor activities may have been dictated by reasons other than the ones just mentioned. Perhaps these leaders expected that the municipal government would give some support to the weeders in exchange for their help in calming down the protesters. An indication that this might have been the case can be seen in the assistance the city gave to the migratory weeders stranded in Vercelli. In 1910 the Vercelli city council awarded the chamber of labor a long coveted subsidy of a thousand lire,[133] doubtless a reward for the chamber's collaboration in ending the May 1909 general strike. This was not the first time that the chamber of labor, with Cugnolio as its secretary, helped to restrain protesting workers. Why was this help rewarded in 1910? Perhaps it was the consequence of the new political climate. On March 7, 1909, the Vercelli clerico-moderate deputy Piero Lucca, an unconditional supporter of the rice growers and the church, was defeated, and Mario Abbiate, the candidate of the new Constitutional Democratic Party (*Partito Democratico Costituzionale*) was elected. The socialists voted for him as "the lesser of two evils." The FRAP expected Abbiate's support in exchange for votes.

Abbiate's election in 1909 is an indication of voters' increasing support for nontraditional candidates in the rice belt, but at the same time it revealed the weaknesses and the difficulties the Socialist Party's political organizations in the rice belt had getting its own candidates elected to parliament.[134] Cugnolio was elected municipal councilor. In Novara the "ministerial" candidate lost to the "protest" candidate. In the 1909 electoral contest, Catholic propaganda efforts also became more visible in the rice belt. Heeding the call of Pius X, Catholics did not put up their own candidates, but instead voted for those who presented the most antisocialist credentials, even if they were Freemasons or Jews, as happened in Vercelli.[135] The Socialist and Constitutional Democratic Parties continued to gain in the 1910 local elections. In July, under the banner of a constitutional association, candidates from the two parties won the majority of several municipal councils in the Vercellese.

"The Eternal Question": The Federterra, the Rice Belt Farm Workers' Federations, and the Issue of Migratory Weeders

The Federterra met again in Bologna on October 31 to November 1, 1909, to discuss the problem of migration to the rice belt. The chamber of labor in Novara sent a delegate, but the federations of the Vercellese and Lomellina decided not to be represented.[136] "After seven years of useless attempts, we have certainly won the right to say that *for the time being* there is nothing to do regarding the immigration of weeders," was the position of the FRAP. Along with the Lomellina federation and the existing Novarese leagues, it tried to intensify its dialogue with groups of unorganized migrant weeders from the neighboring Biellese and Canavese instead.

With this in mind, the three rice-belt federations held two meetings in December 1909.[137] The main topic under discussion was the adverse consequences for the local labor struggle of the January 1909 Federterra national contract: the Federterra migratory squads refused to participate in the strikes of the local *mondariso* and used the excuse that they had signed a contract. Paradoxically, the migrants led by traditional *caporali* managed to weed for higher pay. This happened because the *caporali*, instead of placing their squads early in the season, waited until the time the *monda* was approaching and employers were under pressure to have the fields weeded. Early in 1910 the Federterra was already preparing a new national contract along the lines of the 1909 pact. To this end, they organized a network of placement offices. The wage would be 27 centesimi an hour instead of the 24 of 1909.

In 1910 the Lomellina proletarian federation proved more amenable, at least outwardly, to a dialogue with the Federterra. Altobelli attended the federation meeting on May 15 where she agreed to close contracts with employers only if the local leagues informed the Federterra about the need for migratory weeders in their communes.[138] But in labor circles very few believed that these cordial exchanges would solve the problem of competition from migratory squads.

On October 9, 1910, at the Federterra meeting of Mirandola, its leaders reiterated the call that local federations sign contracts with employers before the end of the year, with the understanding that the Federterra would supply all the migratory squads needed, at wages equal to the ones fixed in the rice belt. For the Lomellina federation this was still equivalent to thinly disguised scabbing. The FRAP again refused to cooperate; once these wages were set, it argued, farmers would begin looking for unorganized migratory weeders who would accept lower pay.[139] Cugnolio declined an invitation to attend a Federterra meeting at Novara to discuss this question on November 22. The invitation came at a highly critical moment for the Federterra: the Lower Emilian rural proletariat was suffering the effects of a severe unemployment crisis, and Altobelli was seeking relief through temporary migration to the rice belt.[140]

On March 2–5, 1911, Cagnoni represented Lomellina in the fourth national congress of the Federterra at Bologna, only to charge it with strikebreaking activity yet again: "I do not understand how the Federterra leadership can recommend Italian workers going abroad to observe the working conditions that they meet abroad, and at the same time insist that we accept its right to import to us rice weeders with a ten-hour schedule and a wage of 27 centesimi an hour, while . . . our [weeders] do not earn less than 30 centesimi an hour and do not work more than eight hours a day." Nino Mazzoni, in the name of the Federterra, could offer in rebuttal only an unsatisfactory reply, adducing "the objective reality that reveals that the idea of a boycott of the rice belt is irreconcilable with the general interests of regional organizations." Another member of the national federation recalled the rice belt organizations "to their duty to overcome the natural and understandable local sensibilities and to ponder the problem with a broad and enlightened approach." Cugnolio, as well as Arturo Rossi, secretary of the chamber of labor in Novara and coordinator of the leagues, was conspicuously absent at Bologna.[141]

There was another factor that helped keep migratory weeders' competition high. Government officials failed to check their documentation at the time of their departure to see whether the mandatory labor contracts and health and birth certificates were in order. This sort of control could easily have prevented many from leaving.[142]

One wonders how many migrant and local weeders were under the age of fourteen, given the frequent references to the problem of underage workers in the labor press.

The situation shows that the socialists could not organize labor in all the regions that furnished unorganized migratory weeders.[143] Organizing these group was a difficult task, considering that, according to 1912 figures, migratory weeders numbered almost forty thousand. Only five thousand of them were organized. Many of them, as the 1909 events show, were ready to disrupt local labor disputes nevertheless.[144]

The Federterra found it difficult to organize workers outside socialist strongholds like the Po valley, the traditional region of the *braccianti* or day field laborers. This failure may be attributed to two related causes. One was the weakness or total absence of Socialist Party sections in electoral colleges lacking masses of wage earners. Only where these masses existed, party sections devoted themselves to organizing workers and related institutions, such as leagues, federations, chambers of labor, People's Houses, and cooperatives, which formed a fragmentary network of "red islands." Second, while the Federterra was very effective in its "red islands," it was less successful in recruiting laborers who worked under land tenure systems other than the one typified by the big commercial farms. Neither did the rice-belt farm workers' federations in their "red islands" reach unorganized migrant weeders with their propaganda, even though migratory weeders were sometimes not too far away (the Biellese, for example, shared a border with the Vercellese). The socialist and labor organizations of the three rice-belt districts were well interconnected, but there were not relations among different party sections and unions in other places. When Argentina Altobelli addressed the Lomellina federation meeting on May 15, 1910, she acknowledged that both the Federterra and the district federations were still very weak. More energy would have improved the situation.

But even if that had been the case, still other factors would have hampered a total change. Employers would have continued taking advantage of labor weakness in times of distress and they would have been supported by the government and the police. Besides, more discipline and organization alone would not have solved one of the problems that moved the farm workers' federations to action: the chronic unemployment of the Po valley, especially in its lower section. Besides suffering from periodic recessions, the growth of Italian industry had slowed down after the 1907 financial crisis.

Unable to keep their own work force fully employed, industries were not at all prepared to absorb the masses of unemployed farm workers who needed to cope with increases in the cost of living. No industries were emerging in the lower Po valley. This would had been a key factor in remedying the job situation. Farmers in the region profited from extensive land reclamation works financed by the Italian government that began in the 1880s and continued in the following decades. But the majority of the beneficiaries neither applied the most adequate methods to take full advantage of the enhanced fertility of the soil nor furthered local industries, preferring instead to invest their earnings outside the area. The Italian government offered no solutions to the structural problems of the Italian economy. Neither the Socialist Party nor its labor organizations had an immediate program to address these same problems. Even if they had had one, it is still an open question whether it stood any chance of implementing the program or solving the problems.[145]

1910: "The Saddest Situation . . ."

The FRAP prepared a plan for the 1910 weeding based on the compromise that ended the 1909 strikes: parties were free to sign contracts for either eight or nine hours. The FRAP therefore urged all *mondine* to rush to register at the leagues for an eight-hour weeding day.[146] With early registration, the *mondariso* would first show the employers their unanimous preference for the shorter workday, and then inform them of the number of weeders available for the season, thereby dissuading them from hiring unneeded migratory labor.

The early round of negotiations between the FRAP and the *Associazione degli Agricoltori* took place in February, but it broke up after disagreements on wages; employers offered an average of 2.50 lire for an eight-hour day, but Cugnolio, for the FRAP, insisted on a 3 lire wage.[147] The FRAP despaired of any favorable agreement, and predicted in *La Risaia* that the employers would precipitate "perhaps the saddest situation the Vercellese workers had gone through in these ten years."[148] In Lomellina, the *agricoltori*, who expected the arrival of numerous migrant weeders, precluded any acceptable negotiation with local weeders. The FRAP foresaw labor foresaking white bread for the cheaper and less nutritious millet loaf.[149] In the following months, workers in the Vercellese and Lomellina complained about the possible closing of the few butcher's stores that had opened after 1900 to supply their growing demand for meat. From 1910 on, there was continual struggle to catch up with price increases.[150]

In May, when the parties in the Vercellese resumed their dialogue, the leagues of Vercelli and other communes finally settled for an average wage of 2.60 lire. The agreement was hard on the *mondariso*, and not simply because the pay was low. In addition, the employers had imposed a sliding scale of wages and a deposit, instead of a uniform wage during the six *monda* weeks and no deposit, as Cugnolio had demanded in the name of the FRAP. In Vercelli, for example, the wages were set as follows: first week, 1.70 lire; second week, 2.30 lire; third week, 2.85 lire; fourth and fifth weeks, 3.10 lire; and sixth week, 2.60 lire. The FRAP was right to distrust a sliding scale; at the end of the third week of weeding, the employers of the commune of Vercelli dismissed the local weeders, just when they were entitled to the highest pay of the season, 3.10 lire. Heavily escorted migratory squads replaced them at the lower rate of 2.50 lire a day.[151]

This was not the only tactic. In the Vercellese and Lomellina the employers began to move migratory weeders, who usually stayed on one farm for the *monda*, from one farm to another, thereby putting more local weeders out of work.[152] Farmers had done this before, but in 1910 they resorted to this maneuver more than ever. In Lomellina the proletarian federation settled for the eight-hour day in exchange for a very low wage, 2.40 lire. The Vercelli and Lomellina agreements speak of a unity of purpose among all the employers of the rice belt. If they yielded on the issue of the eight-hour day, they found other ways to get back at the weeders; they lowered, and, in Vercelli, manipulated, wage scales. The distressing reality bore out the dire predictions of months before.

Protective legislation provided little or no help to the troubled *mondariso*. "For subversives like us," wrote the antireformist Cagnoni in *Il Contadino*, "it is a joy, a satisfaction without limits, to see what conception of the law those in charge of having it observed actually possess." Migrant weeders worked eleven hours a day for six and a half days a week.[153] Most written contracts were not deposited at the mayor's office, as the law prescribed.[154] June 20, 1910, was the farmers' deadline for complying with their obligation to provide adequate shelter for permanent and migratory labor. For each migrant weeder the employers had to furnish a chair and an individual straw mattress.[155] Such regulations, farm workers speculated, might be a good way to improve their conditions because, if the employers decided to invest money in new buildings, migratory weeders would finally have better lodgings. If not, employers would have to dispense with migratory squads and rely on local ones. Rice growers preferred to continue their old ways and hire migrant weeders without providing the dwellings prescribed by the law.

In June 1910 Senator Ricci traveled to Rome to persuade the minister of agriculture to relax the application of the law, while Cugnolio, through deputy Abbiate, continued to demand strict adherence to it.[156] In early September, the FRAP distributed blank forms among workers, so that they could easily keep count of infractions,[157] but finding this was not enough, it invited all the leagues to Vercelli on September 18 for a rally. Cugnolio, at the end of his speech from the balcony of the People's House, submitted the text of a petition to thirty-five hundred demonstrators for their approval. They then marched to present the petition to the subprefect's office. The document demanded compliance with the law, and the immediate dismissal of migratory weeders from farms lacking appropriate lodgings, with an adequate compensation for their losses. It also called for the nomination of labor inspectors. "Convicts sleep on mattresses, workers must not sleep on straw," read one of the several posters carried by demonstrators. Another said, "The law guarantees health and bread."[158]

Despite the FRAP's mobilization during the fall of 1910, authorities brought very few violators to trial and sent no migrant workers home because of a lack of adequate shelters. As judicial sanctions were indefinitely postponed, deputy Montemartini questioned the ministers of the interior and justice in September and December as to whether they intended to prosecute violators of the law.[159] Although the courts began to pass some sentences on those who flouted the law in November, according to *La Risaia* these were all amnestied.[160]

For employers, providing mattresses and chairs for migrant workers was an annoyance and they easily ignored that part of the law. Some magistrates declared it unconstitutional, an opinion shared by the council of state. Employers also counted on the prefects' cooperation; these officials submitted a proposal to the elected bodies of the provinces of Novara and Pavia to do away with this obligation on the pretext that it was impractical and unhygienic.[161] Even the provincial sanitary councils voted unanimously for the abrogation of the regulation. The supreme sanitary council had declared the year before that the mattresses were necessary. But, once summoned to an emergency session attended by only a minority of the councilors, it reconsidered the declaration and finally reversed it.[162] The last battle against the mattresses took place in April 1911, when the provincial councils of Novara and Pavia abolished the rule, and the *mondariso* and all the other migrant workers were indefinitely relegated to sleeping on floors covered with dirty straw.[163]

The Vercellese weeders won only one battle. They wanted a change in the break schedule, the suppression of the 30-minute breakfast rest; the farmers gave in to this. There was still a one-hour lunch break, so that weeders worked from six in the morning until three o'clock in the afternoon, a schedule that they found ideal to fit in with their other duties. But this was not the only reason they preferred this arrangement. Many farmers would shorten every break, and sometimes weeders were left with only ten minutes for breakfast, making a "mockery" of the break, as this description in *La Risaia* shows: "One is forced to hastily nibble that bit of bread standing with legs in the water, seeing, with eager eyes, far, far away, the shade of the trees." In other words, the weeders ended up working longer without pay, a situation that added to their eagerness to do away with the breakfast break.[164]

During these years, 1907–10, the Federterra continued its organizational efforts in the Po valley. It took a series of measures to eliminate the *capisquadre*, but found it difficult to develop a workable and all-embracing program to stop the competition of migratory weeders in the rice fields. Neither the Federterra, nor the local federations of the rice belt, nor the Socialist Party sections could effectively organize some areas of mass migration. In the ring around the rice belt the hold of priests and conservative forces over the working population remained unchallenged, thus precluding any cooperation between the approximately forty thousand unorganized migratory weeders and the local *mondariso*. The proletarian organizations of the rice belt knew where the danger lay and they made important attempts to change the situation despite the growing resistance of the *agricoltori*. Regional unemployment was essentially caused by economic factors beyond their control and their plan to alleviate it proved difficult to implement before World War I. The *mondariso* fought against all these adverse forces, but they found it impossible to withstand them in 1910.

Withstanding Agrarian Militancy and Wars, 1911–15

Although we are women,
We are not afraid.
For the love of our children
We join the league.
                    The League*

The Giolittian System and the Agrarian Classes

The period 1911–15 was characterized by a growing exacerbation of the relations between rice growers and labor. The 1907 law on rice cultivation offered workers certain opportunities to increase their demands and fortify their ranks. But employers had already broadened the antilabor front in 1910 by forming an agrarian-industrial alliance to resist labor activity, even if it was sanctioned by law.

Until 1910, the Giolittian system could balance opposing political forces by restraining and attracting reformist socialists while ensuring the support of industrialists and agriculturalists. Although outwardly still intact, the Giolittian equilibrium became more and more fragile after 1907, because of the economic crisis. This was followed by a recession in 1908 and a weak economic recovery after 1909, characterized by many mergers among industrial enterprises. The rate of industrial growth decreased from 6.7 percent in the years 1896–1908 to 2.4 percent in the years 1908–13, and unemployment rose in some critical periods. The years of accelerated industrial progress were over in Italy and in the rest of Europe as well.

Under these circumstances, not only producers, but also all Italians who cared about the country's modernization, its political and military prestige, and its great-power status, began to question the soundness of a political system that was unable to ensure economic prosperity. The public wavered in its backing of Giolitti. Nevertheless, the prime minister counted on a comfortable majority in the chamber, which ensured his return to office each time he temporarily stepped down (as he did from March 1905 to February 1906, and from December 1909 to March 1911). But the nature of Giolitti's parliamentary support changed after the intervention of clerical forces in the 1909 national elections. Their votes, almost all in favor of government candidates, did not yet endanger any liberal majority, but they contributed to the election of conservative and moderate deputies. Legislators indebted to the Catholics for their seats in parliament were, therefore, obliged to support, or at least not to oppose, Catholic principles.

Agriculturalists were always either extremely critical of Giolitti's policies or directly opposed to them. Did the agrarians' complaints against Giolitti have any real justification? For example, agriculturalists objected to the high property taxes on land, but in fact these taxes were rather moderate and Giolitti had never increased them. The burden of property taxes fell harder on small holdings, but that was of no consequence to owners of big and medium-sized holdings, who formed the core of the influential agrarian groups. In addition, Giolitti never introduced a progressive income tax; he continued to rely heavily on indirect taxes on basic consumer goods instead.

Along with the taxation problem, there was the agriculturalists' alarm about Giolitti's friendly attitude toward reformist socialists. Thanks to an increase in votes for socialists, many were elected to the governments of rural communes and could therefore raise municipal property taxes. Capitalist farmers felt that Giolitti, whom they considered neutral toward socialist and farm worker organizations' actions, was neglecting them and ignoring their interests, leaving them in the hands of their class enemies.

Agriculturalists were also concerned about losing some of their economic, social, and political leverage to the new industrial and financial groups favored by Giolitti's policy of direct intervention in the country's industrial development. Agriculturalists maintained that the government should stick to the liberal rules instead. It is true that Giolitti's measures favored industry over agriculture, but the major contradiction in the agriculturalists' argument lies in the fact that the protective tariff, which furthered industrial growth, had also been in effect for agricultural products since the 1880s and would not be abolished until the end of World War I. Agriculturalists did not want to see this removed.[1] In truth, they were distressed because as in all industrializing countries, their power was becoming increasingly overshadowed by the new industrial and financial groups, in a process that Giolitti was unable to control.

New conditions in the national and international markets initiated this change. During the economic depression at the end of the nineteenth century, commercial agriculture underwent structural changes aimed at raising productivity. With the economic recovery at the turn of the century, commercial farmers found added incentives to increase productivity. Agricultural prices were rising, and more farm products were in demand for the growing urban industrial centers, for international markets, and for industries using agricultural products as raw materials. Improvements in the transportation of agricultural goods, as well as the expansion and modernization of the transportation network, grew simultaneously with demand and new markets.

While they increased their farms' productivity, agriculturalists were also becoming integrated in the process of industrialization, just as industrialists, along with bankers, were finding opportunities to take over the commercial farming sector. Therefore, new developments in industry and banking had repercussions for farming, and vice versa.[2] Agricultural economists and historians such as Colin Clark,[3] Folke Dovring,[4] and Pasquale Villani[5] focus on the relation between industrial and agricultural productivity on a national and international scale. They date to the 1880s the establishment of multiple links between Europe and the world economy, which coincided with the beginning of the formation of industrial monopolies.[6] From then on, city interests embodied in industry and banking began to acquire an increasing share of farmers' income.

How did this occur? The explanation lies in the fact that competition from agricultural producers in other countries forced farmers to increase their output, and such an increase could generally be obtained only at the cost of raising expenditures on items from other sectors of the economy. Endeavoring to raise agricultural production, the farm sector had to intensify its use of goods (fertilizer, insecticide, new equipment and buildings) and services (transportation, credit, insurance) at costs that were rising faster than ordinary costs (salaries, wages, rent, taxation).[7] As a result, Dovring explains, despite the rise in demand for agricultural products, farm income did not grow at the same pace. In other words, even if productivity was increasing in the whole economic system, relative to it farm income would decline. In addition, agricultural prices tended to rise less (or fall more) than other prices. Agricultural markets were more competitive than those of industries,[8] which found ways of controlling prices through cartels.

We may ask ourselves whether or not the declining relative income of the farm sector remained an inexorable fact, following Dovring's conclusions, or whether it applied equally, without exception, to all farm production. All that we can say is that when landholders requested lessees to reduce the surface cultivated with rice in 1907, they refused to do so, surely because rice was the most profitable crop. Furthermore, when leaseholders demanded a lowering of rent, the claim went unheeded, perhaps because landowners doubted lessees' inability to pay. In 1911 rice-field rents were soaring. In some cases, leaseholders were paying from about 25 to 45 percent more to renew their nine-year leases. Rice fields grew slightly smaller in the years preceding World War I, but not necessarily in the rice belt. We read that rice farmers of the Novarese were interested in expanding their rice fields in 1910. In any case, output increase per hectare more than compensated for the reduction.

Still, before World War I Italian agriculturalists were disturbed by several developments, among them the loss of their political power. At the same time, the rate of growth of agricultural production, compared with that of industry, was slowing down. Agricultural production grew 38 percent in 1871–75 and 1911–15. Industrial production, on the other hand, increased 158 percent in the same period.[9]

Focusing on post–World War II Italy, Zangheri states that the importance of landownership and agricultural profits, in the economy as a whole, diminished. Landowners' income and capitalist farmers' profit decreased between 1913 and 1951 from 24.7 percent to 6.4 percent of the national income. But he clarifies that, within the agricultural sector, profit from agricultural production was 24.7 percent in 1951, whereas the profit from capital in the other sectors of the economy was 23.2 percent. Zangheri concludes that despite the advances of industry, financing, and service, landed property held an important position in the economy.

May we say something similar about the agricultural sector in the pre–World War I years? In relative terms it was subordinate to the industrial sector, but perhaps in absolute terms individual rice growers did not see their personal situation worsen.[10] And, after all, were rice growers applying the most progressive methods to further rice production? In the proceedings of the fourth international rice congress at Vercelli in 1912 we find that the delegate from Spain lectured his Italian colleagues on the enormous advantages of the most advanced method of rice transplantation, which enhanced yield, quality, and profit. It was commonly employed in his country, but Italians were not in a hurry to adopt it. Before the war they conducted some tests with the technique and used it somewhat during the war. They introduced it on a wider scale only at the end of the war.[11] Rents, as well as the price of rice, continued to be high, and the tariff protected farmers from foreign competition.

Discussions of the fourth international rice congress at Vercelli (November 5–8, 1912) reveal the rice growers' main concerns, which were similar to those of all commercial farmers; above all, it was the need to make higher investments to increase productivity and quality, and to fight competition. Panelists talked about growers feverishly selecting, importing, and experimenting with new seeds, and requesting government assistance for the enterprise.[12] The exhibition and promotion of new machines put growers under pressure to make the financial decisions necessary to mechanize, or to update the mechanization of as many operations as possible, in a process that would intensify in the interwar period. Luraghi states that in Novara the investment in farming equipment was the highest in Europe. The farm machinery industry's use of the congress as a forum to promote its interests became more evident with the presentation of new factory devices for rice milling and refining.[13]

Rice growing and industry interpenetrated each other on an unequal basis because, as in all industrializing countries, manufacturers who supplied the technical goods, or who processed the crops, were consolidating, eliminating small competitors, regulating marketing, and controlling prices. Italian rice growers, as well as the growers of sugar beets, tomatoes, hemp, and citrus fruits, faced similar problems. Rice had traditionally been milled and refined on the farm, but, at the end of the nineteenth century, big manufacturers, equipped with the latest machines, not only started to purchase and process the local crop but also to export it. By 1905 seven such refineries were able to set the purchase prices from growers and limit the sale of the refined product to keep prices high. The production of chemical fertilizers reached a still higher degree of consolidation in 1910–11, with four plants controlling the whole local market. There was also a high degree of interpenetration between rice farming and financial circles, resulting from agriculturalists' increasing needs for insurance policies and loans. Here again, a few companies dominated the rice-belt insurance business, and a limited number of banks, primarily the Novara Popular Bank (*Banca Popolare di Novara*) took over or crippled older credit institutions.[14]

The pressure exerted by industrialists and bankers was, no doubt, a source of tension for growers, but they avoided open confrontation. Despite their conflicts, the contending groups had other things in common besides supporting the protective tariff. They shared an increasingly critical attitude toward Giolitti, and opposed the Socialist Party and its labor movement, two essential elements in the Giolittian political compromise. "The solidarity of the high industrial and financial bourgeoisie with the landowners, the conservative compromise that has marked a hundred years of the life of the state and of the Italian society," to use Zangheri's words, prevailed over discord.[15]

Three related events in 1910 symbolize a turning point in Italian history and underscore the common interests between agrarian and industrial capitalists, and their endeavor to use their political and economic strength to change Giolitti's policies. On July 1 agriculturalists' associations of the rice belt joined forces with other associations pursuing common ends throughout Italy to found a national confederation, the *Confederazione Nazionale Agraria*. It aimed at destroying workers' resistance and increasing farmers' political influence. With the same goals in mind, the Turin Industrial League, formed in 1906 and converted two years later into the Piedmontese Industrial Federation, became the General Confederation of Industry (*Confindustria*).

The third event took place on December 3–5, when Italian nationalist groups, backed by representatives of important economic interests, founded the Italian Nationalist Association (*Associazione Nazionalista Italiana*), with a program of arms buildup and colonial expansion. The goal was to transform what nationalists called a "proletarian" nation into a rich "capitalist" nation.

From 1910 on, the agrarian and the industrial confederations came together in an agrarian-industrial alliance forming an offensive against both the government and organized labor. Beginning in 1910, their supporters in parliament formed the Agrarian Central Committee and the Industrial Parliamentary Group to further antilabor policies and promote their economic interests in matters of taxation, trade agreements, and protective tariffs. In the same year, delegates from both confederations intensified their efforts to force the government to restructure the supreme labor council in their favor. They wanted the state to allow their two confederations—not the ministry of agriculture, industry, and commerce—to elect employers' representatives, and to include members of nonsocialist unions among the labor representatives, thereby weakening socialist influence on the council. They wanted to contribute to the shaping of other proposed laws that would affect their interests as well, such as the inauguration of the interregional placement offices to regulate labor internal migration, the tribunals of *probiviri* for agriculture, mandatory labor contracts for all workers, an insurance system covering agricultural workers' accidents, and a corps of labor inspectors. This last was the only proposal to become law before World War I.

Close collaboration between the two confederations culminated in 1912 with the founding of the monthly *L'Italia Industriale e Agraria*.[16]

The agenda of the agrarian and industrial confederations stressed antiparliamentarianism, the importance of their economic pursuits to the nation, and the subordination of labor to their interests. This program had much in common with the Italian National Association. This convergence of goals drew the three organizations together, and industrial and agrarian leaders became members of this nationalist grouping on the eve of World War I "as the new 'party of opinion' of the upper bourgeoisie."[17]

These three powerful groups confronted a Socialist Party badly enfeebled by internal conflicts and divisions between reformists and revolutionaries. The party found more obstacles to its campaigns to develop coherent national and labor policies, to defend democratic liberties, to stop price increases, and to reduce unemployment. While the living standards of urban workers deteriorated, the power and surveillance measures of employers organized in their own federations grew. This made joint actions between weeders and city workers in all the more difficult, though this collective action had proved so effective in 1906.

Difficult Years

In 1911 the rice-belt labor organizations came out with a flurry of new plans. One concerned ways of regulating the traffic of migratory weeders; a second, the conclusion of a long-term *monda* pact; a third, the struggle for the enforcement for the first time of a stipulation contained in the 1907 law on rice cultivation; and a fourth, in connection with the preceding one, concerned the attempts to establish placement offices. The FRAP in Vercelli took the initiative in implementing the last three programs. As on prior occasions, rice growers sabotaged the campaigns to implement labor laws. Their resistance grew because they felt that even the enforcement of such an innocuous law as the one on rice cultivation was an encroachment on their rights.

The 1911 *monda* season started with the negotiation of two labor contracts, the first concerning migratory weeders; the second, local *mondariso* in Vercelli. On February 8 the National Federation of Farm Workers (Federterra), which represented migrant labor, and delegates of the agrarian associations of the Novarese, the Vercellese, and the Lomellina drew up a national pact for migratory weeders. The agreement, which stipulated wages of 2.70 lire for a ten-hour day, was signed after the employers pledged to hire organized migratory weeders first, but not enough to cause local unemployment.[18]

In May bargaining for the local weeders' contract took place in the city of Vercelli. The leagues of the commune of Vercelli and the *Associazione degli Agricoltori* negotiated a three-year *monda* contract, fixing wages of 2.75 lire for an eight-hour day, and guaranteeing thirty-six days of work during the weeding season; the employers also agreed to hire local *mondariso* first.[19] In the rest of the Vercelli district, the employers offered the same, or slightly lower wages, but without agreeing to six weeks of work.

Weeders from Ronsecco and Tricerro in the Vercellese went out on strike for higher wages and for a six-week work contract. They won neither of their demands, because the employers already had migratory squads on hand to replace them, so they were left lamenting the poor communication and coordination between the Vercellese leagues and the Federterra. Two squads of the national federation worked at Ronsecco, "and this happened despite Cugnolio's telegram alerting Altobelli about the strike." Once again organized weeders from one region were replacing striking workers in another area.[20]

Despite a promising beginning, the three-year Vercelli contract was signed too late to prevent the arrival of an abundant supply of migrant workers in the commune.[21] Still, the perennial plight of migratory workers was not responsible for the poor, "miserable," 1911 *monda*, which required fewer weeders than usual. That was a consequence of heavy rain and a great scarcity of weeds.[22]

The effects of bad weather lasted into the fall. Those harvesters and threshers fortunate enough to find jobs were paid lower wages than in 1906 (5 lire for men and 3 lire for women); men earned 4.40 lire, women 2.90.[23] In addition, in order to be hired, many had to accept hated piecework contracts (*cottimo*), which the 1906 strike had sought to abolish completely from the region. From then on, harvesters and threshers fought an arduous battle to regain their working conditions of 1906.[24] As we shall see, they suffered a severe setback in 1914.

The 1911 Federterra and Vercelli pacts were not the only new events in the rice belt. The 1907 law on rice cultivation had decreed the creation of conciliation commissions to force both farmers and workers to abide by their contracts. This provision came into effect in 1911. Each commission was to have five members, two elected by farm workers, two by employers, and the fifth, the president, appointed by the four other members. The law also had a unique feature: women could vote and run for office. True to its antireformist stand, the *Federazione Proletaria Lomellina* advised weeders to abstain from elections, because employers would continue breaking contracts, no matter what the commissions ruled. If certain compliant magistrates were declaring the new regulations unconstitutional, like the employers' obligation to supply migratory labor with mattresses and chairs, workers should leave the law aside "without regard for whether the law either antedates or follows our victories," Cagnoni wrote in *Il Contadino*.[25]

On the contrary, the FRAP saw the law as a means to tackle problems of low wages, high unemployment, and a continuing decline in the workers' standard of living. So it encouraged all male and female farm workers over the age of fourteen to register in the electoral lists at the city halls.[26] The FRAP also considered the electoral process an opportunity for labor to exercise its rights, and a practical way to compile public statistics about local weeders, which could be brandished in front of the farmers to stop them from hiring excessive numbers of migratory squads. Thus far, the municipalities had never made estimates of their labor force,[27] but now the opportunity was there to collect the data.

Despite these positive signs, the FRAP's campaign encountered several major stumbling blocks. No woman wanted to run for office, and the two workers' delegates and their substitutes elected in each commune were male. Women's refusal to run for office may have been the result of opposition from men in their households or prompted by the lack of time, a fear of being mocked by male workers if they were elected, or a disinclination to participate in male-dominated bodies, such as the commissions. Aiazza and collaborators write about older Vercelli weeders whom they interviewed in 1976–78: "Even though they have been protagonists of great union and political struggles, 'public' life did not weigh heavily upon their 'private' life, where they continued to fulfill the role that society expected of them."[28] Another source of frustration for the FRAP was the weeders' inability to come up with claims of unjust treatment before the commissions, because they lacked valid contracts. When hiring their squads, the farmers hid behind traditional verbal promises and avoided what they considered cumbersome, compulsory written labor contracts.[29] In this way, of course, they also obviated weeders' complaints about contracts and made the conciliation commissions unnecessary.

All this was taking place against a backdrop of soaring rice-field rents,[30] which may explain the employers' reluctance to increase workers' wages. "You impudently and shamelessly increase land rent and afterward you try to recoup yourself with the skin of those who toil," wrote Carlo Facchinotti in *Il Contadino*.[31] In addition, rice growers, along with all the major *agricoltori* in Italy, were generously funding the new National Agrarian Confederation. The Novara and Vercelli rice growers outdid their fellow agriculturalists in this.[32] The confederation's largest outlay was for strike insurance or, to put it plainly, for hiring strikebreakers during work stoppages. But from 1911 on, rice growers added new counteroffensive tactics to their traditional weapons, such as breaking strikes or circumventing the law to put down weeders' labor actions. The *mondariso* organizations also increased their activity, but they resorted mostly to lawful means.

Thinking of the next year's *monda*, FRAP congratulated itself for at least having signed a three-year pact in the commune of Vercelli. It expected to extend similar agreements to the district as a whole.[33] The FRAP considered this the first step toward an ultimate goal: the introduction of local placement offices (*uffici di collocamento*) in collaboration with the *Associazione degli Agricoltori*. This was one of the most important points in the program of the Federterra.

The FRAP wanted to reduce unemployment through an even distribution of labor in the district. In some communes the work force was small; in others it was too numerous for local needs. Still, if the workers moved to the communes where labor was needed, local workers objected to their arrival because it contributed to lowering wages. The placement office was supposed to establish uniform wage pacts for a whole district to avoid this, and then allocate the surplus labor. Here again, the FRAP reasoned that the placement offices would be adequate to negotiate the written labor contracts required by the 1907 law. In fact, the whole idea of placement offices was appropriate to the spirit of this law.

But first the FRAP wanted to negotiate a three-year *monda* pact that would cover the whole district for 1912. When it proposed this plan to the farmers in 1911, they agreed as long as the leagues submitted to the employers the number of weeders ready to work on each farm before the end of the year.[34] But the FRAP was unable to convince weeders to register early, because, clinging to customs, the women thought that "it is absurd to think of *monda* contracts in November."[35]

In the end, the Federterra did not renew its 1911 national pact. In February 1912 the employers' associations rejected its demands for an eight-hour day and a rise in wages from 27 to 30 centesimi an hour to compensate for increases in the cost of food and railroad fares. Employers found these terms excessive, especially the eight-hour day, which was two hours shorter than the workday fixed by the 1907 law for migratory weeders. The Federterra finally accepted the fact that as long as migrant workers were willing to work longer hours, they would be hired before local weeders. This was something the rice-belt labor federations had pointed out time and time again to the Federterra.

Now that there was no contract, the Federterra declared a boycott of the rice belt and urged the Emilian leagues and chambers of labor to spread the word so that squads would not leave Emilia for the *monda*.[36] Although it welcomed the Federterra boycott as the "ideal solution" to an old problem, the FRAP saw its effects as only partial, because unorganized weeders did not join the boycott as well. While the employers were turning down Federterra terms, they were offering 30 centesimi an hour to unorganized squads from Piacenza and Bobbio. In May the FRAP tried to come to the aid of the Federterra. Using the pages of *La Risaia*, it called upon the Socialist Party sections of Turin, Casale, Ivrea, and Biella to "get out of the city and go to the countryside; we do not merely invoke doctrine, we also have to put it into action." This appeal was reminiscent of the plea of the young socialist organizers of the 1890s and was a reminder of the socialists' duty to instruct unorganized migratory weeders to demand the same conditions the employers had refused the Federterra. But the party and the neighboring socialist sections were completely unresponsive. The FRAP criticized their passivity, despairing that they would never turn the "propaganda of words" into a "mobilization for action"[37] of migratory weeders.

At the root of this attitude was the difficulty of the party and of the Federterra to organize workers outside the so-called classic regions of the massive landless proletariat concentrated in the "red islands." In addition to this, small landholders' and craftsmen's economic power was in decline in the surrounding highlands. Many members of these groups would supplement their reduced income with *monda* wages.

Even without the pact's extension to the entire Vercellese, the *Associazione degli Agricoltori* accepted the eight-hour day in 1912 in order to avoid major labor conflicts. Still there were strikes. The weeders of Casanova Elvo struck for 3 lire a day, but when the employers offered 2.75 lire, the strikers accepted it and resumed work. In Pezzana a long strike ended when seventy-two weeders who were out of work were finally hired. But because they now had a larger work force, employers shortened the *monda* contract of all the squads by several days.[38]

Lomellina and the Novarese were not as peaceful as the Vercellese, where at least there was a pact limiting the length of the workday. Employers there were unwilling to agree to an eight-hour workday. In Lomellina the weeding season started with strikes in numerous communes where workers asked for the eight-hour day and decent wages. Emboldened by the presence of a huge number of unemployed weeders, employers offered 2.30 lire, which was 20 centesimi less than in 1911, and 40 centesimi less than in 1910, for a nine-hour day. Strikers succeeded in winning the eight hours, and in some places even slightly higher wages.

In Ferrera Erbognone there were violent confrontations. On May 24 squads of women and children from 8 to 12 years old formed a human chain on the road to block the arrival of strikebreakers; they suffered serious injuries when carabinieri charged them. Several arrests followed, including that of Eugenio Riba, secretary of the local league, who had not participated in the protest.[39] This was an unusual step but from then on it would become more frequent, as a demonstration of employers' and the government's growing aggressiveness toward labor. To make matters worse, the organized Emilian squads of migratory weeders, which were supposed to boycott the rice belt that year, migrated anyway. Hired by the traditional *capisquadre* for a wage of 27 centesimi an hour,[40] they were motivated by lack of work at home.

If, in 1912, local weeders of the Vercellese could at least reach one of their goals—the eight-hour day—almost without exception harvesters in 1911–12 were still unable to get back what they had won in 1906 and lost in the years thereafter. On August 26 the FRAP declared a general strike of harvesters to win back the 1906 contract, which they would not regain in the pre–World War I years. It was a long, violent protest, which resulted in more than twenty arrests. The strikers won the eight-hour day and wages slightly lower than those of 1906 in only thirteen communes. Employers held out in the rest. They were aided by the decisive intervention of the National Agrarian Confederation, which sent unorganized migrant workers to the scene, who were protected by local police and carabinieri.[41] Possibly they made use of the confederation's excellent insurance fund.

The jurist and historian Guido Neppi Modona has studied how the different Italian governments before Fascism interpreted the section of the criminal code of 1889 (the Zanardelli code) devoted to the regulation of strikes. The code granted the right to strike, but articles 165 and 166 condemned work stoppages in cases where strikers employed violence and threats. Neppi Modona has cited many cases in the nineteenth and twentieth centuries when the executive power interfered with the administration of justice, and caused magistrates to uphold a very rigorous interpretation of the concepts of violence and threat. The justice system in Italy responded to new forms of social struggle by organized labor by applying the code more stringently. This was especially evident after the general strike of 1904.

One of the many examples of this new, more rigid, interpretation of articles 165 and 166 was the tendency to arrest persons not directly involved in a protest, such as the arrest of league secretary Eugenio Riba in Lomellina or the repeated prosecution of socialist journalists for whatever influence they could have exercised on labor unrest through the press. Neppi Modona points to the contrast between the Giolitti government's apparently lenient policy toward labor at the beginning of the century, and the concomitantly stricter jurisprudence that his pressure on the magistrature helped to create. Because of this, he does not see either a change in the relations between political power and justice at the turn of the century of the sort expected from a liberal government, or the "turning point" usually ascribed to the Giolittian era. He concludes that pressure from the executive served to hinder the exercise of the right to strike.[42]

Obstacles to Organization and Legislation

Notwithstanding their unity of purpose, since the early days of struggle each farm workers' federation in the rice belt had acquired a specific identity and characteristics that endured throughout the years. The mobilization campaigns followed the district-by-district expansion of socialism in the last decade of the nineteenth century to compete with the established political groups in national and local elections. Preexisting political boundaries had, therefore, promoted the independent life of each socialist section, and this was something that the decentralized structure of the party did little to counteract. These divisions fostered the individual features of the farm workers' organizations in each district, though on their own initiative they strove to overcome these differences through the innumerable meetings and consultations they held to discuss common strategies.

In 1912 the Novarese, where revolutionary socialists had the majority, still had the weakest organization led by the revolutionary majority. Its leagues, which were coordinated by the chamber of labor, lacked the vigor to reconstitute the federation, which was disbanded after the 1901 strikes.[43] On May 19, 1912, Arturo Rossi, secretary of the chamber of Novara, launched an ambitious program to reorganize the federation: first, to reach a long-term agreement with the Novara farmer's association; and second, to introduce placement offices and a "farm workers' cooperative" to organize the seasonally unemployed and thereby eliminate middlemen. Rossi's proposal, which followed the FRAP guidelines, did not materialize, because the leagues, the foundation of a sound federation, were too weak.[44] Rossi attributed the leagues' decay to (1) the growth of workers' wine circles, set up by the socialists; (2) the depletion of the pool of active and potential labor leaders who emigrated either to towns to seek work in growing industries[45] or overseas, in a flow that accelerated after the economic crisis of 1907, often in the aftermath of unsuccessful strikes; (3) labor's excessive interest in cooperatives, which channeled the fighting spirit of the workers into very limited pursuits.

It was no wonder that Rossi complained that the lack of solidarity among weeders gave the agrarian association of Novara the upper hand. Rossi knew that the agriculturalists could divide the *mondariso* by continuing to promise those who did not join the leagues individual contracts, which they seldom fulfilled afterward.[46] Also, if women did succeed in forming leagues, they dissolved them at the end of the *monda*.[47] A certain Rax, writing in *Il Lavoratore*, echoed Rossi in blaming male workers who frequented wine circles, a typical discussion place for male socialist workers, for the leagues' weaknesses; these workers neglected their own political and labor interests, and also shirked their duty to educate the women of their households, so that they could form leagues.[48] But, although these factors may have had some weight, Rossi did not say that the Novarese political and labor leaders neglected farm workers. Neither Funes, first, nor Gemma, after him, nor Rossi, devoted themselves fully to farm workers' problems, to the extent that Cugnolio and

Cagnoni did in the Vercellese and in Lomellina. Instead, they seemed to be more concerned with the urban workers' federations, which were the backbone of the chamber of labor of Novara, and with political propaganda.

In the two farm workers' strongholds of the rice belt, the Vercellese and Lomellina, the leagues increased their capacity to resist employers' renewed offensives. Cugnolio and the FRAP still had the initiative with regard to strategy and they resorted, whenever possible, to the law to substantiate their claims. Despite Cagnoni's intransigence and distrust of the use of legal means in the struggle, in the Lomellina the organizations often followed the same tactics as those employed in the Vercellese. Cagnoni sometimes had some differences of opinion with Luigi Montemartini, a tireless labor organizer who devoted his efforts to the cause of the rice workers of Pavia and Lomellina. He was a reformist socialist deputy for the district of Stradella (province of Pavia). Cagnoni often voiced his disagreement with Montemartini's reformist views with regard to the role of the party and the methods of the labor struggle.

But labor was suffering under the impact of a profound economic and political crisis. The price of basic commodities had risen steadily since 1909 and by September 1911 it leapt to new heights. In Vercelli the retail price of wine rose from 5 in 1910 to 9 centesimi a liter; the wholesale price of sugar went from 135 to 145 lire the quintal; in Novara that of flour went up from 34.50 to 37.50 lire the quintal. Beef, which workers had begun incorporating into the family diet as wages rose, disappeared from their tables because it was now selling at 1.90 lire a kilogram.[49] Prices increased mainly as a consequence of Italy's military adventure in Africa.

On September 26, 1911, Italy embarked on a colonial war with Turkey for the conquest of Libya, a war that heralded the end of the Giolittian system. The historian Maurizio Degl'Innocenti observed in his book on the Socialist Party and the Libyan war that the influence of big industry on the government determined its decision to acquire new territories to provide more outlets for the Italian industrial monopolies.[50] The lives of the weeders showed no improvement as a consequence of Italy's colonial ventures. On the contrary, the sacrifice of so many lives and the economic crisis that beset the country in the wake of the conflict became new sources of social malaise for the whole Italian proletariat.

The 9-month-old Italian Nationalist Association employed modern propaganda techniques to help carry the day, trying to infuse public opinion with patriotic, bellicose, and jingoistic sentiments that had a strong antisocialist tone. Thus was the Libyan war created, the cause of much division within Italian society. Opposition to the war included Giolittian liberals, the Catholic left, and the majority of the reformist socialists. In general, however, the Socialist Party was subdued, unprepared and lacking resources to combat the nationalistic fanfare of the prowar faction.

The declaration of war caught the Socialist Party by surprise. Its majority staged a general strike of protest on September 27, which had very little repercussions in some parts of the country, such as Vercelli, in part as a consequence of police repression. Rinaldo Rigola, the leader of the CGdL, considered it a failure. Its effect was eclipsed by prowar demonstrations. This episode reveals the inability of the reformist Socialist Party leadership to take the political initiative to mobilize all its resources to develop a strong antimilitaristic and anticolonial movement, or to lessen the conservative influence of the royal court and the military. It had neither its own economic plan, nor alternative schemes for the official policies on banking, finance, and taxation that benefited some sectors to the detriment of others. Other circumstances weakening the party were the decrease in party membership (from forty thousand in 1908 to thirty two thousand in 1910), and the increasingly independent role played by the General Confederation of Labor and the socialist parliamentary group in the decision-making process, to the detriment of the party.

But the General Confederation of Labor itself lost many workers who escalated their militant rejection of reformist guidelines[51] and joined the ranks of the revolutionary syndicalists who split from both the Socialist Party and the CGdL in 1908. In addition, some reformist members, supporters of Leonida Bissolati, approved of the war (Bissolati and his followers were expelled in 1912), but the majority of socialist deputies, under Turati's leadership, withdrew their parliamentary support from Giolitti. The revolutionary wing increased its influence in party matters and took over the party leadership at the 1912 socialist congress at Reggio Emilia. The revolutionary socialists stressed an intransigent line, in which their opposition to alliances with other political groups or with the government were fundamental. Beyond that, they gave scant consideration to ways to bring about changes in the structure of the Italian state, and they failed to analyze the profound evolution occurring in Italy and around the world.

Opposition to Giolitti's liberal policies was gathering strength. The problem was grave because the prime minister's liberal followers, despite being a majority in Italy, had never organized their own political party, which, along with other democratic factions, might have opposed the enemies of the liberal regime.

The shortcomings of social legislation caused labor several disappointments. The regulation that obliged rice growers to provide mattresses and chairs for migratory squads was abolished in 1910. This had fatal consequences in the Vercellese. The straw covering the big shelters' floors constituted a serious fire hazard; these dormitories had few exits, so that, in case of fire, evacuation would be difficult. During the 1912 *monda*, four dormitories caught fire, and in one, two children lost their lives.[52]

Farmers disliked making written contracts,[53] and in the Vercellese they were also getting around the issue of conciliation commissions by refusing to elect representatives to them. Had they attended the conciliation sessions, they would have served as a platform for labor to press for contracts and draw public attention to the farmers' refusal to sign them. So they ignored the law, and, as we have seen, continued to rely on verbal agreements at the beginning of the *monda*. In this way, the farmers could dismiss local weeders after the first weeks of weeding when squads of migratory workers were available. They could do this with impunity and without answering to anyone.

The labor offices also failed to fulfill their legislative role. In 1912 the city of Vercelli set up a municipal labor office, presided over by the mayor or an appointed delegate, with a mandate to alleviate high unemployment. It had to gather information about labor conditions within and outside the district, not solely for statistical purposes but also as a basis for its prime function as a placement office. However, the municipal labor office did not fulfill its duties[54] and was completely useless to the organizers. The socialists consequently raised the old call for farm workers' labor tribunals (*collegi di probiviri*) to replace the conciliation commissions, which, after all, could deal only with contractual agreements. The rice-belt organizers saw no reason why the government could not extend the jurisdiction of the tribunals for industrial workers to the countryside.

Labor legislation in 1912 continued to exclude farm workers from the protection given to workers in industrial and commercial sectors. The list of protective legislation from which farm work was exempt included the laws on woman and child labor (1902), disability insurance (1904), and weekly rest (1907). As an exception, the 1907 law on rice cultivation did grant weeders a rest. The insurance for maternity leave or miscarriage came in 1910, providing 40 lire of com-

The 1912 weeding in Vercelli, Italy, MAIC, *Supplemento al Bollettino del Ufficio del Lavoro*, No 14, Rome, 1912. *Above:* Migratory weeders at work. *Below:* Local weeders at Lunch. (Economics and Public Affairs Division, The New York Public Library, Astor, Lenox and Tilden Foundations.)

The 1912 weeding in Vercelli, Italy, MAIC, *Supplemento al Bollettino del Ufficio del Lavoro*, No 14, Rome, 1912. *Above:* Model women's dormitory, Larizzate estate, Vercelli. *Below:* Migrant weeders' kitchen. *Opposite:* Inside a dormitory. (Economics and Public Affairs Division, The New York Public Library, Astor, Lenox and Tilden Foundations.)

pensation in either case, but also exempted all agricultural workers. Cagnoni, speaking in the July 1908 meeting of the *Federazione Proletaria Lomellina*, rationalized the absurdity: "Economists, deputies, the king himself assert that the economic profile of Italy is overwhelmingly agricultural, to the point that farming employs six million workers, while industry hardly occupies three million," and insisted that the government should eliminate the discrepancy.

"For the pariahs of the soil the law is mute," we read in *Il Contadino*.[55] "Why does the government, which thinks of women industrial workers, not think of women farm workers?" asks a contributor to *La Risaia* in April 1912, when insurance for maternity leave or miscarriage went into effect on April 6. "For the same reason that there is a compulsory insurance for workers' accidents and not for farm workers' accidents," the writer continued. "Who remembers that farm workers exist?" Because the law on rice cultivation forbade pregnant women from working a month before and after giving birth but with no compensation, he mused: "Is it just that, to make up for the prohibition, a provision does not exist to compensate the woman for this forced loss of work?" He thought that insurance for weeders, paid by employers, could easily have been introduced, even though weeding was a temporary job, because weeders were registered in each commune as eligible voters for conciliation commissions, and therefore identifiable as workers.[56] The recognition of such rights for temporary workers was, of course, out of the question then, and generally continues to be so nowadays.

Protective legislation for farm workers, therefore, lagged behind that for industrial labor, despite the fact that the mass mobilization of farm workers in Italy preceded the organization of industrial workers. The same phenomenon occurred in most industrialized nations. What reasons underlay these disparities in protective legislation, and why did not the Socialist Party leadership challenge them? The explanation lies in the fact that this was, to a considerable degree, also the policy of the reformist socialists. The Socialist Party avoided formulating political objectives demanding structural changes and a definite legislative program to supplement the one proposed by the government itself. This resulted partly from the support that the reformist socialists were giving to Giolitti's own initiatives and to the whole reformist system, which were the justification for this mutual understanding.

The majority of reformist socialists shared Giolitti's interest in modernizing and industrializing Italy. Furthermore, they considered it their mission to support rapid industrial development of the sort that in Italy demanded substantial subsidies from the government. They saw a connection between the gradual growth of industrial productivity and the betterment of the workers' standard of living, thanks partly to social legislation, and this was a condition that would make labor more receptive to socialist ideas. Industrialization was, thus, a fundamental lever for the formation of a modern socialist work force, which would spearhead the emancipation of the whole Italian working class. However, this proposition reflected the situation only in northern Italy, where industry was making strides. Both Giolitti and the reformist socialists overlooked the economic, political, social, and cultural development of the south or Mezzogiorno, the poorest region in the peninsula. One of the most notorious consequences of this policy was the widening of the gap between a progressive north and a backward south. For the Socialist Party this made it even more difficult to extend its influence in the south.

This attitude stirred the critics of southern socialists, with Gaetano Salvemini as the most vocal advocate for the progress and democratization of the Mezzogiorno. Here, the prevalent agrarian economic structure was the *latifundium* (large landed estate) where extensive agriculture was practiced. Even the masses of farm and industrial workers that the socialists were so successful in organizing elsewhere were lacking, with few exceptions. The jobless population generally left the country to resettle in America. Local employers, politicians, and pressure groups dominated southern workers and deprived the Socialist Party and its labor organizations of many potential members. One of the limitations of the party in this area was that it had not proposed nationwide structural changes. Salvemini's pleas for reforms like the expropriation of *latifundia* in the south were made in a vacuum.

The upward economic trend at the turn of the century persuaded not only many Italian, but also French and German, socialists to favor big industry and urban workers, and thus to neglect farm workers.[57] In his history of Italian trade unionism, Idomeneo Barbadoro refers to the general mistrust of some urban socialists toward the masses of farm workers in the Po valley, and reports the accusation of the organizer Enrico Dugoni against the "followers of Turati" in 1902 for not having cooperated "in the organization of the Milanese agrarian proletariat, leaving this region in the same situation as the Vendée." Ernesto Ragionieri presents a similar picture in Sesto Fiorentino, a socialist commune in Tuscany. The city government devoted little attention to the conditions of agricultural workers, sharecroppers, or *mezzadri* in their majority, and to their organizations. In 1906 seven thousand sharecroppers went on strike in order to press for changes in their labor contract. The protest ended up in a defeat as a consequence of the shortcomings of socialist activity in favor of the *mezzadri*. From then on, Catholic labor associations would spread in the rural areas of the commune.[58]

More charged with suspicion was the attitude of many socialists toward field laborers of the Mezzogiorno. In 1911 Altobelli declared that the Federterra had to limit its action so far to a homogeneous region—in other words, the Po valley. When the south came under discussion, Turati's conception prevailed, that of "strengthening the movement in the north first, to expand it afterward to the south." To Salvemini's exasperation, Turati "renounced grasping the objective and concrete bond that united the struggle of Italian labor from north to south." His indifference to the agricultural universe of the south is illustrative of his misconceptions about the agrarian question.[59] Until 1910 Turati opposed universal male suffrage. Still, on July 7 he wrote to his partner Anna Kuliscioff: "The great problem is always that blessed universal suffrage, which does not go, does not go, does not go especially in the south, for which it was created and put into the world."[60]

Of course, if the Socialist Party neglected the political and labor education of the rural masses of half the country, the thought of the use they would make of the vote caused it great concern, the same concern, by the way, that was elicited by the idea of extending the vote to women. Kuliscioff was always critical of the mutual understanding between the Socialist Party and Giolitti, and of the support that the party gave to ministerialism (*ministerialismo*). In 1910 she had written to Turati about signs that "the socialist party was degenerating," and about an "involution of our socialist reformism toward a possibilism and a chronic ministerialism." She particularly disapproved of Turati's "grand synthesis of the separation of parliament from the *piazza*."[61] In other words, she reproached him for being immersed in the parliamentary routine while remaining indifferent toward the masses of workers (the *piazza*), with the exception of one particular group, the workers of the industrial north. The Socialist Party's failure to have the benefits of the law extended to farm workers shows the party's detachment from them and their needs, one of the consequences of "the separation of parliament from the *piazza*."

Like Turati, Giolitti was reluctant to go beyond some concessions, like the one that allowed farm workers to organize moderate protests to have their wages, which he deemed too low, increased. Far from realizing his conception of the integration of all classes into one social body, Giolitti seldom aided farm workers with his legislation plans. The revenues from agricultural exports were meant to serve to finance industrial growth, and therefore prices of farm products had to remain low to compete in the international market. This necessitated controlling labor costs. There are some exceptions to the practice of general neglect, however, instances of public works and land reclamation programs proposed by Giolitti to temporarily alleviate the farm workers' unemployment problems. But there was an overall plan to favor industrial over agricultural development. His economic measures furthered industrialization and supported industrial prices and, in some cases industrial wages too, at an artificially high level. He and the social legislation he introduced favored the industrial proletariat.[62] There were, therefore, essential limits to the progress of the reformist course he espoused, which would have required conditions other than the ones prevailing in Italy, with a small industrial development and the presence of a huge agricultural proletariat.[63]

The list of reforms demanded by labor included the modification of the 1907 law on rice cultivation. On June 11, 1912, Cabrini rose in parliament to point out the law's violations: no appointment of government inspectors to monitor the application of the law; no written contracts; no Sunday rest; no age restrictions on weeding; no change in the system of money deposits and withholdings. He insisted on the introduction of a uniform work schedule to facilitate inspection.[64] In July 1913, Rita O. Tintori in *Il Lavoratore* told how girls under fourteen managed to weed, and got around the law by presenting birth certificates of older girls to municipal secretaries.[65] The Federterra lent a hand in this campaign; it collected a series of proposals to be submitted to the government.[66]

Cugnolio suggested that the written contract be simplified to an individual slip for each worker, with a copy for the farmer. Given the impossibility of eliminating the *capisquadre,* he proposed to control them by licensing them as internal migration agents. He also suggested using the proceeds from the fines employers paid when charged with violations to set up more day-care centers for infants. There were already two of these centers, one in Vercelli and one in San Germano Vercellese, run by a charitable institution, to which half of the fines already went.

Another motion proposed that workers provide their own supervisors, as the Bianzè (Vercellese) league and the Federterra had already done. Government inspectors would be appointed for the first time only in 1913. Labor recommended once again a uniform workday of eight hours for both local and migratory weeders, along with the posting of rest breaks, the reintroduction of mattresses in shelters, and compensation of workers or their families for labor-related accidents, among which were malaria or death. With regard to the conciliation commissions and the farmers' refusal to take part in them, there was a motion requesting that the judgment passed by the commissions be considered valid, despite the absence of employers' representatives.[67]

The motion for an eight-hour day for migrant weeders had the backing of the Vercellese municipal doctors who, in August 1912, allowed their findings to be published in *La Risaia.* They confirmed that migrant workers were unaccustomed to local conditions and were therefore the first to fall victim to malaria and other work-related diseases. They concluded that the ten-hour day should be shortened by two hours.[68] The Federterra planned to distribute fliers with this impressive program among the migratory weeders in 1913.[69]

The farmers, however, had another kind of reform in mind. At their fourth international rice congress, renowned specialists, as usual, delivered lengthy expositions on the ways and means of making weeding cheaper.[70] Labor representatives, disapproving of the exclusive class character of the gathering, decided not to attend it. Once more, the Nobel laureate Golgi described the antimalarial campaign in the rice belt. He referred to the controversial nature of the topic, whose discussion was never kept within "the boundaries of scientific medicine and of pure science." Instead it was mixed in with economic and political issues. As a consequence, he complained, "it is difficult to see judgments and discussions that do not become eclipsed by individual or collective passions."[71] He saw no reason for a law requiring employers to provide screens on the shelters as a means of controlling malaria when quinine could do the trick.[72]

Needless to say, the rice growers welcomed Golgi's suggestions with enthusiasm. Giovanni Voli, president of the Novarese *Associazione degli Agricoltori*, voiced their feelings when he exclaimed: "Let us then abolish this hateful, expensive, useless mechanical protection and develop instead therapeutic methods (*bonifica umana*), whose salutary results in our region we have been able to appreciate."[73] Voli himself prepared a study opposing the use of screens, which the Association of Agriculturalists of the Novarese and the Vercellese submitted to the minister of agriculture in December 1912, in the hope of having this requirement finally abolished.[74]

Be that as it may, before World War I parliament did not undertake any reform of the law. In fact, of the two legal developments that favored labor, one was the ruling of the supreme court of appeal (*corte di cassazione*) in Rome on November 21, 1912, affirming that written work contracts were mandatory, thus rejecting the farmers' appeals to abolish them;[75] weeders with a contract would, at least, be in a stronger position to appeal to conciliation commissions in the case of labor disputes. The other was the law of December 22, 1912, prescribing the creation of an official body of labor inspectors.

Despite their repeated attempts to sabotage labor's gains, rice growers in 1913 had to reckon with the supervision of two inspectors sent by the Federterra and three officials headed by Ilario Zannoni, appointed by the government. There was never before a *monda* better overseen than this. In addition, the carabinieri contributed to the surveillance of farms. As a result, farmers paid more penalties than in previous years. However, the number of inspectors was still inadequate and, as Zannoni suggested, the government needed to appoint ten times the 1913 number to fulfill the task properly. The inspectors visited 301 farms, and found irregularities in 119, or 40 percent, of them. The main violations were: the use of kerosene cans or open pails instead of regulation containers with tight lids; the lack of adequate, separate rooms for migratory weeders who fell ill at work to rest in until they received medical assistance; omissions, or irregularities, in the preparation of the work contracts; the lack of such things as adequate dormitories with screens and signs indicating the break schedules; and the failure to provide separate sleeping compartments for men and women. In addition, employers occasionally hired minors under the age of fourteen who used forged birth certificates.[76] In 1914 the Federterra sent two, and the government eight, inspectors—close to a 200 percent increase from 1913. The numbers of infractions rose, as the statistics show, in absolute and relative terms:

Year	Farms	Infractors	Infractions
1913	301	119	185
1914	1,129	601	1,340

In 1913 the inspectors found infractors in 39.55 percent of the farms. In 1914 this proportion increased to 53.23 percent.[77]

The 1913 Weeding

In 1913, following the Libyan war, Italy underwent an economic crisis. This aggravated many agriculturalists' and industrialists' critical attitudes toward the government, as well as their intransigence in dealing with labor. The economic situation upset foreign trade, banking and financial operations, and industry, which was undergoing a crisis of overproduction. The condition of the working class worsened. The contraction of the labor market, caused by a decrease in industrial production, resulted in unemployment, the weakening of industrial workers' organizations and of their capacity to resist wage reductions, and an increase in emigration.

In the years 1912–13 the number of transoceanic emigrants rose from 208,434 to 305,205. This was not enough to solve the domestic problem of labor oversupply, and jobless city workers began to compete with farm workers for agricultural employment.[78] Employers' organizations were strong and were prepared to oppose labor demands.[79] In April 1913, for example, agriculturalists in the Vercellese, Lomellina, and the Novarese joined together in a federation.[80] Their main purpose was to keep wages at the 1912 level, and they were extremely resourceful in doing so.

The first test of the farmers' resolve came in Lomellina, where the leagues pledged not to sign individual contracts, but to negotiate

a single *monda* pact,[81] on the lines of the three-year Vercelli agreement. Rice growers not only turned down that proposal, but also
tried to manipulate local and migratory squads with new, humiliating
demands. In Sartirana, for example, they announced in February that
they would recruit squads for thirty-two days, for eight hours a day,
and for a pay of 30 centesimi an hour. In case the squads finished the
weeding ahead of time, farmers would send them to weed somewhere else, or have them harvest wheat nine hours a day for 3.60 lire
a day before paying them for the season. This arrangement was un-
heard of, and the Sartirana league rejected it outright, because the
weeders did not want to break the tradition of working on only one
farm. They wanted to be paid as soon as they finished with all the
weeds and only after all local men had been hired would they harvest
wheat for 4.25 lire a day.[82]

Although the prevailing wage in Lomellina was 2.40 lire a day,
some leagues did force higher rates through job actions. The women's
league of Valle, for example, was able to impose a wage of 2.70 lire.[83]
At San Giorgio, the weeders went out on strike on May 25; eight days
later they settled for 2.25 lire a day. This was an increase of 15 centesimi over 1912 wages and was won thanks to the solidarity of the
migrant squads.[84] When the carabinieri tried to force the migrant
weeders to proceed to the fields, they refused because they "did not
intend to go to work accompanied by the police like so many ban-
dits." In retaliation, the angry employers took back the bread and rice
they had begun distributing to the migrant squads. But these weeders
did not starve; members of the local leagues used their headquarters
as a kitchen to feed their fellow strikers for the duration of the work
stoppage.[85]

At San Giorgio as well as in several other communes in
Lomellina, employers used another tactic: they lent migratory squads
to one another and transported them from one farm to another according to their needs. Sometimes they did the same with local
squads, for not all the weeders resisted this maneuver as those from
Sartirana did. One squad in Ottobiano had to spend more than two
hours a day walking between that commune and San Giorgio. Then
they weeded for ten hours. After two weeks, they rebelled and refused to go on with the work. Although the law sanctioned a ten-
hour workday for migratory weeders because they spent the night at
the farm, the squads felt that if they had to walk back "home" the law
did not apply to them. Hence, this squad protested, but the San
Giorgio farmers found more docile workers to replace them.[86]

At Goido (Lomellina) a strike broke out because farmers wanted to extend, by an extra hour,[87] the eight-hour day, guaranteed since 1910, but the appearance of local strikebreakers led to the protesters' defeat.[88] The league in Lomello complained about the lack of solidarity of the women and children who went in squads to weed for nine hours a day in the neighboring commune of Ferrera, thereby depriving local weeders there of work. The league blamed not so much the *mondariso* but the Lomello men who allowed this to happen and who had not instilled in their wives and children working-class values and discipline.[89]

In Vercelli the *monda* agreement that expired at the end of 1913 was applied to the whole district, making that locality particularly conflict-free during the weeding. The real setback for labor came at harvest time, when the *Associazione degli Agricoltori* set up its own placement offices, hired migrant squads, and paid lower wages than in 1912 (from 50 to 75 centesimi less). It also imposed longer workdays, some ending at midnight.[90]

In 1913 the Federterra endeavored to cooperate with the local federations. Again, it declared a boycott of the rice belt by refusing to deliver its organized migrant weeders. Employers, in any case, had been offering them only 28 centesimi an hour, while they were hiring the unorganized at 29 and 30 centesimi an hour. Rebellious or striking migratory weeders could be threatened by employers with the loss of all their earnings, as the events of Lomellina showed, and with the employers' refusal to feed them.[91]

The leagues managed to grow despite the increased hostility of the employers and amid an extremely adverse economic situation, while dissension among reformist and revolutionary socialists was reaching a very critical stage. At its national Reggio Emilia congress (July 7–10, 1912), the Socialist Party's revolutionary wing, after winning the majority, had demanded the expulsion of Leonida Bissolati and other reformist deputies who had supported the Libyan war. Cugnolio, practical and independent, referred to the signs of crisis within the party in his own way in 1912. Using the Vercellese labor struggle as an example, and perhaps exaggerating his disdain for political and theoretical debates, he opposed the "true socialist," the one who was "always in contact with the workers," to the "armchair philosopher."[92] In Lomellina, Cagnoni also disapproved of the Socialist Party's neglect of the working class. In 1913, during the third provincial Socialist Party meeting at Pavia, he proclaimed the need to strengthen the links between the party and workers.[93]

While workers and employers played out their moves in the rice fields, the 1912 law granting men almost universal suffrage increased the electorate from 3 to 8 million. This law extended the franchise to all men over the age of thirty, and included all males over twenty-one who were literate. The vote gave the socialists in the rice belt the opportunity to play an important role in molding national and local policies, and this was bound to have a significant effect in the Po valley. In 1913, while five million men prepared themselves to vote for the first time on October 26, party sections proliferated in the rice belt along with cooperatives, youth and women's leagues. As a result of the elections, the number of deputies from four socialist groups increased from forty-one to seventy-eight; fifty-two of these deputies were pledged to the subversion of parliament.

The other big change was the loss of seats by constitutional liberals. They returned with 304 instead of 370 seats, and they owed some of these to the Catholics. This was the outcome of an agreement (the Gentiloni pact) that Giolitti had made with Count Vincenzo Gentiloni in the name of the *Unione Elettorale Cattolica*. Catholics, following the pact's stipulations, supported Giolitti's nominees in those constituencies where Catholic votes alone were not enough to send their own candidates to parliament. In exchange, liberal candidates committed themselves to support Catholic political tenets. The number of Catholic representatives rose from twenty to twenty-nine; the nationalists won six seats. On the left, the republicans decreased from twenty-four to seventeen, while the radicals' number rose from fifty-one to seventy-three.

Thanks to the new franchise, socialist candidates for the chamber won half of the rice-belt seats. The party captured all the constituencies in the Vercellese and many electoral slots in the Novarese and the Lomellina. Cugnolio won the electoral district of Vercelli, Maffi that of Crescentino (Vercellese), and Cagnoni the one of Mortara (Lomellina). This increase in socialist strength encouraged optimism among labor leaders who saw in it a sign of society's advancement along the road to socialism. The FRAP secretary, Cugnolio, expressed this sentiment in the following glowing terms:

> *True Socialists* are never inactive; they advance from one victory to another until the final abolition of wage slavery, until the emancipation of workers from the employers' tyranny, until everybody enjoys the whole product of his labor.[94]

Turati's and many other socialists' negative assessment of workers' capacity to make use of the vote to promote the renewal of Italian society proved unjustified in the Po valley. It was the workers' mobilization for national elections in 1913, and then for local elections in 1914, that infused new blood into the party in the rice belt. Weeders also rallied to the support of the socialist candidates, as will be discussed in chapter 8, p. 275, and contributed to their victory.

Slowly, the rice-belt leagues were following the trend of all the farm workers' leagues in the country, especially those in the Po valley. As can be seen in the following table, after some losses, farm workers' leagues gained new members:[95]

Year	Organized Farm Workers	Organized Industrial Workers[96]
1906	221,913	
1907	273,698	404,533
1908	426,079	508,290
1909	405,149	438,662
1910	390,851	426,183
1911	407,999	449,531
1912	408,148	452,354
1913	468,969	502,698
1914	488,756	473,292

The rise in the number of organized workers between 1912 and 1913 was perhaps the result of increasing labor and political agitation, intensified during the electoral campaign for the 1913 elections. It may also have been a response to the employers' heightened offensive, the acute economic crisis, or, indeed, a product of all three. Strike statistics reveal the effect of all these factors on labor protest actions. The exasperation caused by the crisis did not result in an increasing strike activity, especially in the agricultural sector. From 1909 to 1914, the numbers of both agricultural and industrial work stoppages went down and remained below the 1908 level.

STRIKES FROM 1908 TO 1914 (KINGDOM OF ITALY)

	Agriculture		Industry	
Year	Strikes	Strikers (1000s)	Strikes	Strikers (1000s)
1908	286	173	1,417	200
1909	140	47	931	142
1910	97	26	1,021	173
1911	148	133	1,107	253
1912	176	96	914	144
1913	97	80	813	385
1914	82	49	782	173

The Struggle for the Placement Offices

In 1914 the FRAP had to solve two critical, related problems: one was the renewal of the three-year *monda* pact; the other was the need to define the rights of the Vercellese *mondariso*. When they went to work in another commune and had to stay there overnight, they felt entitled to weed, like any other local *mondariso*, for eight hours, and not for ten, like the migratory weeders.[97] On paper, matters were settled easily. On March 10 the *Associazione degli Agricoltori* agreed to extend the pact for another three years, and this time for the whole Vercellese. The district was divided into three sections, each with different wages, based on those of 1913: 2.80 lire in Vercelli and in communes where the pay had been of 2.75 lire in 1913; 2.60 lire in Santhià and in communes with wages of 2.50 lire; and 2.50 lire in Crescentino, Bianzè, and other communes where wages had been 2.30 lire a day.

Employers promised to hire local before migratory squads. Vercellese weeders migrating from one commune to the other within the district's boundaries would not work more than eight hours a day. March 31 was the *mondine* deadline to register for the weeding. This gave sufficient time to the farmers to hire migrant squads where necessary.[98]

The FRAP admitted that the pact's wages were lower than the 3 lire it considered fair, but it traded lower wages for full employment for all local weeders. It also gained employers' agreement to set up placement offices at harvest time to ensure fair employment practices. For the FRAP, the farmers' acceptance of placement offices was more fundamental than the issue of the 3 lire, just as the winning of the eight-hour day in 1906 had been more important than higher pay.

Given the exceptional importance of the currents of internal migration, organized labor saw the necessity to control the labor market and to establish contacts with the migratory masses through placement offices. This does not mean that employers would be ready to accept them. The offices first appeared in Mantua in the early 1890s; in the following decade they spread through neighboring provinces. The offices were intended to correct three abuses. First, violations of labor accords that often offset the workers' gains of better wages and a shorter workday. Second, discrimination against organized or local workers by employers who preferred unorganized and migrant workers. The third problem was unemployment. The government presented a law project on the creation of interregional placement offices in 1907, which parliament never discussed. In 1910 the Federterra had set the guidelines for their operations and their main purposes: to enforce the fulfillment of labor settlements, taking from employers' hands their monopoly of hiring procedures, and to organize the surplus labor supply into shifts (*turni*), in order to give the whole labor force a chance to work.[99]

Although the problems of low wages, the eight-hour day, and full employment may have appeared to be settled in the Vercellese, there were immediate violations of the pact, as the following examples show. In communes like Rive, *mondariso* who had failed to register before the March 31 deadline for the *monda* remained idle; migrant workers weeded in the fields. In others, like Pezzana, Stroppiana, and Cappuccini, the agriculturalists' *associazione* hired migrant workers. In Caresana weeders went on strike because employers were openly violating the terms of a written pledge to hire local women first.[100] In Tricerro 130 nursing mothers had not found jobs near their homes, the only place they could work under the circumstances. Employers there were even trying to pay 14-year-old workers only two-thirds of a regular weeder's pay.[101]

In Lamporo the weeders struck for a wage raise of 20 centesimi and to force the hiring of local *mondariso* first. A member of the Lamporo league put it this way:

> Certainly employers would have preferred to raise the pay 50 and 60 centesimi to be free from the obligation of hiring *promoters*, as they call our best *compagni*. This is what they always did in the past; but our problem was not a simple wage problem, because we wanted more than the increase. We wanted to get at strikebreaking tactics that rice growers were employing by excluding militant workers.[102]

In May 1914 Cugnolio left Rome for the rice belt to take a direct role in ending the *monda* strikes. He traveled from farm to farm with mediators—the chief of police and the carabinieri marshal—to negotiate with employers to settle the strikes by hiring locals first.[103] In Vinzaglio, in the Novarese, women went on strike for an eight-hour day, although a nine-hour day was still common in that part of the Novarese. Cugnolio advised the women to return to work, because if they held out for the eight hours any longer, the imminent arrival of strikebreakers would deprive them of any work at all in the depressed economy.[104]

Yet strikes continued. In Lomellina the employers spurned attempts to negotiate, but the intense labor and political activity of 1913 prepared the proletariat to fight in 1914. In the winter, in preparation for the 1914 *monda*, leagues began separate talks for the upcoming weeding season.[105] In Candia, for example, the mayor invited employers to sit down with the women's league to iron out an agreement. The rice growers refused, because they knew that the league was very weak and that many of its members would not resist employers' delaying tactics. One of the speakers of the league, acknowledging this frailty, predicted that employers would wait until January when weeders "would sell themselves one by one for lower wages," and when *caporali* could select younger, more vigorous *mondariso*. The league at Semiana complained about local weeders who "committed a disgraceful act" by following the lead of the Candia weeders.[106]

Employers took the same tack when it came to dealing with the much stronger Lomellina leagues, like those of Valle and Mortara.[107] Intransigence on the employers' part reinforced the workers' determination to strike in March. *Il Proletario* reports that the employers' hard line prompted the formation of women's leagues as the strike deadline drew close. Workers felt that employers would be compelled to sign contracts for the *monda* and other agricultural work, and thereby guarantee an eight-hour day and the principle of hiring local farm workers first. The Tromello employers, supported by the mayor and the subprefect, proposed a nine-hour day. In March the Tromello sowers initiated a work stoppage, defying local authorities' threats to arrest their leaders if the workers went out on strike. The protest lasted several weeks because the strikers rejected a settlement proposal whereby employers would grant a 2.40 lire wage for the *monda* provided that the league accepted a nine-hour workday.

On April 8 the Tromello employers were ready to yield on the eight hours, on condition that the agrarian association fix wages on a weekly basis during the *monda*.[108] Naturally, the strikers found this proposal unacceptable and continued their protest until April 15, when the two parties agreed on an eight-hour day, a minimum wage of 2.35 lire (five centesimi less of a wage, equivalent to thirty centesimi an hour), and the condition that farmers would not hire women for the harvest until the whole male work force was employed.[109]

With this proviso the protesters wanted employers to desist from the tactic applied more and more frequently to use women harvesters rather than men, in order to pay lower wages. The leagues were regularly requesting women to refuse to harvest unless they received a pay rate equal to men's. The reality was that women did not always assent willingly to a deal that organized labor condemned as treacherous, but management sometimes imposed an obligation to harvest rice on the *mondine* when they closed weeding contracts.

Employers used some variations of the same maneuver. In Otto-biano workers went on strike early in April in order to bargain for a *monda* settlement. It started when the employers posted their own conditions in the *piazza:* women were to harvest wheat, too, during the *monda,* and for *monda* wages. This was clearly an order for *mon-dariso* to scab, and to deprive their husbands, fathers, and sons of work and of the traditionally higher harvest wages.[110] The work stop-page ended two weeks later, on April 15, when rice growers with-drew the terms that had been unacceptable to the league, and granted an eight-hour day, a 2.50 lire weeding wage, and promised to hire local weeders first.[111] In Gravellona, after much unrest, the parties also reached an agreement for the weeding, setting for thirty-four days, the eight hours, and 2.50 lire a day. However, they did not want to bargain with the newly formed women's league.[112] The farmers yielded but they negotiated only through the mayor, because pride kept them from admitting defeat in front of the women. This they found too humiliating.

Although wages for the *monda* in Lomellina remained lower than in the Vercellese, the workers' real accomplishment was their ability to endure long strikes, to win an eight-hour day and the right to ensure local weeders' employment before migrants, and to avoid, with some exceptions, being used by farmers to depress harvest wages.[113] This was a major achievement when we remember that the *agricoltori* tried to impose unacceptable conditions on the workers, and in many instances they also had the backing of the police, who would try to force workers to accept employers' demands. The Lomellina protest action shows the firmness of all farm workers, as strikes by sowers in April opposed the employers' stratagems to im-pose outright changes in the work procedures of weeding squads. They knew that any change would eventually affect the situation of all the farm workers in the district.

Other signs of employers' growing aggressiveness were the tightening of their own organizations, their willingness to hit leagues at their nerve centers by arresting and harassing their leaders, and the continual violations of the Vercellese three-year *monda* pact. Signifi-cantly, they responded to workers' demands by resorting time and again to the until then unusual and offensive practices of shifting weeders' squads from one farm to another, or by demanding extraor-dinary operations, like harvesting, from them in order to lower wages, cause unemployment, and generate animosity within the workers' ranks. They continued their opposition to the eight-hour *monda* day. As food prices rose and wage levels remained almost unchanged, workers prepared themselves to resist further impairment of their living conditions also.

Two events in the spring and summer of 1914 aggravated social conflicts in the region. One was Red Week; the other, the outbreak of World War I. On June 7, 1914, the Socialist Party leadership joined anarchists and republicans in an antimilitarist rally in Ancona. At the same time, demonstrators were venting their discontent over the deterioration of living conditions, the lack of jobs, employers' intransigence with labor, and police brutality against workers. During the course of the rally, police opened fire on demonstrators, killing three persons and injuring many others. Thousands of industrial and farm workers in all parts of Italy took to the streets to voice their outrage, and the Socialist Party and the General Confederation of Labor then called a nationwide general strike.

The so-called Red Week (June 7–14) erupted in the rice belt during the 1914 *monda*. The Vercelli chamber of labor answered the party's and the confederation's call, and the weeders came out in force, rushing to set up propaganda committees and spreading word of the protest to surrounding areas. Vercelli had two rallies at the people's house, alternating with two marches led by women holding red banners; as they passed the archbishop's palace, the marchers hissed. In the colorful language of *La Risaia*, "the red banners of that poor bleeding contemporary Christ, the Italian people, passed in front of the place where the priests say they exalt the memory of the old Christ, whom legend still describes as yesterday's subversive, yesterday's savior of the exploited and the tyrannized."[114] The image of Jesus Christ as a socialist rebel incarnated justice, equality, and the struggle of the Italian workers.

In Lomellina bands of cyclists spread the news of the strike to most communes. Weeders deserted the fields, shopkeepers kept their shutters closed, and the streetcars of Mortara did not run on June 9 and 10. On June 11 the General Confederation of Labor broke with the extremists among the strike organizers and called off the work stoppage.[115]

It was not the first time that weeders had joined a national protest (they had participated in demonstrations to protest hikes in the cost of living and, in September 1911, to oppose the Libyan war), but this general strike took place during the *monda* season. This total mobilization of the weeders for the general strike is very significant, because it reveals the women's heightened class and political consciousness. This consciousness told them to desert the fields and oppose the shedding of proletarian blood and the assault against public liberties. As their attitude during this national protest shows, they could unite with enthusiasm and discipline to march for the rights they valued most—bread, justice, and peace.

Red Week influenced the results of the local elections of June and July held under the 1912 electoral law for mayors and city and provincial councilors. Nationwide, the electorate reacted against the excesses, confusion, and miscalculated insurrectionism of some episodes of Red Week by favoring moderates such as liberals and Catholics, and nationalists. But in the rice belt, as in other parts of the Po valley, just the opposite took place. This was most remarkable because these candidates ran alone. Following the directives of their intransigent, revolutionary party leadership, they did not enter into any coalitions, and owed their triumph exclusively to socialist votes.

The conquest of the commune was a decisive step in Italian socialism's program for the liberation of society. It was the call that conjured up the tradition of the medieval commune and of the Paris Commune of 1871, "understood as an antibourgeois and antistate experience of self-government." The socialists captured several municipalities in the lower Po valley in the late 1880s and continued their successes in local elections in the following decades, mainly in northern Italy. Each commune they won was an affirmation of local autonomy against the encroachment of the state and an "experimental laboratory" of Italian socialism upon which the structure of the future state would hinge. Public education, child and health care, housing, industry, cooperativism, excise duties, income taxes, public works and services, charitable and savings institutions were objects of experimentation and changes that buttressed labor resistance and education. In 1909–10 "red" communes undertook different initiatives in an attempt to mitigate the effect of constant cost of living increases on the lives of proletarian families.[116]

The Socialist Party revolutionary leaders developed an "intransigent" program of municipal socialism after 1912. By ruling out coalitions with other leftist parties, they asserted the importance of political autonomy in the city administration as the cornerstone of the future democratic system. The socialists won 330 municipalities, including Milan and Bologna, in local elections in 1914, held in a very politicized atmosphere in the wake of Red Week; they more than tripled the number of communes won in 1910. In the Vercellese, thirty-three out of fifty communes went socialist; two district capitals, Novara and Mortara, became "red" communes, and as the editorial in *Il Lavoratore* put it on July 3, the moderates in the Novarese "met their Waterloo."[117]

In the rice belt, among the items on the agenda of their rural "municipal socialism" were more schools with refectories and day-care centers for workers' children.[118] Progressive sectors of Italian society began to reflect on the importance of day-care centers in order to alleviate the impact of poverty upon children of destitute families in the first half of the nineteenth century. Poor working mothers were abandoning their infants in increasing numbers to foundling hospitals or, if not, lacked the time to care for them. Many children grew up suffering from neglect. With state subvention, private charitable groups or individuals, the church, or sometimes manufacturers, set up day-care centers, mainly in northern cities. Thus day care was already a well established institution at the time of the countries' unification.[119]

The commune of Tricerro can give us a good idea of what "municipal socialism" could do. The socialists had already been in power for a year by the time of the 1914 elections. During that year, the socialist city council voted a salary for the town midwife and allowed expectant mothers to use her services free of charge. It also provided a milk subsidy for poor mothers, added a fourth year of schooling for boys, set up a free preschool center, gave clothing to destitute children, and soup and subsidies to the needy.[120]

But although socialist majorities in local communes and towns in the countryside might have improved workers' lives further, the outbreak of World War I, followed by another economic crisis, put an end to "municipal socialism" as it had been planned. The sudden return to the region of thousands of migratory workers from neighboring countries already at war swelled the huge masses of the unemployed. The growing wave of grain speculation increased bread prices. These were some of the tremendous problems awaiting the new municipal administrations. They met this enormous challenge courageously, mainly in the realm of public assistance, but it was a completely different situation from the one they had envisioned at election time.

Antonio Salandra was prime minister by then. Giolitti resigned from his fourth ministry in March 1914 and the Giolittian era came to an end. The conservative Salandra opposed collaboration or compromise with democrats and socialists. He was an advocate of strong government and an enemy of reform; he was disposed to support a policy of repression in dealing with the widespread social turmoil, the upsurge of revolutionary socialist activity, and a very precarious economic situation. It was his government that was to lead Italy into World War I in May 1915. With the radicalization of social and political conflicts during Red Week, Salandra, more than ever, held that compromise was out of the question. However, after the socialist parliamentary and local triumphs, the Vercellese farm workers felt more confident in their ability to win completely on the issue of the placement offices. As previously stated, in March employers had agreed with the FRAP to include the idea of placement offices in a written, districtwide pact, but they had put off any concrete talks until harvest time.

I shall dwell on the struggle at harvest time to the extent that it is related to the weeders' problems. The harvesters' goal was to set up an institution to regulate all farm workers in the Vercellese. The weeders, the largest group and the most prone to fall victim to competition from migrant *mondariso*, would be the main beneficiaries of such an arrangement. The main battle for the 1914 weeding conditions was fought during the sowing in April. Now, the harvesters wanted to fight for the regulation of the 1915 *monda*, but the FRAP overestimated what it could get from farmers. It did not take into consideration that the central government still held the balance, and it decided ultimately on the use of force, wielding power through the prefects and subprefects, and thus outweighing parliamentary and local support. The FRAP engaged in a long, desperate battle in the late summer of 1914, but the rest of Europe was at war too. Against a backdrop of rising unemployment throughout Italy, and the popular fear of Italy's entry into the war, public opinion turned against the workers' demands, viewing them as yet another cause of economic hardship and social unrest. In this tense situation the very resourceful National Agrarian Confederation defeated the FRAP. The confederation was backed to the hilt by the Salandra government.

The strike began on August 26 when employers rejected outright a three-year pact for harvesters, the establishment of placement offices, and some wage increases. Considering the high rate of inflation, these demands were moderate, but moderation had nothing to do with the farmers' desire to crush organized labor. They had lost no time in trying out new antistrike tactics with the central government's help. In his concern for the "right to work," Salandra ordered the national railway to stop trains loaded with strikebreakers. They would stop between stations, closer to the fields. Migrant workers would be escorted under heavy guard from there to the rice fields, and in this way they would avoid confronting strikers. Under these conditions the protest failed.[121]

In March employers in the Vercellese had promised to negotiate a pact with FRAP, which gave them a strike-free season at moderate cost. In the space of less than six months, events larger than those of the rice-belt gains turned the FRAP triumph into a hollow victory, in spite of the socialists' capture of the three electoral districts of the Vercellese in 1913 and of municipal and provincial posts in the 1914 summer elections.

The FRAP defeat was in part the result of labor's confidence in its strength, which had been bolstered by recent socialist successes in local elections, and in the rice growers' word. But the employers' firm stand and the government's extraordinary assistance shattered the hopes of organized farm workers. Those of the Vercellese had hoped to bring about socialism step by step, through partial electoral victories and labor reforms. By then, with the war being fought in Europe, the steady erosion of civil liberties further muzzled organized labor. In August, Salandra had used the war as the excuse to instruct his prefects to prohibit public meetings; in February 1915 the government restrictions extended to private meetings, or any action it regarded as a threat to public order.[122]

The deterioration of living conditions was widespread in the first months of 1915. Mayors of the Vercellese held a special meeting on March 30 to discuss ways of alleviating the distress of the working classes, fearing that their hardships would incite them to protest and threaten public order. The mayors voted to promote, through the mediation of the subprefect, a joint meeting of FRAP and the *Associazione degli Agricoltori* to adjust *monda* wages to the higher cost of living and to rice price increases, which were benefiting rice growers.[123] At the meeting, Cugnolio applauded the plan that substituted "the employment of the political and administrative forces to obtain labor protection," for workers' agitation and strikes. But his optimism was ill-founded. The employers refused to accept the proposal.[124]

The failure of this attempt, the last in neutral Italy, to persuade employers to make concessions through negotiations, shows how difficult it was for local socialists to press labor issues in a changed political situation and amid an antisocialist offensive.[125] Maurizio Degl'Innocenti wrote that "with the Libyan war the painless and gradual growth of socialism inside society gave way to a period of intense social struggle,"[126] of which the August 1914 events in Vercelli are a clear example. The consolidation of conservative forces had limited the rice-belt work force's possibilities of fulfilling its reform program. It limited, too, its part in bringing about the socialization of the land, which was a goal formulated by the Federterra at its very first meeting.

The weeders' struggle stands out as an example of mobilization by a group of women, who tried to improve their labor conditions by challenging the employers' right to perpetuate miserable, unsafe working conditions. In addition, the women forced a measure of recognition from the power structure that had not acknowledged their right to mobilize. In this sense, their struggles for rights and equality did help to consolidate Italian democracy.

Be this as it may, we shall see that whatever setbacks the socialists faced, fifteen years of activity in the rice belt had brought about changes among *mondariso*.

Weeders' Consciousness as Women and Workers

Our brothers, husbands, and sons will never, never depart for war, but only for the revolution.
Weeders of the League of Livorno (Vercellese), April 1915

The Woman Question and the Rise of Feminism

Weeders began their first war-time *monda* job actions and strikes at the end of May 1915. These protests revealed the combative attitude and awareness of common purpose that fifteen years of militancy had given the weeders. During that decade and a half the *mondariso* had changed their perceptions of themselves and of how they fit not only into their immediate surroundings but also into Italy and the world. The process was gradual, to be sure, but we do have clear signs of this process of transformation of the weeders' general perceptions and some yardsticks to measure the change.

One measure is the growth of women's leagues, and the women's interest and degree of participation in political life. In addition, there are articles addressed to weeders in the labor weeklies, some of them written by women but these were not very common. Until it founded *La Difesa della lavoratrice* [Defense of the working woman] in 1912, the Socialist Party had never supported any women's newspaper financially and the socialist press in general very reluctantly published articles by women or on women's issues. Still, articles in the rice-belt socialist press appeared, reproaching men for keeping women in their subordinate status in the family as well as in society, and lectures by women speakers, mostly Socialist Party members, were delivered to women on women's issues. This type of activity reveals the socialist leaders' perception (or lack of it) of the changes in weeders' political awareness. It also shows the socialists' views of the obstacles barring the path to what they called a class consciousness, as well as their own critique of the manner of developing such a consciousness.

Most of these items in the press speak of impatience and frustration with the slow pace of change in weeders' lives, change being described by party members as the women's readiness to join the leagues, pay dues, and heed their organizers' instructions. Socialists often chided weeders and other women workers for their alleged inertia. They seemed to ignore the decades-long labor actions that women staged in the form of strikes, demonstrations, and other forms of protest. Whose fault was it? Some women writers in the socialist weeklies upbraided weeders for their resistance to change, but they blamed men in the Socialist Party too for their indifference toward weeders' issues. Some men writers found fault with men and women, and both sometimes blamed the church and the bourgeoisie for this state of affairs. I shall review the different arguments set forth in this polemic, and see how the debate became more complex in the last years of the Giolittian era. At the same time, I shall try to judge how labor militancy, historical events, political propaganda, community life, and to a certain extent also the press, transformed weeders' lives and enriched their experience as women, as citizens, and as workers.

Arguments the party press advanced were little different from those raised by the woman question, as the debate over the public and private roles of women came to be known in the nineteenth century in Italy and other European countries. With few exceptions, serious analyses of the principles upon which sexual discrimination rested were lacking. The writings and campaigns of the agitator Anna Maria Mozzoni constitute the main exception to the rule. (Chapter 3 contains an exposition of her ideas on women's emancipation.) In the previous generation, many women who participated in the struggle for women's emancipation, such as Giovanna Garcea, Gualberta Alaide Beccari, Erminia Fuà, Aurelia Cimino Folliero, Sara Nathan, and Adelaide Cairoli, believed that they were fighting at the same time for Italy's and for "the woman's Risorgimento," which would result in the emancipation of both women and their native land.[1] Only in the 1890s the term "feminism" will begin to gain currency in Europe and in Americas, and replace the expression "woman's emancipation."[2]

According to the Italian historian Franca Pieroni Bortolotti, the "movement for women's emancipation" in Italy was associated with the idea of a revolutionary social renewal carried out by women and workers. This was in fact how Mozzoni defined it.[3] The "emancipationists" of the Risorgimento were mainly followers of Mazzini, and risked their lives and personal and family stability for the sake of the Italian revolution. Many of these women helped create the image of the "patriot mother," which sketched a sharp contrast in the national imagination to the traditional image of the "angel of the hearth." For Mazzini, "patriot mothers" were politicized women who were devoted to their families but also to the cause of a democratic republic. But women like the revolutionary Adelaide Cairoli or the constitutional monarchist Aurelia Cimino Folliero committed their entire families to revolutionary action. Thus, they became agents of historical change and, in this role, they transcended the Mazzinian ideal of "patriot mother," and, through different approaches to the woman question, succeeded in reaching women of all social classes and helping them improve their situation.

It would had been purposeless to cling to Mazzini's conception of women's emancipation. He ruled out the possibility that women might overcome judicial, political, and social inequalities before the revolutionary renewal of Italian society would give birth to the democratic republic.[4] These women lived a wide range of political experiences and formed political networks that included men or were sometimes structured around women's journals.

Their approach to the woman question ranged from moderate to radical. The proponents of these two tendencies, whom the historian Judith Jeffrey Howard labels respectively "reformers" and "feminists," had a variety of programs for propaganda and action. The "reformers" like Erminia Fuà stressed in general that women should be educated in order to further social progress. Education would enhance their status and prepare them to better fulfill their family duties, which included the need to earn a living, if possible as a teacher. Women should be self-sufficient but shun political involvement. Fuà rejected the views of the more radical "feminists" who upheld the model of the independent, emancipated woman, educated but also politicized, demanding political rights, committed to political, social, and economic change or revolution. "Feminists" also put forward the archetype of the individualist, antifeminine "manwoman."[5]

This simplified delineation of two different approaches to woman's emancipation does not adequately recognize the many other arguments on the place of women and men in Italian society, which adopted aspects of both strands of thought, and added and combined new elements to them.[6] The historian Karen Offen uses the terms "relational" and "individualist" feminism to describe "reformers' " and "feminists' " modes of argument on behalf of women's emancipation since the mid-nineteenth century to the present. Offen points to the prevalence of "relational" over "individualist" arguments in the Western world in the past century.

> They ["relational" arguments] featured the primacy of a companionate, non-hierarchical, male-female couple as the basic unit of society . . . . Relational feminism emphasized women's rights *as women* (defined principally by their childbearing and/or nurturing capacities) in relation to men. . . . By contrast, the individualist feminist tradition of argumentation emphasized more abstract concepts of individual human rights . . . while downplaying, deprecating, or dismissing as insignificant all socially defined roles and minimizing discussion of sex-linked qualities or contributions, including childbearing and its attendant responsibilities.[7]

In her history of the women's press in Italy from 1861 to 1922, Annarita Buttafuoco writes about these two feminist orientations and refers to the "relational" as the one maintaining the principle of "equivalence," and the "individualist" maintaining that of "equality." The principle of "equivalence" extolled the specificity of the feminine experience, celebrating so-called natural characteristics of women, "(sensibility, pacifism, capability for devotion and sacrifice), demanding that these become the guiding values of civilized society and of human relations in general." Motherhood was a symbol of strength and women's moral superiority. The principle of "equality" proclaimed that women and men were equal in order to fight male domination. Men appealed precisely to the different reproductive functions of the two sexes in order to deny women the rights they enjoyed. Mozzoni's approach to the woman question establishes her as the major exponent of this tendency. But Buttafuoco observes that usually there was no clear-cut separation between the two orientations, which were not based on any strong theoretical ground, and that activists and their newspapers sometimes identified with both of them.

These tendencies continued to impress feminism in the twentieth century, when the concept of "equivalence" became more dominant than that of "equality" in feminist thought and action. Pieroni

Bortolotti regards feminism as a more moderate movement than the emancipationist struggle of the previous decades, when its followers were not yet divided into groups representing different theories, political positions, creeds, organizations, and programs. However, Buttafuoco does not detect any loss of vitality or any fundamental change in this emancipationist ferment until the period from 1911, when Italy entered the Libyan war against Turkey, to the beginning of World War I. It was then that a group of women responded to the official call for women to join in the war effort on the civilian front by adopting a new posture. They identified themselves with, and began to work for, the state's nationalistic goals, once and for all obliterating the internationalist and pacifist ideals that so far all feminist associations had stood for. The split foreshadowed the disbanding of the feminist movement in the Fascist era.[8]

In the decades following unification, women became more and more visible in Italian society. In increasing numbers they were taking agricultural, industrial, teaching, and a variety of other jobs in the tertiary sector. Notwithstanding their different orientations, emancipationists felt the need to work for the transformation of society and for shaping it according to a feminine ethic. They had to cope with economic, educational, legal, and cultural discrimination against women. Women worked for little or no remuneration at all. The legal and educational systems and the official culture ratified and crystalized sexual inequalities into something more tangible than tradition. It was against this that activists of different persuasions fought a relentless battle.

Shortly after unification, the civil code of 1865, which defined the legal position of all women in Italy, became a great source of disappointment. Like its counterparts in western Europe and the United States, the code sanctioned the principles of male domination. The Italian code remained almost unchanged in its basic provisions for more than fifty years. If married, women exercised fewer rights than their husbands and became minors under their guardianship. Married women property owners needed their husband's authorization when making decisions about their property that went beyond simple administration. A married woman also needed her husband's consent to carry out any "public act," including participating in charitable work, joining a woman's association, or subscribing to a newspaper.[9]

Mozzoni attacked the civil code, for she regarded the legal subjection of women and the male absolutism it endorsed as the basis of the authoritarian political and social structure that she wanted to see abolished.[10] Radical and moderate women's networks shared Mozzoni's claims and campaigned for the amendment of family law. Their ideas on motherhood informed their campaigns. They criticized the absolute legal impunity with which men could seduce women and father "illegitimate" children. Seduction and paternity suits were illegal in all but some exceptional cases, and feminist groups called for laws ensuring the general right to search for paternity. Buttafuoco states that paternity suits would have allowed single or unmarried mothers to claim the right to endure their condition with dignity, without being overwhelmed by feelings of guilt:

> To maintain the dignity of motherhood in or out of wedlock meant, in theory, to upset the very meaning . . . of the family . . . —grounded on man's control of reproduction and on women's and male minors' dependence—because the value of motherhood itself, above all the potential autonomy of the relation mother-child, the possibility of building up *another* family . . . independently from the presence of the man, were affirmed and extolled.[11]

The majority of the activists also wanted to introduce divorce legislation and eliminate the blatant difference in the position of men and women in the definition of adultery in the criminal code. "For a married woman," explains Jeffrey Howard, "this meant any encounter with a man other than her husband. For a man, it necessitated not only keeping a concubine, but also doing so without a shred of discretion."[12]

The field of education was correspondingly limited for women. The Casati law of 1859 introduced two years of compulsory education and admitted women into normal schools. Minister of education Francesco De Sanctis established separate institutes of higher education for women in 1878. In 1874 the universities opened their doors to women students, at first only as auditors but nevertheless stirring the hostility of male students. In any case, the first Italian woman lawyer, Lidia Poët, was denied the right to exercise her profession in 1883 despite a battle fought by emancipationists around the issue. The feminist Teresa Labriola, also a lawyer, suffered the same fate. As in the case of Poët, the court of appeals canceled her name from the law list in 1913.[13]

Cultural and scientific realms helped to validate the sexist notions that underlay the codes. They perpetuated traditional prejudices against women by providing them with a "scientific" basis. The most advanced cultural groups in Italy at this time embraced the philosophy of positivism. Scientists of the positivist school of criminal anthropology studied women's psychophysical characters and "demonstrated" their inferiority by measuring skulls and weighing brains. Women's smaller crania and beardless faces reflected infantilism and little intelligence. According to Cesare Lombroso (1836–1909), the most outstanding scientist of this school of criminology, women were less intelligent and more indolent; they also had less moral sensitivity and no special artistic, scientific, or professional inclination. As we shall see below, gynecological studies served to reinforce these misrepresentations of women. In addition, the idealist philosopher Benedetto Croce denied any validity to the woman question.[14]

Positivist philosophy, along with its misogynist cultural prejudices, permeated the Socialist Party. The party officially assumed that the problem of women's discrimination in society, in the family, and in the work place would find an automatic solution only with the establishment of a new socialist order. It generally dismissed feminist issues as middle-class concerns. Because of this, many socialist feminist groups had to carry out their actions in favor of women of the lower classes without the party's assistance. In 1881 Mozzoni founded a women's league in Milan (*Lega promotrice degli interessi femminili*). Emancipationists set up several more leagues in other Italian cities. The socialist Emilia Mariani, active in the Turin league, was one of the main promoters of a federation of leagues in 1896.

Another women's association was the Women's Union (*Unione femminile*), founded by the seasoned feminist and socialist Ersilia Maino Bronzini in Milan in 1899, and transformed into the National Women's Union (*Unione femminile nazionale*) in 1905. Although not all the members of the *Unione* were socialists, the association directed an intensive campaign almost exclusively among women and children of the working class and persons living in destitution in urban and rural Italy. It also fought for the principle of equal wages for equal work. Maino, its founder, maintained that women's struggle should be centered in their "difference," in their specific role of mothers, to gain the recognition so far denied to them by society. She exposed the Socialist Party's lack of concern for the need of proletarian mothers. The *Unione femminile* always had uneasy relations with the Socialist Party because it was, after all, a multiclass group and the party despised the class bias of its middle-class members.[15]

Argentina Altobelli was also a socialist, a feminist, and a workers' organizer. Deeply involved in the battles of the agricultural proletariat, she was one of the co-founders of the Federterra in 1901 and its secretary from 1906 to 1926. She was a highly respected member of the Socialist Party and was appointed to its executive in 1908. During her emancipationist campaigns in favor of divorce, women's suffrage, and their participation in political and union life, she sometimes had to contend with the opposition of male party members.[16]

The party opposed socialist women's attempts to create a separate women's group until 1912. It based its resistance on the notion that such a group would pursue feminist ends. Because feminism was a cross-class movement, it could become a disruptive issue for a party that stressed class conflict.[17] Finally, the first women's newspaper sponsored by the party saw the light in January 1912. During the Reggio Emilia national congress in July of the same year, Anna Kuliscioff, the most prestigious woman in the party, convoked the first women's congress also. This gave life to the National Union of Socialist Women (*Unione nazionale delle donne socialiste*). Kuliscioff explained that far from espousing a "socialist feminism" that stood in opposition both to socialist theory and to the principle of the class struggle, the *Unione* would deal exclusively with the organization of women workers.[18]

The failure of the Socialist Party to recognize the cause of the woman, by addressing the special ethical, political, economic, cultural, or psychological causes of their inferior status for so many years, had to do in part with ideas still prevalent in Italian society about women's work—that it should be essentially domestic work and was the natural outcome of women's biological destiny. Therefore, activities outside the home were unacceptable, in conflict with the dominant ideology, and were frequently seen as an exceptional and temporary phenomenon.[19]

But it had to do also with the position of many socialist leaders and of Kuliscioff, the most influential woman in the party, regarding women's oppression. She distanced herself from Mozzoni during the inaugural congress of the Italian Socialist Party in 1892. Mozzoni remained outside the party, while Kuliscioff, and with her the whole leadership of the Socialist Party, never proposed any special program for proletarian women. They drew the line between feminism and socialism, and emphasized instead the need to organize and protect women.

Pieroni Bortolotti asserts that "in 1892 the Italian socialists had, among other things, liquidated the campaign for women's emancipation."[20] Kuliscioff's "contradictions," to use Maria Casalini's words, responded to her interest in preserving harmony within the party, beset as it was, like other European socialist parties, with antifeminist prejudices. To avoid hostility from the party and the public at large, she had to set aside the feminist premises she had expounded two years earlier in her lecture "Il Monopolio del uomo." The lecture met with strong resistance from party members and from then on Kuliscioff tried to avoid in-depth discussions of the controversial issues she raised in "Il Monopolio," such as the structure of the family. She called it an economic question that would be settled with the advent of a socialist economic system, and geared her policy on the woman question toward conciliation between the "individualist" and "relational" orientations.[21]

Claire LaVigna concludes that Kuliscioff approached the woman question with an attitude of Marxist ambivalence. Describing her at the Zurich congress of the Second International in 1893, LaVigna observed: "Kuliscioff's old loyalties to her sex could emerge, and she moved an amendment to that motion [factory legislation, protecting mainly women labor] to include the 'principle: for equal labor equal salary between the two sexes.' " But a month later at the Reggio Emilia national congress of her own party, she voted with the majority to table that same amendment in order to avoid divisive issues, "which might alarm the leaders of the workers' movement, whom she was carefully courting."[22] In 1897 she publicly declared her independence from the feminist movement, for its members were only concerned with freedom for women of the middle class and made clear her intention to give precedence to socialism over feminism.[23]

For several years Kuliscioff focused the party's attention on protective legislation for women. Her campaign for the law on child and woman labor is a clear example of this tendency. She prepared a draft that provoked a heated debate (see chapter 3, p. 73). Protests rose from the socialist and emancipationist camp, with Mozzoni attacking the principle of "protection" for women that would further ensure their inferior status, mollify their labor militancy, limit their labor opportunities, and offer employers a pretext to exclude them from the factories that employed a high proportion of women. As Buttafuoco explains, this was the dawn of the era of heavy industry in Italy, and big entrepreneurs were successfully competing against small industries that employed a high percentage of children and women.[24] Women lost many of the new jobs. The modern factory entrepreneur avoided hiring protected labor, and because of this women missed the opportunity to become a skilled labor force. In fact, Evelyne Sullerot noted that Italy had "the worst record in dealing with the whole question of women work" in the 1960s,[25] a situation that LaVigna ascribes to the Italian socialists' reluctance to let women compete for better-paying and more skilled jobs. Kuliscioff sacrificed the cause of the woman worker for the sake of proletarian unity.[26] Pieroni Bortolotti observes:

> A political animal at bottom, Kulisciocff had understood that to launch the password of the limitation of woman factory work at the beginning of the century meant to meet the most secret desires of the majority of male workers, who would interpret it (as they in great part did) as the start of their wives' "return to the home," whereas the old password of women's emancipation had perhaps awakened in this majority the justified fear of seeing the authority of the head of the household contested by that of the employer.[27]

The chambers of labor were the most active in campaigning for the law. Despite its objections to the draft, the *Unione femminile* also supported it. It questioned the absence of a stipulation of equal wages for equal work in it. Kulisciocff had decided not to include it despite the many voices in its favor. Many feminists reasoned that without such a clause, the bill would perpetuate the disadvantages of women vis-à-vis male workers.[28] In any case the Socialist Party showed little interest in the draft and socialist deputies gave it scant support in parliament. On June 12, 1902, parliament finally passed a law on woman and child labor, but one proposed by the liberal government and much milder in tone than the socialist draft.[29] And the law made no provisions for women agricultural workers.

Only in 1910 did Kulisciocff reemerge as a feminist, when she began campaigning for women's right to vote. Women's suffrage and the Socialist Party had a rather involved history. We can trace the first petition to enfranchise women back to the 1870s. The radical Mozzoni submitted to parliament the first petition, which was supported by several thousand signatures, in 1877. From then on, she continued to draft new petitions. But the Socialist Party did not give serious consideration to women's suffrage even after it included the women's right to vote in its minimum program of 1900. In 1904 the republicans instead took the lead, not surprisingly because Mozzoni herself became influential in republican circles, and had the issue of the women's vote presented by its main advocate in parliament, deputy Roberto Mirabelli. The fact that in 1907 the socialist deputy Andrea Costa refused to sign Mirabelli's second proposal gives an idea of the deep roots that antifeminist prejudice had in the Socialist Party, a prejudice it had absorbed from Italian culture and that it conveyed to the workers' federations. The Mirabelli episode reveals, according to Pieroni Bortolotti, that "regarding the women's question there was an entire zone of Italian socialism essentially more backward than bourgeois democracy itself."[30]

In 1905 the newspaper *Unione femminile*—the press organ of the Women's Union—published the results of an inquiry on the issue of women's vote that it had conducted in 1903. The indifferent or negative tone of many of the answers, especially if penned by socialists, upset the survey's organizers. Maino replied privately to some of the respondents, among them the socialist deputy Ivanoe Bonomi, who in his answer had pointed to womens' immaturity as an impediment to their exercising the right to vote. She retorted: "Where stupidity is concerned, it is found in both men and women. Why must one make an exception of her? With your theory, to be truly honest, one would have to disenfranchise three-fourths of the men who have the vote."[31]

Italian feminists formed the first prosuffrage committee at Milan in 1905. More committees sprang up in many cities including Rome, the seat of the central committee, while Mozzoni prepared a new petition to submit to parliament in 1906. Despite the massive presence of socialist women among the agitators, Kuliscioff denied them her support, and condemned them for allying themselves with bourgeois groups. At the same time Kuliscioff discouraged other more hesitant socialist women from joining the campaigners, thus closing off the possibility of the committees having what many socialist women wanted—a definite socialist imprint. Kuliscioff's attitude, Buttafuoco observes, contributed to the fragility of the Italian suffrage movement, which was continually beset with divisions, misunderstandings, contradictions, and mutual distrust.[32]

In 1910, when Kuliscioff began championing the cause of the vote for women, she met with great resistance within the party. Her chief opponent was her companion, Filippo Turati. He was even leery of giving the franchise to male peasants from the Mezzogiorno. For Turati, these men—and all women—were easy prey for manipulative priests and landowners. He argued too that women did not show any interest in getting the vote, and therefore they could wait.

Echoes of Turati's opinion had reached the rice belt, where a contributor by the name of Consuelo mocked Turati in 1906 in *Il Lavoratore*: "Turati, the holy man of piecemeal reform (*riformette*), opposes the extension of the vote to women because, according to this high priest of reformism, the female sex's vote would weaken socialist forces at the ballot box." Consuelo urged women to shake off their age-old inertia, and participate in the fight for the right to vote.[33] Kuliscioff launched a decisive attack on Turati and the party, blaming the socialists for the alleged unpreparedness of women to exercise the right to vote.[34] Kuliscioff hoped that the polemic would also serve to close the gap between the party and its rank and file, bringing the former closer to the latter in order to "infuse a new youth into our party," which she perceived in a profound crisis:

> The Socialist Party in Italy suffers from premature old age. . . . That is why youth does not come to it and seeks other ways. Those who still come, and, for lack of higher idealistic content, give themselves to the most vulgar anticlerical propaganda, which goes against the sentiments of the masses and drives them away, would find—in a strong agitation for truly universal suffrage without restrictions—an oxygenated air for their moral lungs, a food for their eagerness for expansion and for work, and then they would flow back, numerous and ardent, into the ranks, and restore life to us.[35]

Kuliscioff's campaign succeeded in changing the party's stance on the vote for women in the 1911 socialist national congress of Modena. Socialist women working in the prosuffrage committees thought that the Modena resolution would strengthen their position within the organization. However, the party attached a provision asking them to disassociate themselves from prosuffrage committees, which counted nonsocialist women among their members, in the name of socialist unity. It threatened recalcitrants, such as the fiery suffragist Emilia Mariani, with expulsion. The measure weakened the committees and the suffrage movement in Italy.[36]

The socialist parliamentary group chose Turati and Treves to introduce the amendment of the bill on universal male suffrage extending the right to vote to women on May 15, 1912. But the defeat of this amendment, also proposed by Mirabelli and Sydney Sonnino, was predictable.[37] However, the party's late support for the women's vote was a triumph for Kuliscioff, albeit tarnished by disappointments. She carried out a brilliant campaign, but the agitation for universal suffrage failed to arouse a general enthusiasm for women's vote, nor did it infuse into the party the new life it badly needed. Worst of all, women were left without the weapon that Kuliscioff and many feminists considered essential for the defense of their economic, social, and political goals.[38] But the socialist parliamentary bloc, which had doubled in size after the 1913 elections, made no move to further women's suffrage.

With its insights, initiatives, hesitancies, difficulties, and contradictions, the party press of the rice belt reflects all this flux of thought and action on the woman question. It is repetitious in its attention to the same questions and the same solutions. Its editors were undoubtedly well aware of the difficulties involved in reaching a community of women, a high percentage of whose members were either illiterate or not in the habit of reading. Therefore, we must assume that only a small proportion of the writing reached its intended audience, and in many cases only by word of mouth.

Workers' newspapers also published articles and letters by women, possibly members of local Socialist Party sections, urging women to organize. Generally, women writers seemed more dissatisfied with other women than with men. These calls probably responded to a plan aimed at stirring women out of what the authors criticized as their lethargy toward political and labor problems. This was a process that was taking much more time than that of awakening men's socialist consciousness. If these letter writers were party members, might not some of them have been unwilling to challenge male socialists' authoritarian attitudes and the party's inadequacies in its handling of the woman question?

On July 21, 1906, Libera Costa in *La Risaia* appealed to weeders' sense of class solidarity as a means to prevent their being dragged like stupified beasts of burden "along the road to the Calvary of this life" by "the class sucking the blood and sweat of the proletariat." Women, Costa wrote, had to free themselves from male domination also. Women lived "here as a doll, there as a servant, everywhere as property." Yet she concluded by urging women, rather contradictorily, to stop opposing men's political interests in order to help them in their liberation struggle,[39] to avoid being controlled mentally by men who exploited women, and to heed the calls of male socialist politicians and labor organizers instead, many of whom were members of their own families.

Her message hinted strongly at many weeders' opposition to men's political and league activities, which had been encouraged by the church. In June 1910 a writer for *La Risaia*, signing herself simply as "a woman," hoped that women would abandon all attachment to superstitions and pay more attention to the teachings of the Socialist Party—the only party that had done anything positive for women, especially mothers compelled to work to feed their children, and thus forced to leave them alone at home.

Another writer, Marietta Cagna, identifying herself as a mother of three, a socialist, and an anticlerical, wrote in 1911 that the blame for the worsening financial situation of the workers' family lay with the wives, because they not only refused to join the leagues but also verbally abused their husbands when they returned home from socialist meetings. Cagna never missed going to these meetings with her husband, for she thought that her presence there helped strengthen the labor movement.[40] But Cagna did not propose ways of helping women with child care or other obligations during the meeting times.

Some men also encouraged women to unlearn old habits and join leagues. In Costanzara a male league member complained: "and you, women . . . still pay attention to what the priest says; if he says that women who have husbands in the league are consorting with the Antichrist, you agree; if he says that you have to run away unless he quits the league, you agree." The writer, instead, urged women to join the league alongside their husbands; and, in this way, "there will be victory for us."[41]

In 1902 a Lomellina contributor to *Il Contadino* presented opposing reasons as to why women had to organize: on the one hand, to earn wage increases, necessary because the workers' families could not survive only on men's earnings; and the other, to limit women's work. Employers were hiring increasing numbers of women in the place of men. This was a dangerous trend from the economic point of view, the writer reasoned, because it caused men's unemployment, and from the moral point of view, because it kept women away from the home, to which they had to dedicate as much time as possible. But there was a third consideration: unorganized women committed acts of disorder at weeding time.

A month later the same writer (presumably) explained that women should understand that so far men have considered them "inferior beings under guardianship," and, if unorganized, they "will continue to be [slaves] in the proletarian family." Instead, "the organized woman becomes a conscious citizen . . . men's companion."[42] Were the weeders actually convinced that the mere act of organizing would transform them from "slaves" into "companions"? Perhaps they feared that by joining an organization they would have to surrender whatever control they had over the allocation of their time and over labor opportunities to organized men, many of them family members, for benefits they could hardly imagine.

More appeals to women were published in times of economic distress, as in March 1908, when many men were leaving the rice belt to look for work elsewhere. A male contributor to *La Risaia* called on women to join leagues and fight for better wages and full employment, and to turn a deaf ear to the priest's plea for resignation to economic hardship.[43] Men appealed continually to weeders to change "medieval outlooks" or abandon "superstitious beliefs."

F. A. C., writing in *La Risaia*, thought weeders were weak because they did not imitate men in joining organizations to fight for their rights; they needed to raise their heads high to "breathe in freer and purer air." For him, the priests and the bourgeoisie were the oppressors; the priests preached resignation and taught prayer, and the bourgeoise "have made your lives miserable and mean . . . inside and out of the home, after having already corrupted you when you were young." Such submissiveness helped these class enemies to subjugate still more male workers. Women, F. A. C. concluded, needed men to guide them in setting up leagues.[44]

In January 1915 a certain Carlo Borgo went a step further in this argument. He called upon socialist husbands to help women fight against social and economic injustices. "It is, therefore, one of the socialist's highest duties to instruct and educate our children's educators, to tear them away from the crooked claw of the clergy that has held them fast since birth."[45]

Men also blamed themselves for being directly responsible for the women's lack of militancy and for stopping them from joining leagues. A certain Chaughi explained in *Il Contadino* that the status of women could rise only as a result of a broader and more radical process: "After all, the man looks down on the woman," and condemns her to slavery. This ought to end, but only if the woman is in full possession of herself and wants to be free. This amounts to a profound revolution, leading to changes such as the end of religion, wars, prostitution, violence, and the oppression of the weak by the strong.[46] Also in *Il Contadino* the anonymous author of "The Revolution at Home" thought of achieving social redemption by another means. He drew a very somber picture of socialist husbands who extolled the ideas of equality and justice among their friends, and then went back home to assume the role of master and order his "slave" to serve him, and, if he was drunk, even abusing her verbally and physically. The writer indicted the husbands:

> Then you will cry that the woman is not with you in the long struggles fought for the conquest of justice, that she is a slave of the old ideas and of religious and priestly prejudices. . . . But it

is your fault. You yourselves have erected a barrier between your ideals and her. . . . She cannot understand the battle for equality because at home you are the master and she is the slave.

Therefore, as the first step toward final victory, husbands should establish relations of justice, freedom, and equality in the family and make "the revolution at home."[47]

An unsigned article in *La Risaia* criticized the members of the San Grisante league for employing their wives and daughters in more stable jobs, but for miserable pay, instead of enlisting them in the leagues to fight for better wages.[48] In 1912, at a meeting of Novarese farm workers, a delegate insisted that "the weakness of women's organization is due to the complete indifference of male farm workers."[49] Women were not unaware of the role of men in mobilizing them or in convincing women of the need to join leagues in order to agitate for better conditions during the *monda*. This was the sense of the resolution of the 1913 meeting of the women's league of Ceretto (Lomellina): "All the male comrades have the duty to urge wives, daughters, and sisters to register with the league on Sunday, April 6."[50] In Lomello (Lomellina), a male league member ruefully observed that some of his fellow workers, who seem "honorable, decent socialists, permit their daughters and wives to commit the highest treason—that is, to act as strikebreakers."[51]

These varied press sources show that, as at the turn of the century, the main deterrents to women's organizing continued to be the church and men's attitudes in the home. The voice of the priests penetrated into the sanctuary of the family, and even interfered with men's labor militancy. Men inhibited the activities of women, which they feared might disrupt the family hierarchy that assured its male members their authority and their right to make decisions for the women of the household. What changed during the years immediately before World War I was the growing number of both women and men voicing disapproval of traditional attitudes. They expressed their dismay about the rank-and-file's slow rate of change, and about the enormousness of the task they faced. Women's leagues organized slowly and men still continued to represent them at their own league meetings.

In the wake of the 1906 strikes, there was a flurry of weeders' organizational activity. A league of five hundred women was organized in the commune of Vercelli, but its two secretaries were men.[52]

At Asigliano (Vercellese), where organizers asked women to rip off "the mask that blindfolded" their eyes and mobilize like men, the weeders responded and formed a league run exclusively by women.[53] At the end of 1906 in the Vercellese there were about seven leagues, but in the Novarese there was only one, in Lumellogno.[54] But, in any case, at the 1906 national meeting of rice workers, the rice-belt organizers expressed regrets that weeders were unable to send women delegates and no women delegates attended the regional meeting of rice workers at Vercelli a week later.[55] The absence of rice-belt women from labor meetings shows how difficult it was to overcome the traditional patterns of behavior sanctioned by the majority of men, by the church, with some exceptions by the party leadership, and, of course, held by the weeders themselves. In contrast, many Emilian weeders, inspired by the organizing activity of the indefatigable Emilian labor leader Argentina Altobelli, and with a longer tradition of mobilization, readily participated in labor associations' militancy.

After 1907, women's leagues declined as the economic recession that followed the 1907 financial crisis deepened, but they also lost support in response to increasing agrarian militancy. In 1911 there was a change in this pattern. At Trino (Vercellese) weeders won the eight-hour day, thanks to the energetic activity of Vercelli organizers who managed, momentarily, to break the sway of the local priest over the workers. This victory, however, culminated only in the establishment of a men's league (and the men, as elsewhere, represented the weeders in the organization),[56] and, a year later, the opening of a People's House in the town by the Socialist Party. But, as *La Risaia* points out, the church had enough power over the majority of women so that at the time of the opening of this house many weeders gathered at the opening celebrations, but only to jeer at the socialists. *La Risaia* took the weeders to task for scorning male socialist workers:

> The priest preaches that if you do not abandon the People's House you will be excommunicated; they do not want young men and women to have fun together. But where were their protests when their young men and women were compelled, by necessity, to sleep together in the fields after weeding? . . . And, after all, when women have to get married, it is better that they find partners at the People's House than in the fields or at church.[57]

The Catholic Church, the Socialist Party, and the Family

As ambivalent as male socialists were on the women's question, the Catholic Church remained another obstacle in the way of weeders' organization. The church failed in its attempts to set up Catholic leagues in the rice belt, but it increased its political and moral authority over people living in the lands surrounding the Po valley with other systems of farming and land tenure. There were no masses of wage earners, the ones socialists were successful with, and the women who lived in these regions made up the majority of the migrant weeders. In *Il Contadino* we read complaints about the "obnoxious undertaking" of the Lomellina clergymen, who sought employment for squads put together by priests of the area of Piacenza, Bobbio, and Milan. The wages and the length of the workday agreed upon were so unfavorable to the migrant women that the socialist newspaper claimed that the priests were siding with the *agricoltori*, and doing "everything possible to ruin the cause of the exploited." It was not uncommon for rice-belt federations to accuse priests of organizing squads of strikebearers.[58] So the church's organizing did directly affect conditions of labor in the rice belt.

But the chief influence of the church lay elsewhere, in its centuries-old hold on the faithful, particularly women. Although, as I said, its influence was beginning to weaken in the rice belt, priests still exercised sway over the more pious in the confessional booth and through antileague sermons delivered from their pulpits on Sundays. In *Il Contadino*, "bi-gi" indicted the priest at Ottobiano who denied absolution to a group of women league members, condemning them to *eternal damnation (sic)* until they handed their union cards over to him.[59]

In response, the socialists launched anti-Catholic and anticlerical campaigns in an attempt to neutralize the church's influence.[60] They diffused the notion of Jesus Christ as the advocate of the oppressed and the incarnation of justice and equality, and counterposed to it an image of the church as the defender of privilege and exploitation, especially in the countryside. They also developed the program of municipal socialism, with its emphasis on secular elementary education and the laicization of the city's institutions. This type of action was a continuation of a nineteenth-century tradition aiming at the laicization of society. This was understood as the rejection of all church interference in the state and society, and the defense of the natural, human, and rational values that developed outside and in contrast to Catholic tradition.

For political reasons related to the destruction of the pope's temporal power and the papal condemnation of Italian nationalism, the founders of the nation supported secularization. The laicization program of the Italian Socialist Party in the pre–World War I period had its roots in both the secular policies of the bourgeois liberal rulers of united Italy and in international, atheistic, and scientific political and cultural currents. Radicals and democrats who embraced rationalistic ideas spread their creed through Masonic lodges. Free thinking (*libero pensiero*) societies were founded in many European cities (Brussels and Siena by 1863). In addition, their ideas were disseminated through publications and the First International. The first prominent supporters in Italy were the *garibaldini* or sympathizers of Garibaldi (1807–82), the popular hero of Italian struggle for unification. Many of these radicals, champions of the principles of universal brotherhood and popular emancipation from all types of authority, militated also in anarchist and socialist groups and in the first workers' organizations.[61]

At the turn of the century the socialists' anticlerical propaganda intensified with the church opposition to the proliferation of socialist leagues. After 1904 Catholics became increasingly involved in politics and in labor organizing,[62] and slowly sought a political agreement with Giolitti, which they actually reached at the time of the 1913 national elections. This was a reversal of the secular and anticlerical stand that had prevailed since the time of the Risorgimento.

Despite the hostility between clergy and organized labor, many weeders remained regular churchgoers. "One might even argue that women were less tempted to secularization, for the new bourgeois world was primarily male-dominated," explains Eric Hobsbawm.[63] Jane and Peter Schneider refer to the rivalry between men and the church, who both upheld the ideals of domesticity, for the control of women in Sicily. They wrote: "As the Church reached out to women, men doubled their efforts to control them."[64] Similar conflicts occurred in rural France at the turn of the century where, according to Roger Magraw, "not only was churchgoing seen as diminishing manhood and independence, but the priest was viewed with suspicion as a rival to the husband, as a threat to a man's control over his womenfolk."[65]

A contributor to *Il Contadino* affirmed that "the priest always meddles in politics, and his politics consists of disunifying the family . . . and especially of making the woman the instrument of his political and economic aims." The Sartirana (Lomellina) league called on women to join it and offered this encouragement: "Maybe you feel ashamed of entering our hall, and don't you know that the league is formed by your own fathers and brothers? So, cheer up! and come to register."[66] The women's response to this and other articles on the subject never appeared in the newspapers, so we may only speculate that some weeders preferred to stay away from a union structure that duplicated the authoritarian family structure.

The fact that there was a multitude of weeders and of women farm workers in the Po valley who did decide to change their faith and become socialists, must be considered a remarkable event in Italy. But as already noted, the widespread allegiance of Italian women to the church stopped many male Socialist Party members from supporting the vote for women. The socialist Maino wrote in her introduction to the 1905 volume that contained the results of the inquiry conducted by the newspaper *Unione femminile* on votes for women:

> Read the statistics, you men who want to deny us the right to vote because we are irresponsible and slaves of the priest, and you will see that the education of youth, our education, was left in his hands *by you,* and that today he is hastily making a monopoly out of it. And it was not women who allowed this to happen.[67]

There was an inconsistency between the Socialist Party's plan to emancipate the oppressed and its failure to liberate women from their inferior status. In contrast, the church was consistent in its teachings if only because it promised deliverance after death. That is why Kuliscioff attacked not the church but the Socialist Party for its position on women when she began to militate in favor of women's suffrage. "The party," she wrote, "deplores the religious penchant in women which disguises, after all, the unconscious yearning for . . . an imaginary redemption from slavery, for attaining the ideal of motherhood, symbolized in the adoration of the Virgin Mary."

If women are chained to the church it is the party's fault. "What has the Socialist Party done to bring women down from heaven to earth, to translate fantasy into reality . . . and to be less deceptive toward women than religion, less priestly than the priests?"[68]

Nevertheless, Kuliscioff acknowledged the achievements of the organizers in the Po valley[69] and saw these as a step in the right direction. In the speech she prepared for the 1910 party congress, she acknowledged this ambivalence in the party's attitude. The party addressed women workers less directly than it did men; the party had to assist women not only as workers, but also as mothers, wives, daughters, and sisters, as part of a family in a society that relegated them to a dependent role.

Cosetta Lazzari, talking about the support women needed from the Socialist Party, touched on the same idea:

> Certainly women are a field to cultivate; but we cannot pretend that they will suddenly desert the churches and the religion that welcome them; nor can we look to them to join anticlerical associations that neglect or even exclude them. It is necessary not to forget this basic rule of thumb in winning women over to our cause: women eventually will have to escape the clutches of church domination. In order to help them in this, we have to assist them in remolding religious conviction into a belief in doing things here and now. This is what I call social education.[70]

We also find echoes of this in Giselda Brebbia's 1913 speech to the Vercelli women at the People's House. The public applauded when she said that it would be cruel to keep back women who had no consolation in this world from seeking comfort in the church. When women could find in the family the joys they were entitled to, and men would abandon the taverns, then, according to Brebbia, the influence of the church would end.[71] Women went to church hoping to find the assistance they could not find elsewhere, as well as to forget economic and social pressures and have a respite from a long exhausting day.

Weeders who embraced socialist ideas sometimes turned socialist celebrations into ceremonies typical of the Catholic Church. The imposing 1906 protest demonstration at Vercelli against the cancellation of the Cantelli regulation was a case in point. Here weeders, accompanied by other women sympathizers and children, donned the clothes they kept for festivals and marched solemnly, as though they were parading in a religious procession.[72] This was the ritual they were much more familiar with.

This slow conversion touched other celebrations too. We read how couples began more frequently to marry in civil ceremonies only, how they did not baptize their children, and gave them nontraditional names, such as Libero, or how some Italians abandoned the use of Catholic funeral rites. In Lomellina, a devout farmer angrily fired a work squad because, while weeding, the women were singing an irreverent popular song recounting a certain Father Riva's breach of the code of sexual behavior.[73] The socialists thought that they should fill the social void for women who left the church. Consequently, they set up People's Houses, or in their absence, league halls, where women could meet friends, socialize, shop in the cooperative stores that they housed, discuss problems, and request assistance to solve them. As a member of the San Grisante (Vercellese) league pointed out in 1907, if the women made the decision to join the leagues, they would "learn," contrary to common wisdom, "that socialists do not want the disappearance of religion," but a better religion.[74]

We read in *Il Contadino* that in Gravellona (Lomellina), "the priests set you [the women] traps wherever they can; the recreational center of Saint Agnes is one of these; . . . it is there that you start being taught to stay away from the leagues and from the socialists." In Sartirana the members of the league complained: "We ask young women why they recall the league only during Carnival, when the administration allows its use as a ballroom? To dance with an empty stomach because of the scant and wretched meals, and with broken bones, must certainly not be the greatest pleasure. . . ! Get organized." Thus, People's Houses were proposed as a substitute for churches. And the People's Houses were—as a speaker at the inauguration of the Tricerro's People's House called it—"a symbol of the new idea, which in contrast to the temples of the past, does not stand for superstition . . . and in contrast to the barracks, does not stand for brutal force or for fratricidal war."[75]

Socialist symbols replaced other Christian images, and bourgeois ones, such as official national heroes, as well. Working men and women heroes took the place of saints and notables consecrated by the establishment in the socialist pantheon. In Bianzè socialists transformed the celebration of St. Valerio Peasant, the patron saint, into a party festivity. Solemn ceremonies were held on the anniversary of the executions of Giordano Bruno, and (after October 12, 1909) the Spaniard Francisco Ferrer, two champions of free thinking. Liberal circles and labor associations in Europe staged protests against Ferrer's execution by the Spanish government.[76] He became an international martyr to antimilitarist agitation in the years before World War I. A military court condemned him to death after holding him responsible for a wave of antimilitarist protests, followed by a week of mass rioting, the "Tragic Week," in Barcelona.

Democrats in Mortara held a demonstration to protest Ferrer's execution on October 16. It ended with the league members marching to city hall to demand that the mayor hang the flag at half-mast for eight days. After shouting in vain for ten minutes, the women—"the most excited" in the crowd—cried: "Everybody to the mayor's!" In front of the mayor's house they brandished their clogs in their hands and threatened, "out with the flag willy-nilly!" When they saw that the mayor was trying to escape, they challenged him, saying: "The flag is not yours; we have paid for it; out with the flag, out with the mourning!" The demonstrators left only after the mayor hoisted the flag and they were assured that the city government had canceled a public concert scheduled for that day.[77] As a result of the women's outcry, the city of Mortara, albeit reluctantly, mourned the execution of the Spanish internationalist.

We also see a notably decreasing birth rate, despite the church's reminders to the weeders that birth control was a sin. "The parish priest," according to a member of the Cappuccini Vercellese league writing in 1910, "goes so far as to stick his nose in where it doesn't belong." At Sunday Mass, this priest referred to the "monstrous, malicious practices among spouses in town" because the number of births was declining. By not procreating, married couples were living in grave sin. The writer suggests why there was a decline in births: in the past, workers were bent under the sway of the church and of the powerful; they had large families, and became victims of hunger, illiteracy, crime, and other social hardships. Furthermore, he continued (from the vantage point of 1910), "bread did not cost 45 centesimi a kilogram, and . . . the question of the high cost of living did not exist."[78]

This article in a socialist newspaper is rather noteworthy because the party in general gave scant consideration to the issue of birth control or neo-Malthusianism, as it came to be known in the nineteenth century. In Italy two groups campaigned for population control through contraception: the lay moderates gathered around Giuseppe Prezzolini and the journal La Voce [The voice], founded in 1908, and the anarchists, among them Pietro Gori, Francesco Saverio Merlino, and Luigi Fabbri. For different reasons, they were concerned with limiting the size of the proletarian family. Anarchists founded a neo-Malthusian league in 1913. But with some exceptions, neither the circle around La Voce nor the anarchists linked their arguments on contraception to any discussion of changes in the conditions of women in the family and society. Women continued to be mothers or future mothers of fewer children, thanks to men's initiative, a circumstance that allowed women to be better and more conscientious mothers and have healthier children. Very few women took part in the debates. Most of the times eugenic interests prevailed over feminist concerns for women's sexuality. Seldom was a voice "raised to proclaim the legitimacy of womanly selfishness," that is, the use of contraception which would make motherhood a fully responsible choice.

The enemies of contraception included religious associations, the medical establishment, moralists, and nationalists, these last stressing the importance of maintaining Italy's population growth in view of the gradual drop of the fertility rate since 1862, which occurred mainly in the north. The country needed soldiers and workers to maintain its power and attempt colonial adventures. Moralists referred to the liberating aspects of contraception as moral perversion, egoism, eroticism, and lust. Most physicians opposed abortion and contraception, and advanced the argument, among others, that women did not have sexual needs apart from reproductive activities. The great representatives of the Italian positivist school of science, such as Lombroso, proved experimentally "that women lacked sensitivity and sexual needs, and that it did not pay to discuss their proverbial frigidity." The true feminism or true valorization of women would consist, instead, in the glorification of their biological role.

Gynecology, well established as a special academic discipline in the nineteenth century, emphasized the biological approach to womanhood. The distinguished socialist gynecologist Tullio Rossi-Doria affirmed not only that "the vegetative life must prevail in the woman," but also that a woman who left her home to work in a factory was going against biology.[79]

Feminists were too weak to fight back and take the risk of questioning the centrality of the woman's maternal function, for society in general would condemn this in the same way it had denounced woman's right to vote, or the calls for civic equality. Feminists dealt cautiously with issues of sex education and birth control, in part because of their own unpreparedness to discuss them. In part, they felt threatened. Encircled as they were "by church, conservative parties, and also by the sometimes equally acute moralism of socialists," they realized that any talk of birth control would hurt the image of respectability they were trying to construct.[80] If feminists kept silent, Italian socialists officially never disavowed Rossi-Doria's position, which on the issue of women's work coincided with that of many male socialists who resented women's competition in the work force. Rossi-

Doria, as well as a large sector within the party, supported the passage of protective labor legislation for women that would raise the cost of women's labor and encourage employers to hire men instead. For many years, the majority of socialist leaders revealed their lack of preparation to deal with the issue of contraception and sexual education, declaring that these topics belonged to the private sphere. For only two years, from 1912 to 1914, did the party journal *Critica Sociale* introduce a lively and comprehensive debate on neo-Malthusianism, which the war interrupted. The articles touched on subjects such as prostitution, virginity, sexual ethics, and contraception.[81]

Inasmuch as no political, social, or religious institution offered sexual education to rice-belt workers, they alone had the responsibility for decisions they took in matters of birth control. As in other Italian regions, mothers generally kept daughters completely ignorant about topics such as the reproductive cycle. M. B., a Vercellese weeder born in 1895, explained when she was interviewed in 1976 that, when adult women were talking about the subject and girls appeared on the scene, they used to say "Keep quiet. It is foggy," and changed the topic. N., also born in the Vercellese in 1909, declared: "We neither heard any talk about sex at home, in the stable, or in the rice field, nor were we taught anything about childbirth, and we came to know something when our wedding was imminent, through some friends who were already married."[82] Nuto Revelli's interviews with women of Cuneo in the north and Campania in the south reveal also the same degree of unawareness. The onset of menstruation came as a surprise or, better said, as a shock to the majority of the interviewees. Not even older sisters told younger ones about their own experience.[83] With no access to methods to control fertility, they turned to abortion, practiced by a friend or a midwife, or even self-practiced.[84]

Despite all the People's Houses, new symbols, heroes, and celebrations, those socialist champions of change, the propagandists who helped organize weeders, never spoke of altering the structure of the male-dominated family.

"Your true friend," writing for *Il Proletario* in 1913, thought that women had to understand that they had rights and needed to unite with other women to achieve them; if left alone, they could only become society's slave. The author—like many other women—describes woman as "a husband's servant"; yet neither she nor other women writers advocated the change in family relations that would allow her to enjoy full rights. After all, for these writers, the major thrust of their remarks was the need to organize for the battle to end bourgeois exploitation.[85] Their silence on the family issue parallels the party's caution in dealing with this topic.

After she opted to abandon the polemic on family reform in 1892, Kuliscioff had been advising moderation. Weeders were of course far from envisioning any form of social structure other than the family in which to bring up their children, for they were economically dependent first of all. They had to accept their subordinate role at home, and their responsibilities as breadwinners in the fields and factories. The civil code and Italian culture in general sanctioned male domination in the society and in the family. The two institutions that competed for influence over weeders' lives—the Catholic Church and the Socialist Party—bolstered this domination.

This may explain why weeders acted with such autonomy as part of the working class and with such constraint as family members. We may find other reasons too. The Biellese, then a district in the province of Novara, was an important textile center. The Biellese mills employed mostly women, involved in numerous strikes; they were "very combative as for social struggles, but very timorous and irresolute in their everyday behavior and in the family, and hesitant to engage in any political activity."[86]

In contrast, anarchist feminists in nineteenth-century Argentina, most of them European immigrants, mainly from Italy, developed a radical critique of the family and its authoritarian structure. The Italian anarchist Errico Malatesta went into exile in Argentina in 1883. His Italian-language paper, La Questione Sociale, published works on women's issues and attracted all-woman groups of militant anarchists. Some of them tried to reach a wider female audience and founded the newspaper La Voz de la Mujer [The woman's voice] in 1896. Although mostly identified with the Spanish community, its editors published articles (some in Italian) on international anarchist feminism and writings by Spanish, French, and Italian activists, including Mozzoni. Despite the universal appeal of its arguments, the newspaper failed, because it expressed criticism of the family in terms

> too outrageous for the mainstream. . . . Most women . . . would have been scandalized by attacks on the church and family and by the explicit discussion of sexuality. To many women, the family was a site of oppression, but it was also a locus of relative security in a rapidly changing world in which they had few alternatives. The abolition of marriage without other radical

changes in their position would have left women even more exposed, threatening not greater freedom but possible loss of "financial" help and status in the eyes of the community.[87]

Weeders felt the obligation to preserve life, to nurture their children.[88] Like many other women, they knew that economic conditions precluded the possibility of carrying on this mission alone, and they clung to the family as the place where they could fulfill the duties that their beliefs dictated. M. B., a weeder from Vercelli born in 1895, stated in 1976 that women submitted completely to the authority of their husbands. V. B., a man, affirmed: "Women could not raise their heads. They were treated like dirt. Women were the most victimized persons: they had to obey their father, their brothers, and their mother-in-law when they got married."[89]

The Law of Universal Male Suffrage and Weeders' Wider Concerns

The socialist and workers' leaders' criticisms of weeders' attitudes, as well as their appeal to organize, seem to imply that many of the difficulties in the labor struggle were due to the *mondariso*'s attitude. However, we can see that in the late 1940s and in the 1950s the Union of Italian Women (*Unione donne italiane* or UDI), a women's organization of the left founded in 1944, was still fighting to eliminate the injustices to which women field workers were subject. The UDI appealed to the *mondine*, too, to raise their consciousness as workers and as women for the struggle for emancipation: concretely, by establishing child care centers for migrants' children, and building a sense of solidarity between migratory and local *mondariso*. After more than three decades and under changed circumstances, many of the old problems remained.[90]

In the pre–World War I period, workers' leaders demanded a committment from the weeders. A contributor to *Il Contadino* told women to "join the league, devote some time to the reading of our newspaper and of socialist pamphlets. Educate yourself, become conscious,"[91] without mentioning who would assist women in this endeavor, or if these readings offered anything of interest for them. Angelica Balabanoff advised them that if husbands were uncouth and brutal, instead of complaining, wives had to advise them to join socialist organizations. Women would still remain in a condition of inferiority, of course, but at least they would have a free man as a husband. (Balabanoff, the revolutionary socialist who spent several years in Switzerland organizing Italian women emigrants, always dismissed feminist principles, which she considered of interest only to the middle class.)

In *Il Contadino* an optimistic writer urged women to form leagues in order to pull husbands, brothers, and lovers behind them.[92] Many appeals called on mothers to fulfill their mission by educating socialist children, but they had to stop being slaves to their own prejudices in order to accomplish this. Then, according to a certain Cesarina Ciccotti-Borelli, a wife could say to her husband: "Here I am, I am your true wife, I am twice yours: in the faith that took us to our marriage, and in the faith that guides us to the conquest of the future."[93]

Another journalist indicted the mothers who, influenced by priests, forbade their daughters to attend the inauguration of the banner of the women's league.[94] The article "Proprietà e militarismo" urged mothers to rebel against the government that sent their sons to wars to serve a fatherland that belonged "to the masters and the capitalists."[95]

Organizers burdened weeders with more responsibilities when men of their families began to emigrate overseas. In times of economic hardship, the labor movement was unable to improve workers' situation. This weakness was due, they argued, to a lack of women's support. Throughout the men's stay in America, the number of new departures or family separations seemed to hinge upon women's allegiance to the leagues.[96] "Compagne!" wrote a contributor from Sartirana, "the emigration continues and you remain alone. Recognize that it is your turn to support the struggle, and if you do not want to retreat, your interest must be that of joining the league in place of your migrating husband, son, or brother."[97]

Instead, the situation created by Italian capitalist development was at the root of the workers' troubles. It transformed the inhabitants of the Po valley into a mass of landless workers and also indirectly affected economic and social conditions in regions surrounding the rice belt, which were apparently untouched by the capitalist mode of production. But these regions, like the Po valley, became a reservoir of cheap labor; industry, with its irregular pace of growth, was unable to absorb the overabundant workers. Neither the government nor the Socialist Party, and least of all the weeders, had a solution for this structural problem. Competition for jobs was inevitable, and this eased the way for employers' maneuvers to reduce wages and impose harsher working conditions.

Weeders became part of the working class against this backdrop.

The spurts of protest in the last years of the nineteenth century, which preceded the formation of the leagues, already speak of their class consciousness, explicit in their refusal to accept employers' tactics. From 1901 on, the weeders pursued concrete goals, ones they considered vital for their lives and those of their families and community, such as a shorter workday and full employment. The first socialist labor organizations were taking root by then and they assisted weeders in shaping a campaign intimately related to the labor struggle in the entire region. One of the results of this cooperation was the gain of a shorter workday, an unusual victory that put weeders ahead of the majority of workers throughout the world at that time.

Socialist campaigns on health care taught them to reject employers' assurances that rice fields were healthy places, and that with quinine to cure malaria there was no need to limit the workday. The *mondariso* were aware that long hours of weeding could harm them in many ways and that malaria was only one of the hazards they were exposed to. Weeders took quinine distributed free of charge when they contracted malaria. This does not mean at all that they trusted doctors and medicines in general. Older farm workers that Aiazza and collaborators interviewed in 1976–78 remembered that they either refused to go to the doctor or to the hospital when they and their children were sick or, if they went and the treatment did not succeed, resorted to healers who treated them with prayers and herbal concoctions. They also relied on pharmacists who were "the repositories of a popular medicine with which the people identified," rather than on physicians, "the repositories of a science completely unknown to them, and who furthermore were also mighty and a center of power (in many towns doctors held political office)." When the *mondine* suffered from dermatitis of the hands and legs caused by contact with certain weeds or the chemicals that polluted the water, they used a treatment consisting of rubbing the ailing skin with garlic, alcohol, gasoline, or "black salve."[98]

By pursuing specific plans the weeders were also changing the consciousness and the working conditions of many migratory squads. Even the government, yielding to the general outcry caused by the weeders' actions, took the exceptional step of passing the law on rice cultivation of 1907 that put a legal limit on the workday of both local and migratory *mondariso*.

The men of their families generally kept them out of labor organizations and meetings, as well as political activities. Considered from another angle, perhaps men's presence in organizations and activities deterred weeders from participating in them. Their reluctance to join contrasted sharply with the tremendous initiative they employed in declaring strikes, or in staging other forms of protest. They relied on direct action and, it must be said, none of the weeders' critics ever accused them of hesitancy or apathy when they resorted to it. No doubt they caused organizers plenty of trouble during the weeding campaigns! In Lomellina, organized women had to pay the same dues as men, 10 centesimi a month. *Il Contadino* explained:

> The organized women who are being affected by this decision must not be alarmed and use it as a pretext to leave the organization. They have to convince themselves that the women's leagues cause the federation higher expenditures and much bigger disturbances than the men's leagues, and that the central committee was not and will not be able to pay the organized women continuous and efficient assistance . . . until the women were persuaded to put the federation in the position of meeting their just demands.[99]

This is a rather uncommon resolution, because generally women paid lower union dues, and the organizers used this as an excuse to ignore their labor problems. In the rice belt, the leagues' negotiations with farmers and migratory squads for each *monda* season were costly and time-consuming.

But the breakthrough in women's militancy came about concurrently with other critical historical events in 1911–12. In 1911 the General Confederation of Labor launched a call for more intensive work among proletarian women and the Socialist Party finally founded a women's biweekly, *La Difesa della lavoratrice*. In 1912 the party held the first socialist women's congress, and its members decided to organize the National Union of Socialist Women (*Unione nazionale delle donne socialiste*). In May of that year the government passed the law on universal male suffrage. It is possible that the combination of all these developments, and also the distressing situation workers were living through as a consequence of the ongoing economic crisis, brought about an outburst of political activities among the working masses. All these factors created a climate of rising expectations that stirred weeders to propaganda and labor activities in a drive that neither the agrarian counteroffensive nor the economic recession could dampen.

In 1912 the party set up sections and People's Houses in Tricerro (Vercellese) and Vespolate (Novarese),[100] which attracted weeders too. This new energy produced a weeder's league in September 1912 at Nicorvo (Lomellina). On the day of the inauguration the *mondariso* marched, according to *La Plebe*, without "fear . . . of carrying openly their banner, symbol of their union along the city streets."[101] The numbers of Lomellina women's leagues continued to increase in 1913: in April there were seven (with a total of 414 members), in addition to three "mixed" leagues.[102] (The twenty-three men's leagues had around nineteen hundred members.) While the weeders participated in the 1913 electoral campaign and contributed much to the impressive socialist triumphs in the rice belt, they also joined the leagues. The urgency of their organizing drives was underlined by the increasing incidence of agrarian anti-labor violence. In December 1914 women's leagues in Lomellina numbered seventeen, with 1,439 members,[103] while there were twenty-eight men's leagues, with 4,332 members. On January 25, 1914, weeders from Livorno Piemonte (Vercellese) formed their own league, with a membership of 250.[104]

At its June 7 meeting the league's president, Antonietta Camerano, introduced the main speaker, Paolina Perrone, a socialist from Turin.[105] The significance of the meeting lay not so much in Perrone's call for women to find salvation in socialism, but in the organizing of a conference by women, for women, and whose main speaker was a woman. This would have been unimaginable a few years earlier. A higher degree of literacy in Piedmont and Lombardy by 1913 may have contributed to the weeders' politicization.

Another woman speaker was Giselda Brebbia, a socialist teacher from Milan and, along with Angelica Balabanoff, acting editor of *La Difesa della lavoratrice*.[106] Between June and December 1911 Brebbia visited different communes and gave speeches on "women and socialism," or "women and the labor movement." She continually pointed out the need to give women the vote, to allow them to participate fully in public life, and to provide all of them with maternity insurance.[107] In April 1913 she attended the Socialist Youth Congress at Abbiategrasso (Lomellina), and urged young hearers to intensify their propaganda efforts, oral or written, toward women to win them over to socialism.[108]

Alma Dolens (a.k.a. Teresita Pasini), an active suffragist and one of the most prominent Italian pacifists, lectured on the topic of women's organization during her speaking tours in the region. At the inauguration of Vespolate (Novarese) People's House in 1912, she delivered a speech in which she encouraged women to participate in the class struggle; she urged the men not to consider their wives as "either obedient servants or devoted lovers," but as affectionate companions.[109] Alma Dolens continued to speak at party events in 1913, sometimes with Margherita Sarfatti (the future sponsor of cultural affairs in Milan under Fascism).[110]

On May 10, 1914, women formed a Women's Socialist Section at Vercelli.[111] Later in the year, Brebbia addressed them on "Women in Economic and Political Life." She strongly urged that women, as breadwinners, should learn about economy and politics, and struggle side by side with men. Many women attended the lecture,[112] and their presence may be viewed as a sign of an awakening interest in new approaches to their own political, social, and economic problems.

Yet the 1912 electoral law excluded women from the vote. It would have been useless to expect Giolitti to enfranchise women. He maintained that women could not vote because all their public acts required prior authorization by their spouses, as if women had to have their husbands' authorization to work in the factory, as the socialist Claudio Treves argued at the chamber in June 1913. We may add that the 1907 law on rice cultivation recognized the ability of the weeders between fifteen and twenty-one, in other words minors, to sign their own labor contracts, in violation of the civil code that declared invalid any deed or contract subscribed by minors without parental authority.[113] Thus, women's militancy, and legislation responding to this militancy, were making the civil code obsolete long before it was actually reformed.

However, farm workers' federations expected women to assist in the October 1913 elections, as can be seen in the following appeal in *La Risaia:* "Women weeders! Urge your men to vote for Modesto Cugnolio. For without him you would still be laboring long in the fields and receive the same miserable pay you did years ago." This demand had a double thrust: first, to urge women to persuade their men to vote for socialist candidates; second, to counter priests' calls from the pulpit not to vote for socialists, and particularly not for Cugnolio, the FRAP leader.[114]

We have an example of how women played a role, albeit indirect, in the administrative elections of Gravellona (Lomellina) in June 1914. Women not only urged their men to vote for socialist candidates but they also attended socialist rallies (including one at which Brebbia spoke), marched in parades, and sang socialist songs during the campaign.[115] Their cooperation in organizing the June 1914 general strike (Red Week) to protest the police killing of antimilitaristic demonstrators in Ancona is a sign of their interest in playing a larger role in public life, and of their concern about issues transcending the limits

of the rice belt, such as those related to national policies. I wish to
recall here the Mortara weeders' determination to commemorate the
execution of Francisco Ferrer in 1909. Although we have no direct
testimony of what weeders thought about women's suffrage, it may
be assumed that, because many of them campaigned so enthusi-
astically at election time, some of the *mondariso* would have liked to
cast their own ballots.

The suffragist and pacifist Alma Dolens celebrated the energy
with which Italian women of all classes and places joined in propaganda drives in factories and rural dwellings. Her observation is not
without a premonitory note: "Let us rejoice at the fact that the woman
demonstrated that she has a political consciousness to anyone who
insists on denying it. Before worrying about the criteria with which
the majority of women would go to the polls, let's worry about
whether the deputies who have incurred a debt of gratitude to their
allies, the suffragists, will remember it, breathing the soporific air of
Montecitorio [the chamber of deputies]."[116]

Pietro Campastri from Valle (Lomellina) set forth his thoughts
on women's duties in June 1914, directly before the local elections. He
asked women to help get socialists elected to the local administration.
Women would then have to stay away from the fields and stop competing with men for jobs, he reasoned. Without women in the fields,
men could get higher wages and, of course, with socialists in the local
government, they would have strong allies in negotiating a fair contract. With improved living conditions, women could stay at home
and act as full-time mothers to their children, something they could
not do before.[117] There is no doubt that many men thought the same
way, but we do not know whether there were women who shared
this view and considered weeding unappealing work, preferring to
work only in the home.

This fundamental question underlies specific debates on wom-
en's roles, such as their duties in election campaigns, their allegiance
to the hearth or to organized labor battles: How can women participate in public life? In 1913 Cosetta Lazzari spoke at the second Italian
anticlerical students' congress on the need to encourage women to
take part in public life and to take a special interest in social questions.
Only through active participation in public affairs would women dispel the "myth of their own inferiority" and get the same rights as
men, she argued.[118] At least some weeders might have been exposed
to the subject; *Il Proletario* of Mortara published her speech.

In April 1915, on the eve of Italy's entry into World War I, Maria
Goia, a workers' organizer and one of the acting editors of *La Difesa*

della lavoratrice, called upon weeders to take to the streets in support of the Socialist Party's stand for neutrality. She urged them to take over the town *piazza,* the traditional preserve of men, to support nonintervention in the war:

> Women should never be absent from public life, women should not allow half of humanity to determine the destiny of the other half. But if there ever was a moment when silence was a crime, it is now, oh mothers, wives, sisters, women of Italy. . . . It is up to you to save civilization. . . . Join the socialists in the denunciation of war.[119]

Goia's message may have articulated aloud what many weeders felt in their hearts about the war. The socialists and the Catholics took an energetic antiwar stand, and the April 1915 prefects' special reports on the state of public feeling in the event of war shows that this was the position of the majority of the Italian workers. All the European belligerent countries had the support of their workers with the exception of Italy. Italian labor was the only one to refrain from supporting the war. Nowhere else in Europe did proletarian women raise their voices to oppose the war, a circumstance that makes the weeders' stand on Italian intervention quite exceptional.[120]

In addition, weeders had to cope with severe problems whose roots were in the past, but which were becoming increasingly serious: cost of living increases, new offensive tactics by employers, and a rising rate of unemployment. Instead of demoralizing the workers, the situation encouraged them to close their ranks. Women's consciousness had changed. For example, in April 1915 Vercellese employers sent an urgent message to communes and leagues because they sensed that Italy was going to end its neutrality at any moment and enter the world war. Employers called on all weeders to be ready to replace men on the farms in case of mobilization, and to enter their names in a special register.[121] Weeders responded to the call for registration and to the entire scheme with indignation and mockery.

The Dessana league chided the farmers for their "honey-coated words" in invoking the defense of the fatherland and the rice growers' grain. Could they, asked the weeders, make these "gentlemen believe that we have forgotten their past blandishments, including those they lavished on us during the last strike?" This was an ironic reference to the hardship they suffered during the 1914 harvest strike. The farmers' appeal to patriotism came after their recent rejection of the mayors' proposal for an increase in *monda* wages (on March

30). The weeders considered this invitation to be little more than a "mockery" of the Vercellese proletariat.[122] Additionally, there was the concern that farmers might take advantage of the general atmosphere of fear at the time, so that in hiring women they would drive down men's wages.[123]

Women had come a long way. Now they responded to the farmers' request with irony, scorn, and a bit of their own mockery in a manner that shows a self-assertiveness that years of struggle in the leagues had developed. It also reveals how the women's world had transcended narrow concerns of the home and the village to touch on concerns of the world at large, as the Livorno (Vercellese) women's league retorted:

> Gentlemen, do you think we women can commit such an ignominy? This is too much, you insult us. We, women of Livorno, say to you: our brothers, husbands, and sons will never, never depart for the war, but only for the revolution.[124]

Conclusion

Focusing on the history of the weeders from 1861 to 1915 makes it possible to appreciate the results of mobilization in an important rural sector of the Italian labor force. Farmers with large investments in the rice belt created a huge female proletariat, and this women's wage-labor force made sacrifices, risking health and well-being for the sake of employers' profits. Weeders, as wage workers, had to accustom themselves to the conditions dictated by their employers, but also had to accept certain necessary precepts regarding authority, discipline, and belief. These were imposed upon women, at varying times and on different occasions, by employers, government officials, police, the church, and the men of their own communities and families. They represented, in fact, the whole economic, political, and social structure of Italy in the lives of the women.

At the turn of the century, the Italian economy was flourishing and many Italians, including those in the government, expected a peaceful era of sustained economic progress, which would benefit all social classes. This, therefore, would alleviate or do away with unrest among the workers. At the same time the reformist socialists, who held the majority in the party, advocated a minimum program that tied the betterment of the working class to successful industrial development and the passage of social reforms. This decision was based on the party's analysis of the Italian political and economic climate at the time. A liberal regime would help pave the path to socialism. It saw two processes, one in the countryside and one in the city, already creating the objective preconditions for the end of the capitalist mode of production. In the countryside, the land concentration process was producing the prerequisites for a socialist transformation of society, while a high degree of industrialization was giving rise to similar conditions in the cities.

Weeders, as well as all the rural workers in the Po valley, bore the brunt of much of the economic and social dislocations of this period. They mobilized to act against the particular conditions created by these changes. In this they were assisted by the Socialist Party. In the rice belt, employers could hire weeders from outside the region to replace the disobedient local *mondariso*, break their resistance, and artificially create a mass of jobless weeders. This tactic compounded the problem of structural unemployment in the rice belt, which resulted from the scarcity of employment opportunities in industry and the lack of agricultural jobs during the winter. The absence of a more diversified agriculture and of other forms of land tenure systems aggravated the problem of unemployment.

During their mobilization the weeders became part of a class and they caused a similar transformation in the agriculturalists, who changed from a group simply conscious of its professional and social status, accustomed to taking all its privileges for granted, into an organized interest group that formed federations and lobbying groups to counteract the workers' power. Rice growers acted in this way not only for economic reasons, but also as a matter of principle, extending their attacks to Prime Minister Giovanni Giolitti's social policies, which had fostered the weeders' mobilization.

The weeders' labor actions were among the most radical that farm workers carried on in pre–World War I Italy. A comparison of the collective actions of other groups of women of working-class families in Europe and in the United Stated reveals that they all had common traits. Like the weeders, women headed labor protests and demonstrations on their own, defending their autonomy from unions' directives. They defied the employers, the government, the army, and the police when their female consciousness led them to struggle for conditions that they deemed just and necessary for themselves, their families, and their communities. Weeders had a clear class consciousness and by withstanding employers' conditions they became vital participants in the labor struggle of the Po valley. Their claim for better health served to ignite social conflict. But they had also a female consciousness that gave their collective action solidarity, motivation, impetus, and independence that organizers and party members, not to speak of the rest of Italian society, often misunderstood or disdained as something illegitimate. Neither gender, nor the nature of weeding itself—unstable, temporary farm work, combining local and migratory women—was an unsurmountable obstacle to change for weeders.

Similarly, the economic, social, and political circumstances under which women's mobilization took place did not prove an effective barrier to the force of weeders' demands. An aggressive foreign policy and a slowdown in industrial growth contributed to the crisis-ridden period that antedated World War I. The economic slump caused by the Libyan war and the consolidation of employers' militant antilabor confederations were some of the events presaging the end of an era. Even the Italian feminist movement split between opponents and supporters of the two wars. But the *mondariso* closed their ranks and expanded the scope of their public concerns. As they fought the battle for social progress, for peace and justice in the rice fields, they achieved rights that transformed their lives.

Notes

Chapter 1

1. The following works deal with the history of rice growing in Italy: Paolo Bodo, *Le consuetudini, la legislazione, le istituzioni del vecchio Piemonte* (Turin: G. Giappichelli, 1950); Luigi Messedaglia, "Per la storia delle nostre piante alimentari: il riso," *Rivista di Storia delle Scienze Mediche e Naturali*, 20 (Jan.-Feb. and March-April 1938); Emilio Motta, "Per la storia della coltura del riso in Lombardia," *Archivio Storico Lombardo*, 4th ser., 4 (1905); Novello Novelli and Giovanni Sampietro, "La risicoltura in Italia," in *La risicoltura e la malaria nelle zone risicole d'Italia*, edited by Italy, Ministero dell'Interno e Ministero dell'Economia Nazionale (Rome: Provveditore generale dello Stato, Libreria, 1925).

2. Aldo de Maddalena, *Prezzi e aspetti di mercato in Milano durante il secolo XVII*, Università Commerciale "Luigi Bocconi," Istituto di storia economica diretto da Armando Sapori. Serie Studi, vol. 1 (Milan: Malfasi, 1950), p. 43. Rice was mentioned as a familiar crop in a letter of Duke Galeazzo Sforza in 1476.

3. Messedaglia, "Per la storia delle nostre piante alimentari," pp. 52–57. Very soon merchants were exporting rice beyond the Alps (see Motta, "Per la storia della coltura del riso," p. 395).

4. Novelli and Sampietro, "La risicoltura in Italia," p. 12.

5. Ibid., p. 20.

6. Fernand Braudel, *The Mediterranean and the Mediterranean World in the Age of Philip II*, trans. Siân Reynolds, vol. 1 (New York: Harper & Row, 1972), pp. 69–70.

7. Carlo Cipolla, "Per la storia delle terre della 'bassa' lombarda," *Studi in onore di Armando Sapori* (Milan: Istituto Editoriale Cisalpino, 1957), pp. 668–69. After 1540 the new Spanish rulers found out that rice export favored their

balance of trade and helped to mitigate the impact of scarcity of food in bad years (see de Maddalena, *Prezzi*, p. 48).

8. Novelli and Sampietro, "La risicoltura in Italia," p. 26.

9. Ibid., p. 20.

10. Pieraldo Bullio, "Problemi e geografia della risicoltura in Piemonte nei secoli XVII e XVIII," *Annali della Fondazione Luigi Einaudi*, 3 (1969), p. 57.

11. Luigi Faccini, *L'economia risicola lombarda dagli inizi del XVIII secolo all'Unità*. Studi e Ricerche, 6 (Milan: SugarCo, 1976), p. 12.

12. Eusebio Buffa, *Il Canale Cavour e il progresso economico e sociale del Novarese e della Lomellina*, Associazione irrigazione Est-Sesia, Banca Popolare di Novara, Camera di Commercio di Novara, Camera de Commercio di Pavia, Ente Nazionale Risi (Pavia: Editrici Fusi, 1968), p. 125.

13. Raimondo Luraghi, "Wage Labor in the 'Rice Belt' of Northern Italy and Slave Labor in the American South—a First Approach," *Southern Studies*, 16, no. 2 (1977), 116. For the political, economic, and social effects of the introduction of capitalist agriculture in Italy, see Emilio Sereni, *Il capitalismo nelle campagne (1860–1900)* (Turin: Einaudi, 1968, 2nd. ed.), pp. 147–48 and passim.

14. Messedaglia, "Per la storia," pp. 52. Novelli and Sampietro mention the Italian provinces where, in different periods, rice has been or is now farmed: Alessandria, Cuneo, Novara, Turin, Bergamo, Brescia, Cremona, Mantua, Milan, Pavia, Padua, Rovigo, Udine, Venice, Verona, Vicenza, Bologna, Ferrara, Modena, Parma, Piacenza, Ravenna, Reggio Emilia, Lucca, Massa Carrara, Pisa, Perugia, Rome, Campobasso, Teramo, Naples, Catania, and Syracuse; see "La risicoltura in Italia," p. 19.

15. Bullio, "Problemi e geografia della risicoltura," p. 55.

16. Novelli and Sampietro, "La risicoltura in Italia," p. 6.

17. Salvatore Pugliese, "Produzione, salari e redditi in una regione risicola italiana," *Annali di Economia*, 3 (1926–1927) (Milan: Università Commerciale "Luigi Bocconi," 1927), p. 76; Rosario Romeo, *Cavour e il suo tempo (1810–1842)* (Bari: Laterza, 1969), p. 152.

18. Bullio, "Problemi e geografia," pp. 49–50; Romeo, *Cavour*, pp. 147, 621–22, 642–43. See also chapters 1 and 2 in *Cavour*, Tome I (1842–1854), and chapters 9 and 10 in Tome II (Bari: Laterza, 1977).

19. Raffaele Pareto, *Relazione a S. E. il Ministro di Agricoltura, Industria e Commercio (Luigi Torelli) sulle Bonificazioni, Risaie ed Irrigazioni* (Milan: Tipografia e Litografia degli Ingegneri, 1865), p. 232.

20. For the history of the Cavour canal, see Buffa, *Il Canale Cavour*, and Cesare Marchetti, *Cenni storici e descrittivi circa al Canale Cavour ed ai suoi Diramatori e Subdiramatori di proprietà demaniali* (Turin: Stamperia reale della ditta G. B. Paravia e C. di I. Vigliardi, 1878). The canal was 82 kilometers long, running from the Po to the Ticino rivers (see Marchetti, *Cenni storici*, p. 4).

21. Pareto, *Relazione*, p. 21.

22. Novelli and Sampietro, "La risicoltura in Italia," p. 22; Salvatore Pugliese, *Due secoli di vita agricola. Produzione e valore dei terreni, contratti agrari, salari e prezzi nel Vercellese nei secoli XVIII e XIX* (Milan: Fratelli Bocca, 1908), pp. 123–28.

23. Buffa, *Il Canale Cavour*, pp. 152–53.

24. Pareto, *Relazione*, pp. 266–69.

25. Buffa, *Il Canale Cavour*, p. 220.

26. Pugliese, *Due secoli*, p. 165.

27. Buffa, *Il Canale Cavour*, pp. 136–37.

28. Novelli and Sampietro, "La risicoltura in Italia," p. 26.

29. Novelli and Sampietro, "La risicoltura in Italia," pp. 31–32.

30. Pugliese, *Due secoli*, pp. 126–27. For the effects of the crisis on the Italian agriculture in general, see Sereni, *Il capitalismo nelle campagne*, pp. 233–41.

31. Lucio Villari, "Il capitalismo della grande depressione. La crisi agraria e la nuova economia (1873–1900)," *Studi Storici*, 10, no. 1 (Jan.-March 1979), 27–36. The Italian parliamentary inquiry on agriculture (*Inchiesta Jacini*) was voted in 1877, and its results published between 1881 and 1885; the acts of the British Parliamentary Royal Commision on Agriculture, between 1894 and 1896. The *Société Agricole* of Paris promoted research on the rural crisis in 1879. The German statistics on farms and agricultural workers of 1881 and 1895, and the American census of 1890, fall into this same category. Protective tariffs were established by Italy in 1878; by Germany in 1879, by France in 1881, and many other countries; among the exceptions were the Low Countries, Belgium, and Great Britain.

32. Pugliese, *Due secoli*, p. 269.

33. Market prices of rice per hectoliter (2.838 bushels), compared to the prices of wheat showing the downward trend of prices from 1873 on, followed by a slow recovery in the last years of the century. Pugliese, *Due secoli*, pp. 274–75:

	Price			Price	
Year	Rice	Wheat	Year	Rice	Wheat
1860	25.49	20.00	1880	29.81	24.38
1861	27.35	22.88	1881	24.21	21.03
1862	25.59	21.32	1882	24.22	20.06
1863	24.32	19.13	1883	23.40	18.19
1864	25.66	18.94	1884	24.64	16.92
1865	25.53	17.20	1885	21.95	16.35
1866	27.64	19.21	1886	23.45	16.22
1867	29.30	24.19	1887	24.62	16.39
1868	28.23	25.59	1888	26.37	16.72
1869	25.79	19.30	1889	25.86	17.13
1870	22.61	20.25	1890	25.34	17.28
1871	25.46	23.15	1891	29.14	19.33
1872	30.13	25.47	1892	26.29	18.10
1873	31.62	26.94	1893	22.71	14.94
1874	30.33	27.63	1894	21.62	14.74
1875	25.19	19.25	1895	22.37	15.43
1876	29.61	20.81	1896	25.00	16.02
1877	30.70	24.53	1897	28.89	20.31
1878	28.52	22.75	1898	25.77	17.59
1879	28.97	22.63	1899	25.29	17.88

34. "Brusone," *Enciclopedia Italiana*, 1930, VII, 1, p. 989. The parasite that caused *brusone* was, according to some plant pathologists, *Piricularia oryzia*, according to others, *Bacillus oryzia*.

35. Pugliese, "Produzione," p. 81. Here the index numbers indicating rent fluctuations are as follows:

1709–19	1861	1871	1881	1891	1901	1906
100	648	886	1249	910	914	1080

In 1906 the *affituario* paid an average rent of 200.40 lire per hectare.

36. Novelli and Sampietro, "La risicoltura in Italia," pp. 30–31.

37. Ibid., pp. 55–57. In 1910 one finds the smallest rice productive areas of the pre–First World War period (143,000 hectares). It went up slightly in 1914 (146,300 hectares).

38. Pugliese, *Due secoli*, p. 269.

39. Luraghi, "Wage Labor in the 'Rice Belt' of Northern Italy," p. 126;

Enzo Busca, *L'economia risicola italiana in cento anni di cronaca* (Milan: Rizzoli, 1961), p. 5.

40. Sereni, *Il capitalismo*, p. 253; Villari, "Il capitalismo della grande depressione," p. 35.

41. Novelli and Sampietro, "La risicoltura," p. 57.

42. Pugliese, "Produzione," p. 88.

43. Faccini, *L'economia risicola lombarda*, p. 18.

44. Alessandro Visconti, *La pubblica amministrazione nello stato milanese durante il predominio straniero (1541–1796)* (Rome: Athenaeum, 1913), pp. 265–66.

45. Quoted in Franco Della Peruta, *Società e classi popolari nell'Italia dell'Ottocento* (Syracuse: Ediprint, 1985), p. 240n.

46. De Maddalena, *Prezzi e aspetti di mercato*, p. 52. Visconti quotes the same edict in *La pubblica amministrazione*, p. 266, but dated April 24, 1599.

47. Luraghi, "Sulle origini del movimento contadino nella pianura padana irrigua: il Vercellese," *Nuova rivista storica*, 60 (Sept.-Dec. 1956), 492.

48. Giuseppe Prato, *L'evoluzione agricola nel secolo XVIII e le cause economiche dei moti del 1792–98 in Piemonte*, Reale Accademia delle Scienze di Torino (anno 1908–1909) (Turin: Vincenzo Bona. Tipografo di S.M. e dei RR. Principi, 1909), p. 58; Pugliese, *Due secoli*, p. 197.

49. Prato, *L'evoluzione agricola*, p. 58.

50. Luigi Bulferetti and Raimondo Luraghi, *Agricoltura, industria e commercio in Piemonte dal 1790 al 1814*, Pubblicazione del Comitato torinese dell'Istituto per la storia del Risorgimento, nuova serie, 3 (Turin: Palazzo Carignano, 1966), pp. 73–75. In Ravenna, in the low Po valley, where the formation of a rice field required a patient and elaborate technique of mud sedimentation, the dissolution of the rural patriarchal society was the topic of the study of Sergio Nardi, "Bonifiche e risaie nel Ravennate (1800–1860)," in *Atti del II Convegno di studi Gramsciani tenuto a Roma nei giorni 19–21 marzo 1960*, Nuova biblioteca di coltura, 34 (Rome: Editori Riuniti, 1962).

51. Pugliese, *Due secoli*, pp. 43–52.

52. Luigi Bulferetti and Raimondo Luraghi, *Agricoltura, industria e commercio in Piemonte dal 1814 al 1848*, Pubblicazione del Comitato torinese dell'Istituto per la storia del Risorgimento, nuova serie, 4 (Turin: Palazzo Carignano, 1966), p. 48.

53. Faccini, "I lavoratori della risaia fra '700 e '800. Condizioni di vita, alimentazione, malattie," *Studi Storici*, 15 (July-Sept. 1974), 559.

54. Louis de Jaucourt, "Riz," *Encyclopédie ou Dictionnaire raisonné des sciences, des arts et des métiers, par une société de gens de lettres. Mis en ordre et publié par M. Diderot et quant à la partie mathématique, par M. d'Alembert,* 14 (1765), p. 306.

55. Faccini, "I lavoratori della risaia," p. 547. The author calculates that several tens of thousands of temporary workers were engaged in the different operations of the rice fields in the eighteenth century.

56. Busca, *L'economia risicola italiana,* p. 8.

57. Oreste Bordiga and Leopoldo Silvestrini, *Del riso e della sua coltivazione. Studio di economia rurale* (Novara: Tipografia della Rivista di Contabilità, 1880), p. 210.

58. Italy, *Atti della Giunta per la Inchiesta agraria e sulle condizioni della classe agricola,* Stefano Jacini, chairman (15 vols.; Rome: Forzani & Co., 1881–85), VIII, part 1, 566; hereafter cited as *Inchiesta Jacini.*

59. Karl Julius Beloch, *Bevölkerungsgeschichte Italiens* (3 vols.; Berlin: Walter de Gruyter, 1961), III:225. Italy, Direzione Generale della Statistica, *Censimento della popolazione del regno d'Italia al 31 decembre 1881* (3 vols.; Rome: Tipografia Bodomiana, 1883–84) I:102.

60. Italy, Direzione Statistica, *Censimento 1881,* III:262–63.

61. Francesco Coletti, *La popolazione rurale in Italia e i suoi caratteri demografici, psicologici e sociali. Raccolta di studi* (Piacenza: Federazione Italiana dei Consorzi Agrari, 1925), pp. 114 and 118.

62. Società Umanitaria, *Pubblicazioni,* no. 5, febbraio 1904. Dott. Giovanni Lorenzoni dell'Università di Innsbruck, *I Lavoratori delle Risaie. Inchiesta sulle condizione del lavoro nelle risaie della Lomellina, del Vercellese e del Novarese* (Milan: Ufficio del Lavoro, 1904), p. 24. Pugliese calculates that in Larizzate (Vercellese) in 1901 about one *mondariso* was needed to weed 1.28 hectare in forty days. This was the ratio when the rice field was already two or three years old. New fields needed about two weeders for the same surface. See Pugliese, *Due secoli,* p. 102.

63. Novelli and Sampietro, "La risicoltura in Italia," pp. 106–10.

64. Società Umanitaria, *Pubblicazioni,* no. 5, p. 23.

65. Pugliese, *Due secoli,* p. 121. Yield in a farm of 191 hectares around 1905 was 50 quintals per hectare in a new field, 40 quintals in the second year, and 34 quintals in the third. This was considered a large farm.

66. Ibid., pp. 102–5.

67. Michele Lecce, "Un'azienda risiera veronese nel XVII e XVIII

secolo," *Economia e storia,* 6 (Jan.-March 1959). Lecce describes the *monda* performed exclusively by women.

68. Giovan Battista Spolverini, *La coltivazione del riso* (2nd ed.; Verona: A. Carattoni Stampator del Seminario Vescovile, 1763), pp. 103–7.

69. Novelli and Sampietro, "La risicoltura in Italia," p. 55.

70. Pugliese, *Due secoli,* pp. 234–39 and 242–43. This author makes detailed cost of living calculations in households of farm workers, both permanent and temporary, and includes lists of prices of basic needs.

71. For the proportion of women employed, and for the proportion of women in the employed population, see Pierfrancesco Bandettini, "The Employment of Women in Italy, 1881–1951," *Comparative Studies in Society and History,* 2 (1959–1960), pp. 369–73.

72. Cynthia B. Lloyd, ed., *Sex, Discrimination, and the Division of Labor* (New York: Columbia University Press, 1975), p. 4. The contributors to the volume stress the complications in assessing the weight of discrimination in the labor market. See, for example, Harriet Zellner, "Determinants of Occupational Segregation," pp. 126 and 143.

73. Heidi Hartmann, "Capitalism, Patriarchy, and Job Segregation by Sex," in Martha Blaxall and Barbara Reagan, eds., *Women and the Workplace. The Implications of Occupational Segregation* (Chicago: University of Chicago Press, 1976), pp. 137 and 140–47; Ruth Milkman, "Organizing the Sexual Division of Labor: Historical Perspectives on 'Women's Work' and the American Labor Movement," *Socialist Review,* 10 (Jan.-Feb. 1980), 95–150.

74. On the subject of the division of labor by sex, see the special number of *Signs: Journal of Women in Culture and Society,* 7, no. 2 (1981). See also Kate Young, Carol Wolkowitz, and Rosalyn McCullagh, eds., *Of Marriage and the Market* (London: CSE Books, 1981); Lourdes Benería, ed., *Women and Development. The Sexual Division of Labor in Rural Societies* (New York: Praeger, 1982); Benería and Martha Roldán, *The Crossroads of Class and Gender* (Chicago: University of Chicago Press, 1987); Eleanor Leacock and Helen I. Safa, eds., *Women's Work. Development and the Division of Labor by Gender* (South Hadley, Mass.: Bergin and Garvey, 1986), pp. 267–84.

75. Patricia Hilden, *Working Women and Socialist Politics in France, 1880–1914* (New York: Oxford University Press, 1986), pp. 90–91 and 276; Jane Lewis, *Women in England, 1870–1950: Sexual Division and Social Change* (Sussex: Wheatsheaf Books, 1984), p. 164; Joy Parr, "Disaggregating the Sexual Division of Labour: A Transatlantic Case Study," *Comparative Studies in Society and History,* 30, no. 3 (July 1988), 528–29 and 533.

76. Faccini, ed., *Uomini e lavoro in risaia, Il dibattito sulla risicoltura nel '700 e nell '800* (Milan: Franco Angeli, 1976), p. 16.

77. *Il Congresso Risicolo Internazionale, Atti*, Mortara, 1–3 ottobre 1903 (Mortara: Cortellezzi, 1903), p. 211.

78. Antonio Aldini, "Osservazioni sul discorso pubblicato per le stampe dal Marsigli col titolo 'Delle risaie e dei pessimi loro effetti,'" in Faccini, *Uomini e lavoro in risaia*, p. 124.

79. Novelli and Sampietro, "La risicoltura in Italia," p. 107.

80. Joan Wallach Scott, *Gender and the Politics of History* (New York: Columbia University Press, 1988), pp. 28–32.

81. Janice Fanning Madden, "Discrimination and Male Market Power," in Lloyd, *Sex Discrimination*, p. 154.

82. Pugliese, *Due secoli*, p. 215; August Bebel, *Women under Socialism* (trans. Daniel De Leon) (New York: Labor News Press, 1904), p. 168. Bebel observed the depressing effect of women's employment upon men's wages.

83. Pugliese, *Due secoli*, p. 220. Pugliese's indexes illustrate wage fluctuations between 1866 and 1905:

Years	Women's Wages	Men's Wages
1866–1870	100	100
1871–1875	122	116
1876–1880	130	109
1881–1885	144	100
1886–1890	116	91
1891–1895	118	92
1896–1900	140	102
1901–1905	160	119

(The table shows the faster increase of women's wages.)

84. Pugliese, *Due secoli*, pp. 217 and 219; *Inchiesta Jacini*, VIII, part 1, 683.

85. Pugliese, *Due secoli*, pp. 220–21.

86. Pugliese, "Produzione," p. 161.

87. Gianverardo Zeviani, "Il riso e il giavone," in Faccini, *Uomini e lavoro in risaia*, p. 156.

88. Francesco Puccinotti, "Delle risaie in Italia e della loro introduzione in Toscana," in Faccini, *Uomini e lavoro in risaia*, p. 156.

89. Colombi, La Marchesa (Maria Antonietta Torriani Torelli-Viollier), *In risaia. Racconto di Natale* (Milan: Galli, 1890, 4th ed.), pp. 58–60.

90. Novelli and Sampietro, "La risicoltura in Italia," p. 119.

91. *Inchiesta Jacini*, VI, part 2, 87.

92. Società Umanitaria, *Pubblicazioni*, no. 5, pp. 26–27.

93. Ibid., p. 34. The national census of 1911 contains the classification of women over nine years old by occupations in the communes of Novara and Vercelli. The domestic servants form one of the largest groups of non-agricultural employed women, 1,001 in Novara and 746 in Vercelli, out of a total of 22,569 in Novara and 13,896 in Vercelli. Figures for dressmakers were 1,060 in Novara and 750 in Vercelli. Cotton textile workers were well represented only in Novara (1,462 women). There were 1,977 (Novara) and 2,919 (Vercelli) wage earners in agriculture. See Italy, Direzione Generale della Statistica, *Censimento della popolazione del regno d'Italia al 10 giugno 1911* (5 vols.; Rome: Bertero, 1914–15), IV:62. Domestic servants continued to participate in the weeding during the 1950s (interview with Lucia Minerbi Flegenheimer).

94. Louise A. Tilly and Joan W. Scott, *Women, Work, and Family* (New York: Holt, Rinehart and Winston, 1978), p. 15.

95. Marchesa Colombi, *In risaia*, pp. 17–33, passim. Carlo Livi, "Della coltivazione," p. 244. For information on this novelist, see Benedetto Croce, *La letteratura della nuova Italia. Saggi critici* (6 vols., 4th ed.; Bari: Laterza, 1957), V:71–72.

96. Marchesa Colombi, *In risaia*, p. 67.

97. Wanda Aiazza, Francesca Fontana, and Piera Gaia, "Vercelli e la Bassa: evoluzione storica, economica, sociale e culturale" (diploma thesis, Scuola per Assistenti Sociali del Comune di Casale Monferrato, 1978), p. 224. The authors held interviews with several weeders between November 1976 and April 1978.

98. Ibid., pp. 213, 216, 217, and 224.

99. Gaudenzio Gramegna, "Delle risaie e della loro influenza sull'umana salute," in Faccini, *Uomini e lavoro in risaia*, p. 197.

100. Pugliese, *Due secoli*, p. 218.

101. Pugliese, "Produzione," p. 158.

102. Aiazza, "Vercelli e la Bassa," p. 213.

103. Pugliese, *Due secoli*, p. 243.

104. Aiazza, "Vercelli e la Bassa," p. 215.

105. Pugliese, "Produzione," p. 189.

106. Aiazza, "Vercelli e la Bassa," p. 214.

107. *Inchiesta Jacini*, VIII, part 1, 683; Massimo Livi-Bacci, *A History of Italian Fertility During the Last Two Centuries* (Princeton: Princeton University Press, 1977), pp. 256–57. Weaning orphans (*fanciulli da pane*) were sometimes also trusted to families of peasants and artisans. Insights on the issue of expansion of industrial production in Italy and the problems of disintegration of workers' families in urban centers, of foundlings, and of wet nursing are given in Franco Della Peruta, "Infanzia e famiglia nella prima metà dell'ottocento," *Studi Storici* (July-Sept. 1979), 473–91.

108. Aiazza, "Vercelli e la Bassa," pp. 158 and 162. The authors present a table comparing births and foundlings in the city of Vercelli (p. 158):

Year	Births	Foundlings	Percentage
1871	928	86	9.26
1876	1,006	64	6.36
1881	1,022	76	7.43
1886	1,052	73	6.93
1891	980	72	7.34
1896	890	68	7.64
1901	768	51	6.64
1906	714	43	6.02
1911	619	38	6.13
1916	431	15	3.48

On the history of the London Foundling Hospital in the eighteenth century, see Valerie Fields, *Wet Nursing. A History from Antiquity to the Present* (Oxford: Basil Blackwell, 1988), pp. 159–89. Women from Cuneo in northern Italy used to go to France to employ themselves as wet nurses for a higher pay than in Italy. See Nuto Revelli, *L'anello forte* (Turin: Einaudi, 1985), p. 226.

109. *Inchiesta Jacini*, VIII, part 1, 628.

110. G. Manzino, "Mercato di carne umana," *Il Contadino*, Oct. 6, 1911, p. 2.

111. Aiazza, "Vercelli e la Bassa," pp. 212–13.

112. Francesco Coletti, "Dell'emigrazione italiana, 1861–1911," in *Cinquanta anni di storia italiana* (publication made under the auspices of the government edited by the Reale Accademia dei Lincei) (Milan: Hoepli, 1911), III:193. For weeders' attitudes in the 1940s and 1950s, see Maria Michetti, Margherita Repetto, and Luciana Viviani, *Udi: laboratorio di politica delle donne* (Rome: Cooperativa Libera Stampa, 1984), p. 121. The song "L'amarezza delle mondine" [The bitterness of the *mondine*] is in the collection *Canti della protesta femminile*, edited by Agata Currà, Giuseppe Vettori and Rosalba Vinci (Rome: Newton Crompton, 1977), p. 132.

113. Società Umanitaria, *Pubblicazioni*, no. 5, pp. 26–34, passim. This inquiry makes frequent references to married women, both local and migrant.

114. Novelli and Sampietro, "La risicoltura in Italia," p. 106. The figures for both age groups among the migratory weeders were respectively 15,883 and 15,364.

115. Livi-Bacci, *A History of Italian Fertility*, p. 164.

116. Novelli and Sampietro, "La risicoltura in Italia," p. 188.

117. Jacini, *La proprietà fondiaria e le popolazioni agricole in Lombardia: studi economici* (Milan: Borroni e Scotti, 1854), pp. 102–3.

118. *Inchiesta Jacini*, VIII, part 1, 627 and 861.

119. Carlo Cipolla, "Four Centuries of Italian Demographic Developement," in D. V. Glass and D. E. C. Eversley, *Population in History. Essays in Historical Demography* (Chicago: Aldine, 1965), pp. 579 and 583–84.

120. Livi-Bacci, *A History of Italian Fertility*, pp. 264–66.

121. Germana Muttini Conti, *La popolazione del Piemonte nel secolo XIX* (Turin: ILTE, 1962; 2 parts), part 2, p. 137.

122. Marchesa Colombi, *In risaia*, pp. 17–33, passim.

123. Novelli and Sampietro, "La risicoltura in Italia," p. 183.

124. Ugo Giusti, *Caratteristiche ambientali italiane Agrarie-Sociali-Demografiche, 1815–1942*, Istituto Nazionale di Economia Agraria, Studi e Monografie, no. 27 (Rome: Failli, 1943), pp. 314–15; Pugliese, *Due secoli*, p. 56. Family size in the Vercellese in the years 1838 and 1848 were respectively 4.81 and 4.65.

125. Livi-Bacci, *A History of Italian Fertility*, pp. 253–62. He explains that "it has also been suggested that, in many instances, breast-feeding was coupled with sexual taboos" (p. 253). On breast-feeding as a means of child spacing, see Mayling Simpson-Hellert, "Breastfeeding and Human Infertility," *Bibliography Series, Technical Information Services. Carolina Population Center* (March 1975, no. 9), p. 1.

126. Personal interview with Francesca Fontana, Vercelli, July 1978,

127. On Spolverini, see Giulio Natale, "Spolverini, Giovan Battista," *Enciclopedia Italiana*, 1936, XXXII, p. 407.

128. Spolverini, *La coltivazione del riso*, pp. 103–8.

129. Ibid., pp. 109–10.

130. Ibid., p. 116.

131. Arthur Young, *Travels during the years 1787, 1788, and 1789. Undertaken more particularly with a view of ascertaining the Cultivation, Wealth, Resources, and National Prosperity of the Kingdom of France*, vol. 2 (2nd ed., printed for W. Richardson, 1794), p. 237. This volume contains sections on Young's travels in Italy and Spain.

132. Aldini, "Osservazioni sul discorso pubblicato per le stampe," in Faccini, *Uomini e lavoro in risaia*, p. 124. Faccini focuses this anthology on the debate about rice farming during the more than a century and a half that preceded the unification of Italy. On Aldini, see also Renato Zangheri, "Un dibattito sulle risaie bolognesi agli inizi della Restaurazione," in *Convegno di studi sul Risorgimento a Bologna e nell'Emilia (27–29 febbraio 1960). Communicazioni, Bollettino del Museo del Risorgimento*, Bologna, 5 (1966), 1183–1210.

133. Bordiga and Silvestrini, *Del riso e della sua coltivazione*, p. 236.

134. E. J. Hobsbawm calls attention to the important role played by social medicine in Britain, not only for connecting social distress to economic changes, but also for bequeathing posterity such rich information on the lives of the laboring poor. See *The age of Revolution, 1789–1848* (New York: Mentor Books, 1962), p. 242 and footnote. A similar case can be made for Italy, where we find many physicians who studied the situation of the lower classes subject to new economic conditions. They often became members of the Socialist Party and militants in the labor movement. See Tommaso Detti, "Medicina, democrazia e socialismo in Italia tra '800 e '900," *Movimiento operaio e socialista*, 2, new series (1979), 3–49, and *Fabrizio Maffi. Vita di un medico socialista* (Milan: Franco Angeli, 1987), p. 36.

135. Zeviani, "Il riso e il giavone," in Faccini, *Uomini e lavoro in risaia*, p. 76.

136. Anonymous, "Delle risaie e dei loro pessimi effetti," Faccini, *Uomini e lavoro in risaia*, pp. 107–8.

137. Faccini, *Uomini e lavoro in risaia*, p. 103; Zangheri, "Un dibattito," pp. 1184–90.

138. *Inchiesta Jacini*, VIII, part 1, 749; Luraghi, "Wage Labor," p. 117.

139. *Inchiesta Jacini*, VI, part 2, 179; Mary Gibson, *Prostitution and the State in Italy, 1860–1915* (New Brunswick: Rutgers University Press, 1986), p. 20. On women's urban migration, see Louise A. Tilly, "Urban Growth, Industrialization, and Women's Employment in Milan, Italy, 1881–1911," *Journal of Urban History*, 3 (1977), 467–84.

140. Coletti, "Dell'emigrazione italiana, 1861–1911," p. 193.

141. Studies on illegitimacy in Italy reveal that it has never had a major

impact on the fertility of the population. Here, as well as in most European countries, reproduction takes place mainly within marriage. See Livi-Bacci, *A History of Italian Fertility,* p. 69.

142. Novelli and Sampietro, "La risicoltura in Italia," p. 108.

143. Girolamo Alghisi, "Memoria sui mezzi di prevenire le malattie dei coltivatori del riso," in Faccini, *Uomini e lavoro in risaia,* pp. 71–72.

144. Giacomo Besozzi, "Della risicoltura in ordine all'igiene e all'economia," in Faccini, *Uomini e lavoro in risaia,* p. 205.

145. Achille Ghezzo, Giuseppe Montanari, and Clemente Sancasciani, "Sulla coltivazione del riso in rapporto alla salubrità," in Faccini, *Uomini e lavoro in risaia,* p. 218.

146. Carlo Livi, "Della coltivazione del riso in Italia," in Faccini, *Uomini e lavoro in risaia,* p. 244.

147. Mario Panizza (Deputy to Parliament), *Risultati dell'Inchiesta istituita da Agostino Bertani sulle condizioni sanitarie dei lavoratori della terra in Italia* (Rome: Stabilimento tipografico italiano, 1890), pp. 20–21. On the history of this inquiry, see Alberto Caracciolo, *L'Inchiesta Agraria Jacini* (Turin: Einaudi, 1958 and 1973), pp. 17–57, passim; Panizza, *Risultati,* pp. xxiii–lxvi, and 1–19, and 232. On the general health condition of Italian workers after unification, see Della Peruta, *Società e classi popolari nell'Italia dell'ottocento,* pp. 197–237.

148. Italy, Ministero di agricoltura, industria, e commercio, "Sulla pellagra nella provincia di Pavia. Relazione della Camera di Commercio di Pavia," *La pellagra in Italia, Annali,* 18 (1880), p. 437. The publications of the Ministry of Agriculture, Industry, and Commerce will hereafter be cited as Italy, MAIC.

149. *Inchiesta Jacini,* VIII, part 1, 686.

150. Panizza, *Risultati,* p. 233.

151. *Inchiesta Jacini,* VIII, part 1, 684.

152. Carlo Livi, "Della coltivazione," p. 244.

153. Bordiga and Silvestrini, *Del riso e della sua coltivazione,* p. 236.

Chapter 2

1. Novelli and Sampietro, "La risicoltura in Italia," p. 112.

2. Jacini, *La proprietà fondiaria,* pp. 223–24.

3. Gaudenzio Gramegna, "Delle risaie e della loro influenza sull'umana

salute," *Uomini e lavoro in risaia*, p. 198. Gramegna was a municipal doctor at Novara. He published his work in 1852.

4. Alghisi, "Memoria sui mezzi di prevenire le malattie," pp. 72–73.

5. Giovanni Capsoni, *Della influenza delle risaie sulla salute umana* (Milan: Stabilimento Libraio Volpato, 1851), p. 83. On aqua vitae and wine consumption in Italy, see Della Peruta, *Società e classi popolari*, pp. 215–16.

6. Stefano Somogyi, *L'alimentazione nell'Italia unita, Storia d'Italia, V, parte I, I documenti* (Turin: Einaudi, 1973), pp. 843–55.

7. *Inchiesta Jacini*, VI, part 2, 23; Gramegna, "Delle risaie," p. 198.

8. *Inchiesta Jacini*, VIII, part 1, 650–51.

9. Ibid., VI, part 2, 174.

10. Gramegna, "Delle risaie," p. 198.

11. *Inchiesta Jacini*, VIII, part 1, 868.

12. Bordiga and Silvestrini, *Del riso*, p. 233.

13. *Inchiesta Jacini*, VIII, part 1, 573, 650–51, and 868.

14. Bordiga and Silvestrini, *Del riso*, p. 233; Faccini, "I lavoratori della risaia," p. 557.

15. Marchesa Colombi, *In risaia*, pp. 32–33.

16. Bordiga and Silvestrini, *Del riso*, p. 234.

17. "Dalla risaia", *Il Contadino*, June 27, 1902, p. 2.

18. Società Umanitaria, *Pubblicazioni*, no. 5, p. 115.

19. Giacomo Besozzi, *Della risaia e specialmente di quelle del Novarese, del Vercellese e della Lomellina nei rapporti colla salute pubblica* (Turin: Tipografia Subalpina di Artero e Cotta, 1857), p. 77.

20. Faccini, *Uomini e lavoro in risaia*, pp. 27–28.

21. Giovanni Momo, "Cenni dei danni che soffre il pubblico per la troppa estesa coltivazione del riso," in Faccini, *Uomini e lavoro in risaia*, p. 149.

22. Alghisi, "Memoria sui mezzi di prevenire," p. 70.

23. Jacini, *La proprietà fondiaria*, p. 223.

24. Società Umanitaria, *Pubblicazioni*, no. 5, pp. 117–19.

25. Bordiga and Silvestrini, *Del riso*, p. 232; *Inchiesta Jacini*, VI, part 2, 85; VIII, part 1, pp. 686 and 868; Pugliese, "Produzione," p. 189.

26. *Inchiesta Jacini*, VI, part 2, 144.

27. Bordiga e Silvestrini, *Del riso*, p. 238.

28. *Inchiesta Jacini*, VI, part 2, 85.

29. Novelli and Sampietro, "La risicoltura in Italia," p. 113; *Inchiesta Jacini*, XV, *Relazione finale sui risultati dell'Inchiesta*, by Stefano Jacini, 241.

30. *Inchiesta Jacini*, VI part 2, 179, and 94; VIII, part 1, 868.

31. Novelli and Sampietro, "La risicoltura in Italia," p. 112.

32. *Inchiesta Jacini*, VIII, part 1, 868.

33. Ibid., p. 686.

34. Ibid., VI, part 2, 176, and VIII, part 1, 684.

35. Ibid., VIII, part 1, 626; Jacini, *La proprietà fondiaria*, p. 102.

36. *Inchiesta Jacini*, VIII, part 1, 863 and 866.

37. W. Aiazza, "Vercelli e la Bassa," p. 196.

38. *Inchiesta Jacini*, VIII, part 1, 750 and 862–63.

39. Romeo, *Cavour e il suo tempo (1842–1854)*, Tome I (Bari: Laterza, 1977), pp. 133–34.

40. Ibid., p. 133n.

41. *Inchiesta Jacini*, VI, part 2, 82 and 95.

42. Muttini Conti, *La popolazione del Piemonte nel secolo XIX*, part 1, pp. 70–71.

43. Un maestro, "I mondarisi e l'istruzione obbligatoria," *La Plebe*, April 14–15, 1900, p. 2. *La Plebe*, a Pavia socialist weekly, founded in 1890, brought news from the district of Lomellina.

44. *Inchiesta Jacini*, VIII, part 1, 616–17 and 749.

45. Ibid., p. 867.

46. Romeo, *Cavour e il suo tempo*, Tome I, p. 75.

47. Ibid., p. 110. On rural theft, see also Federico Bozzini, *Il furto campestre: una forma di lotte di massa nel veronese e nel veneto durante la seconda metà del'800* (Bari: Dedalo, 1977.)

48. *Inchiesta Jacini*, VI, part 2, 82–83.

49. Coletti, *La popolazione rurale*, pp. 114 and 118–19.

50. Aiazza, "Vercelli e la Bassa," p. 217.

51. Coletti, *La popolazione rurale*, p. 115; *Inchiesta Jacini*, VIII, part 2, 865; Pugliese, *Due secoli*, p. 242; idem, "Produzione," pp. 156 and 161.

52. Coletti, *La popolazione rurale*, p. 115.

53. *Inchiesta Jacini*, VI, part 2, 82, and VIII, part 2, 876.

54. Guido Neppi Modona, *Carcere e società civile, Storia d'Italia*, V, part 2, *I documenti* (Turin: Einaudi, 1973), pp. 1917–20, 1928–29, and 1937–38.

55. Raimondo Luraghi, "Wage Labor in the 'Rice Belt' of Northern Italy and Slave Labor in the American South—A First Approach," *Southern Studies*, 16, No. 2 (1977), 115.

56. Ibid., pp. 110 and 119–26. Although I do not agree with Luraghi's opinion, his idea of drawing such a poignant parallel between the two work forces indicates the deep impression that the conditions of rice-field workers made on the Italian historian. However, if we focus on the comparison of slaves with women, and not only the *mondariso*, we shall see that by the mid-nineteenth century the most prominent advocates of women's emancipation considered women's status equal to that of slaves in America.

57. Novelli and Sampietro, "La risicoltura," p. 124.

58. Società Umanitaria, *Pubblicazioni*, no. 5, pp. 39–43, 61, and 63.

59. Marchesa Colombi, *In risaia*, p. 70.

60. The following works mention itineraries of migratory weeders: *Inchiesta Jacini*, VIII, part 1, 556–57 and 626–30; Pugliese, *Due secoli*, pp. 196–97; Bordiga and Silvestrini, *Del riso*, p. 210; Panizza, *Risultati dell'Inchiesta*, p. 221.

61. Italy, Ministero delle communicazioni, *Sviluppo delle ferrovie italiane dal 1839 al 31 dicembre 1926* (Rome: Tipografia Ludovico Cecchini, 1927), pp. 12–40. There was a strong interest on the part of the rice farmers for the widening of the transportation network, which becomes evident in the frequent petitions that they made to the government for the building of new lines and roads, as stated in Italy, MAIC, *Notizie intorno alle condizioni dell'agricoltura negli anni 1878–79* (3 vols.; Rome: Stamperia reale, 1882), III:880.

62. Capsoni, *Della influenza delle risaie*, p. 11.

63. On the evils of rice farming and its restrictive legislation, see Momo, "Cenni dei danni che soffre il pubblico per la troppa estesa coltivazione del riso," p. 149; Paolo Bodo, *Le consuetudini, la legislazione, le istituzioni del vecchio Piemonte*, pp. 273–74; Faccini, *L'economia risicola lombarda*, p. 164.

64. Decreto del Regno d'Italia del 3 febbraio 1809, Archivio di Stato di Milano, Fondo Agricoltura, in Faccini, *Uomini e lavoro in risaia*, pp. 91–93.

65. Luigi Dal Pane, *Economia e società a Bologna nell'età del Risorgimento* (Bologna: Zanichelli, 1969), p. 95.

66. Quoted in Bodo, *Le consuetudini, la legislazione, le istituzioni del vecchio Piemonte*, p. 282.

67. Quoted in Giuseppe Giardina, "La malaria in risaia," in *La risicoltura e la malaria nelle zone risicole d'Italia*, p. 151. On the conservatives' attack on rice farming during the Restoration, see Faccini, *Uomini e lavoro in risaia*, p. 103.

68. Giardina, "La malaria in risaia," pp. 135, 138, and 150.

69. Bordiga and Silvestrini, *Del riso*, p. 235.

70. *Inchiesta Jacini, Relazione finale*, XV, part 1, 97–98.

71. *Ibid.*, VI, part 1, 117–18.

72. Panizza, *Risultati dell'Inchiesta*, pp. 20–21, 42, 221, and 232; see also *Inchiesta Jacini*, VIII, part 1, 682–84.

73. Giardina, "La malaria," pp. 197–99 and 202; Francesco Pezza, *Saggio di demografia storico-sanitaria di un comune risicolo d'Italia (Mortara)* (Mortara: Cortellezzi, 1899), pp. 130–31.

74. Momo, "Cenni dei danni che soffre il pubblico per la troppa estesa coltivazione del riso," p. 149; Amletto Rizzi, *Aspetti economici e sociali di Novara e del Novarese, 1750–1870*, Cronistoria Novarese no. 11 (Novara: Stabilimento Tipografico Cattaneo, 1951), p. 114. Rizzi indicates that in 1825 the Novarese consumed only one-eighteenth of the rice produced; this proportion for wheat was one-half; for rye, five-sixths; and for oats, two-thirds. On the destruction of rice fields, see Faccini, *Uomini e lavoro*, pp. 13–14.

75. Alfonso Corradi, *Annali delle epidemie occorse in Italia dalle prime memorie fino al 1850* (4 vols.; Bologna: Gamberini e Parmeggiani, 1865–94), IV, *Dall'anno 1701 al 1801*, pp. 1641–57, passim.

76. Panizza, *Risultati dell'Inchiesta*, p. 229.

77. Bordiga and Silvestrini, *Del riso*, p. 246.

78. Italy, MAIC, "Sulla pellagra," pp. 408–12, 140, and 436–37.

79. *Inchiesta Jacini*, VIII, part 1, 682–84; Marchesa Colombi, *In Risaia*, p. 66.

80. Italy, *Atti del Parlamento Subalpino, Discussioni* (Camera dei Deputati), 2nd period (16 Oct. to 28 Dec. 1848), pp. 676–88, passim.

81. Ibid., IV Legislatura (23 Nov. 1850 to 27 Feb. 1852), pp. 1535–47, passim.

82. Ibid., 1848, pp. 676–77, 687, and 1538.

83. Ibid., 1848, p. 688. The inquirers of the *Inchiesta Jacini* also observed that the hospitals and free medical services in the rice belt, offered by poorly paid municipal doctors, were inadequate and sometimes manipulated by powerful local politicians (VIII, part 1, 682–84).

84. Italy, *Atti del Parlamento Italiano, Discussioni* (Camera dei Deputati, 2nd ed., 8th Legislative Session, 1861–62), vol. 1 (Rome: Eredi Botta, 1881), p. 2303.

85. "Atti dell'Accademia del Comizio Agrario di Milano," Jan.-Feb. 1867, in Enzo Busca, *L'economia risicola italiana*, p. 4.

86. Italy, Camera dei Deputati, *Raccolta dei documenti stampati per ordine della Camera*, 9th Legislative Session, 1865–66 (18 November to 30 October 1866), vol. 1 (Florence: Eredi Botta, 1866), pp. 1–7. The text of the bill appears as document no. 105.

87. Bordiga and Silvestrini, *Del riso*, pp. 213–15 and 222–23.

88. Italy, MAIC, "Sulla pellagra nella provincia di Pavia," p. 432.

89. Denis Mack Smith, ed., *The Making of Italy, 1796–1870* (New York: Harper and Row, 1968), p. 172.

90. Luraghi, "Sulle origini del movimento contadino nella padana irrigua: il Vercellese," p. 172.

91. Jacini, *La proprietà fondiaria*, pp. 244–52, passim.

92. *Inchiesta Jacini*, VIII, part 1, 750, and part 2, 869.

93. On the shortcomings of social legislation in Italy in the nineteenth century, see Giancarlo Jacteau, "Le origini della legislazione sociale in Italia. Problemi e prospettive di ricerca," *Movimiento operaio e socialista*, 5, no. 2–3 (1982), 289–301.

94. Rodolfo de Mattei traces the use of the locution "social question" in Italy in "La prima coscienza in Italia d'una 'questione sociale,' " in *Storia e politica internazionale. Rassegna trimestrale dell'Istituto per li studi di politica internazionale*, 21 (March 1943), 97–109. The Italian Catholics began to deal in depth with the social question in 1889.

95. *Inchiesta Jacini*, VIII, part 1, 536, 874, and 1035–36.

96. "Cronache vercellesi," Federbraccianti, ed., CGIL provinciale Vercelli (mimeographed work, Vercelli, 1969), pp. 1–6.

97. Noi, "Società Operaie di Mutuo Soccorso," *La Plebe*, Jan. 20–21, 1900, p. 1.

98. *Inchiesta Jacini,* VI, part 2, 178, and VIII, part 1, 686, 810–11, 875, 962, and 1039–45.

99. Ibid., VIII, part 2, 876, 895, 1040–41, and 1044.

100. Ibid., VI, part 2, 179–80.

101. Ibid., XV, part 1, 106 and 248.

102. The population active in agriculture was 57.6 percent in 1871 (8,652,000 inhabitants), 59.1 percent in 1901 (9,611,000 inhabitants), and 55.8 percent in 1921 (9,841,000 inhabitants). In 1921 this sector in France comprised 41.5 percent of the population; in Germany, 30.5 percent; in Britain, 7.1 percent. See Renato Zangheri, ed., *Lotte agrarie in Italia. La Federazione nazionale dei lavoratori della terra, 1901–1926* (Milan: Feltrinelli, 1960), pp. xiv–xv.

103. Giuliano Procacci, *La lotta di classe in Italia agli inizi del secolo XX* (Rome: Editori Riuniti, 1970), p. 81.

104. On the grind tax uprisings, see Nello Rosselli, *Mazzini e Bakounine, 1860–1872* (Turin: Bocca, 1927), pp. 215–54; Renzo del Carrià, *Proletari senza revoluzione* (4 vols.; Rome: Sanelli, 1975), I:141–58; Maurice P. Neufeld, *Italy: School for Awakening Countries* (Ithaca: Cayuga Press, 1961), pp. 166–74.

105. Zangheri, "I moti del macinato nel Bolognese," Zangheri ed., *Le campagne emiliana nell'epoca moderna* (Milan: Feltrinelli, 1960), pp. 136–38; "Andrea Costa e le lotte contadine del suo tempo," *Movimento operario,* I (Jan.-Feb. 1955, no. 1), pp. 3–7.

106. Daniel L. Horowitz, *The Italian Labor Movement* (Cambridge: Harvard University Press, 1963), pp. 40–41. The electoral law of 1882 raised the number of male voters from half of million to over two million.

107. On the anarchist movement, see Enzo Santarelli, *Il socialismo anarchico* (Milan: Feltrinelli, 1973).

108. Only after 1894 did official statistics record the sex of the strikers. The figures for the period 1894–1898 are as follows:

Year	Strikes	Men	Women
1894	8	3,861	887
1895	7	1,705	60
1896	1	100	. . . .
1897	12	16,600	7,535
1898	36	5,376	2,576

See Sergio Zaninelli, ed., *Storia del movimento sindacale italiano*, vol. 1: *Le Lotte nelle campagne dalla grande crisi agricola al primo dopoguerra 1880–1921* (2 vols.; Milan: Celuc, 1971), p. 171.

109. Giampiero Carocci, *Agostino Depretis e la politica interna italiana dal 1876 al 1887* (Turin: Einaudi, 1961), p. 535; Gastone Manacorda, *Il socialismo nella storia d'Italia* (2 vols.; Bari: Laterza, 1972), I:153–59.

110. Luigi Preti, *Le lotte agrarie nella valle padana* (Turin: Einaudi, 1955), p. 124; Del Carrià, *Proletari*, I:251.

111. Zangheri, "Andrea Costa," p. 25.

112. Luigi Arbizzani, *Sguardi sull'ultimo secolo. Bologna e la sua provincia. 1859–1961* (Bologna: Galileo, 1961), p. 66.

113. Preti, *Le lotte agrarie*, p. 125.

114. Anselmo Marabini, *Prime lotte socialiste* (Rome: Rinascita, 1949), p. 140.

115. Zangheri, "Andrea Costa," p. 25. On Massarenti, see Gianna Mazzoni, "Molinella e Giuseppe Massarenti nell'età giolittiana," *Movimento operario e socialista*, 20 (1974, no. 4), 317–51.

116. Arbizzani, *Sguardi*, p. 94.

117. Anthony Cardoza, *Agrarian Elites and Italian Fascism. The Province of Bologna, 1901–1926* (Princeton: Princeton University Press, 1982), pp. 90–91.

118. Zangheri, *Lotte agrarie*, p. lxv.

119. Idomeneo Barbadoro, *Storia del sindacalismo italiano dalla nascita al fascismo*, I, *La Federterra* (Florence: La Nuova Italia, 1973), pp. 59 and 80–83.

120. *Inchiesta Jacini*, VI, part 2, 84.

Chapter 3

1. Ugo Fedeli, *Luigi Galleani. Quarant'anni di lotte revoluzionaire (1891–1931)* (Cesena: Edizione L'Antistato, 1956), pp. 33–44; Pier Carlo Masini, "La giovinezza di Luigi Galleani," *Movimento Operario*, new series, 6 (May-June 1954), 4, no. 3, 445–58.

2. Mariella Nejrotti, "Le prime esperienze politiche di Luigi Galleani (1881–1891)," *Anarchici e anarchia nel mondo contemporaneo. Atti del convegno promosso dalla Fondazione Luigi Einaudi (Torino, 5, 6 e 7 dicembre 1969)* (Turin: Fondazione Luigi Einaudi, 1971), pp. 208–16.

3. Gastone Manacorda, *Il movimento operario italiano attraverso i suoi congressi (1853–1892)* (Rome: Editori Riuniti, 1963), pp. 186–87.

4. Felice Anzi, *Il movimento operaio socialista italiano (1882–1894)* (Milan: Avanti, 1946), p. 43.

5. In 1885 thirty thousand workers had joined the POI. All the members of its central committee were arrested on June 23, 1886, after Depretis issued the dissolution decree (ibid.).

6. The official count numbered eighty demonstrators and two policemen killed, four hundred fifty persons wounded, and hundreds of imprisoned political offenders (Neufeld, *Italy,* pp. 221–22).

7. "Propaganda e organizzazione. Novara," *Lotta di classe,* July 1–2, 1893, p. 4; "La macchia nera si allarga," ibid., July 15–16, 1893, p. 3; "Propaganda e organizzazione. Novara," ibid., Sept. 16–17, 1893, p. 3; "Novara," ibid., Dec. 30–31, 1893, p. 4; "Novara", ibid., April 13–14, 1895, p. 3; "Novara," ibid., May 4–5, 1895, p. 4. *Lotta di classe,* a weekly founded in Milan on July 31, 1892, was directed by Filippo Turati and Anna Kuliscioff. They also published the bimonthly *Critica Sociale.*

8. "Una riunione socialista della provincia di Novara," ibid., June 13–14, 1896, p. 2; "Novara. Propaganda. Violenze poliziesche," ibid., Jan. 9–10, 1897, p. 3.

9. "Propaganda e organizzazione. San Germano Vercellese," ibid., July 22–23, p. 3; "San Germano Vercellese. Propaganda," ibid., August 17–18, 1895, p. 3; "Vercelli," ibid., March 14–15, 1896, p. 2.

10. Quoted from Maffi's letter of Dec. 1904, in Detti, *Fabrizio Maffi,* p. 72. See also pp. 71–74 and 82. On the issue of relations between city and countryside at the beginning of the twentieth century, see Procacci, *Lotta di classe,* pp. 120–22.

11. Detti, *Fabrizio Maffi,* pp. 84–88; "Il movimento contadino nel vercellese," *Lotta di classe,* Oct. 31-Nov. 1, 1896, pp. 3–4.

12. "Vercelli. Processo," ibid., Feb. 13–14, 1897, p. 4; "Vercelli. Processo e assoluzione," ibid., Aug. 15–16, 1897, p. 3.

13. Rosaldo Ordano, "Modesto Cugnolio," *Figure* (Vercelli: S.E.T.E., 1977), p. 18.

14. Detti, *Fabrizio Maffi,* pp. 101–2.

15. "Santhià. Scioglimento," *Lotta di classe,* Feb. 6–7, 1897, p. 3; "Lezioni e revincite," ibid., March 27–28, 1897, p. 1; "Il Congresso provinciale della Federazione socialista della Provincia di Novara," ibid., May 22–23, 1897, p. 2.

16. "La campagna maledetta," ibid., June 10–11, 1893, p. 1.

17. Detti, *Fabrizio Maffi*, pp. 63–64; "La Sicilia nella Provincia di Pavia," *Lotta di classe*, May 12–13, 1894, p. 2. These were the communes where socialist sections came into existence: Sannazzaro (400 members), Balossa Bigli (150 members), Ferrera Erbognone (300 members), Ottobiano (400 members), Lomello (450 members), Mede (1,100 members), Parona (50 members), Sartirana (450 members), Valle, Zeme, Breme, Pieve del Cairo, and Doma.

18. *Lotta di classe*, May 12–13, 1894, p. 2; "Pavia. Nuovi soprusi," ibid., May 26–27, 1894, p. 3.

19. For Lomellina, see "Propagandiamo i mondarisi," *La Plebe*, June 2–3, 1894, p. 1; "Terzo Congresso Provinciale. Broni, 6 gennaio 1897," ibid., Jan. 9–10, 1897, pp. 1–2; Don José, "Da Mortara," ibid., May 19, 1897; "I mondarisi," ibid., May 22–23, 1897, p. 3; "Per completare l'opera del giornale," and Tito, "La lega di resistenza fra contadini, la piccola proprietà e la mezzadria," ibid., Aug. 14–15, 1897, p. 2; "I mondarisi," ibid., May 27–28, 1899, p. 1; Noi, "Per la organizzazione economica. Da Mortara," ibid., Dec. 23–24, 1899, p. 1, and Jan. 13–14, 1900, p. 1. *La Plebe*, a socialist weekly of the province of Pavia, printed news from its district of Lomellina. It was founded in 1890.

20. Detti, *Fabrizio Maffi*, p. 88.

21. Procacci, *La lotta di classe*, p. 120.

22. *Cronache vercellesi*, pp. 10–12.

23. Ibid., pp. 16–17.

24. Ibid., pp. 26–30.

25. Nejrotti, "Le prime esperienze politiche di Luigi Galleani," pp. 210 and 212–13.

26. Mary Nolan, "Women and Socialism in Germany" (Binghampton Women's History Lecture Series, State University of New York, Feb. 19, 1981, unpublished paper), pp. 1–5. On women and socialism in Europe, see Charles Sowerwine, "The Socialist Women's movement from 1850 to 1940," Renate Bridenthal, Claudia Koonz, and Susan Stuard, eds., *Becoming Visible. Women in European History*, 2nd ed. (Boston: Houghton Mifflin, 1987), pp. 404–26. On the relationship between German socialist feminists and the Social Democratic Party, see Jean H. Quataert, *Reluctant Feminists in German Social Democracy, 1885–1917* (Princeton: Princeton University Press, 1979).

27. See as an example the article by Francesco De Luca, "La donna dell'avvenire ed il sentimento di pietà. (A proposito del movimento femminile)," *Lotta di Classe*, March 6–7, 1897, p. 1.

28. Claudio Giovannini, "L'emancipazione della donna nell'Italia postunitaria: una questione borghese?" *Studi Storici*, 23, no. 2 (April-June 1982), 378–79; Franca Pieroni Bortolotti, *Socialismo e questione femminile in Italia, 1892– 1922* (Milan: Mazzota, 1974), p. 82; Procacci, *La lotta di classe*, p. 30.

29. Patricia Hilden, *Working Women and Socialist Politics in France, 1880– 1914* (Oxford: Clarendon Press, 1986), p. 189.

30. This theory was developed by Friederich Engels, August Bebel, and Clara Zetkin. Bebel's book, *Women under Socialism*, written in 1879, was translated in 1892 and widely read in Italy. See Nolan, "Women and Socialism in Germany," pp. 1–5.

31. Procacci, *The Italian Working Class from the Risorgimento to Fascism. Three Lectures* (Cambridge, Mass.: 1979, mimeographed copy), monograph no. 1, p. 4.

32. Anna Maria Mozzoni, *La donna e suoi rapporti sociali* (Milan: Tipografia Sociale G. Ferrari, 1864).

33. Franca Pieroni Bortolotti, *Sul movimento politico delle donne. Scritti inediti*, Annarita Buttafuoco, ed. (Rome: Utopia, 1987), pp. 26–33.

34. Mozzoni, *La liberazione della donna*, Pieroni Bortolotti, ed. (Milan: Mazzota, 1975), p. 58. Also quoted in Giovannini, "L'emancipazione della donna," p. 367. On socialism and feminism, see also Pieroni Bortolotti, *Socialismo*.

35. Pieroni Bortolotti, *Socialismo*, p. 78.

36. Mozzoni, "La trasformazione del lavoro domestico," *Rivista critica del socialismo*, 1 (Feb. 2, 1899), quoted in Pieroni Bortolotti, *Socialismo*, pp. 96 and 101n, and Mozzoni, *La liberazione*, p. 27.

37. Mozzoni, *La liberazione*, pp. 207–8 and 214.

38. Quoted in Pieroni Bortolotti, *Socialismo*, pp. 76 and 80–81. See also Maria Casalini, *La signora del socialismo italiano. Vita di Anna Kuliscioff* (Rome: Editori Riuniti, 1987), p. 157. On the origins of the campaign for the law on women's and children's labor launched by Kuliscioff and the *Gruppo femminile socialista* of Milan, see "Proteggiamo la donna! Proteggiamo i fanciulli!" *Lotta di classe*, Nov. 20–21, 1897, pp. 2–3; Casalini, *La signora del socialismo italiano*, pp. 155–61; Pieroni Bortolotti, *Socialismo*, pp. 96–97.

39. For Anna Kuliscioff's important role in the Italian Socialist Party, see Claire LaVigna, "Anna Kuliscioff: From Russian Populism to Italian Reformism, 1873–1913" (Ph.D. dissertation, University of Rochester, 1971), and Maria Casalini, *La signora del socialismo italiano*.

40. La Redazione, "Programma," *Rivista internazionale del socialismo*, 1, no. 1 (May 15, 1880), 3.

41. Anna Kuliscioff, *Il monopolio dell'uomo* (Milan: Critica Sociale, 1894), pp. 27–28; LaVigna, "Anna Kuliscioff," p. 227. Casalini analyzes this lecture in *La signora del socialismo italiano*, pp. 95–103.

42. Anna Kuliscioff, *Monopolio*, pp. 27, 40, 41, 48, 51, and 52 (also quoted in LaVigna, "Anna Kuliscioff," p. 228).

43. Kuliscioff, "Il sentimentalismo nella questione femminile," *Critica Sociale*, 2 (May 1, 1892), 143. Quoted in LaVigna, "Anna Kuliscioff," p. 233.

44. Quoted in Giovannini, "L'emancipazione," p. 380, and in Maria Casalini, "Femminismo e socialismo in Anna Kuliscioff, 1890–1907," *Italia contemporanea* (April-June 1981), 25.

45. LaVigna, "Anna Kuliscioff," p. 233.

46. Ghino di Tacco, "Nostre correspondenze. Dall'Emilia. Lega socialista," *Lotta di classe*, Sept. 3–4, 1892, p. 3; "Alla campagna!" ibid., March 11–12, 1893, p. 1.

47. Una donna, "Le donne e il partito operaio-socialista," *Lotta di classe*, Oct. 1–2, 1892, p. 1. See also "Dalle provincie. Pavia. Conferenza Berenini," ibid., March 11–12, 1893, p. 4; "Alla campagna!" ibid., March 11–12, 1892, p. 1; Una fanciulla, "Alle fanciulle," ibid., April 29–30, 1893, p. 2; "Milano operaia. Conferenza femminile," ibid., July 29–30, p. 3; "Borghesia e proletariato femminile," ibid., April 28–29, 1894, p. 2.

48. O. G., "Alle donne," *La Risaia*, Feb. 9, 1901, p. 4; Gigetto, "Alle donne contadine," ibid., June 15, 1901, pp. 3–4; and O. G., "Alle donne vercellesi," ibid., Dec. 14, 1901, p. 3.

49. Procacci, *Lotta di classe*, pp. 84–85.

50. Ibid., p. 91.

51. Manacorda, *Il Socialismo*, I:248.

52. Alessandro Schiavi, "Due anni di agitazioni proletarie," *Riforma Sociale*, 9, no. 2 (Feb. 15, 1902), 153–80; Ivanoe Bonomi, *Questioni urgenti* (Genoa, 1902).

53. Napoleone Colajanni, "Il movimento agrario in Italia," *Rivista d'Italia*, 5, no. 11 (Nov. 1902), 729. In 1901 there were in Italy 629 agricultural strikes, with 222,985 strikers involved, the highest number in the history of the country. There had been 27 strikes in 1900 and 9 in 1899. The preceding record was in 1885, with 62 strikes and 8,857 participants (Procacci, *La lotta di classe*, p. 77).

54. "5. Congresso Provinciale Socialista, Pavia, 18 febbraio 1900," *La Plebe*, Feb. 24–25, 1900, pp. 1–2.

55. Bertoldo, "Per la organizzazione dei mondarisi," ibid., March 3–4, 1900, pp. 1–2.

56. "Per la organizzazione dei mondarisi," ibid., March 17–18, 1900, p. 1.

57. Barbadoro, *Storia del Sindacalismo Italiano*, p. 202.

58. "Ancora i mondarisi dell'Oltrepò," *La Plebe*, April 7–8, 1900, p. 1.

59. Un maestro, "I mondini e l'istruzione obbligatoria," ibid., April 14–15, 1900, p. 2.

60. "III. Congresso Socialista Provinciale," *Il Lavoratore*, Dec. 15, 1900, p. 2.

61. Ordano, *Modesto Cugnolio*, p. 18.

62. "La reazione," *La Plebe*, Dec. 22–23, 1900, p. 2. On the repercussions of the Genoa strike in Vercelli, see "La Camera del lavoro a Vercelli," *La Risaia*, Feb. 2, 1901, pp. 3–4.

63. Renato Brocchi, *L'organizzazione di resistenza in Italia* (Macerata: Libreria Editrice Marchigiana, 1907), p. lxxiv.

64. Carocci, *Agostino Depretis e la politica interna italiana dal 1876 al 1887*, p. 535; Procacci, *La Lotta di classe*, pp. 89–93.

65. Gi, "L'organizzazione dei contadini," *La Plebe*, Nov. 10–11, 1900, p. 3. The expression used here is "league of resistance or improvement" (*lega di resistenza o miglioramento*); by April 1901 the word "resistance" is definitely dropped in *La Plebe*. See also "Catechismo del contadino," *La Risaia*, Dec. 8, 1900, pp. 2–3.

66. Angelo Bertolini, *Gli scioperi agricoli in Italia. Monografia inviata alla "Société des agriculteurs de France," nell'occasione della Esposizione Universale di Parigi del 1900* (Rome: Tipografia dell'Unione Cooperativa Editrice, 1900), in Zaninelli, ed., *Storia del movimento sindacale italiano*, vol. 1, pp. 169–70.

67. "Atti della lega di miglioramento," *La Plebe*, May 18–19, 1901, p. 1.

68. Procacci, *La lotta di classe*, pp. 86–87.

69. Ibid., p. 130.

70. Archivio di Stato di Novara, busta 2032. *Camera del lavoro. Statuto della Camera del lavoro*, Novara, 1901.

71. "La Camera del lavoro a Vercelli," *La Risaia*, Feb. 2, 1901, pp. 2–3; "Camera del lavoro e politica," *Il Lavoratore*, Aug. 24, 1901, p. 1.

72. Brocchi, *L'organizzazione di resistenza*, pp. clxxviii–clxxx.

73. "La proclamazione della Camera del lavoro," *Il Lavoratore*, March 9, 1901, p. 1.

74. "Catechismo del contadino," *La Risaia*, Dec. 8, 1900, p. 2.

75. "Camera del lavoro," *Il Lavoratore*, March 23, 1901, p. 1, and "La Camera del lavoro a Vercelli," *La Risaia*, Feb. 2, 1901, pp. 3–4. The chamber did not always succeed in obtaining the subsidies. In January 1902, the chamber of labor of Novara was denied funds, with the excuse that the city had to support the new official labor bureau ("L'Ufficio circondariale di lavoro a Novara," *Il Lavoratore*, Jan. 25, 1902, p. 2).

76. Claudio Treves, "La funzione della Camera del lavoro (Da un discorso al Consiglio Comunale di Torino)" *Il Lavoratore*, May 11, 1901.

77. "La proclamazione della Camera del lavoro," ibid., March 9, 1901, p. 1.

78. Procacci, *La lotta di classe*, pp. 93–95.

79. Ibid., pp. 60 and 62–64.

80. La Redazione, "Al lettore," *La Risaia*, Dec. 1, 1900, p. 1.

81. "Propaganda spicciola. Il fine del socialismo. Che cosa vogliono i lavoratori," *Il Lavoratore*, March 30, 1901, p. 1.

82. "Il giornale dei risaiuoli. Dove un Contadino parla col suo padrone del nostro giornale," *La Risaia*, Dec. 1, 1900, p. 1; "Come si onorano i nostri santi," ibid., Dec. 8, 1900, p. 2; "Catechismo dei contadini," ibid., p. 3; "Qui si conta di un padrone che se la prende colle Camere del lavoro," ibid., May 25, 1901, pp. 1–2; Eugenio Ciacchi, "Propaganda spicciola. I. Le nostre leghe," *Il Lavoratore*, June 29, 1901, p. 1.

83. Gi, "L'organizzazione dei contadini," *La Plebe*, Nov. 10–11, 1900, p. 2; "La Camera del lavoro a Vercelli," *La Risaia*, Feb. 2, 1901, p. 1.

84. Gi, "L'organizzazione dei contadini," *La Plebe*, Nov. 10–11, 1900, p. 2; "Il proletariato agricolo," *Il Lavoratore*, March 30, 1901. The other region, beside the Po valley, where the leagues flourished, was Puglia, called "the Emilia of the Mezzogiorno" (Brocchi, *L'organizzazione di resistenza*, p. lxxv).

85. "Pei contadini," *La Risaia*, Dec. 1, 1900, p. 3. The same list of requests is repeated in the number of Dec. 15, 1900, and Feb. 2, 1901. *La Risaia* published also a standard model of league constitution, generally used in the Po valley; in the initial assembly, the workers elected the secretary, the trea-

surer, and the administrative council of three members for one year; regular assemblies met every other month. The members of the leagues had to reach agreements with the farmers on contracts and wage rates, and then watch their fulfillment; provide legal aid to the members in litigations for violation of pacts; and find jobs for the unemployed. The low dues paid by the workers served only to cover stationery expenses ("Le leghe di miglioramento agricole," ibid., Feb. 9, 1901, p. 3; "Programma e statuto di una lega di contadini," ibid., March 16, 1901, p. 4).

86. Gigetto, "Il mercato del lavoro," ibid., April 6, 1901, p. 1; "Ai contadini. Un avviso interessante," ibid., April 13, 1901, p. 4; "Movimento operaio," ibid., April 6, 1901, p. 1; "Ai contadini," ibid., April 20, 1901, p. 4.

87. "Nella risaia. Albano Vercelli," ibid., Feb. 2, 1901, pp. 2–3; "Nella risaia. Asigliano," ibid., Feb. 2, 1901, p. 3.

88. "Ai contadini," ibid., March 20, 1901, p. 4.

89. "Ai contadini," ibid., April 20, 1901, p. 4.

90. "Ai contadini," ibid., March 2, 1901, p. 4; "Ai contadini," ibid., April 20, 1901, p. 4. Giolitti declared at the chamber in the following month that the leagues and their goals were legal; the farmers had the right to transport workers from another place as strikebreakers, but he advised the farmers to grant the increases the leagues demanded, because these were small and just. In any case, the government would respect the right to work. "Le dichiarazioni del ministro dell'interno circa le Leghe," ibid., May 4, 1901, p. 1.

91. "Per l'organizzazione delle mondarisi," ibid., June 22, 1901, p. 4; "Ai contadini," ibid., April 27, 1901, p. 4.

92. "Per la monda del riso," ibid., May 11, 1901, p. 4. The number of the league members does not appear in the newspaper.

93. *Cronache vercellesi*, pp. 31 and 33–34.

94. The history of the agrarian elites of the rice belt remains to be written. A related study, Anthony Cardoza's *Agrarian Elites and Italian Fascism*, presents significant insights into the policies of the agrarian employers' associations in Bologna, which in the pre–World War I era already foreshadowed those typical of agrarian Fascism, the force that changed Mussolini's nascent movement into a real power.

95. Facchinetti, *"La lotta di classe,"* p. 344. One of the first acts of the association was to evict all the permanent workers suspected of having joined the leagues.

96. *Cronache vercellesi*, p. 36. I shall use the terms "rice grower," "agriculturalist," "farmer," "employer," "entrepreneur," agrarian classes, or *agricoltore* to refer to the agricultural entrepreneurs. I exclude the word "owner,"

because only few employers were landowners. The majority of the rice farmers were leaseholders.

97. S. L. "Ufficio del lavoro e Camera del lavoro," *La Risaia*, March 23, 1902, p. 2; "Mistificatori!" ibid., April 20, 1901, p. 1; "La Camera del lavoro," ibid., June 1, 1901, p. 4; "L'Ufficio municipale del lavoro," *Il Lavortore*, June 8, 1901, p. 1; "L'enorme fiasco dell'on. Lucca e del suo Ufficio del lavoro in Vercelli," ibid., June 22, 1901; "L'Ufficio circondariale di Lavoro a Novara," ibid., Jan. 25, 1902, p. 2.

98. "L'enorme fiasco dell'on. Lucca e del suo Ufficio del lavoro in Vercelli," ibid., June 22, 1901, p. 1.

99. "I fatti di Albano," *La Risaia*, May 25, 1901, p. 2; Italy, MAIC, Direzione generale della statistica, *Statistica degli scioperi avvenuti nell'industria e nell'agricoltura durante l'anno 1901* (Rome: Bertero, 1904), pp. 83 and 318.

100. *Cronache vercellesi*, p. 35.

101. "Stroppiana," *La Risaia*, June 1, 1901, p. 4.

102. Italy, MAIC, *Statistica degli scioperi, 1901*, pp. 90 and 319.

103. Ibid., p. xxxix. The official statisticians stated that they found it difficult to calculate the number of strikes, while they spread from commune to commune, or even from farm to farm, and ending in the same way, without synchrony. Similar comments are made by Giuliano Procacci in "Geografia e struttura del movimento contadino della Valle padana nel suo periodo formativo (1901–1906)," *Studi Storici*, 5, no. 1 (Jan.-March 1964), p. 44, now in *La lotta di classe*, p. 78.

104. "L'enorme fiasco dell'on. Lucca e del suo Ufficio del lavoro in Vercelli," *Il Lavoratore*, June 22, 1901, p. 1.

105. "Nella risaia. Crova," *La Risaia*, July 6, 1901, p. 3.

106. "Importantissimo. Alle squadre forestiere," ibid., June 1, 1901, p. 4.

107. Gibson, *Prostitution and the State in Italy*, p. 164.

108. "Per l'organizzazione delle mondarisi," *La Risaia*, June 22, 1901, p. 4.

109. *Cronache vercellesi*, pp. 34, 37, 38, and 39.

110. "Vercelli e la Bassa," p. 118.

111. Italy, MAIC, *Statistica degli scioperi, 1901*, pp. 88–90 and 317–20. About 35 strikes were recorded by the MAIC in the district of Novara that year. Another source, the declaration of Romolo Funes, secretary of the cham-

ber of labor of Novara, tells about 126 or 127 strikes within three months ("Resoconto stenografico del primo congresso nazionale dei lavoratori della terra," Zangheri, ed., *Lotte agrarie*, p. 22).

112. "L'organizzazione economica dei contadini," *La Plebe*, March 23–24, 1901, p. 2. In April the federation was already set up. "In provincia. Da Mortara. Organizzazione economica in Leghe di miglioramento," ibid., April 6–7, 1901, p. 3; "La funzione civile delle leghe," ibid., April 20–21, 1901, p. 2; "Le leghe di miglioramento in Lomellina. Il dovere dei compagni," ibid., April 27–28, 1901, p. 2; "Camera del lavoro: organizzazione di contadini e braccianti," ibid.; C. C. "Ai contadinia di Lomellina," ibid., May 18–19, 1901, p. 1.

113. "Atti della lega di miglioramento," ibid., May 4–5, 1901, p. 1. Later on the *Comizio agrario* agreed upon a wage scale, which, in any case, was not used by the farmers ("Da San Giorgio," *La Plebe*, June 15–16, 1901, p. 3; "Importantissimo," *La Lega dei Contadini. Supplemento mensile del Giornale La Plebe*, June 8, 1901, p. 2). This monthly supplement of *La Plebe*, covering the activities of the rural leagues, began its publication on April 21, 1901. See also "La questione dei mondarisi," ibid., p. 3.

114. "I sindaci. Osservazioni pei contadini," ibid., May 25–26, 1901, p. 1; "Da Ferrera Erbognone," ibid., June 1–2, 1901, p. 3.

115. "Da San Giorgio Lomellina," ibid., June 1–2, 1901, p. 3; "Da San Giorgio Lomellina," ibid., July 13–14, 1901, p. 3; "Da Ottobiano," ibid., June 29–30, 1901, p. 3.

116. "Da Mortara," ibid., June 1–2, 8–9, and 15–16, 1901, p. 3.

117. "Il solenne comizio della fratellanza," *La Lega dei Contadini*, July 13, 1901, pp. 1–3.

118. Italy, MAIC, *Statistica degli scioperi, 1901*, pp. 111–15 and 367–74. The wages for the *monda* fluctuated between 1 and 1.80 lira, and the workday was between 10 and 11 hours long. In one place, Scaldasole, it was twelve and a half in spite of the strike that 150 weeders staged in June 7 to have it shortened. Only one strike in Gambolò was crowned with complete success. Two hundred weeders asked to be hired before the migrants, and were finally employed after a four-day strike (Italy, MAIC, *Statistica scioperi, 1901*, pp. 373–74).

119. "Il Comizio delle leghe dei contadini rinviato," *La Plebe*, Aug. 24–25, 1901, p. 1; Un Lavoratore, "Contadini, unitevi," ibid., 1–2. The league dues were 5 centesimi a month and, for the weeders, 15 centesimi a year. In Mantua the federation had three hundred leagues and forty thousand members. See also, A. Omodeo and E. Zolla, "Relazione sulla organizzazione economica," *La Plebe*, Aug. 31-Sept. 1, p. 1.

120. "Da San Giorgio," *La Plebe*, June 15–16, 1901, p. 3; "Discussione aperta," *La Lega dei Contadini*, Supplemento no. 5, Aug. 17, 1901, p. 1.

Chapter 4

1. "Le risaiuole di Vercelli," *La Risaia*, Aug. 10, 1901, p. 3.

2. "Movimento operaio. Le mondarisi vercellesi," ibid. The article closed by inviting the weeders to report to the chamber of labor on the following Sunday to put the league in motion again.

3. Gabriella Facchinetti, "La lotta di classe nelle zone risicole del novarese e del vercellese," p. 346.

4. "Bollettino del lavoro," *La Risaia*, June 29, 1901, p. 2.

5. "Resoconto stenografico del primo congresso nazionale dei lavoratori della terra," Zangheri, *Lotte agrarie*, pp. 79–80.

6. Michela Figurelli, "Il movimento contadino nel pavese dal 1894 al 1904," *Braccianti e contadini*, p. 266.

7. "La lega dei padroni in Lomellina," *La Plebe*, July 20–21, p. 2.

8. "Da San Giorgio," ibid., Aug. 3–4, 1902, p. 3; Rocco Guida, contadino, "L'Ufficio del Lavoro," *La Lega dei Contadini*, Sept. 25, 1901, pp. 2–3.

9. Archivio di Stato di Novara, Biblioteca 78. *Lettera di presentazione a S. E. il Presidente del Consiglio dei Ministri del Memoriale dell'Associazione*, Vercelli, June 11, 1901, pp. 1–2.

10. *Atti del I. Congresso Risicolo Internazionale. Novara, 17–19 ottobre 1901* (Novara: Fratelli Miglio, 1902), pp. 100–101.

11. Italy, MAIC, *Statistica delle organizzazioni dei lavoratori e notizie sulle organizzazioni padronali al 1 gennaio 1910* (Rome: Officina Poligrafica Italiana, 1911); also in Zaninelli, *Storia del movimento sindacale italiano*, pp. 276, 278, and 283.

12. "La grande associazione degli agricoltori. Il progetto di Statuto," *La Risaia*, Jan. 15, 1902, p. 2.

13. Giuseppe Emanuele Modigliani, "Lo sviluppo del capitalismo agrario in Italia," *Critica Sociale*, 8–9 (1898–99), 88–90. Now in Manocorda, *Il socialismo nella storia d'Italia* (Bari: Laterza, 1972), I:253. See also Maria Adelaide Salvaco, "Riflessi parlamentari delle lotte emiliane," Zangheri, ed., *Le campagne emiliane*, p. 215.

14. Modigliani, "Lo sviluppo," p. 256.

15. "Il 1º Congresso Regionale dei Contadini del Piemonte," *La Risaia*, Aug. 10, 1901, p. 4; Procacci, *La lotta di classe*, p. 99–100; Detti, *Fabrizio Maffi*, p. 127.

16. Gaetana Gallina, Teresa Vasori, "Per i mondarisi," *La Lega dei Contadini*, Sept. 25, 1901, p. 2.

17. Luigia Rolandi, Antonio Minchiotti, "Per le donne obbligate," ibid.

18. "1º Congresso delle leghe fra i lavoratori della terra di Lomellina," ibid., Oct. 30, 1901, pp. 1–2.

19. Figurelli, "Il movimento contadino nel pavese," p. 269. Figurelli dwells on the "evangelical" style of *La Lega dei Contadini*, a tone shared also by *La Risaia*. Some articles of *La Lega* exhorted the workers to practice the Christian precepts of mutual love by forming their associations; others criticized the failure of the parish priests to apply Christian doctrines.

20. "Resoconto stenografico del primo congresso nazionale dei lavoratori della terra," Zangheri, *Lotte agrarie*, p. 18.

21. Brocchi, *L'organizzazione della resistenza in Italia*, p. lxxxvi.

22. Zangheri, *Lotte agrarie*, pp. lviii–lxiii; Procacci, *La lotta di classe*, pp. 123–29.

23. On this debate, see Zangheri, *Lotte agrarie*, pp. lxv–lxxxii, and Alberto Caracciolo, "Questione agrarie e movimento socialista nella campagna," in Mario Spinella, Alberto Caracciolo, Ruggero Amaduzzi, Giuseppe Petronio, eds., *Critica Sociale* (3 vols.; Milan: Feltrinelli, 1959), II:47–147.

24. "Resoconto stenografico," Zangheri, *Lotte agrarie*, p. 104.

25. Procacci, *La lotta di classe*, pp. 125–26. See also Claudio Treves, "Debbono le Camere del lavoro diventare socialiste? A proposito di un voto del congresso dei lavoratori della terra," *Critica Sociale*, 11, no. 12 (Dec. 1901), 353–55; Filippo Turati, "Variazione sul tema dell'articolo precedente," ibid., 355–58; "Resoconto stenografico," Zangheri, *Lotte agrarie*, pp. 67–72.

26. Zangheri, *Lotte agrarie*, "Resoconto stenografico," pp. 73–85.

27. "La risaia," *La Risaia*, Aug. 3, 1901, p. 3.

28. "Orari di monda," ibid., Jan. 11, 1902, p. 4.

29. Ardis Cameron, "Bread and Roses Revisited: Women's Culture and Working-class Activism in the Lawrence Strike of 1912," in Ruth Milkman, ed., *Women, Work and Protest. A Century of U.S. Women's Labor History* (Boston: Routledge and Kegan Paul, 1985), p. 44.

30. Hilden, *Working Women and Socialist Politics in France*, p. 262.

31. Alice Kessler-Harris, "Where are the Organized Women Workers?" *Feminist Studies*, 3, no. 1/2 (Fall 1975), 101–2.

32. Società Umanitaria, *Pubblicazioni*, no. 5, p. 28.

33. Luigi Moranino, *Le donne socialiste nel biellese (1900–1918)* (Vercelli: Istituto per la storia della Resistenza in provincia di Vercelli "Cino Moscatelli," 1984), p. vi.

34. Flora, "Educhiamo alle donne," *La Risaia*, Feb. 21, 1903, p. 3.

35. Maurizio Degl'Innocenti, *Geografia e istituzioni del socialismo italiano, 1892–1914* (Naples: Guida, 1983), pp. 34–36.

36. Aiazza, "Vercelli e la Bassa," p. 204.

37. Robert Michels, *Il proletariato e la borghesia nel movimiento socialista italiano. Saggio di scienza sociografico-politica* (Turin: Bocca, 1908), p. 138.

38. Procacci, *Lotta di classe*, p. 97.

39. Carocci, *Giolitti e l'età giolittiana* (Turin: Einaudi, 1961), pp. 67–68.

40. On Cuneo women's temporary migration, see Nuto Revelli, *L'anello forte. La donna: storie di vita contadina* (Turin: Einaudi, 1985), pp. 117–19 and 208–9. In the year 1905, 182,750 women and 676,250 men took part in internal migration. The following year, 112,191 women migrated abroad, mostly to neighboring countries (see Zangheri, *Lotte agrarie*, pp. 191 and 193).

41. On figures for organized agricultural workers, see "L'organizzazione nazionale dei contadini dal novembre 1901 all'aprile 1906," Zangheri, *Lotte agrarie*, pp. 135–38. Robert Michels stressed that the majority of the migrant weeders came from places where socialist ideas had not taken roots, like Piacenza, Bobbio, or Voghera (*Il proletariato e la borghesia*, pp. 181–82).

42. "Per la monda del riso in Piemonte e Lomellina. Alle risaiole," *Cronaca del lavoro. Bollettino Mensile della Federazione Italiana delle Camere del Lavoro e della Federazione Nazionale dei Lavoratori della Terra*, 1, no. 2 (Feb. 1902), 27.

43. "Il Congresso delle risaiole," *La Risaia*, Feb. 8, 1902, p. 3; "Il Congresso Circondariale dei lavoratori della terra," *Il Lavoratore*, Feb. 8, 1902, p. 1.

44. "Atti della Federazione circondariale fra le Leghe dei Contadini di Novara," *Il Lavoratore*, March 15, 1902, p. 1, and April 12, 1902, p. 1.

45. "9 marzo. Decisione di sciopero," *Cronache vercellesi*, p. 96. "A quando lo sciopero?" ibid.

46. "Atti ufficiali della FRAP. Consiglio Generale della Federazione del 29 maggio 1902," *La Risaia*, June 7, 1902, p. 3.

47. Il Segretario. Stefano Viglongo, "Spettabile Associazione degli Agricoltori Vercellesi. Città," ibid., Nov. 15, 1902, p. 3; "Il bene degli umili. Per la monda," ibid., Jan. 31, 1903, p. 3.

48. "Lo sciopero di Sartirana," *Il Contadino*, March 21, 1902, pp. 1–2; "San Giorgio Lomellina," *La Plebe*, March 29–30, 1902, p. 3.

49. "San Giorgio Lomellina," ibid., June 14–15, 1902, p. 3.

50. "La voce delle risaie," *La Risaia*, Jan. 3, 1903, p. 3.

51. "Il Congresso Nazionale delle Risaiole in Guastalla," *Il Lavoratore*, Nov. 22, 1902, p. 1.

52. "Il Congresso dei Lavoratori Lomellini, Mortara, Nov. 16, 1902," *Il Contadino*, Nov. 21, 1902, pp. 1–2; "Secondo congresso dei Contadini della Regione risicola Piemontese," *La Risaia*, Jan. 3, 1903, p. 2.

53. Una donna a nome di 132 mondine, "Il voto di 132 mondine," ibid., June 21, 1902, p. 2.

54. "Il congresso dei contadini," *Cronache vercellesi*, p. 56; Procacci, *La lotta di classe*, p. 97.

55. Facchinetti, "La Lotta di classe nelle zone risicole del novarese e del vercellese," *Braccianti e contadini nella valle padana, 1880–1905* (Rome: Editori Riuniti, 1975), p. 345.

56. Rosaldo Ordano, "Modesto Cugnolio," *Figure* (Vercelli: S.E.T.E., 1977), pp. 17–24.

57. Detti, *Fabrizio Maffi*, p. 127.

58. "I dissensi nel partito," *Il Lavoratore*, Sept. 14, 1901, p. 1. The Novarese socialists were critical of the reformists who were backing the Giolitti government at the time of the "slaughter" of Berra Ferrarese.

59. Figurelli, "Il movimento contadino nel pavese dal 1894 al 1904," p. 281n. The leagues of Lomellina led an independent life from the chamber of labor of Pavia, dominated by the reformists. On Cagnoni, see also Michela Figurelli, "Cagnoni Egisto," in Franco Andreucci and Tommaso Detti, *Il movimento operaio italiano, Dizionario biografico, 1853–1943* (Rome: Editori Riuniti, 1975), I:447.

60. Sergio Soave, "Socialismo e socialisti nelle campagne dal 90 alla grande guerra" in Aldo Agosti and Gian Mario Bravo, eds., *Storia del movimento operaio, del socialismo e delle lotte sociali in Piemonte, II. L'età giolittiana, la guerra e il dopoguerra* (Bari: De Donato, 1979), p. 186.

61. "Preti," *La Risaia*, March 30, 1901, p. 2; "La miseria dei preti," ibid., Aug. 3, 1901, p. 3.

62. On the affinities socialists found between socialism and the Christian faith, see Detti, *Fabrizio Maffi*, pp. 66–67.

63. "Catechismo del contadino," *La Risaia*, Dec. 8, 1900, p. 2.

64. "Il proletariato agricolo," *Il Lavoratore*, March 30, 1901, p. 1; "Borgomanero," ibid., May 11, 1901, p. 1.

65. "La lettera di un contadino," *Le Lega dei Contadini*, July 13, 1901, p. 4.

66. "Alle donne," *La Risaia*, Feb. 9, 1901, p. 4; Virgoletta, "Alle donne," ibid., May 25, 1901, p. 1; Gigetto, "Alle donne contadine," ibid., June 15, 1901, pp. 3–4; Nina S., "Per le donne," *Il Lavoratore*, July 20, 1902, pp. 1–2; Flora, "Educhiamo alle donne," *La Risaia*, Feb. 21, 1903, p. 3.

67. Celle, "L'organizzazione fra le donne e necessaria," *La Risaia*, Nov. 1, 1901, p. 3.

68. Temma Kaplan, "Other Scenarios: Women and Spanish Anarchism," Renate Bridenthal and Claudia Koonz, eds., *Becoming Visible. Women in European History* (Boston: Houghton Mifflin, 1977), p. 413.

69. Quoted in Aurelia Camparini, "Lotte sociali e organizzazioni femminili, 1880–1926," in Agosti and Bravo, *Storia del movimento operaio*, p. 138.

70. Sándor Agócs, *The Troubled Origins of the Italian Catholic Labor Movement, 1878–1914* (Detroit: Wayne State University Press, 1988), pp. 22, 30, 39, 81, and 87–88.

71. "Galliate. All'erta, o mondarisi!" *Il Lavoratore*, June 8, 1901, p. 3; Eugenio Ciacchi, "Propaganda spicciola, I. Le nostre leghe," ibid., June 29, 1901, p. 2 and July 6, 1901, p. 2; Bertolino, "La mistificazione delle Leghe cattoliche del lavoro," ibid., Aug. 10, 1901, p. 2.

72. "Per una lega cattolica del lavoro," *Il Vessillo di S. Eusebio*, Aug. 24, 1901, p. 1; "Lega cattolica del lavoro," ibid., Sept. 7, 1901, p. 1; "Lega cattolica del lavoro," ibid., Sept. 28, 1901, p. 1; "Lega cattolica del lavoro," ibid., Oct. 19, 1901, p. 1; "Lega cattolica del lavoro," ibid., Nov. 9, 1901, p. 1; "Lega cattolica del lavoro. Sezione femminile," ibid., April 4, 1903, p. 1.

73. "Tromello," *Il Contadino*, Jan. 31, 1902, p. 2.

74. Agócs, *The Troubled Origins*, p. 189.

75. *Atti del I. Congresso Risicolo Internazionale*, p. 67.

76. Ibid., pp. 76–82.

77. Archivio di Stato di Novara, busta 2011. *Circa la protezione meccanica nella lotta contro la malaria*, pp. 2 and 5.

78. "Il chinino gratis ai nostri contadini," *La Risaia*, Sept. 20, 1902, p. 3.

79. "Alle leghe dei contadini," *Il Lavoratore*, Feb. 22, 1902, p. 2.

80. "Secondo congresso dei Contadini della Regione risicola Piemontese," *La Risaia*, Jan. 3, pp. 2–3.

81. "Per la legge sul lavoro delle donne e dei fanciulli," *Cronaca del lavoro*, 1, no. 1 (Jan. 1902), 4. The law prohibited the work of children under the age of twelve and it limited the workday of children between twelve and fifteen to eleven hours, and that of women over fifteen, to twelve hours. No girls of any age and no boys under thirteen could be employed in underground work. Only boys over fifteen and adult women could be employed in dangerous and unhealthy jobs. This was the only law introduced by the socialists and approved by parliament. On the origins of the campaign for this law, launched by Kuliscioff and the *Gruppo femminile socialista* of Milan, see "Proteggiamo la donna! Proteggiamo i fanciulli!" *Lotta di classe*, Nov. 20–21, 1987, pp. 2–3, and Pieroni Bortolotti, *Socialismo*, pp. 96–97.

82. Enzo Balboni, *Le origini della organizzazione amministrativa del lavoro* (Milan: Giuffrè, 1968), p. 45.

83. Facchinetti, *"La lotta di classe,"* p. 235.

84. Figurelli "Il movimento contadino nel pavese," p. 283.

Chapter 5

1. Società Umanitaria, *L'Umanitaria e la sua opera* (Milan: Cooperativa grafica degli operai, 1922), pp. 14–18. See also Enrico Decleva, "Socialismo e etica del lavoro: la Società Umanitaria," in Maurizio Degli Innocenti, ed., *Filippo Turati e il socialismo europeo* (Naples: Guida, 1985) pp. 159–93.

2. Ilario Zannoni, *Società Umanitaria*, Milano. Segretariato per l'emigrazione interna. *Gli Uffici di Collocamento per i contadini migranti in Italia* (Imola: Cooperativa Tipografica Editrice P. Galeati, 1907), p. 10.

3. Società Umanitaria, *Pubblicazioni*, no. 5, pp. 3–9 and 15.

4. Ibid., pp. 125–31.

5. "Atti ufficiali della FRAP," *La Risaia*, Feb. 7, 1903, p. 2. On the workers' campaign to enforce legislation, see "L'agitazione nel paese per la applicazione del regolamento Cantelli circa le risaie e il chinino di Stato," ibid., April 11, 1903, p. 2.

6. Italy, *Atti del Parlamento Italiano, Discussioni* (Camera dei Deputati), 21st Legislative Period, 2nd Session (1902–4), vol. 7 (Rome: Tipografia della Camera dei Deputati, 1903), p. 6029.

7. Ibid., pp. 6036–38, 6040, and 6042.

8. Ibid., p. 6044–45.

9. "Pei nostri contadini," *La Risaia*, May 9, 1903, p. 3. "Pei nostri contadini," ibid., May 23, 1903, p. 3; "Pei nostri contadini," ibid., May 30, 1903, p. 3.

10. "Per i lavori nelle risaie," June 23, 1903, in *Cronache vercellesi*, p. 61.

11. Italy, Consiglio Provinciale di Novara. *Atti*, Session of Aug. 19, 1903. *Modificazioni al regolamento sulla coltivazione del riso*, pp. 130–31.

12. "In difesa dei mondarisi," *Cronaca del Lavoro*, 4, no. 1 (Jan. 1904), 24.

13. Italy, Consiglio Provinciale di Novara. *Atti*, Session of Dec. 30, 1903, p. 383; Session of Aug. 10, 1903, pp. 134–37.

14. Ibid., pp. 138, 142, and 144. On the session of the Pavia provincial council, see "Consiglio Provinciale. Seduta 27 giugno," *Il Contadino*, July 3, 1903, pp. 1–2.

15. "Un medico che esercisce fra le risaie vercellesi. I medici in difesa dei contadini. Alla vittoria! La scienza non si prostituisce," *La Monda*, Aug. 14, 1903, p. 2. The editors did not disclose the name of the physician, presumably a municipal doctor, not to put him in danger of losing his job. Not all municipal doctors were so outspoken as this anonymous writer. Some hesitated to give their opinion on the value of the Cantelli regulations. Cugnolio observed that they were under the influence of the entrepreneurs and preferred to remain silent (see "Il Congresso di domenica," ibid., Aug. 29, 1903, p. 1).

16. Italy, Consiglio Provinciale di Novara. *Atti*, Session of Aug. 10, 1903, p. 152; Session of Dec. 30, 1903, pp. 378–89.

17. *Atti del II. Congresso Risicolo Internazionale, Mortara, 1–3 ottobre 1903* (Mortara: Cortellezzi, 1903), p. 144.

18. Ibid., pp. 209–11 and 215.

19. Ibid., pp. 209, 232–34, and 236–37.

20. Ibid., p. 244.

21. Ibid., pp. 245–55.

22. Società Umanitaria, *Pubblicazioni*, no. 5, p. 1.

23. Ibid., p. 11. The agents studied, in 114 rice communes, 911 large and middle-sized farms (small property was disregarded), covering 64,619 hectares, each one covering an average extension of 71 hectares. Of the 911

farms, 154 were managed by the landowners, and 757 by leaseholders (see ibid., p. 165). The figures on the composition of the labor force are as follows:

	Number of Squads		Number of Weeders	
Total	1,238	(100.00%)	76,145	(100.00%)
Local	799	(64.54%)	39,921	(53.43%)
Migratory	439	(35.46%)	36,224	(46.57%)

A local squad had an average of 49 members; a migratory one, of 82. The distribution by sex and age was as follows:

women	57,048	(74.92%)
men	14,193	(18.64%)
children	4,904	(6.44%)

Among the grown-ups there were some artisans and many "old men and women over fifty" (12.50 percent.) Of the 39,921 local weeders, 1,902 (4.86 percent) were permanent workers in the farms, and 37,214 (95.14 percent) free. The rate of women to men and children in the local and migratory squads was as follows:

	Local Squads	Migratory Squads
Women	76.04%	71.45%
Men	17.93%	21.61%
Children	6.03%	6.94%

(See ibid., pp. 24–28.)

Figures for the weeding of 1904 can be found in Italy, MAIC, Ufficio del Lavoro, *Le condizioni di lavoro nelle risaie*, Pubblicazioni dell'Ufficio del Lavoro, Serie B, no. 8 (Rome: Tipografia Nazionale G. Bertero, 1906), pp. 91–190. This was an inquiry on labor conditions in the rice fields to assist legislators in the preparation of the new law.

24. Ibid., pp. 29 and 33–34.

25. Ibid., pp. 117–19, 132, and 142.

26. Ibid., pp. 152–61.

27. "Si cammina," *La Monda*, June 13, 1903, p. 1; "Ministero dell'Interno. Consiglio Superiore di Sanità," ibid., Aug. 22, 1903, p. 2. The whole session of June 8 of the supreme sanitary council is reprinted in this article.

For the discussion of the Cerruti project in the superior labor council, see Italy, MAIC, Consiglio Superiore del Lavoro, *Atti*, Session of Sept. 15, 1903, pp. 34–47; Session of March 3, 1904, pp. 36–49; Session of May 19, 1904, pp. 15–16.

28. "Il prezzo della monda," *La Risaia*, April 4, 1903, p. 3; "Per il prezzo della monda," ibid., May 23, 1903, p. 2.

29. "Per nostri contadini," June 6, 1903, p. 1; "Lettera Aperta," *Il Contadino*, June 12, 1903, p. 4.

30. Società Umanitaria, *Pubblicazioni*, no. 5, p. 67.

31. "Sempre per la monda," *La Monda*, June 13, 1903, p. 3; "Le contravvenzioni pel regolamento sulle risaie," ibid., June 30, 1903, p. 3.

32. "Le vicende della monda," ibid., May 30, 1903, p. 3; "Sempre la monda," ibid., June 13, 1903; "Il contadino di Ronsecco," ibid., June 13, 1903, p. 3; Alessandro Schiavi, *Per le otto ore in risaia. Inchiesta sugli scioperi della primavera del 1904* (Milan: Editore l'Ufficio del Lavoro dell'Umanitaria, 1904), p. 17 (this is another inquiry made by the labor bureau of the Humanitarian Society); "Da Villanova Monferrato: Sempre sul regolamento Cantelli," *La Monda*, Oct. 1, 1904, p. 2.

33. "In risaia," *Cronache vercellesi, 1871–1905*, June 23, 1903, p. 63.

34. "Le contravvenzioni pel Regolamento sulle risaie," *La Monda*, July 30, 1903, p. 3; "Violazioni constatate," *Il Contadino*, June 12, 1903, p. 4.

35. "Sorvegliate," *La Monda*, May 30, 1903, p. 3; "Ultime notizie," ibid., May 30, 1903, p. 3; and Italy, *Atti del Parlamento Italiano*, Discussioni (Camera dei Deputati), 21st Legislative Period, 2nd Session, June 3, 1903 (1902–1904), vol. 9 (Rome: Bertero, 1903), 8553–56.

36. "Sempre per la monda," *La Monda*, June 13, 1903, p. 3; "Il tradimento contro i mondini del Vercellese," ibid., June 20, 1903, p. 3; "Le contravvenzioni del Regolamento sulle risaie," ibid., June 20, 1903, p. 3; "I padroni minacciano il governo," ibid., June 27, 1903, p. 2.

37. "Non ce ne importa," ibid., June 27, 1903, pp. 2–3; "I padroni," ibid., p. 3; "Ai contadini del Vercellese," ibid., July 25, 1903, p. 2.

38. "La nostra campagna," ibid., June 27, 1903, p. 3; "Ai contadini del Vercellese," ibid., July 25, 1903, p. 2; "Agricoltori assolti," ibid., "Importantissimo," ibid., "Ai contadini del Vercellese," ibid., and "Cozzo," *Il Contadino*, June 26, 1903, p. 2.

39. The FRAP collected 15,000 signatures. See "Il congresso di domenica," *La Monda*, Aug. 29, 1903, p. 1; "Il Memoriale della Federazione Regionale Agricola Piemontese ai Ministri dell'Interno e d'Agricoltura, Indus-

tria e Commercio," ibid., p. 2. The weeders' song, "Le mondine contro la cavalleria" [The weeders resisting the cavalry], chronicles the events of Ferrera Erbognone (see Currà, *Canti della protesta femminile*, pp. 149–50 and 227).

40. "Barbarie," *Il Contadino*, June 19, 1903, p. 1; "L'orario dei mondarisi," *La Plebe*, June 20–21, 1903, p. 3; "Per i mondarisi," ibid., June 27–28, 1903, p. 1. This article, with the subtitle "Non vogliamo neanche gli scrupoli di coscienza," explains how the entrepreneurs called for a session of the provincial council of Pavia to ask for either the suppression or the modification of the Cantelli regulations.

41. "L'errore della autorità," *La Monda*, Sept. 26, 1903, p. 1; "Il congresso dei risaiuoli a Milano," ibid., Nov. 21, 1903, p. 1. See the records of this assembly in "La difesa dei mondarisi," *Cronaca del Lavoro*, 4, no. 1 (Jan. 1904), pp. 23–37. Representatives of the national federations of workers (Federterra), of the Humanitarian Society, of several chambers of labor, and the leagues dwelt on a series of modifications to the Cerruti law project, which they intended to present to the government.

42. "Il Consiglio generale della FRAP," *La Monda*, Oct. 31, 1903, p. 1.

43. "Un brano degli atti del Consiglio Superiore del Lavoro," ibid., Dec. 5, 1903, p. 1, and December 19, 1903, p. 2; "I progetti di regolamenti di lavoro per la risaia," ibid., Dec. 19, 1903, pp. 1–2, and Jan. 2, 1904, p. 2.

44. "Atti ufficiali della FRAP. L'Assemblea del Consiglio generale," ibid., Jan. 9, 1904, p. 1. A journalist of *La Risaia* stated that the farmers introduced the hourly pay to induce the *mondariso* to work as many hours as possible and so violate the law. (See "Ai contadini. Attenzione! Attenzione! Attenzione! Come si prepara la battaglia," ibid., April 15, 1905, p. 2; "L'opera della FRAP," ibid., May 20, 1905, p. 1.)

45. "Il Comizio di Novara rinviato," *La Monda*, Jan. 30, 1904, p. 2; "Ultimissime. I Consigli dell sanità e del lavoro," ibid.

46. "Atti ufficiali della FRAP," ibid., Feb. 27, 1904, p. 1; "Scampoli della questione delle risaie," ibid., Feb. 27, 1904, pp. 1–2.

47. "Ai contadini. Avvertenza importantissima," ibid., Feb. 27, 1904, p. 3; "Il comizio di domenica," ibid., March 5, 1904, pp. 1–2.

48. "Atti ufficiali della FRAP. L'Assemblea del Consiglio Generale," ibid., Jan. 9, 1904, p. 1; "Il Congresso del Comitato Esecutivo della Federazione Nazionale e delle Federazioni Provinciali dei Lavoratori della Terra a Mantova," ibid., Feb. 13, 1904, p. 1.

49. Italy, *Atti del Parlamento Italiano. Discussioni* (Camera dei Deputati), 21st Legislative Period, 2nd Session (1902–1904), February 24-March 26, 1904, vol. 12, March 10, 1904 (Rome: Bertero, 1904), 12,416–18; "Intorno alla legge

sulle risaie," *La Monda*, March 12, 1904, p. 1; "La risaia davanti alla legge," ibid., March 19, 1904, p. 1; "Atti ufficiali della FRAP," ibid., April 16, 1904, p. 1; "Il lavoro nelle risaie. Seduta del 12 maggio alla Camera dei deputati," ibid., May 21, 1904, p. 2. In March 1904 the provincial council of Novara voted modifications to the Cantelli regulations to cancel out all protective measures to the workers. The alarmed socialist deputies interrogated Giovanni Giolitti, then premier and minister of the interior, on whether he intended to approve such modifications with royal decree. His answer was in the negative, adducing that he would back the passage of the Cerruti project. In April and May it was the turn of the provincial council of Pavia to change the regulations. The undersecretary of the interior, Ugo di Sant'Onofrio, questioned on the subject by the socialist deputies, stated that the changes would not be approved by the government.

50. "Padroni tra due fuochi. La Cassazione di Roma dichiara costituzionale il Regolamento Cantelli," ibid., March 5, 1904, pp. 2–3; "Il comizio di domenica," ibid., March 5, 1904, pp. 1–2. In spite of the acquittal of the farmers violating article 14, the cassation court in Rome confirmed in March 1904 the constitutionality of the 1866 law and its regulations. In 1906 there appeared a curious article in *La Risaia*, in which its author compared the indifference of the mayors and the subprefects toward article 14 with their zeal in posting and enforcing other rules advantageous to the entrepreneurs. There was one forbidding the sale in the public market of Cappucini, in the Vercellese, of fish not reaching a certain length. The entrepreneurs of the fishermen's society made them observe the regulation, affecting poor fishermen selling fish for the poor, who could afford to eat polenta and cheap fish. The catch was from the canals that were being drained in any case, and the fish would have gone to waste if not caught. (See "Bisogna misurare il pesce! Contro i poveri Cappuccinatti," ibid., March 10, 1906, p. 2.) Workers often complained about suffering prosecution for committing a trespass, such as stealing firewood. Little girls tending geese in Candia (Vercellese) had them "confiscated" by a guard because the animals ran away into a private field. When the girls' tears and their mothers' entreaties to the guard did not mollify him, the women began to hit him with their sticks while the girls took their geese back (Candia, *"Il Contadino*, Oct. 6, 1905, p. 2). On the same subject, see "Pieve del Cairo," ibid., June 27, 1904, p. 2; "Nicorvo," ibid., June 12, 1908, p. 2.

51. "La nostra idea," *La Monda*, Feb. 20, 1904, p. 1; "Il Congresso di Bologna," ibid., April 16, 1904, p. 2.

52. "Per la monda del riso," *Il Contadino*, April 8, 1904, p. 1; "Otto ore di lavoro nella monda," *La Monda*, May 14, 1904, p. 2; "Il grande sciopero della monda. La grande fabbrica dei rivoluzionari," ibid., May 21, 1904, p. 1.

53. "Cronaca dello sciopero," ibid., May 21, 1904, pp. 1–2.

54. "Cronaca dello sciopero," ibid., May 28, 1904, p. 1. Five women of Bianzè received similar sentences to those of Lignana (see "Echi dello sciopero," ibid., June 11, 1904, p. 2). In Quinto Vercelli four women had a suspended sentence of ten days (see "L'ultimo processo dei contadini," ibid., Aug. 6, 1904, p. 2; "Per le vittime dello sciopero," ibid., June 4, 1904, p. 1).

55. "Lo sciopero prosegue a Santhià," ibid., June 4, 1904, p. 1; "Echi dello sciopero," ibid., June 11, 1904, p. 2.

56. "Echi dello sciopero," ibid., June 18, 1904, p. 2.

57. Alessandro Schiavi, Per le otto ore in risaia, p. 8.

58. "Echi dello sciopero," La Monda, June 18, 1904, p. 2.

59. "Atti ufficiali della FRAP," ibid., July 30, 1904, p. 1.

60. Italy, Atti del Parlamento Italiano. Discussioni (Camera dei Deputati), 21st Legislative Period, 2nd Session (1902–1904), vol. 14, June 9, 1904 (Rome: Bertero, 1904), 13,578–80.

61. Schiavi, Per le otto ore, p. 6; "L'agitazione dei contadini," Il Lavoratore, May 28, 1904, p. 1; "Borgolavezzaro," ibid., May 28, 1904, p. 3; "Vespolate," ibid.

62. "Borgolavezzaro," Il Lavoratore, June 4, 1904, p. 3.

63. "Federazione Proletaria Lomellina," Il Contadino, June 17, 1904, p. 1; Schiavi, Per le otto ore, p. 6. In 1903, 15,560 migratory weeders traveled to Lomellina. In 1904 they were three thousand fewer (see ibid., p. 11).

64. Ibid., pp. 12–15; "Il nostro trionfo," Il Contadino, June 17, 1904, p. 3.

65. "Sannazzaro," La Plebe, June 25–26, 1904, p. 3.

66. Schiavi, Per le otto ore, p. 15; "Bravi forestieri," Il Contadino, June 10, 1904, p. 1.

67. "Atti ufficiali della FRAP," La Monda, July 30, 1904, p. 1.

68. Ibid., p. 17. Here are the work schedules and wages of the local weeders in 1903 and 1904 published by Schiavi (pp. 4 and 16):

	1903	
	Length of workday	Wages (in lire)
Novarese	9 hrs. 45 min.	1.82
Vercellese	9 hrs.	1.82
Lomellina	10 hrs.	1.82

	1904 Length of workday	Wages (in lire)
Novarese	9 hrs.	2.00
Vercellese	8 hrs.	2.00
Lomellina	9 hrs.	1.80

69. Zannoni. Società Umanitaria. Milano. Segretariato per l'emigrazione interna. *Gli Uffici di Collocamento per i contadini migranti in Italia*, pp. 49–50.

70. Pico, "Ufficio di collocamento per i mondatori di riso," *Il Lavoratore*, Jan. 21, 1905, pp. 1–2.

71. "I pericoli di una istituzione," *La Risaia*, Jan. 7, 1905, pp. 1–2.

72. "Il Congresso Nazionale dei Lavoratori della risaia," ibid., Jan. 31, 1905, pp. 2–3; "Convegno dei rappresentanti della Federazione delle leghe circa l'emigrazione delle risaiuole in Lomellina e nel Vercellese. Bologna, 16 maggio 1905," ibid., May 20, 1905, p. 1. This congress was called by Argentina Altobelli, the secretary of the Federterra. See also "Un uomo a mare," *Il Contadino*, June 9, 1905, pp. 1–3.

73. Disc, "Gli emissarii dell'Ufficio di Collocamento pei mondarisi," *Il Lavoratore*, May 20, 1905, pp. 1–2.

74. "Ufficio di collocamento," *Il Contadino*, Aug. 25, 1905, p. 2; "L'Ufficio di collocamento dell'Umanitaria," *La Risaia*, Nov. 18, 1905, p. 1; Gavroche, "Calano i corvi," *Il Contadino*, Nov. 17, 1905, p. 1; "Noi e l'Umanitaria," ibid., Nov. 24, 1905, p. 1; "L'Umanitaria al bivio," ibid., Dec. 8, 1905, p. 1.

75. "Per istituire un Collegio di Probiviri a Vercelli," *La Risaia*, Aug. 19, 1905, p. 1; "Il Comizio pei 'Probiviri,'" ibid., Oct. 21, 1905, p. 2; "Cose del partito ed interessi dei lavoratori," *La Plebe*, Sept. 30, 1905, p. 1.

76. Ernesto Ragionieri, *La storia politica e sociale, Storia d'Italia* (Turin: Einaudi, 1976), vol. 4, part 3, 1976.

77. "Per la legge sulla risaia," *La Risaia*, Dec. 31, 1904, p. 2. On Giolitti's alignment with the conservatives, see also Carocci, *Giolitti e l'età giolittiana*, pp. 84–85 and 95.

78. "Il Congresso Nazionale dei Lavoratori della risaia," *La Risaia*, Jan. 31, 1905, pp. 1–2.

79. "Per una lege sulle risaie," ibid., March 4, 1905, pp. 1–2; "Per il lavoro in risaia. Il progetto Fracassi e l'onorevole Montemartini," *La Plebe*, March 4–5, 1905, p. 1; "Per la legge sulle risaie," ibid., March 4–5, 1905, p. 2.

80. "Giolitti tradiva i lavoratori della risaia," *La Risaia*, April 1, 1905, p. 2;

"Vogliono la pelle," *Il Contadino*, April 7, 1905, p. 1; "Ai contadini. Attenzione! Attenzione! Attenzione! Come si prepara la battaglia," *La Risaia*, April 15, 1905, p. 2; Landmann, "Il progetto barbaro ritirato," ibid.; "Losche manovre," *Il Contadino*, April 14, 1905, p. 1.

81. "Per la legislazione delle risaie. Il nuovo tentativo degli agricoltori contro l'interesse dei contadini," *La Risaia*, Dec. 16, 1905, p. 2; "Consiglio Provinciale," *La Plebe*, April 14, 1905, p. 2.

82. "Per la legge sul lavoro nelle risaie," *La Risaia*, March 10, 1906, p. 2; "La sottoscrizione dei contadini per le otto ore nella monda e per la giornata limitata," ibid., March 10, 1906, p. 3.

83. "Per il lavoro nelle risaie," *La Plebe*, June 9, 1906, p. 3.

84. "Il Congresso di domenica," *La Monda*, Aug. 29, 1903, p. 1.

85. See, for example, "Il Comizio di Novara rinviato," ibid., Jan. 30, 1904, p. 2.

86. "I progetti di regolamento di lavoro per la risaia," *La Monda*, Dec. 19, 1903, pp. 1–2; "I progetti di regolamenti di lavoro per la risaia," ibid., Jan. 2, 1904, p. 2.

87. "Atti ufficiale della FRAP. L'Assemblea del Consiglio Generale," ibid., Jan. 9, 1904, p. 1.

88. "Per una legge sulle risaie," *La Risaia*, March 4, 1905, pp. 1–2.

89. "Lo sciopero a San Germano Vercellese," ibid., March 11, 1905, p. 2.

90. Doctor bonus, "La campagna antimalarica. Speranze. Illusioni," ibid., March 11, 1905, pp. 2–3.

91. "L'igiene nelle risaie. La relazione Grassi", ibid., April 29, 1905, p. 2. The title of Grassi's report is *Relazione dell'esperimento fatto nel 1904 in Olevano (Lomellina) nel podere Drovanti, per iniziativa del Congresso Internazionale di Risicoltura del 1903* (offprint from "L'Agricoltura Moderna," no. 6–10, 1905). See ibid., p. 21.

92. "Stringiamoci insieme," *La Risaia*, May 6, 1905, p. 1.

93. Francesco Costa, "Ai risaiuoli," ibid., June 3, 1905, p. 2; "Gli agricoltori dicono," ibid., June 3, 1906, p. 2.

94. The program of mobilization of the FRAP can be followed in these articles: "Atti ufficiali della FRAP," ibid., April 1, 1905, p. 1; "Ai contadini ed operai disorganizzati," ibid., April 1, 1905, p. 2; "Propaganda," ibid., April 15, 1905, p. 1; "Corrispondenze. Buronzo: Ai disorganizzati," ibid., May 13, 1905, p. 3; "Per la imminente campagna risicola," ibid., May 13, 1905, pp. 2–3; "Corrispondenze," ibid., May 13, 1905, p. 3.

95. A journalist of *La Risaia* expressed the general disappointment with the role of parliament in Italy: "We think that we live in a regime where the will of Parliament commands. Not at all. There are a thousand ways to deceive this will" ("Leggi e regolamenti," ibid., May 13, 1905, p. 1).

96. "Convegno dei rappresentanti delle Federazioni delle leghe circa l'emigrazione delle risaiuole in Lomellina e nel Vercellese," ibid., May 20, 1905, p. 1.

97. "La questione del mondariso," *Il Contadino,* May 5, 1905, p. 2; "Alle risaiole che vengono in Lomellina," ibid., June 1, 1905, p. 2; "Si fa eseguire il Regolamento Cantelli," ibid., May 23, 1905, p. 1; "Nella imminenza della monda," ibid., May 27, 1905, p. 1. Unemployment was widespread also in Emilia, in the recruitment zones of the migratory weeders. See "Atti ufficiali della FRAP," ibid., June 3, 1905, p. 1; "Il momento terribile," ibid., June 22, 1905, p. 1; "Per i mondarisi," *La Plebe,* May 27, 1905, p. 1; "L'andamento della monda," *La Risaia,* June 3, 1905, p. 3; "Denunciate! Denunciate!" ibid.; "Correspondenza. Bianzè," ibid.; "Il consiglio generale dell'11 Giugno," *Il Contadino,* June 16, 1905, p. 2.

98. "Castelnovetto," *Il Contadino,* July 28, 1905, p. 3.

99. "Atti ufficiali della FRAP," *La Risaia,* June 3, 1905, p. 1; "Corrispondenze. Bianzè," ibid., June 3, 1905, p. 2; "Otto ore di lavoro. La vittoria di Tricerro," ibid., June 10, 1905, p. 1; "L'agitazione di Monticello," *Il Lavoratore,* June 10, 1905, p. 2; "I vantaggi dell'organizzazione," ibid., July 1, 1905, p. 1; "Atti ufficiali della FRAP," *La Risaia,* Oct. 28, 1905, p. 1. In the commune of Strella the total earnings of the *monda* increased from 87 lire in 1904 to 102 lire in 1905.

100. Angelica Balabanoff, "Perchè vogliamo le otto ore," *La Risaia,* June 3, 1905, pp. 1–2; "La compagna Balabanoff," ibid., June 3, 1905, p. 2. (See also Balabanoff's article dedicated to women workers of Novara, "Su compagne!" *Il Lavoratore,* Oct. 7, 1905, p. 1.)

101. "Atti ufficiali della FRAP," *La Risaia,* May 26, 1906, p. 1; "Le otto ore di monda," ibid.; "I due ordini del giorno," ibid., June 3, 1906, p. 1; "Il regolamento Cantelli non è un vecchiume," ibid., June 3, 1906, p. 1; "Fatte otto ore di monda," ibid., June 3, 1906, p. 2.

102. The numerous labor conflicts in the rice belt at the end of May and the beginning of June are reported in "La grave agitazione per le 8 ore di monda," ibid., June 3, 1906, pp. 1–3; and in *Cronache vercellesi,* 1906–1909, pp. 4–14.

103. A. Gionino, "Contadini malvaggi," *La Risaia,* July 21, 1906, p. 1.

104. Adolfo Fiorani, *Se otto ore vi sembran poche* (Commune di Vercelli: Assesorato alla Coltura, 1976), p. 7. On the 1906 Vercelli general strike, see

also Elda Gentili Zappi, "'If Eight Hours Seem Few to You . . .' Women Workers' Strikes in Italian Rice Fields, 1901–1906," in Barbara J. Harris and JoAnn K. McNamara, *Women and the Structure of Society* (Durham, N.C.: Duke University Press, 1984), pp. 206–14.

105. Ibid., pp. 7 and 13–16.

106. "Come si svolse lo sciopero a Santhià," *La Risaia,* June 9, 1906, pp. 2–3.

107. "La serrata dei metallurgici vercellesi," ibid., June 3, 1906, p. 3; "Gli operai panattieri," ibid.

108. "Le mondarisi di Vercelli," ibid., June 3, 1906, p. 1.

109. Fiorani, *Se otto ore vi sembran poche,* pp. 39–40.

110. "Ultime notizie sull'agitazione proletaria a Vercelli. Lo sciopero generale," *La Risaia,* June 3, 1906, p. 4; Fiorani, *Se otto ore vi sembran poche,* pp. 16–20.

111. Ibid., Fioriani, *Se otto ore vi sembran poche,* pp. 48–51.

112. "Alle leghe federate," *Il Contadino,* June 2, 1905, p. 1; "Confienza," ibid., p. 2; "Vittorie di mondarisi," ibid., June 22, 1906. On women textile workers at Biella, see Moranino, *Le donne socialiste nel biellese (1900–1918),* pp. 15–18.

113. Preti, *Le lotte agrarie,* p. 124.

114. Alberto Caracciolo, *Il movimento contadino nel Lazio (1870–1922)* (Rome: Edizioni Rinascita, 1952), pp. 105–11.

115. Frank M. Snowden, *Violence and Great Estates in the South of Italy. Apulia, 1900–1922* (Cambridge: Cambridge University Press, 1986), p. 67. The *Avanti!* article is cited in ibid., pp. 67–68.

116. Moranino, *Le donne socialiste,* p. 57.

117. Hilden, *Working Women and Socialist Politics,* p. 136.

118. Alice Kessler-Harris, *Out to Work. A History of Wage-Earning Women in the United States* (New York: Oxford University Press, 1982), p. 160.

119. Ardis Cameron, "Bread and Roses revisited: Women's culture and working-class activism in the Lawrence strike of 1912," in Ruth Milkman, ed., *Women, Work and Protest* (Boston: Routledge & Kegan Paul, 1985), p. 43. On the Lawrence strike, see also Meredith Tax, *The Rising of the Women. Feminist Solidarity and Class Conflict (1880–1917)* (New York: Monthly Review Press, 1980), pp. 241–74.

120. Kessler-Harris, *Out to Work,* p. 160.

NOTES

121. Hilden, *Working Women and Socialist Politics*, pp. 48–49 and 64; Cameron, "Bread and Roses revisited," pp. 44–45.

122. Kaplan, "Female Consciousness and Collective Action: The Case of Barcelona, 1910–1918," *Signs*, 7, no. 3 (Spring 1982), pp. 545–48.

123. Louise Tilly, "Paths of Proletarianization: Organization of Production, Sexual Division of Labor, and Women's Collective Action," ibid., 7, no. 2 (Winter 1981), p. 29.

124. On the Biella workers, see Moranino, *Le donne socialiste nel biellese*, p. 24: on the Lawrence strike, see Tax, *The Rising of the Women*, p. 249; on collective action of working-class women in Barcelona, see Kaplan, "Female Consciousness and Collective Action," pp. 551–66.

125. Kaplan, *Anarchists of Andalusia, 1868–1903* (Princeton: Princeton University Press, 1977), p. 204. On the role of the chambers of labor in the general strike, see Procacci, *La lotta di classe*, pp. 420 and 423.

126. "L'agitazione proletaria nel Vercellese," *La Risaia*, June 9, 1906, pp. 1–3; "Come si svolse lo sciopero a Santhià," ibid., June 9, 1906, pp. 2–3.

Chapter 6

1. "Festa di campagna a Trino pro mondarisi carcerati," *La Risaia*, June 30, 1906, p. 2.

2. "Salasco," ibid., July 21, 1906, p. 3; La Commissione, "Sottoscrizione pei carcerati in seguito allo sciopero generale," ibid., Oct. 6, 1906, p. 1.

3. "Per gli arrestati", ibid., June 16, 1906, p. 1.

4. Fiorani, *Se otto ore vi sembran poche*, pp. 103–25.

5. "L'abolizione del Regolamento Cantelli"; A. Gionino, "Fu?"; "La proposta di Asigliano," *La Risaia*, Aug. 11, 1906, p. 1.

6. Italy, MAIC, *Bollettino dell'Ufficio del Lavoro*, no. 6 (July-Dec. 1906) (Rome: Officina Poligrafica Italiana, 1907), 499–502.

7. Italy, MAIC, "Congresso dell'Unione Agraria Italiana," *Bollettino dell'Ufficio del Lavoro*, no. 5 (Jan.-June 1906) (Rome: Officina Poligrafica Italiana, 1906), 1177.

8. "L'abolizione del Regolamento Cantelli," *La Risaia*, Aug. 11, 1906, p. 1; "Il grandioso movimento contro l'abolizione del Regolamento Cantelli e per la tariffa e l'orario nella mietitura del riso," ibid., Aug. 18, 1906, p. 2; "Federazione Regionale Agricola Piemontese. Grande corteo di protesta con-

tro l'abolizione del Regolamento Cantelli," ibid., Aug. 18, 1906, p. 2; Un contadino fuori lega, "La parola d'un contadino," ibid., Aug. 18, 1906, p. 2; Francesco Costa, "Cinque anni di manovre contro il lavoro," ibid.

9. "Alla Camera del lavoro. Lega contadina di Vercelli," ibid., Aug. 11, 1906, p. 2.

10. *Cronache vercellesi*, p. 28.

11. "Atti ufficiali della FRAP," *La Risaia*, Aug. 11, 1906, p. 2; La Lega di Stroppiana, "Come si svolse lo sciopero a Stroppiana," ibid., Aug. 18, 1906, p. 2; Zanvercelli, Luigi, segretario della Lega, "Crescentino," ibid., Sept. 1, 1906, p. 2; La Lega, "Lamporo," ibid.; Cino Cini, "Borgovercelli," ibid.; "Brarola," ibid.

12. "Sciopero generale a San Germano," *Cronache vercellesi*, p. 30; "I fatti di Santhià," ibid., p. 36.

13. Ibid., p. 32.

14. Eraldo Gilardino, Segretario Circolo Socialista e Lega di Resistanza, "Balzola," *La Risaia*, Sept. 1, 1906, p. 2.

15. L'agitazione vittoriosa dei contadini," *Il Lavoratore*, Sept. 8, 1906, p. 1.

16. "Lumellogno. Per la vita della Federazione dei contadini," ibid., Oct. 27, 1906, p. 2.

17. Petrini, "Per la ricostruzione della Federazione dei contadini del Novarese," ibid., Aug. 25, 1906, p. 2; "Per la ricostruzione della Federazione dei contadini. Manette, carceri e mitraglia," ibid., Sept. 1, 1906, p. 1.

18. "La agitazione vittoriosa dei contadini," ibid., Sept. 8, 1906, p. 1.

19. "In Lomellina," *Cronache vercellesi*, p. 47.

20. *Atti del Terzo Congresso Risicolo Internazionale, Pavia, 27, 28, 29 ottobre 1906* (Milan: Stabilimento Lito-Tipografico Giuseppe Abbiate, 1907), pp. 56–57.

21. *Cronache vercellesi*, p. 30; "L'Associazione degli agricoltori del Vercellese alle consorelle ed al Parlamento," ibid., p. 40.

22. "La nomina di una commissione," *Cronache vercellesi*, p. 39; "La nuova commissione," ibid., p. 45; "Una commissione camorristica. Risaioli boicottatela," *Il Lavoratore*, Sept. 1, 1906, p. 1.

23. "Un biasimo all'opera del governo. Nel Comitato del Consiglio superiore del lavoro," *Cronache vercellesi*, p. 42; "L'adunanza di martedì dell'Associazione Agricoltori," ibid., p. 44.

24. "Il memoriale degli agricoltori alla Commissione d'inchiesta," ibid., p. 48; Francesco Costa, "Ancora il Memoriale degli agricoltori," *La Risaia*, Oct. 20, 1906, p. 2.

25. "Il memoriale degli agricoltori alla Commissione d'inchiesta," *Cronache vercellesi*, pp. 49–50.

26. La Lega di Olcenengo, "Fosche previsioni," *La Risaia*, Sept. 29, 1906, p. 1.

27. *Atti del Terzo Congresso Risicolo*, pp. 56–57 and 266.

28. "Le proposte della Commissione dei proprietari ed affittavoli del Vercellese," *Cronache vercellesi*, pp. 55–56; "Le deliberazioni dei proprietari," *La Risaia*, Dec. 22, 1906, p. 3; "Tra proprietari e fittabili," ibid., Dec. 29, 1906, p. 2; La Lega contadini di Vercelli, "Ai signori proprietari e conduttori di fondi del Comune di Vercelli," ibid., Dec. 29, 1906, p. 2; "La riduzione della risaia," *Il Contadino*, Feb. 1, 1907, p. 1.

29. Ibid.; "Adunanza delle due Commissioni di proprietari e fittavoli," *Cronache vercellesi*, p. 59; "Un appello ai proprietari ed agricoltori," ibid., p. 60.

30. Cardoza, *Agrarian Elites*, p. 119.

31. "Tra agricoltori e contadini," *La Risaia*, Sept. 29, 1906, p. 1; "Fra contadini e agricoltori," ibid., Oct. 6, 1906, p. 1; "Fra contadini e agricoltori," ibid., Oct. 28, 1906, p. 1; "Fra contadini e agricoltori," ibid., Nov. 3, 1906, p. 1; "Attenzione," ibid., Nov. 3, 1906, p. 1; "Fra contadini e agricoltori," ibid., Nov. 10, 1906, p. 1.

32. "L'assemblea dei proprietari di fondo del Vercellese, Novembre 24," *Cronache vercellesi*, p. 54.

33. "I risultati del Congresso dei lavoratori del riso," *La Plebe*, Dec. 22, 1906, p. 1.

34. Ibid.

35. "A proposito di immigrazione in risaia," *La Risaia*, Nov. 1, 1908, p. 1; "Il Congresso dei risaiuoli di Piacenza," ibid., Nov. 14, 1908, p. 1.

36. "A proposito di immigrazione in risaia," ibid., Nov. 1, 1908, p. 2; "Il Congresso dei risaiuoli. Piacenza," ibid., Nov. 14, 1908, p. 1.

37. "Congresso regionale dei lavoratori della risaia di Novara, Mortara e Vercelli," ibid., Dec. 19, 1906, p. 2.

38. Italy, MAIC, "Congresso nazionale di lavoratori della terra," *Bollettino dell'Ufficio del Lavoro*, no. 7 (Jan.-June 1907) (Rome: Officina Poligrafica Italiana, 1908), 466.

39. La Lega, "San Germano," "Oldenico," and "Castelletto Cervo," *La Risaia*, Feb. 16, 1907, p. 3; "Sartirana," *Il Contadino*, Feb. 8, 1907, p. 2; "Emigrare!" ibid., Feb. 22, 1907, p. 1.

40. Un compagno, "San Grisante," *La Risaia*, Feb. 16, 1907, p. 3.

41. Uno della Lega, "Carisio," ibid., Feb. 16, 1907, p. 3.

42. A. Gionino, "Storia d'un delitto morale," ibid., March 23, 1907, p. 1; A. Gionino, "Buonafede . . . volpina," *La Risaia*, June 1, 1907, p. 2.

43. "Lo sciopero generale" and "Le notizie dello sciopero," *Cronache vercellesi*, pp. 60–68; "Il lavoro del compagno Aroldi," *La Risaia*, March 9, 1907, p. 1; "La questione dello sciopero" and "Previsione sullo sciopero," ibid., March 23, 1907, p. 1.

44. "Le trattative cogli agricoltori," ibid., March 23, p. 1.

45. "Atti ufficiali della FRAP," ibid., March 30, p. 1.

46. "La situazione," ibid., April 13, 1907, p. 1; "Le notizie dello sciopero," *Cronache vercellesi*, p. 68; "Guai ai vinti" and "Notizie dello sciopero," ibid., March 30, 1907, p. 1; "Federazione Regionale Agricola Piemontese," ibid., April 6, 1907, p. 1.

47. "Lavoratori! Emigrate!!" ibid., Oct. 19, 1907, p. 1; "Attenzione! Contadini!" ibid., Jan. 18, 1908, p. 1; A. Gionino, "Il loro giuoco," ibid., Feb. 15, 1908, p. 1; La lega, "Lega contadini di Vercelli," ibid., Feb. 22, 1908, p. 2; "Il guadagno d'un contadino di Vercelli secondo la tariffa dei patroni," ibid., March 7, 1908, p. 2; Ogi, "Mutiamo tattica," ibid., March 14, 1908, p. 2; A. Gionino, "I moderni feudatari," ibid., March 21, 1908, p. 2; "Per le donne" and "Abbandonando la patria," ibid.

48. "Viva la forca," *Il Lavoratore*, March 9, 1907 p. 1; "Agitazione dei contadini del Novarese," ibid., March 16, 1907, p. 2; "Contadini krumiri vergognatevi!" ibid., March 16, p. 2. In Lomellina there were strikes in Robbio and Confienza. See "Confienza e Robbio," *Il Contadino*, March 22, 1907, p. 2.

49. "Le otto ore di monda," *La Risaia*, June 8, 1907, p. 1; "Le otto ore," ibid., June 15, 1907, p. 1.

50. "Sannazzaro," "Lo sciopero di Olevano," and "Mede," *Il Contadino*, May 31, 1907, p. 2; "Ceretto," ibid., June 2, 1907, p. 1; Italy, MAIC, "Notizie sulle condizioni di occupazione," *Bollettino dell'Ufficio del Lavoro*, no. 8 (July-Dec. 1907) (Rome: Officina Poligrafica Italiana, 1908), 58.

51. "San Giorgio," *Il Contadino*, June 7, 1907, p. 2; "Mortara" and "Sannazzaro," ibid., June 14, 1907, pp. 2 and 3.

52. "La situazione," *La Risaia*, April 13, 1907, p. 1; A. Gionino,

"Buonafede . . . volpina," ibid., June 1, 1907, p. 2; Italy, MAIC, "Mercato del lavoro," *Bollettino dell'Ufficio del Lavoro*, no. 8, pp. 80–82.

53. "Violazione alla legge sul lavoro in risaia," *Il Lavoratore*, June 6, 1908, pp. 1–2.

54. A. Gionino, "I moderni feudatari," *La Risaia*, March 21, 1908, p. 2; "Abbandonando la patria," ibid.

55. Valerio Castronovo, *Economia e società in Piemonte dall'Unità al 1914* (Milan: Banca Commerciale Italiana, 1969), pp. 252–56.

56. Alessandro Roveri, *Dal sindacalismo rivoluzionario al fascismo. Capitalismo agrario e socialismo nel ferrarese (1870–1920)* (Florence: La Nuova Italia, 1972), pp. 156–57.

57. See on this matter *Atti del Terzo Congresso Risicolo*, pp. 243 and 269.

58. La Critica Sociale, "La legge del tradimento," *Critica Sociale*, 17, no. 5 (March 1, 1907), 66.

59. *Atti del Terzo Congresso Risicolo*, pp. 204–8.

60. Ibid., pp. 236–37 and 249.

61. Ibid., p. 250.

62. Ibid., pp. 282–83.

63. Ibid., pp. 286–90.

64. Ibid., pp. 293–94 and 296.

65. Angiolo Cabrini, *La legislazione sociale (1859–1913)* (Rome: C. A. Bontempelli, 1913), p. 161; La Critica Sociale, "La Legge del tradimento," pp. 65–66.

66. See on the topic "All'attacco," *La Risaia*, March 9, 1907, p. 1; "Otto ore di monda," ibid., May 11, 1907, p. 1; P.M., "La legge forca," ibid., May 25, 1907, p. 2; "La legge sulla risaia in Senato," ibid., June 29, 1907, p. 1; "Ai lavoratori della risaia," *Il Lavoratore*, March 2, 1907, p. 1; "Viva la forca!" ibid., March 9, 1907, p. 1; "Contadini!" ibid.; Atta Troll, "Da Alicante alla risaia," ibid., March 16, 1907, p. 1; "Tregua di Dio," ibid., March 30, 1907, p. 1; "Il progetto forca," ibid., May 25, 1907, p. 1; "Gli onorevoli del Vaticano contro i lavoratori della risaia," ibid., June 1, 1907, p. 3; "Per le risaie," *La Plebe*, Feb. 2, 1907, p. 1; "Contro la legge forca," *Il Contadino*, March 19, 1907, p. 1.

67. "Contro la legge-capestro," *La Risaia*, March 30, 1907, p. 1; "Comizio protesta," *Il Lavoratore*, April 20, 1907, p. 1; "L'imponente comizio contro la Legge del tradimento," ibid., April 27, 1907, p. 2; "Contro la legge sulla risaia," *La Plebe*, March 30, 1907, p. 1.

68. "La legge forca non passerà," ibid., May 1, 1907, p. 1. "La festa d'inaugurazione della 'Casa del Popolo,'" *La Risaia*, May 11, 1907, p. 1; "L'inaugurazione della 'Casa del Popolo,'" ibid., May 25, p. 1.

69. Filippo Turati, "Le utopie dei conservatori. La controrelazione nel disegno di legge per la risicoltura," *Critica Sociale*, 17, no. 10 (May 16, 1907), 155 and 157. The Giolitti law project of February 21 was published in Italy, MAIC, *Bollettino dell'Ufficio del Lavoro*, no. 7, 537–53. The modified text, presented to the chamber on April 21, is in ibid., no. 8, pp. 1055–98.

70. "La legge sulle risaie," *La Risaia*, May 25, 1907, p. 1.

71. A farmer's obligation to provide drinking water to labor might be interpreted as an elementary duty. To our surprise, we read in *The New York Times* (Feb. 7, 1987, pp. 1 and 7), in an article by Kenneth B. Noble, "U.S. told to set Sanitation Rule for Field Hands. Court Acts to guarantee facilities for 500,000." "A Federal appeals court ruled here today that the Labor Department must issue guidelines requiring farmers to provide toilets, drinking water and other sanitary facilities for field workers." He adds that "the decision was a victory for farmworkers and their advocates who had sought for more than 14 years to require farmers to provide such facilities. Farm workers contend that unsanitary conditions in the field have led to disease and that workers cannot wash off the residues of the pesticides that blanket the fields." The explanation for the delays was government neglect and the strong opposition of the growers, who argued that these improvements were unnecessary and that "the link between the fields and disease is unproved. Growers also oppose the rules for reasons of cost."

72. Turati, "Le utopie," pp. 156–57.

73. La Critica Sociale, "Trappola smontata," *Critica Sociale*, 17, 11 (June 1, 1907), 161–62.

74. Luigi Montemartini, "Per la legge sulla risicoltura," *Il Contadino*, May 31, 1907, p. 1.

75. "Studiando e tentando," *La Risaia*, Jan. 25, 1908, p. 1; "La 'Nuova Gazzetta Vercellese' ed i contadini," ibid., Feb. 1, 1908, p. 1.

76. "Ai contadini!" ibid., Feb. 8, 1908, p. 1; "La tariffa pei contadini," ibid., Feb. 15, 1908, p. 1; A. Gionino, "Il loro giuoco," ibid., Feb. 15, 1908, p. 1.

77. A Gionino, "I moderni feudatari," ibid., March 21, 1908, p. 2; "Per le donne" and "Abbandonado la patria," ibid.

78. "Le trattative per lo sciopero," ibid., May 30, 1908, p. 2.

79. "Lo sciopero della monda," ibid.; Landmann, "Alle organizzazioni proletarie del vercellese," ibid., June 13, 1908, p. 2; "L'Associazione di cartone," ibid., p. 1.

80. "A Ronsecco ed Olcenengo," ibid. The boycott was a widespread labor tactic in the Po valley.

81. "Le otto ore vinte a Pezzana e ai Cappuccini," ibid.

82. "La nostra vittoria," ibid., June 20, 1908, p. 1.

83. Landmann, "Alle organizzazioni proletarie del Vercellese," ibid., June 13, 1908, p. 2; S. G. "Solidarità. Casanova Elvo," ibid.

84. "La cronaca degli scioperi," *Cronache vercellesi*, p. 75.

85. "Il cerchio si chiude," *La Risaia*, March 6, 1909, pp. 1–2.

86. "Dove si lavora otto ore," *Il Contadino*, June 26, 1908, p. 1; "Mede," ibid., p. 2; "Pieve del Cairo" and "La legge sulla risaia," ibid., July 24, 1908, p. 1.

87. "Ottobiano," *Il Contadino*, June 5, 1908, p. 2; "Balossa Bigli," ibid., June 19, 1908, p. 2; "Sartirana," ibid., July 3, 1908, p. 2; "Garlasco," ibid., Dec. 8, 1908, p. 3.

88. "La legge sulla risaia," ibid., July 10, 1908, p. 2; "Alla vigilia del Congresso," ibid., Jan. 15, 1909, p. 1.

89. Argentina Altobelli, "Federazione Nazionale Lavoratori della Terra. Per le mondine emigranti nelle provincie di Novara e Pavia," *La Risaia*, May 30, 1908, p. 2; "Trino," ibid., June 20, 1908, p. 2.

90. "La grande questione degli orari in risaia," ibid., Aug. 8, 1908, pp. 1–2; "Ancora dei riposi in risaia," ibid., Sept. 12, 1908, pp. 1–2; "Le risposte pervenute dalle Leghe," ibid., Sept. 12, 1908, p. 3; "Sempre in torno ai riposi," ibid., Sept. 26, 1908, p. 1; "La diplomazia in risaia. A proposito dei riposi," ibid., Oct. 17, 1908, p. 1; "Ai lavoratori della risaia," *Il Lavoratore*, Nov. 14, 1908, p. 1; "Il Regolamento Provinciale per la risicoltura," *Il Contadino*, Nov. 20, 1908, p. 1.

91. "Gli igienisti danno ragione alla 'Risaia,'" *La Risaia*, Oct. 17, 1908, p. 1.

92. See, for example, "Il regolamento delle risaie in Consiglio," *La Plebe*, Feb. 12, 1909, p. 1.

93. "Consiglio Superiore del Lavoro," *La Risaia*, June 19, p. 2.

94. "La legge sulle risaie affamatrice dei contadini," ibid., June 27, 1908, p. 1.

95. "Il comizio di domenica," ibid., July 4, 1908, pp. 1–2.

96. "Teoria e pratica," ibid., July 11, 1908, p. 2; Modesto Cugnolio, "L'idea di Cugnolio," ibid., July 11, 1908, p. 1.

97. Ibid.

98. "Intorno alla legge sulle risaie," ibid., July 18, 1908, p. 1.

99. "Posizione equivoca," *Il Lavoratore*, July 4, 1908, p. 1.

100. "Teoria e pratica," *La Risaia*, July 4, 1908, p. 2; "Sono decisamente contrario," ibid. See also Detti, *Fabrizio Maffi*, pp. 131–132, and Soave, "Socialismo e socialisti," p. 203.

101. Gavroche, "Un contradittorio a proposito della legge sulla risicoltura," *Il Lavoratore*, Aug. 1, 1908, p. 1.

102. "Intorno alla legge sulle risaie," *La Risaia*, July 18, 1908, p. 1. See also "In risaia. Il martirio dei nostri bambini," ibid., June 26, 1909, p. 1; A. Gionino, "In risaia. I figli della strada," ibid., July 17, 1909, p. 2.

103. Modesto Cugnolio, "Socialisti per ridere," ibid., Aug. 1, 1908, p. 1.

104. Modesto Cugnolio, "Una vittoria dei contadini vercellesi proclamata in un documento ufficiale," *Critica Sociale*, 12, no. 24 (Dec. 16, 1912), 376–77. For more information about Cugnolio, see ACS, Ministero dell'Interno, Casellario Politico Centrale, Dossier 1555; for Egisto Cagnoni and Luigi Montemartini, see respectively, Dossiers 932 and 3373. See also their biographies in *Il Movimento operaio italiano. Dizionario biografico*, 4 vols. (Rome: Editori Riuniti, 1978). Enrico Ferri formed the integralist bloc in 1904 in order to avoid a split between the reformist and the revolutionary socialists. In the Vercellese, Fabrizio Maffi, the physician who had set up the first socialist organizations in Bianzè in 1894, shared Cugnolio's integralist ideas. See Detti, *Fabrizio Maffi*, pp. 127 and 136; Procacci, *La lotta di classe*, pp. 311–12.

105. "La diplomazia in risaia. A proposito dei riposi," *La Risaia*, Oct. 17, 1908, p. 2; "Non ci sono leggi per il lavoro," ibid., March 26, 1910, p. 1.

106. "La mondatura dei risi nelle nostre campagne," ibid., April 17, 1909, p. 1.

107. "Congresso per le modificazioni alla legge sulle risaie. Garlasco 9 maggio 1909," *Il Contadino*, May 21, 1909, pp. 1–2.

108. Italy, *Atti del Parlamento Italiano, Discussioni* (Camera dei Deputati), 23rd Legislative session (1909–13), March 11, 1912, vol. 15, p. 17,859. On the issue of European farm workers' internal migrations, see Pasquale Villani, "Campagne," in *La dimensione continentale*, in Gian Carlo Jocteau and Nicola Tranfaglia, eds., vol. 4 of *Storia d'Europa*, Bruno Buongiovanni, ed. (Florence: La Nuova Italia, 1980–81), 1448; and Italy, MAIC, *Bollettino dell'Ufficio del Lavoro*, Supplemento, no. 16 (Rome: Officina Poligrafica Italiana, 1912), pp. 18, 36, and 43–45.

109. Zangheri, *Lotte agrarie*, pp. xliii and 193.

110. "A proposito di immigrazione in risaia," *La Risaia*, Nov. 1, 1908, p. 2; "Il Congresso dei risaiuoli di Piacenza," ibid., Nov. 14, 1908, p. 1.

111. "Per la prossima monda," ibid., Jan. 16, 1909, p. 1; "Quello che si sta facendo nei paesi donde ci vengono i mondarisi forestieri," ibid., Feb. 6, 1909, p. 1; "Il pomo della discordia," *Il Contadino*, March 19, 1909, p. 1. See also Soave, "Socialismo e socialisti," p. 199.

112. "La mondatura dei risi nelle nostre campagne," *La Risaia*, April 17, 1909.

113. Egisto Cagnoni, "La legge sulla riasia," *Il Contadino*, March 26, 1908, pp. 1–2; "La legge sulla risaia," ibid., July 3, 1908, p. 2.

114. Idomeneo Barbadoro, *Storia del sindacalismo italiano dalla nascita al fascismo;* I, *La Federterra* (Florence: La Nuova Italia, 1973), pp. 188 and 215–20; Argentina Altobelli, Relazione al III congresso, in Zangheri, *Lotte agrarie,* pp. 167–68.

115. "L'emigrazione dei mondarisi in Lomellina", *Il Contadino*, March 17, 1911, p. 1; "Il Congresso di Bologna," *La Risaia*, April 10, 1909, pp. 1–2; "Il fiasco padronale," *Il Contadino*, April 9, 1909, p. 1.

116. See, for example, "Il Segretariato per le migrazioni interne nell'anno 1906," *L'Umanitaria*, 3, no. 27 (March-April 1907), p. 1.

117. "Lo sciopero nei paesi," *La Risaia*, June 10, 1909, p. 1.

118. "Trattative cogli agricoltori in Municipio," ibid., Jan. 23, 1909, p. 1.

119. "Le tariffe di lavoro per il 1909. La rottura delle trattative," ibid., Jan. 30, 1909, p. 2; "L'Associazione degli Agricoltori ha parlato," ibid., Feb. 20, 1909, pp. 1–2.

120. "Il nuovo fallimento delle trattative per le otto ore di monda," ibid., April 24, 1909, p. 1.

121. "Contadini!" ibid., May 8, 1909, p. 1.

122. "Lo sciopero per le 8 ore nella monda" (May 22–23), *Cronache vercellesi,* p. 81; "Agitazioni e scioperi," *Il Contadino*, May 28, 1909, p. 1; "Agitazioni e scioperi," ibid., June 4, 1909, p. 1.

123. "La cronaca degli scioperi" (May 28), *Cronache vercellesi,* pp. 82–83.

124. "La giunta municipale," *Cronache vercellesi,* p. 83.

125. "La giornata di ieri"; "Il Prefetto di Novara. Le trattative in sotto-prefettura"; "Il comizio alla Casa del Popolo"; and "Gli arresti," ibid., p. 84.

126. "La cronaca degli scioperi," ibid., p. 85.

127. "Alla Camera del Lavoro," ibid., p. 86.

128. "Per una Cooperativa Metallurgica," *La Risaia*, March 27, 1909, p. 3.

129. "31 maggio. Raggiunto l'accordo per le ore 8,30, con l'impegno delle 8 ore per il 1910," ibid., pp. 86–87.

130. "31 maggio. Raggiunto l'accordo," ibid., p. 87.

131. "I mondarisi," *La Plebe*, June 4, 1909, p. 1.

132. "Constatazioni," *Il Contadino*, Aug. 13, 1909, p. 1.

133. "Il sussidio alla Camera del Lavoro," *La Risaia*, March 10, 1910, p. 1.

134. "L'Associazione degli Agricoltori ha parlato" and "Il prefetto di Novara," ibid., Feb. 20, 1909, pp. 1–2; "Lavoratori del Vercellese!" ibid., March 6, 1909, p. 1; "Il cerchio si chiude," ibid.; "Dopo le elezioni," ibid., March 27, 1909, p. 2.

135. "La grande vittoria di Vercelli," ibid., May 22, p. 2.

136. "Alle leghe e Circoli dei lavoratori della terra," *Il Lavoratore*, Nov. 6, 1909, p. 2; "Congresso dei lavoratori della terra," *La Risaia*, Nov. 6, 1909, p. 2.

137. "L'assemblea della FRAP," ibid., Dec. 11, 1909, p. 1; "Pei lavoratori delle risaie," *La Plebe*, Dec. 10, 1909, p. 1.

138. "VIII Congresso dei Lavoratori Lomellini. Mortara 15 maggio 1910," *Il Contadino*, May 18, 1910, pp. 1–2.

139. "Per la monda futura," *La Risaia*, Oct. 15, 1910, p. 1; "Per il contratto di risaia," *Il Contadino*, Dec. 23, 1910, p. 2.

140. "L'eterna questione," *La Risaia*, Dec. 24, 1910, p. 1.

141. "L'emigrazione dei mondarisi in Lomellina," *Il Contadino*, March 17, 1911, p. 1. "IV Congresso Nazionale di lavoratori della terra," *La Risaia*, March 11, 1911, p. 1.

142. Modesto Cugnolio, "L'emigrazione nelle risaie del Vercellese," ibid., April 9, 1910, p. 1.

143. Modesto Cugnolio, "L'emigrazione nelle risaie del Vercellese," ibid., April 9, 1910, p. 1. Figures of wages for the different types of squads can be seen in "La monda del riso nel Vercellese," ibid., May 14, 1910, p. 1. See also Detti, *Fabrizio Maffi*, pp. 127–31.

144. "In provincia. Il convegno per la monda del riso," *La Plebe*, Jan. 27, 1912, p. 1.

145. Ernesto Ragionieri, *La storia politica e sociale*, 1905–6; on unemployment and industrial development, see Luciano Cafagna, "The Industrial Revolution in Italy, 1830–1914," in *The Emergence of Industrial Societies* in *The Fontana Economic History of Europe*, Carlo Cipolla, ed., vol. 4, part 1 (Sussex, England: Harvester Press, 1976), p. 322; Zangheri, *Lotte agrarie*, pp. xiv–xviii; Giorgio Porisini, *Bonifiche e agricoltura nella bassa valle padana (1860–1915)* (Milan: Banca Commerciale Italiana, 1978), pp. 184–86.

146. "Le trattative per le otto ore di monda," *La Risaia*, Dec. 18, 1909, p. 1; "Per le otto ore," ibid., Dec. 15, 1909, p. 1; "La questione della monda," Feb. 5, 1910, p. 1; "Ai mondarisi," ibid., Feb. 5, 1910, p. 1.

147. "Per la monda," ibid., Feb. 19, 1910, p. 1; "La rottura delle trattative per la monda," ibid., Feb. 26, 1910, p. 1.

148. "Monda del riso," *Il Contadino*, March 4, 1910; "La tariffa degli agricoltori per la monda," *La Risaia*, March 12, 1910, p. 1.

149. Ibid.

150. Modesto Cugnolio, "L'emigrazione nella risaia," *La Risaia*, April 9, 1910; "La monda del riso nel Vercellese," ibid., May 14, 1910, p. 1; "Il rincaro della vita," *Il Contadino*, Nov. 25, 1910, p. 1.

151. "La rottura delle trattative per la monda," *La Risaia*, May 14, 1910, p. 1; "Il patto per la monda a Vercelli," ibid., June 4, 1910, p. 1; "Salasco," ibid., June 11, 1910, p. 2; Detti, *Fabrizio Maffi*, p. 133; Soave "Socialismo e socialisti," p. 204.

152. La Lega, "In risaia," *La Risaia*, June 25, 1910, p. 2; "Attenzione," ibid., June 25, 1910, p. 1; "E la legge?" *Il Contadino*, June 17, 1910, p. 2; "Vergognosa constatazione," ibid.; "A stagione finita," ibid., July 15, 1910, p. 1.

153. Ibid.; "Robbio," ibid., July 1, 1910, p. 3.

154. "In risaia," *La Risaia*, June 11, 1910, p. 1.

155. "Ai proprietari di terreni coltivati a riso," ibid., April 23, 1910, p. 1; "Ai lavoratori della terra del Vercellese. Attenzione! Fate osservare la legge ed i regolamenti," ibid., June 18, 1910, p. 1.

156. Ibid.

157. "Lettera aperta all'on. Abbiate," ibid., Sept. 3, 1910, p. 1; "Importantissimo," ibid., Sept. 3, 1910, p. 2.

158. "La grande manifestazione di domenica," ibid., Sept. 24, 1910, p. 2.

159. Italy, *Atti del Parlamento Italiano*, *Discussioni* (Camera dei Deputati),

23. Legislative Session (1909–1913), Dec. 19, 1910, vol. 9, 11, 111–13. See also "La propaganda pratica e le contravenzioni in risaia," *La Risaia*, Oct. 1, 1910, p. 1; "Una interrogazione per le risaie," ibid., Oct. 7, 1910, p. 2.

160. "Le prime condanne per contravvenzioni al Regolamento sulle risaie," ibid., Nov. 12, 1910, p. 1; "Per la prossima monda," ibid., Feb. 18, 1911, p. 2.

161. "I pagliericci sospesi," ibid., Jan. 28, 1911, p. 1; "Consigli Communali," ibid., March 11, 1911, p. 1; Soave, "Socialismo e socialisti," p. 200; "L'ultima trovata," *Il Contadino*, Feb. 3, 1911, p. 1.

162. Italy, *Atti del Parlamento Italiano*, ibid., June 9, 1911, vol. 13, 15,438–40; "Il Consiglio Sanitario Provinciale," *La Risaia*, March 11, 1911, p. 1.

163. "La questione dei pagliericci al Consiglio Provinciale di Novara," ibid., April 8, 1911, p. 1.

164. "Le ore di riposo nella risaia," ibid., July 8, 1911, p. 2; "La monda nel Vercellese," ibid., May 21, 1910, p. 1; "Andate alla monda alle sei," *La Risaia*, June 25, 1910, p. 1. See also Soave, *"Socialismo e socialisti,"* pp. 203–4.

Chapter 7

> *La lega
> Sebben che siamo donne,
> paura non abbiamo:
> per amor dei nostri figli
> in lega ci mettiamo.
> Currà, *Canti della protesta femminile*, p. 144.

1. Francesca Socrate, "L'organizzazione padronale agraria nel periodo giolittiano," *Quaderni Storici*, 12, no. 3 (Sept.-Dec. 1977), 609.

2. Folke Dovring, *Land and Labor in Europe in the Twentieth Century. A Comparative Survey of Recent Agrarian History* (The Hague: Martinus Nijhoff, 1965), p. 3. On the issue of economic policies during the Giolittian era, see Frank J. Coppa, *Planning, Protectionism, and Politics in Liberal Italy: Economics and Politics in the Giolittian Age* (Washington, D.C.: Catholic University of America Press, 1971).

3. Colin Clark, *The Conditions of Economic Progress*, 3rd ed. (London: MacMillan, 1957).

4. Dovring, *Land and Labor in Europe*.

5. Villani, "Campagne,"

6. Ibid., p. 1449.

7. Clark, *The Conditions of Economic Progress*, pp. 277–79.

8. Dovring, *Land and Labor in Europe*, pp. 382–83.

9. Pugliese, "Produzione, salari e redditi," p. 76; "Per le risaie del Novarese," *Bollettino Federale Agrario*, Dec. 15, 1910, p. 1; Camillo Daneo, *Breve storia dell'agricoltura italiana, 1860–1970* (Milan: Mondadori, 1980), p. 95.

10. Zangheri, "A trent'anni dalle leggi di riforma fondiaria. Un commento," *Studi Storici*, 20, no. 3 (July-Sept. 1979), pp. 515–16.

11. *Atti del IV Congresso Risicolo Internazionale.* Vercelli, 5–8 novembre 1912 (Vercelli: Gallardi e Ugo, 1913), pp. 46-55.

12. Ibid., pp. 44–55.

13. Ibid., pp. 147–99, passim. See Luraghi, "Wage Labor," p. 126n.

14. Valerio Castronovo, *Economia e società in Piemonte dall'Unità al 1914*, pp. 263–68. On the interpenetration between industrial and agrarian interests in Bologna, see Anthony Cardoza, *Agrarian Elites and Italian Fascism*, pp. 136–37. On post–World War I history of rice production, see Donata Briante, "Amminstrazione e mediazione degli interessi: l'Ente nazionale risi," *L'amministrazione nella storia moderna*, nuova serie, 3, vol. 2 (Milan: Giuffrè, 1985), pp. 1513–47.

15. Zangheri, "A trent'anni dalle leggi di riforma," pp. 516–17.

16. "Note della capitale," *Bollettino Federale Agrario*, March 15–April 1, 1910, p. 2; "Confederazione nazionale agraria," ibid., June 10, 1910, p. 1. On the formation and activities of the agrarian-industrial alliance, see Cardoza, *Agrarian Elites*, pp. 180–90.

17. Cardoza, *Agrarian Elites*, p. 192. Cardoza quotes Castronovo's expression in "Il potere economico e fascismo," Guido Quazza, ed., *Fascismo e società italiana* (Turin: Einaudi, 1973), p. 54.

18. See Zangheri, *Lotte agrarie*, pp. 293–94; Italy, MAIC, *Bollettino dell'Ufficio del lavoro*, no. 17, 1911 (Rome: Officina poligrafica italiana, 1912), p. 78; "Per la prossima monda," *La Risaia*, Feb. 18, 1911, p. 2.

19. Italy, MAIC, *Bollettino dell'Ufficio del lavoro*, no. 17 (Jan.-June 1912), 78; "Il compromesso di Vercelli," *La Risaia*, May 27, 1911, p. 1; "Alla Casa del Popolo," ibid.

20. "Rive," ibid., June 17, 1911, p. 1; "Gli scioperi di Ronsecco e di Tricerro," ibid., June 10, 1911, p. 1.

21. "Per la monda del riso," ibid., Sept. 16, 1911, p. 1.

22. "Le ore di riposo nella risaia," ibid., July 8, 1911, p. 1.

23. Riccardo Bachi, *L'Italia economica nell'anno 1911. Annuario della vita commerciale, industriale, agraria, bancaria, finanziaria, e della politica economica. Anno III* (Turin: Società tipografico-editrice nazionale, 1912), p. 89; "Atti ufficiali della FRAP," *La Risaia*, Sept. 9, 1911, p. 1.

24. Bachi, *L'Italia economica nell'anno 1912. Annuario della vita commerciale, industriale, agraria, bancaria, finanziaria, e della politica economica. Anno IV* (Turin: Società tipografico-editrice nazionale, 1913), p. 155.

25. "L'ultima trovata," *Il Contadino*, Feb. 3, 1911, p. 1; Carlo Facchinotti, "La strozzatura di un regolamento," ibid., March 10, 1911, p. 1; "Le commissioni di conciliazione in risaia," March 31, 1911, p. 1.

26. "Lavoratori e lavoratrici della risaia andate ad inscrivervi in Municipio!" *La Risaia*, Feb. 11, 1911, p. 1; "Contadine alle urne!" ibid.

27. "La questione della monda," ibid., Feb. 25, 1911, p. 1.

28. "Il risultato delle elezioni del 2 Aprile," ibid., April 8, 1911, p. 1; Aiazza, "Vercelli e la Bassa," p. 178.

29. "La risaia fuori della legge," ibid., Sept. 23, 1911, p. 1; "Contadini! Attenti!" ibid., Oct. 7, 1911, p. 1; "Il lavoro della Commissione di Conciliazione in risaia," ibid., Oct. 28, 1911, p. 1.

30. Pugliese, "Produzione, salari e redditi," p. 76.

31. Facchinotti, "La strozzatura di un regolamento," *Il Contadino*, March 10, 1911, p. 1.

32. Italy, MAIC, *Bollettino dell'Ufficio del Lavoro*, no. 18 (July-Dec. 1912) (Rome: Officina poligrafica italiana, 1912), p. 67.

33. "Per la monda del riso," *La Risaia*, Sept. 16, 1911, p. 1; "Per la monda del 1912," ibid., Oct. 21, 1911, p. 1.

34. "Il problema della campagna," ibid., April 27, 1912, p. 1.

35. "Alle mondarisi di Vercelli," ibid., Oct. 28, 1911, p. 1; "Alle leghe," ibid., Nov. 4, 1911, p. 1; "Il Consiglio federale di domenica 5 corrente," ibid., Nov. 11, p. 1; "Alle leghe contadine," ibid.

36. "Per la prossima monda," ibid., Feb. 24, 1912, p. 1; "Contro i mondarisi emiliani," ibid., March 2, 1912, p. 1; "Le risaie del Piemonte e della Lomellina," ibid., April 13, 1912, p. 4.

37. "Una buona decisione," ibid., May 4, 1912, p. 1.

38. Italy, MAIC, "Dati statistici sui lavoratori delle risaie del Vercellese raccolti dall'Ufficio municipale del lavoro di Vercelli (Stagione di monda 1912)," *Supplemento al Bollettino del Ufficio del Lavoro*, no. 14 (Rome: Officina Poligrafica Italiana, 1912), p. 58.

39. "Agitazione in risaia," *La Plebe,* May 25, 1912, p. 1; "L'azione dell'on. Cabrini in difesa della legge sulla risicoltura," ibid., June 15, 1912, p. 1; "In risaia" and "Lavoro delle leghe," ibid., June 22, 1912, p. 1.

40. "Per il crumiraggio," *Il Lavoratore,* June 8, 1912, p. 2; Italy, MAIC, "Dati statistici," p. 40.

41. ACS, Polizia Giudiziaria, 1912, Scioperi 13089. Dossier 45. Associazione fra gli Agricoltori del Vercellese, Relazione del Consiglio direttivo all'Assemblea ordinaria autunnale dei Soci nell'annata 1912, p. 7. On the harvesting strike in the Vercellese, see "Sciopero generale in campagna," *La Risaia,* Aug. 24, 1912, p. 1; "La situazione dello sciopero," ibid., Aug. 31, 1912, p. 1; "Attorno all'agitazione dei mietitori," ibid.; "Il grande sciopero delle risaie," ibid., Sept. 14, 1912, p. 1; "Lo sciopero," ibid., Sept. 21, 1912, p. 1; "I processi per lo sciopero del taglio dei risi," ibid., March 22, 1913, p. 2.

42. Neppi Modona, *Sciopero, potere politico e magistratura, 1870–1922* (Bari: Laterza, 1969), pp. 79–81, 159, 163, and 168–69.

43. On the structure of the socialist party, see Degl'Innocenti, *Geografia e istituzioni del socialismo italiano, 1892–1914* (Naples: Guida, 1983), p. 155. See also "Per la conquista di un patto di lavoro agricolo," *Il Lavoratore,* June 21, 1912, p. 2.

44. "I lavoratori della terra del Novarese a Congresso," ibid., May 25, 1912, p. 2; "Agitazione per la conquista di un patto di lavoro agricolo," ibid., June 8, 1912, p. 2; "Agitazione per la conquista di un patto di lavoro agricolo," ibid., June 21, 1912, p. 2.

45. "La grande manifestazione socialista di Vespolate," ibid., Aug. 23, 1912, pp. 1–2.

46. "Per la conquista di un patto di lavoro agricolo," ibid., June 21, 1912, p. 2; "La conferenza del maestro Fietti a Trino," *La Risaia,* May 11, 1912, p. 1; "I Lavoratori della terra del Novarese a Congresso," *Il Lavoratore,* May 25, 1912, p. 1.

47. "Per la conquista di un patto di lavoro agricolo," ibid., June 21, 1912, p. 2.

48. Rax, "In risaia," ibid., May 25, 1912, p. 2.

49. Bachi, *L'Italia economica nell'anno 1911,* pp. 217–20. On price increases from 1907 on, see Rinaldo Rigola, *Storia del movimento operaio italiano* (Milan: Domus, 1947), pp. 377–83. On prices in Vercelli, see "Il vitto dei contadini," *La Risaia,* Sept. 30, 1911, p. 1.

50. Degl'Innocenti, *Il socialismo italiano e la guerra di Libia* (Rome: Editori Riuniti, 1983), p. 15.

51. Ragionieri, *La storia politica e sociale. Storia d'Italia*, 4, part 3, *Dall'Unità a oggi*, pp. 1950–51, and Richard Webster, *The Cross and the Fasces. Christian Democracy and Fascism in Italy* (Stanford: Stanford University Press, 1960), pp. 30–31. On the general strike of September 27 in Vercelli, see Degl'Innocenti, *Il socialismo*, pp. 40–42, and Detti, *Fabrizio Maffi*, p. 135.

52. Italy, MAIC, *Bollettino dell'Ufficio del Lavoro*, no. 17, p. 78; "I dormitori trappola," *La Risaia*, July 20, 1912, p. 2.

53. See for example, "La tattica turca," ibid., June 29, 1912, p. 1.

54. Italy, MAIC, "Uffici communali, mandamentali, e provinciali del lavoro esistenti in Italia al 1º gennaio 1916," Supplemento al *Bollettino dell'Ufficio del Lavoro*, no. 30 (Rome: Officina Poligrafica Italiana, 1916), pp. 81–82; "L'Ufficio Municipale del lavoro," *La Risaia*, April 13, 1912, p. 3.

55. "Federazione proletaria lomellina", *Il Contadino*, July 31, 1908, p. 2; "L'assicurazione pei lavoratori della agricoltura," ibid., Nov. 6, 1908, p. 1. See also Giovanni Pieraccini, *Le Assicurazioni contro gli infortuni in agricoltura* (Florence: L. Niccolai, 1911); now in Zangheri, *Lotte agrarie*, pp. 260–87, and Cabrini, *La legislazione sociale*, p. 159.

56. "Lire quaranta ad ogni parto od aborto non procurato," *La Risaia*, April 13, 1912, p. 2. On insurance against accidents, see also "Per l'assicurazione dei contadini contro gli infortuni," ibid., Jan. 3, 1914, p. 1.

57. See Castronovo, *La fase espansiva in età giolittiana, Storia d'Italia*, 4, part 1 (Turin: Einaudi, 1975), pp. 79–81; *Cultura e sviluppo industriale. Storia d'Italia*, Annali 4, *Intellettuali e potere*, Corrado Vivanti, ed. (Turin: Einaudi, 1981), pp. 1268–70; Giuseppe Are, "Socialismo, liberismo e capitalismo industriale nell'età giolittiana," *Critica Storica*, 8, no. 4 (July-Aug. 1969), 401–3; Jocteau, "Le origini della legislazione sociale in Italia. Problemi e prospettive di ricerca," *Movimento operaio e contadino*, 5, no. 2–3 (1982), 290, and Gaetano Salvemini, "Movimento socialista e questione meridionale," now in Manacorda, *Il socialismo nella storia d'Italia*, I:317–30.

58. Barbadoro, *Storia del sindacalismo*, I:155, and Ragionieri, *Storia di un comune socialista. Sesto Fiorentino* (Rome: Editori Riuniti, 1976), pp. 148–52 and 168.

59. Barbadoro, *Storia*, p. 180; Zangheri, *Lotte agrarie*, p. lxxix.

60. Quoted in LaVigna, "Anna Kuliscioff," p. 312.

61. Quoted in ibid., pp. 303–5.

62. Carocci, *Giolitti*, pp. 48–50; Maria Casalini, "Femminismo e socialismo in Anna Kuliscioff, 1890–1907," *Italia Contemporanea*, no. 143 (June 1981), 40.

63. Carocci, *Giolitti*, p. 67.

64. "La Risaia alla Camera dei deputati," *La Risaia*, June 15, 1912, p. 2. See also "L'azione dell on. Cabrini in difesa della legge sulla risicoltura," *La Plebe*, June 15, 1912; "La nostra Camera del lavoro e il problema della risaia," *Il Lavoratore*, June 21, 1912, p. 1.

65. Rita O. Tintori, "A proposito della legge sulle risaie," ibid., July 30, 1913, p. 1.

66. "Per modificare la legge sulle risaie," *La Risaia*, July 13, 1912, p. 1.

67. Ibid.; on the need of the law reform, see "Pei mondarisi," *La Plebe*, July 20, 1912, p. 2.

68. "I medici contro la legge delle risaie," *La Risaia*, Aug. 3, 1912, p. 1.

69. "Per modificare la legge sulle risaie," ibid., March 29, 1913, p. 2.

70. *Atti del IV Congresso Risicolo Internazionale. Vercelli, 5–8 novembre 1912* (Vercelli: Gallardi e Ugo, 1913), pp. 57–93, 104–21, and 147–78.

71. Camillo Golgi, "Bonifica umana o profilassi chininica in risaia," *Atti del IV Congresso Risicolo*, p. 202.

72. Ibid., pp. 211–22.

73. Ibid., p. 251.

74. Archivio dello Stato di Novara, Dossier 2011. Congresso risicolo dall'anno 1911–1913. *A S. E. il Presidente del Consiglio dei Ministri, Ministro dell'Interno ed a S. E. il Ministro di Agricoltura, Industria e Commercio*, Rome, Dec. 20, 1912.

75. "Per il collocamento dei mondarisi vercellesi," *La Risaia*, Jan. 4, 1913, p. 1.

76. "Attenzione," *La Risaia*, June 7, 1913, p. 1; "Contro la violazione della legge di risaia," *La Plebe*, June 7, 1913, p. 2; "Le ispezioni in risaia per la monda del riso," *Il Lavoratore*, May 29, 1913, p. 1; "Mondarisi!" *Il Lavoratore*, May 30, 1913, p. 2; "Stage!" *Il Lavoratore*, Aug. 1, 1913, p. 1; "Le contravvenzioni in risaia," *La Risaia*, July 19, 1913, p. 1; "Come è osservata la legge sulla risaia," *Il Proletario*, June 6, 1913, p. 1; Ilario Zannoni, *Ispezioni compiute in risaia durante i lavori di monda del 1913*. Estratto dal "Bollettino dell'Ispettorato dell'industria e del lavoro," vol. 6, no. 7–8, July-Aug. 1913 (Rome: Officina Poligrafica Italiana, 1914), p. 244.

77. Argentina Altobelli, "Le ispezioni in risaia per la monda del riso," *Il Lavoratore*, May 29, 1914, p. 1; Ilario Zannoni, *Ispezioni compiute in risaia durante i lavori di monda del 1914*. Estratto dal "Bollettino dell'Ispettorato dell'industria

e del lavoro," vol. 6, no. 7–8, July-Aug. 1914 (Rome: Officina Poligrafica Italiana, 1915), pp. 189–95.

78. Bachi, *L'Italia economica nell'anno 1913. Annuario della vita commerciale, industriale, agraria, finanziaria e della politica economica. Anno V* (Turin: Società tipografico-editrice nazionale, 1914), pp. vii, x, xv, and on unemployment and urban decline, see also "Perchè i disoccupati sappiano," *Il Proletario*, June 6, 1913, p. 2, and "La Libia contro l'Italia? Disoccupazione operaia e politica sociale del lavoro (Discorsi socialisti alla Camera)" *Critica Sociale*, XXIII, No. 12 (June 16, 1913), 167–85.

79. Bachi, *L'Italia economica nell'anno 1913*, p. xv.

80. "Un contratto di lavoro in risaia," *La Risaia*, April 5, 1913, p. 1.

81. "I contratti per la monda dei risi," *Il Proletario*, March 21, 1913, p. 2.

82. "Sartirana," ibid., May 30, 1913, p. 3.

83. "Valle," ibid., May 30, 1913, p. 3.

84. "Fine dello sciopero," ibid.

85. "San Giorgio," ibid., June 6, 1913, p. 3.

86. Ibid.; "San Giorgio," ibid., June 13, 1913, p. 3.

87. "Per la conquista delle otto ore," ibid., May 30, 1913, p. 2.

88. "Goido," ibid., June 13, 1913, p. 3.

89. "Lomello," ibid., June 6, 1913, p. 3.

90. "Di male in peggio," *La Risaia*, Aug. 16, 1913, p. 1; "I lavoratori delle risaie e l'Ufficio di Collocamento," ibid., Aug. 23, 1913, p. 2.

91. La Federazione Nazionale Lavoratori della Terra, "La incetta delle mondine," *Il Proletario*, May 9, 1913, p. 1.

92. Modesto Cugnolio, "Una vittoria dei contadini vercellesi proclamata in un documento ufficiale," Caracciolo, *Questione agraria e movimento socialista nella campagna*, p. 284.

93. "Il terzo Congresso provinciale socialista," *Il Proletario*, Feb. 6, 1914, p. 1.

94. Modesto Cugnolio, "Una vittoria dei contadini vercellesi," pp. 281–84. On Maffi's thoughts on univeral suffrage, see Detti, *Fabrizio Maffi*, pp. 139–40.

95. See Italy, MAIC, Ufficio del Lavoro, *Supplemento al Bollettino dell'Ufficio del Lavoro*, no. 20, 1914, pp. 7–17.

96. Ibid., pp. 148–49; Adolfo Pepe, *Storia della CGdL dalla fondazione alla guerra di Libia, 1905–1911* (Bari: Laterza, 1972), Appendix II, and *Storia della CGdL dalla guerra di Libia all'intervento, 1911–1915* (Bari: Laterza, 1971), Appendix II.

97. "Il Consiglio Federale di domenica 12 corrente," *La Risaia,* Jan. 17, 1914, p. 1.

98. "Il contratto della monda per tutto il vercellese," ibid., March 14, 1914, p. 1.

99. Zangheri, *Lotte agrarie,* p. xlv; Emilio Dugoni and Nino Mazzoni, *Gli uffici di collocamento. La loro utilità. Norme, moduli, istruzioni per l'impianto e funzionamento degli uffici* (Ravenna: La Romagna, 1910); now in Zangheri, *Lotte agrarie,* pp. 219–27; Barbadoro, *Storia del sindacalismo,* I:202–3; "Il contratto della monda per tutto il vercellese," *La Risaia,* March 14, p. 1.

100. "L'on. Cugnolio fra i contadini," ibid., May 30, 1914, p. 2.

101. Ibid.

102. La Lega, "Lo sciopero dei mondarisi a Lamporo," ibid., May 30, 1914, p. 1.

103. "L'on. Cugnolio fra i contadini," ibid., May 30, 1914, p. 2.

104. "Lo sciopero a Vinzaglio," ibid., May 30, 1914, p. 1; "Intermezzo," ibid., June 6, 1914, p. 1.

105. Un giovane socialista, "Confienza," *Il Proletario,* Jan. 17, 1914, p. 2.

106. La Lega, "Candia," ibid., Jan. 17, 1914, p. 2, and Jan. 24, 1914, pp. 2–3; La Lega, "Semiana," ibid.

107. La Lega, "Valle," ibid., Feb. 13, 1914, p. 2.

108. La Sezione Socialista, "Tromello," ibid., Jan. 24, 1914, p. 2; "Per la conquista delle otto ore," ibid., March 28, 1914, p. 2; "Gli scioperi per la conquista delle otto ore," ibid., April 11, 1914, p. 2.

109. "La vittoria dell'organizzazione. Le otto ore conquistate! Tromello," ibid., April 18, 1914, p. 2.

110. "Ottobiano," ibid., April 3, 1914, p. 2.

111. "La vittoria dell'organizzazione," ibid.

112. "Gravellona," ibid., April 11, 1914, p. 2.

113. About women competing with, and depressing men's wages, see "Valle," ibid., June 6, 1914, p. 2.

114. "Lo sciopero generale di protesta per gli eccidi proletari," *La Risaia,* June 13, 1914, p. 1.

115. "Il proletariato lomellino risorge," *Il Proletario,* June 13, 1914, pp. 2–3.

116. Degl'Innocenti, *Geografia e istituzioni,* pp. 102–6 and 122–23.

117. Degl'Innocenti, "Il comune nel socialismo italiano, 1892–1922," in Degl'Innocenti, ed., *Le Sinistre e il governo locale in Europa* (Pisa: Nistri-Lischi, 1984), pp. 24–25. See also Ernesto Ragionieri, "La formazione del programma amministrativo socialista in Italia," *Movimento operaio,* 5, no. 5–6 (Sept.-Dec. 1953), 685–749; "Lo sciopero generale di protesta," *Il Lavoratore,* July 3, 1914, p. 1.

118. Paolo Moro, "Gli asili baliatici in risaia," *Il Proletario,* July 5, 1914, p. 2; "I socialisti al Comune (Il nostro programma scolastico)," ibid., July 24, 1914, p. 2.

119. On the history of day care in Italy, see Della Peruta, "Infanzia e familia nella prima metà dell'ottocento," pp. 473–78 and 487–91; Cristina Sideri, "Asili infantili di carità: aspetti della fondazione di un'opera pia milanese," *Il Risorgimento,* 34, no. 2 (June 1982), 98–119; "Le origini degli asili infantili e l'esperienza milanese," *Studi Bresciani,* new series (May-Aug. 1984), pp. 7–19. On the Socialist Party's and worker's interest in the issue of education and child care, see Tina Tomasi, "Istruzione popolare e scuola laica nel socialismo riformista," *Scuola e società nel socialismo riformista (1891–1926). Battaglie per l'istruzione popolare e dibattito sulla questione femminile* (Florence: Sansoni, 1982), pp. 9, 16, and 18–19.

120. "Tricerro," *La Risaia,* June 13, 1914, p. 2.

121. ACS, *Polizia Giudiziaria. Scioperi,* 1914. Dossier 11415.

122. Ragionieri, *La storia politica e sociale,* pp. 1977–78.

123. "La riunione dei Sindaci del Vercellese," *La Risaia,* April 3, 1915, pp. 1–2.

124. Ibid.; ACS, Polizia Giudiziaria, 1915, Scioperi, Dossier 176.

125. Barbadoro, *Storia del sindacalismo,* II, *La CGdL,* p. 315.

126. Degl'Innocenti, *Geografia e istituzioni,* p. 30.

Chapter 8

1. Pieroni Bortolotti, *Sul movimento politico della donna. Scritti inediti,* Annarita Buttafuoco, ed. (Rome: Utopia, 1987), p. 22.

2. Karen Offen, "Defining Feminism: A Comparative Historical Approach," *Signs*, 14, no. 11 (Autumn 1988), 126–27.

3. Pieroni Bortolotti, *Sul movimento politico*, pp. 33–34.

4. Eugenio Garin, "La questione femminile (Cento anni di discussioni)," *Belfagor*, 17, no. 1 (1962), 26–27.

5. Judith Jeffrey Howard, "Patriot Mothers in the Post-Risorgimento: Women After the Italian Revolution," in Carol R. Berkin and Clara M. Lovett, eds., *Women, War, and Revolution* (New York: Holmes and Meier, 1980), pp. 245–46, 248, and 250; Annarita Buttafuoco, *Cronache femminili. Temi e momenti della stampa emacipazionista in Italia dall'Unità al fascismo* (Siena: Università degli studi di Siena, 1988), pp. 27–33.

6. On the problem of classifying the different kinds of "feminisms," see Offen, "Defining Feminism," pp. 128–34.

7. Ibid., pp. 134–36.

8. Pieroni Bortolotti, *Sul movimento politico*, pp. 33–34; Buttafuoco, *Cronache femminili*, pp. 10–13 and 41.

9. Women readers of feminist newspapers frequently requested the editors to remove their names from the subscribers' list to elude their husbands' surveillance. See Buttafuoco and Marina Zancan, eds., *Svelamento. Sibilla Aleramo: una biografia intelletuale* (Milan: Feltrinelli, 1980), p. 140.

10. Howard, "The Civil Code of 1865 and the Origins of the Feminist Movement in Italy," in Betty Boyd Caroli, Robert F. Harney, and Lydio F. Tomasi, eds., *The Italian Immigrant Woman in North America* (Toronto: Multicultural History Society of Ontario, 1978), p. 17.

11. Buttafuoco, *Cronache femminili*, p. 47.

12. Howard, "The Civil Code," pp. 14–18 and 19.

13. Maria Giuseppina Manfredini, "Evoluzione della condizione giuridica della donna nel diritto pubblico," *Società Umanitaria, L'emancipazione femminile in Italia. Un secolo di discussioni, 1861–1961* (Florence: La Nuova Italia, 1962), pp. 177 ànd 179–80.

14. Garin, "La questione femminile," pp. 28–34. On the application of the findings of the Italian school of criminological anthropology, see Gibson, *Prostitution and the State in Italy*, pp. 135–41, and Claire LaVigna, "The Marxist Ambivalence toward Women: Between Socialism and Feminism in the Italian Socialist Party," in Marilyn J. Boxer and Jean H. Quataert, eds., *Socialist Women* (New York: Elsevier, 1978), p. 164. On Benedetto Croce's opinion on feminism, see "Un'inchiesta sul femminismo," *Nuova antologia di lettere, scienze ed arti*, 5th series, 154, no. 952 (July-Aug. 1911), p. 123.

15. On Ersilia Maino Bronzini, see Buttafuoco, *Le Mariuccine. Storia di un'istituzione laica. L'Asilo Mariuccia* (Milan: Franco Angeli, 1985), and *Cronache femminili*, pp. 147–48 and passim.

16. On Altobelli, see *Il movimento operaio italiano. Dizionario biografico*, I:49–52.

17. Buttafuoco, *Cronache femminili*, p. 65.

18. Ibid., p. 245; LaVigna, "The Marxist Ambivalence," p. 151.

19. Sandra Puccini, "Alcune idee sul lavoro femminile: cultura egemonica e ideologie progressiste," in Giulietta Ascoli, ed., *La questione femminile in Italia dal 1900 ad oggi* (Milan: Franco Angeli, 1979), pp. 42 and 48.

20. Pieroni Bortolotti, *Sul movimento politico*, p. 9.

21. Ibid., pp. 35 and 213; Casalini, *La signora*, p. 101.

22. LaVigna, "The Marxist Ambivalence," pp. 155–56.

23. Ibid., pp. 148-49.

24. Buttafuoco, *Cronache femminile*, pp. 59 and 63.

25. Quoted in LaVigna, "The Marxist Ambivalence," p. 170.

26. Ibid., p. 172.

27. Pieroni Bortolotti, *Sul movimento politico*, p. 36.

28. Buttafuoco, *Cronache femminili*, p. 64.

29. Pieroni Bortolotti, *Socialismo*, pp. 96–97.

30. Pieroni Bortolotti, "Anna Kuliscioff e la questione femminile," in *Anna Kuliscioff e l'età del riformismo. Atti del Convegno di Milano, dicembre 1976* (Rome: Mondo Operaio, Edizioni Avanti!, 1978), pp. 105 and 108–11.

31. Cited in Buttafuoco, *Cronache femminili*, p. 151. Even in the post–World War II period male opposition to women's suffrage continued among some members of Italian leftist parties.

32. Ibid., pp. 189, 196–202, and 209–11.

33. Consuelo, "La donna e il suffragio universale," *Il Lavoratore*, Jan. 6, 1906, p. 1.

34. A. K., "Suffragio universale," *Critica Sociale*, 20, no. 6–7 (March 16-April 1, 1910), 82–84; "Ancora del voto alle donne. Suffragio universale a scartamento ridotto," no. 8 (April 16, 1910), 113–15; "Per conchiudere sul voto alle donne," no. 9 (May 1, 1910), 130; see also "Proletariato femminile e Partito

socialista. Relazione al Congresso socialista, 21–25 ottobre 1910," no. 18–19 (Sept. 16-Oct. 1, 1910), 273–78. Kuliscioff's arguments on universal suffrage and Turati's replies were published by *Critica Sociale* in a pamphlet: Filippo Turati, Anna Kuliscioff, *Il voto alle Donne, polemica in famiglia per la propaganda del suffragio universale in Italia* (Milan: C.S., 1910). See also LaVigna, "Anna Kuliscioff," pp. 305–23.

35. Anna Kuliscioff, "Ancora del voto alle donne," *Critica Sociale*, 20, no. 8 (April 16, 1910), p. 114; also in LaVigna, "Anna Kuliscioff," p. 310.

36. Buttafuoco, *Cronache femminili*, pp. 229–32.

37. See Bortolotti, "Anna Kuliscioff," p. 126.

38. LaVigna, "Anna Kuliscioff," pp. 320–21.

39. Libera Costa, "Il dovere della donna lavoratrice," *La Risaia*, July 21, 1906, p. 2; Wanda, "Alle risaiole," *Il Lavoratore*, Dec. 1, 1906, p. 1.

40. Una donna, "Alle donne," *La Risaia*, June 11, 1910, p. 2; Marietta Cagna, "La voce di una donna," *La Risaia*, June 3, 1911, p. 2.

41. Uno della lega, "Costanzara," *La Risaia*, June 1, 1907, p. 2. See also Pietro Dalmasso, "Alle donne," ibid., May 1, 1908, p. 2; Gino, "Donne organizzatevi," ibid., July 4, 1908, p. 2; Leonida Bissolati, "La donna operaia e la organizzazione del lavoro," *Il Contadino*, April 3, 1903, p. 1; "Ceretto," ibid., March 31, 1911, p. 2.

42. "Alle donne," ibid., Feb. 7, 1902, p. 1; "Alle donne," ibid., Feb. 28, 1902, p. 1.

43. "Per le donne," *La Risaia*, March 14, 1908, p. 2.

44. F.A.C., "Alle donne risaiole," ibid., May 28, 1910, p. 2.

45. Carlo Borgo, "Diamo una coscienza alle donne," *La Risaia*, Jan. 16, 1915, p. 2.

46. Chaughi, "La schiavitù delle donne," *Il Contadino*, March 10, 1905, p. 2.

47. "La rivoluzione in casa," ibid., March 9, 1906, p. 2. See also Lucifero, "Di chi la colpa?" ibid., March 13, 1908, pp. 1–2; Lucifero, "Organizza: tua madre, tua moglie, tua sorella," ibid., March 27, 1908, pp. 1–2.

48. "San Grisante," *La Risaia*, Feb. 16, 1907, p. 2.

49. "Congresso dei rappresentanti le organizzazioni dei Lavoratori della Terra," *Il Lavoratore*, Jan. 3, 1913, p. 1.

50. "Ceretto. Riunione femminile," *Il Proletario*, April 4, 1913, p. 2. See also Una Donna, "Alle donne," *Il Proletario*, Aug. 21, 1914, p. 3.

51. "Lomello," *Il Proletario*, June 6, 1913, p. 2.

52. "Lega contadina di Vercelli," *La Risaia*, Aug. 11, 1906, p. 2; "Ai signori propietari e conduttori di fondi del Comune di Vercelli," *La Risaia*, Dec. 29, 1907, p. 1; "Alla Camera del Lavoro," *La Risaia*, Jan. 12, 1907, p. 1.

53. "Asigliano," *La Risaia*, Aug. 18, 1906, p. 1.

54. "Lumellogno," *Il Lavoratore*, Nov. 19, 1906, p. 2.

55. "Atti ufficiali della FRAP," *La Risaia*, Dec. 8, 1906, p. 1; "Congresso Regionale dei lavoratori della risaia," *La Risaia*, Dec. 29, 1906, p. 2.

56. Un compagno, "Trino. Viva le 8 ore di lavoro!" *La Risaia*, June 10, 1911, p. 2.

57. "Cose di Trino. A quelle donne," *La Risaia*, May 17, 1912, p. 2.

58. "Carne di strettoio,", *Il Contadino*, May 29, 1902, p. 2; "Cureggio," *Il Lavoratore*, June 8, 1912, p. 1; "I preti contro i contadina," *La Risaia*, Nov. 23, 1912, p. 1; "I protettori dei crumiri," ibid., Oct. 3, 1914, p. 1; "Crumiraggio cattolico," *Il Contadino*, Feb. 5, 1904, p. 2. In 1911 Lomellina priests enlisted what the socialist organizers in that region considered strikebreakers in the Novarese highlands to disrupt a labor protest action in Sartirana. See "Le canagliate nere," ibid., March 24, 1911, p. 2.

59. Bi-gi, "Ottobiano," ibid., May 12, 1905, p. 2.

60. "Dovere presente," *La Risaia*, June 11, 1910, p. 1.

61. Ragionieri, *Storia di un comune socialista. Sesto Fiorentino*, p. 177. Degl'Innocenti, *Geografia e istituzioni del socialismo italiano*, pp. 88–92 and 99–101; Hobsbawm, *Workers: Worlds of Labor* (New York: Pantheon, 1984), pp. 33–49; Carlo Ginzburg, "Folklore, magia, religione," vol. 1 of *Storia d'Italia* (Turin: Einaudi, 1972), pp. 666–69; Arnaldo Nesti, *"Gesù socialista." Una tradizione popolare italiana (1880–1920)* (Turin: Editrice Claudiana, 1974), pp. 39–44 and 78–84.

62. "Contro la invasione. Cattolici-clericali," *La Risaia*, Feb. 16, 1907, p. 1; "Il grande convegno di Robbio Lomellina," *La Risaia*, May 8, 1908, p. 2; "Manifestazione anticlericale," *Il Lavoratore*, Sept. 17, 1909, p. 1; "L'Associazione degli Agricoltori ha parlato," *La Risaia*, Feb. 20, 1909, pp. 1–2; "Manifestazione anticlericale," *La Risaia*, Sept. 17, 1909, p. 1.

63. Hobsbawm, *Workers: Worlds of Labor*, p. 43.

64. Jane and Peter Schneider, *Culture and Political Economy in Western Sicily* (New York: Academic Press, 1976), p. 96.

65. Roger Magraw, "Popular Anticlericalism in Nineteenth-Century Rural France," in Jim Obelkevich, Lyndal Roper, and Raphael Samuel, eds., *Disciplines of Faith* (London: Routledge & Kegan Paul, 1987), p. 361.

66. G.P., "La donna," *Il Contadino*, Dec. 30, 1904, pp. 1–2.

67. Cited in Buttafuoco, *Cronache femminili*, p. 152.

68. Anna Kuliscioff, "Ancora del voto alle donne," *Critica Sociale*, 20, no. 8 (April 16, 1910), 114.

69. See Kuliscioff, "Proletariato femminile e Partito socialista," p. 278.

70. Cosetta Lazzari, "La Donna, l'Anticlericalismo e la Questione Sociale. Relazione al 2. Congresso Studentesco Anticlericale Italiano," *Il Proletario*, Aug. 8, 1913, p. 2.

71. "La donna nella vita economica e politica. Giselda Brebbia alla Casa del Popolo," *La Risaia*, Dec. 26, 1914, p. 1.

72. "La dimostrazione di domenica. La formazione del corteo," *Cronache vercellesi*, p. 28.

73. "Senza prete! Un matrimonio civile ad Olcenengo," *La Risaia*, Feb. 8, 1908, p. 1; "Ceretto," *Il Contadino*, May 12, 1911, p. 3; "Zeme," ibid., June 30, 1911, p. 3. See also Ragionieri, *Storia di un comune socialista*, pp. 180–81. On the song of Father Riva, see "Cergnago," *Il Contadino*, July 17, 1908, p. 2. According to Nesti the song became a sort of anticlerical anthem in the years 1907–1910. See his book *"Gesù socialista,"* pp. 33–34. During the weeding, the *mondine* sang a repertory that included protest songs, such as the one on the eight-hour day in 1906, old and new rice belt songs, some referring to local episodes and to traditional customs, and others imported from other regions. See Aiazza, "Vercelli e la Bassa," pp. 246–50; Emilio Tron, "Canti di mondariso della valle padana," *Il mondo agrario tradizionale nella valle padana. Atti del convegno di studi sul folklore padano. Modena, 17–19 marzo 1962* (Florence: Olschki, 1963), pp. 365–77, and Currà, *Canti della protesta femminile*, passim.

74. "San Grisante," *La Risaia*, Feb. 16, 1907, p. 2.

75. "Gravellona," *Il Contadino*, Feb. 7, 1908, p. 2; "Sartirana," ibid., April 10, 1908, p. 2; "Inaugurazione della Casa del Popolo di Tricerro," *La Risaia*, July 20, 1912, p. 2. On the functions of the People's House in a Tuscan city, see Ragionieri, *Storia di un comune socialista*, p. 183.

76. On the festivities of St. Valerio in Bianzè, see Detti, *Fabrizio Maffi*, p. 85. On Francisco Ferrer, see "Luce e tenebre," *La Risaia*, Oct. 14, 1911, p. 2; "Inaugurazione della lapide a Francisco Ferrer," ibid., Oct. 14, 1911, p. 2.

77. "Mortara. Per l'umanità offesa," *Il Contadino*, Oct. 22, 1909, p. 2.

78. "Cappuccini V. I delitti dei cappuccinati," *La Risaia*, June 4, 1910, p. 2.

79. Rosanna De Longis, "In difesa della donna e della razza," *Nuova*

Donnawomanfemme, no. 19–20 (Winter-Spring 1982), 164, 166–67, and 172–73; Susanna Bucci, "La guerra tra il pane e l'amore," ibid., 180 and 183–84.

80. Buttafuoco, *Cronache femminili,* pp. 123–25.

81. Bucci, "La guerra tra il pane e l'amore," p. 188.

82. Aiazza, "Vercelli e la Bassa," pp. 220 and 231.

83. Nuto Revelli, *L'anello forte. La donna: storie di vita contadina* (Turin: Einaudi, 1985), pp. 7, 19–21, 28, 47, 59, 256, and 476.

84. Aiazza, "Vercelli e la Bassa," pp. 220–31; and Revelli, *L'anello,* pp. 47 and 89–90. On abortion in Italy during Fascism, see Luisa Passerini, "Donne operaie e aborto nella Torino fascista," *Italia Contemporanea,* no. 151–52 (Sept. 1983), 83–109; Denise Detragiache, "Un aspect de la politique démographique de l'Italie fasciste: la répression de l'avortement," *Mélanges de L'Ecole Française de Rome. Moyen Age. Temps Modernes,* 92 (1980–1982), 691–735.

85. Una vostra vera amica, "Lavoratrici, organizzatevi!" *Il Proletario,* June 13, 1913, p. 3.

86. On the socialist debate over the family, see Puccini, "Alcune idee sul lavoro femminile," pp. 55–63. On women textile workers, see Luigi Moranino, *Le donne socialiste nel biellese (1900–1918)* (Vercelli: Istituto per la storia della Resistenza in provincia di Vercelli "Cino Moscatelli," 1984), p. 84.

87. Maxine Molyneaux, "No God, No Boss, No Husband. Anarchist Feminism in Nineteenth-Century Argentina," *Latin American Perspectives,* issue 48, vol. 13, no. 1 (Winter 1986), 123, 127, 131, and 142–43.

88. Temma Kaplan, "Female Consciousness and Collective Action; The Case of Barcelona, 1910–1918," *Signs,* 7, no. 3 (Spring 1982), 545–46.

89. Aiazza, "Vercelli e la Bassa," pp. 211 and 219. Far from being a historical artifact, weeders' conjugal relations have some common points with those of women doing industrial homework in Mexico City in the 1980s. According to a recent study, these women endure marital oppression in order not to condemn their children to a life of deprivation. For both groups of women, hard work and sacrifices remain "unrecognized or devalued." (See Lourdes Benería and Martha Roldán, *The Crossroads of Class and Gender. Industrial Homework, Subcontracting, and Household Dynamics in Mexico City* (Chicago: University of Chicago Press, 1987), pp. 156 and 160.

90. Michetti, *Udi: laboratorio politico delle donne,* pp. 93–94, 121–22, and 156–57.

91. "Semiana," *Il Contadino,* May 11, 1904, p. 2.

92. Angelica Balabanoff, "Alla moglie del proletario," ibid., Dec. 8,

1905, p. 2; "Le donne nella lega," ibid., June 6, 1906, p. 1. See also "Candia," ibid., June 10, 1901, p. 1.

93. Cesarina Ciccotti-Borelli, "Madri, spose, sorelle," ibid., Aug. 18, 1905, p. 2. See also "La donna e il socialismo," ibid., March 13, 1903, p. 2; Valentina A., "Alle madri," ibid., April 6, 1906, p. 2.

94. "Parona," ibid., June 24, 1904, p. 4.

95. "Proprietà e militarismo. Alle madri," ibid., Dec. 3, 1909, p. 1. See also Giselda Brebbia, "Alle madri!" ibid., Nov. 10, 1911, p. 2.

96. "Sartirana," ibid., Feb. 9, 1906, p. 1; "Sartirana," ibid., April 13, 1906, p. 2; "San Giorgio," ibid., July 22, 1910, p. 2; "Ferrera Erbognone," ibid., Feb. 10, 1911, p. 2.

97. "Sartirana," ibid., Oct. 19, 1906, p. 2.

98. Aiazza, "Vercelli e la Bassa," pp. 196–98.

99. "Si rammenta," *Il Contadino*, Aug. 6, 1909, p. 2.

100. LaVigna, "The Marxist Ambivalence," 177n; Buttafuoco, *Cronache femminili*, p. 245. On the new People's Houses, see "Inaugurazione della Casa del Popolo di Tricerro," *La Risaia*, July 20, 1912, p. 1; "La grande manifestazione socialista di Vespolate," *Il Lavoratore*, Aug. 23, 1912, p. 1. On these developments, see also Detti, *Fabrizio Maffi*, p. 139.

101. "Un esempio per le donne contadine," *La Plebe*, Sept. 11, 1912, p. 2.

102. "Prelevamento tessere," *Il Proletario*, April 4, 1913, p. 2.

103. "Prelevamento tessere," *Il Proletario*, Dec. 5, 1914, p. 2. Illiteracy rates for men and women went down from 37 percent in 1881 to 13 percent in 1911 in Lombardy, and from 32 percent to 11 percent between the same years in Piedmont. See Martin Clark, *Modern Italy, 1871–1982* (London and New York: Longman, 1984), p. 36.

104. "Livorno Piemonte," *La Risaia*, June 6, 1914, p. 1.

105. "Livorno," *La Risaia*, June 13, 1914, p. 2.

106. ACS, Casellario Politico Centrale, Dossier 828 (Giselda Brebbia).

107. ACS, Ministerio dell'Interno. Ufficio Riservato. Direzione Generale di Pubblica Sicurezza. Dossier 18, 1911 (Prefettura al Ministero dell'Interno).

108. "Il Congresso Interprovinciale giovanile socialista di Abbiategrasso," *Il Proletario*, April 4, 1913, p. 2.

109. "La grande manifestazione socialista di Vespolate," *Il Lavoratore*, Aug. 23, 1912, p. 1.

110. "La festa proletaria di Ferrera Erbognone," *Il Proletario*, April 11, 1913, p. 2. On Alma Dolens, see *Biographical Dictionary of Modern Peace Leaders* (Westport, Conn.: Greenwood Press, 1985), pp. 220–21.

111. "Una Sezione Socialista femminile," *La Risaia*, May 16, 1914, p. 1.

112. "La donna nella vita economica e politica. Giselda Brebbia alla Casa del Popolo," *La Risaia*, Dec. 26, 1914, p. 1.

113. Pieroni Bortolotti, "Anna Kuliscioff e la questione femminile," pp. 126–27.

114. "Donne mondarisi!" *La Risaia*, Oct. 18, 1912, p. 2; "Ronsecco," *La Risaia*, Nov. 1, 1912, p. 2.

115. "La Vittoria socialista nel Mandamento di Gravellona," *Il Proletario*, July 5, 1914, p. 2.

116. Quoted in Buttafuoco, *Cronache femminili*, p. 218.

117. Pietro Campestri, "Valle. Per le nostre donne," *Il Proletario*, June 6, 1914, p. 3.

118. Cosetta Lazzari, "La Donna," p. 2.

119. Maria Goia, "Donne, siate con noi contro la guerra!" *Il Proletario*, April 17, 1915, p. 2.

120. See Brunello Vigezzi, "Le 'Radiose Giornate' del maggio 1915 nei rapporti dei Prefetti," *Nuova Rivista Storica*, 43, no. 3 (Sept.-Dec. 1959), 313–40, and 44, no. 1 (Jan.-April 1960), 54–111; James A. Young, "The Consulta and the Italian Peace Movement," in Solomon Wank, ed., *Doves and Diplomats* (Westport, Conn.: Greenwood Press, 1978), pp. 156–58, 160, and 165.

121. "Lavoratrici dei campi!" *La Risaia*, April 24, 1915, p. 3.

122. "Desana," *La Risaia*, April 24, 1915, p. 2.

123. Ibid.

124. "La verità scotta," *La Risaia*, April 24, 1915, p. 2.

Bibliography

The sources listed here do not include information obtained during personal interviews held in Italy in July and August 1978. Maria Pia Rinaldi Mariani (*Archivio Centrale dello Stato*, Rome), Giovanni Silengo (*Archivio dello Stato di Novara*), Carmine Ziccardi (*Archivio di Stato di Pavia*), Rosaldo Ordano (Municipal Library of Vercelli), Wanda Aiazza (Vercelli), Francesca Fontana (Vercelli), and Piera Gaia (Vercelli), with their expertise and their insights into the political, social, and economic developments in the rice belt, offered me invaluable assistance.

It is necessary to emphasize the importance that local socialist and labor newspapers have in this attempt at exploring the weeders' history. Without their existence, this research would have been almost impossible. Although there are alternate sources, there are some gaps in the unpublished materials held in the rice-belt archives and in the *Archivio Centrale dello Stato* in Rome. The dossiers entitled *Polizia Giudiziaria* (Judiciary Police), and *Ministero dell'Interno. Ufficio Riservato* (Ministry of the Interior, Private Bureau) are very incomplete. They contain reports the prefects were obliged to submit to the *Direzione Generale della Pubblica Sicurezza* (General Division of Public Safety of the Ministry of the Interior) concerning strikes, protests, and resistance actions. The lacunas in these archival holdings (specifically for the provinces of Novara and Pavia) limit the researcher's access to the official version of the events through which the weeders became a visible group on the national scene.

The bibliography lists neither the authors nor the titles of articles of the rice-belt newspapers cited in the book's text and notes.

Primary Sources

Manuscript Materials

In the Italian State Archive (Archivio Centrale dello Stato), located in the EUR district of Rome, I consulted the following categories of documents:

Ministero dell'Interno. Direzione Generale, Pubblica Sicurezza, Vecchio Casellario Politico Centrale: Dossiers 828 (Giselda Brebbia), 932 (Egisto Cagnoni), 1555 (Modesto Cugnolio), and 3373 (Luigi Montemartini).

Ministero dell'Interno. Direzione Generale, Pubblica Sicurezza, Ufficio Riservato: Dossier 18, 1911.

Ministero dell'Interno. Polizia Giudiziaria, Scioperi: Dossiers 45 (1912), 158 (1913), and 176 (1915).

A second archival source was the Novara State Archive, where I consulted the following documents:

Archivio di Stato di Novara: Dossiers 78 (Biblioteca), 2011, and 2032.

Official Publications

Atti del I. Congresso Risicolo Internazionale. Novara, 17–19 ottobre 1901. Novara: Fratelli Miglio, 1902.

Atti II. Congresso Risicolo Internazionale. Mortara, 1–3 ottobre 1903. Mortara: Cortellezzi, 1903.

Atti del Terzo Congresso Risicolo Internazionale. Pavia, 27–29 ottobre 1906. Milan: Stabilimento Lito-Tipografico Giuseppe Abbiate, 1907.

Atti del IV Congresso Risicolo Internazionale. Vercelli, 5–8 novembre 1912. Vercelli: Gallardi e Ugo, 1913.

I Lavoratori delle Risaie. Inchiesta sulle condizioni del lavoro nelle risaie della Lomellina, del Vercellese e del Novarese. Giovanni Lorenzoni, chairman. Società Umanitaria, Pubblicazioni no. 5, Feb. 1904. Milan: Ufficio del lavoro, 1904.

Italy, Consiglio Provinciale di Novara, Atti.

Italy, Ministero di agricoltura, industria e commercio. "Sulla pellagra nella provincia di Pavia. Relazione della Camera di Commercio di Pavia," La pellagra in Italia. Annali, 18 (1880).

————. Direzione Generale della Statistica. *Censimento della popolazione del regno d'Italia al 31 dicembre 1881.*

————. Direzione Generale della Statistica. *Censimento della popolazione del regno d'Italia al 10 giugno 1911.*

————. *Notizie intorno alle condizioni dell'agricoltura negli anni 1878–79.*

————. *Statistica delle organizzazioni e dei lavoratori e notizie sulle organizzazioni padronali al 1 gennaio 1910.*

————. Ufficio del lavoro. *Bollettino* no. 7, Jan.-June 1907.

————. Ufficio del lavoro. *Bollettino* no. 8, July-Dec. 1907.

————. Ufficio del lavoro. *Bollettino* no. 17, Jan.-June 1912.

————. Ufficio del lavoro. *Supplemento al Bollettino,* no. 14, 1912.

————. Ufficio del lavoro. *Supplemento al Bollettino,* no. 16, 1912.

————. Ufficio del lavoro. *Supplemento al Bollettino,* no. 20, 1914.

————. Ufficio del lavoro. *Supplemento al Bollettino,* no. 30, 1916.

Italy, Ministero delle communicazioni. *Sviluppo delle ferrovie italiane dal 1839 al 31 dicembre 1926.* Rome: Tipografia Ludovico Cecchini, 1927.

Italy, Ministero dell'Interno e Ministero dell'Economia Nazionale. *La risicoltura e la malaria nelle zone risicole d'Italia.* Rome: Provveditore generale dello Stato, Libreria, 1925.

Italy, Parlamento. *Atti della Giunta per la Inchiesta agraria e sulle condizioni della classe agricola.* Stefano Jacini, chairman. 15 vols. Rome: Forzani & Co., 1881–85.

————. *Atti del Parlamento Subalpino. Discussioni* (Camera dei deputati), 2nd period, Oct. 16-Dec. 28, 1848, and 4th period, Nov. 23, 1850-Feb. 27, 1852.

————. *Atti parlamentari. Discussioni* (Camera dei deputati), 8th (1861–62), 21st (1902–4), and 23rd (1909–13) Legislative Sessions.

————. *Raccolta dei documenti stampati per ordine della Camera,* 9th Legislative Session, 1865–66.

————. *Risultati dell'Inchiesta istituita da Agostino Bertani sulle condizioni sanitarie dei lavoratori della terra in Italia.* Edited by Mario Panizza (Deputy to Parliament.) Rome: Stabilimento tipografico italiano, 1890.

Zangheri, Renato, ed. *Lotte agrarie in Italia. La Federazione nazionale dei lavoratori della terra, 1901–1926.* Milan: Feltrinelli, 1950.

Zaninelli, Sergio, ed. *Storia del movimento sindacale italiano*, vol. 1. *Le lotte nelle campagne dalla grande crisi agricola al primo dopoguerra. 1880–1921*. Milan: Celuc, 1971.

Zannoni, Ilario. *Gli Uffici di Collocamento per i contadini migranti in Italia*. Società Umanitaria, Milan. Segretariato per l'emigrazione interna. Imola: Cooperativa Tipografica Editrice P. Galeati, 1907.

———. *Ispezione compiuta in risaia durante i lavori di monda del 1913*. Estratto dal "Bollettino dell'Ispettorato dell'industria e del lavoro," 6, no. 7–8 (July-Aug. 1913). Rome: Officina poligrafica italiana, 1914.

Newspapers and Periodicals

Annali di Economia.

Archivio Storico Lombardo.

Bollettino Federale Agrario, biweekly newspaper of the Interprovincial Agrarian Federation.

Busca, Enzo. *L'economia risicola italiana in cento anni di cronaca*. Milan: Rizzoli, 1961.

Il Contadino, weekly of the Lomellina leagues.

Critica Sociale, biweekly organ of reformist socialists.

Cronaca del Lavoro, monthly bulletin of the Italian Federation of the Chambers of Labor and of the National Federation of Farm Workers.

Cronache vercellesi. Federbraccianti, CGIL provinciale, Vercelli, ed. (mimeographed).

L'Illustrazione italiana, conservative weekly.

Il Lavoratore, weekly organ of the Socialist Party and of organized labor in Novara.

Lega dei Contadini, Supplemento mensile del giornale La Plebe, monthly supplement of *La Plebe*, socialist newspaper of Pavia.

La Lotta di classe, Socialist Party weekly of Milan.

La Monda, weekly organ of the Vercellese leagues.

Nuova antologia di scienze ed arti.

La Plebe, socialist weekly of Pavia.

Il Proletario, socialist and labor weekly of Mortara.

La Riforma Sociale.

La Risaia, socialist and labor weekly of Vercelli.

Rivista d'Italia.

Rivista di Storia delle Scienze Mediche e Naturali.

Rivista Internazionale del Socialismo.

Spinella, Mario; Amaduzzi, Ruggero; and Petronio, Giuseppe, eds. *Critica Sociale.* 3 vols. Milan: Feltrinelli, 1959.

L'Umanitaria, Società Umanitaria monthly organ for farm workers.

Il Vessillo di S. Eusebio, Catholic weekly of Vercelli.

Books and Pamphlets

Aldini, Antonio. "Osservazioni sul discorso pubblicato per le stampe dal Marsigli col titolo 'Delle risaie e dei pessimi loro effetti.' " *Uomini e lavoro in risaia. Il dibattito sulla risicoltura nel'700 e nell'800.* Luigi Faccini, ed. Milan: Franco Angeli, 1976.

Alghisi, Gerolamo. "Memoria sui mezzi di prevenire le malattie dei coltivatori del riso." *Uomini e lavoro in risaia. Il dibattito sulla risicoltura nel'700 e nell'800.* Luigi Faccini, ed. Milan: Franco Angeli, 1976.

Anonymous. (Angeli, Luigi) "Delle risaie e dei loro pessimi effetti." *Uomini e lavoro in risaia. Il dibattito sulla risicoltura nel'700 e nell'800.* Luigi Faccini, ed. Milan: Franco Angeli, 1976.

Bachi, Riccardo. *L'Italia economica nell'anno 1911. Annuario della vita commerciale, industriale, agraria, bancaria, finanziaria, e della politica economica.* Anno III. Turin: Società tipografico-editrice nazionale, 1912.

———. *L'Italia economica nell'anno 1912. Annuario della vita commerciale, industriale, agraria, bancaria, finanziaria, e della politica economica.* Anno IV. Turin: Società tipografico-editrice nazionale, 1913.

———. *L'Italia economica nell'anno 1913. Annuario della vita commerciale, industriale, agraria, bancaria, finanziaria, e della politica economica.* Anno V. Turin: Società tipografico-editrice nazionale, 1914.

Bebel, August. *Women under Socialism.* Translated by Daniel De Leon. New York: Labor News Press, 1904.

Beloch, Karl Julius. *Bevölkerungsgeschichte Italiens.* 3 vols. Berlin: Walter de Gruyter, 1961.

Bertolini, Angelo. "Gli scioperi agricoli in Italia. Mongrafia inviata alla 'Société des agriculteurs de France' nell'occasione della Esposizione Universale di Parigi del 1900." Rome: Tipografia dell'Unione Cooperativa Editrice, 1900, in Sergio Zaninelli, ed., *Storia del movimento sindacale italiano*. vol. 1. *Le lotte nelle campagne dalla grande crisi agricola al primo dopoguerra, 1880–1921*. Milan: Celuc, 1971.

Besozzi, Giacomo. *Della risaia e specialmente di quelle del Novarese, del Vercellese e della Lomellina nei rapporti colla salute pubblica*. Turin: Tipografia subalpina di Artero e Cotta, 1857.

――――. "Della risicoltura in ordine all'igiene e all'economia." *Uomini e lavoro in risaia. Il dibattito sulla risicoltura nel'700 e nell'800*. Luigi Faccini, ed. Milan: Franco Angeli, 1976.

Bonomi, Ivanoe. *Questioni urgenti*. Genoa, 1892.

Bordiga, Oreste, and Silvestrini, Leopoldo. *Del riso e della sua coltivazione. Studio di economia rurale*. Novara: Tipografia della Rivista di Contabilità, 1880.

Brocchi, Renato. *L'organizzazione di resistenza in Italia*. Macerata: Libreria Editrice Marchigiana, 1907.

Cabrini, Angiolo. *La Legislazione sociale (1859–1913)*. Rome: C. A. Bontempelli, 1913.

Capsoni, Giovanni. *Della influenza delle risaie sulla salute umana*. Milan: Stabilimento Libraio Volpato, 1851.

Coletti, Francesco. "Dell'emigrazione italiana, 1861–1911." *Cinquanta anni di storia italiana*. vol. 8. Reale Academia dei Lincei, ed., under auspices of the Italian government. Milan: Hoepli, 1911.

――――. *La popolazione rurale in Italia e i suoi caratteri demografici, psicologici e sociale. Raccolta di studi*. Piacenza: Federazione Italiana di Consorzi Agrari, 1925.

Colombi, La Marchesa [Maria Antonietta Torrianai Torelli-Viollier.] *In risaia. Racconto di Natale*. 4th ed. Milan: Galli, 1890.

Corradi, Alfonso. *Annali delle epidemie occorse in Italia dalle prime memorie fino al 1850*. 4 vols. Bologna: Gamberini e Parmeggiani, 1856–94.

Dugoni, Emilio, and Mazzoni, Nino. "Gli uffici di collocamento. Le loro utilità. Norme, moduli, istruzioni per l'impianto e funzionamento degli uffici." Ravenna: La Romagna, 1910. Renato Zangheri, ed., *Lotte agrarie in Italia. La Federazione nazionale dei lavoratori della terra, 1901–1926*. Milan: Feltrinelli, 1960.

Ghezzo, Achille; Montanari, Giuseppe; and Sancasciani, Clemente. "Sulla coltivazione del riso in rapporto alla salubrità." *Uomini e lavoro in risaia. Il dibattito sulla risicoltura nel'700 e nell'800*. Luigi Faccini, ed. Milan: Franco Angeli, 1976.

Giardina, Giuseppe. "La malaria in risaia." *La risicoltura e la malaria nelle zone risicole d'Italia*. Italy, Ministero dell'Interno e Ministero dell'Economia Nazionale, ed. Rome: Provveditore generale dello Stato, Libreria, 1925.

Giusti, Ugo. *Caratteristiche ambientali italiane Agrarie-Sociali-Demografiche, 1815–1942*. Istituto Nazionale di Economia Agraria. Studi e monografie no. 27. Rome: Failli, 1943.

Golgi, Camillo. "Bonifica umana o profilassi chininica in risaia." *Atti del IV Congresso Risicolo Internazionale*. Vercelli, 5–8 novembre 1912. Vercelli: Gallardi e Ugo, 1913.

Gramegna, Gaudenzio. "Delle risaie e della loro influenza sull'umana salute." *Uomini e lavoro in risaia. Il dibattito sulla risicoltura nel'700 e nell'800*. Luigi Faccini, ed. Milan: Franco Angeli, 1976.

Grassi, Battista. *Relazione dell'esperimento fatto nel 1904 in Olevano (Lomellina) nel podere Dovranti, per iniziativa del Congresso Internazionale di Risicoltura del 1903*. Offprint from *L'Agricoltura Moderna*, no. 6–10 (1905).

Jacini, Stefano. *La proprietà fondiaria e le popolazioni agricole in Lombardia: Studi economici*. Milan: Borroni e Scotti, 1854.

Kuliscioff, Anna. *Il monopolio dell'uomo*. Milan: Critica Sociale, 1894.

Livi, Carlo. "Della coltivazione del riso in Italia." *Uomini e lavoro in risaia. Il dibattito sulla risicoltura nel'700 e nell'800*. Luigi Faccini, ed. Milan: Franco Angeli, 1976.

Marabini, Anselmo. *Prime lotte socialiste*. Rome: Rinascita, 1949.

Marchetti, Cesare. *Cenni storici e descrittivi circa al Canale Cavour ed ai suoi Diramatori e Subdiramatori di proprietà demaniali*. Turin: Stamperia reale della ditta G. B. Paravia e C. di I. Vigliardi, 1878.

Michels, Robert. *Il proletariato e la borghesia nel movimento socialista italiano. Saggio di scienza sociografico-politica*. Turin: Bocca, 1908.

Momo, Giovanni. "Cenni dei danni che soffre il pubblico per la troppo estesa coltivazione del riso." *Uomini e lavoro in risaia. Il dibattito sulla risicoltura nel'700 e nell'800*. Luigi Faccini, ed. Milan: Franco Angeli, 1976.

Mozzoni, Anna Maria. *La donna e i suoi rapporti sociali*. Milan: Tipografia Sociale G. Ferrari, 1864.

————. *La liberazione della donna.* Franca Pieroni Bortolotti, ed. Milan: Mazzota, 1975.

Novelli, Novello, and Sampietro, Giovanni. "La risicoltura in Italia." *La risicoltura e la malaria nelle zone risicole d'Italia.* Italy, Ministero dell'Interno e Ministero dell'Economia Nazionale. Rome: Provveditore generale dello Stato, Libreria, 1925.

Pareto, Raffaele. *Relazione a S. E. il Ministro di Agricoltura, Industria e Commercio (Luigi Torelli) sulle Bonificazioni, Risaie ed Irrigazione.* Milan: Tipografia e Litografia degli Ingegneri, 1865.

Pezza, Francesco. *Saggio di demografia storico-sanitaria di un comune risicolo d'Italia (Mortara).* Mortara: Cortellezzi, 1899.

Pieraccini, Giovanni. *Le assicurazzioni contro gli infortuni in agricoltura.* Florence: L. Nicolai, 1911. In Renato Zangheri, ed. *Lotte agrarie. La Federazione nazionale dei lavoratori della terra, 1901–1926.* Milan: Feltrinelli, 1960.

Prato, Giuseppe. *L'evoluzione agricola nel secolo XVIII e le cause economiche dei moti del 1792–98 in Piemonte.* Reale Accademia delle Scienze di Torino (Anno 1908–1909). Turin: Vincenzo Bona, Tipografo di S. M. e dei RR. Principi, 1909.

Puccinotti, Francesco. "Delle risaie in Italia e della loro introduzione in Toscana." *Uomini e lavoro in risaia. Il dibattito sulla risicoltura nel'700 e nell'800.* Luigi Faccini, ed. Milan: Franco Angeli, 1976.

Pugliese, Salvatore. *Due secoli di vita agricola. Produzione e valore dei terreni, contratti agrari, salari e prezzi nel Vercellese nei secoli XVIII e XIX.* Milan: Fratelli Bocca, 1908.

Rigola, Rinaldo. *Storia del movimento operaio italiano.* Milan: Domus, 1947.

Schiavi, Alessandro. *Per le otto ore in risaia. Inchiesta sugli scioperi della primavera del 1904.* Milan: Editore l'Ufficio del Lavoro dell'Umanitaria, 1904.

Società Umanitaria. *L'Umanitaria e la sua opera.* Milan: Cooperativa grafica degli operai, 1922.

Spolverini, Giovanni Battista. *La coltivazione del riso.* 2nd ed. Verona: A. Carattoni Stampator del Seminario Vescovile, 1763.

Visconti, Alessandro. *La pubblica amministrazione nello stato Milanese durante il predominio straniero (1541–1796).* Rome: Athenaeum, 1913.

Young, Arthur. *Travels during the years 1787, 1788, and 1789. Undertaken more particularly with a view of ascertaining the Cultivation, Wealth, Resources, and*

National Prosperity of the Kingdom of France. II, 2nd ed., n.p.: Printed for W. Richardson, 1794.

Zeviani, Gianverardo. "Il riso e il giavone." *Uomini e lavoro in risaia. Il dibattito sulla risicoltura nel'700 e nell'800.* Luigi Faccini, ed. Milan: Franco Angeli, 1976.

Articles

Colajanni, Napoleone. "Il movimento agrario in Italia." *Rivista d'Italia,* 5, no. 11 (Nov. 1902).

La Critica Sociale. "Trappola smontata." *Critica Sociale,* no. 11 (June 1, 1907).

Croce, Benedetto. "Inchiesta sul feminismo." *Nuova antologia di lettere, scienze e arti,* 154, no. 952 (July-Aug. 1911).

Cugnolio, Modesto. "Una vittoria dei contadini vercellesi proclamata in un documento ufficiale." *Critica Sociale,* 12, no. 24 (Dec. 16, 1912).

A. K. Kuliscioff, Anna. "Ancora del voto alle donne. Suffragio universale a scartamento ridotto." *Critica Sociale,* 20, no. 8 (April 16, 1910).

_____. "Per conchiudere sul voto alle donne." *Critica Sociale,* 20, no. 9 (May 1, 1910).

_____. "Proletariato femminile e Partito socialista. Relazione al Congresso Socialista, 21–25 ottobre 1910." *Critica Sociale,* 20, no. 18–19 (Sept. 16-Oct. 1, 1910).

_____. "Suffragio universale." *Critica Sociale,* 20, no. 6–7 (March 16–April 1, 1910).

Messedaglia, Luigi. "Per la storia delle nostre piante alimentari: il riso." *Rivista di Storia delle Scienze Mediche e Naturali,* 20 (Jan.-Feb. and March-April 1938).

Modigliani, Giuseppe Emanuele. "Lo sviluppo del capitalismo agrario in Italia." Gastone Manacorda, ed. *Il socialismo nella storia d'Italia,* I. Bari: Laterza, 1972.

Motta, Emilio. "Per la storia della coltura del riso in Lombardia." *Archivio Storico Lombardo,* 45th ser., 4 (1905).

Pugliese, Salvatore. "Produzione, salari e redditi in una regione risicola italiana." *Annali di Economia,* 3 (1926–27). Milan: Università Commerciale "Luigi Bocconi," 1927.

La Redazione. "Programma." *Rivista internazionale del socialismo.* 1, no. 1 (May 15, 1980).

Schiavi, Alessandro. "Due anni di agitazione proletarie." *Riforma Sociale*, 9, no. 2 (Feb. 15, 1902).

Treves, Claudio. "Debbono le Camere del lavoro diventare socialiste? A proposito di un voto del congresso dei lavoratori della terra." *Critica Sociale*, 11, no. 12 (Dec. 16, 1901).

Turati, Filippo. "Le utopie dei conservatori. La controrelazione nel disegno di legge per la risicoltura." *Critica Sociale*, 17, no. 10 (May 16, 1907).

Secondary Sources

Books and Pamphlets

Agócs, Sándor. *The Troubled Origins of the Italian Catholic Labor Movement, 1878–1914*. Detroit: Wayne State University Press, 1988.

Agosti, Aldo, and Bravo, Gian Maria, eds. *Storia del movimento operaio, del socialismo e delle lotte sociali in Piemonte*. 2 vols. Bari: De Donato, 1979.

Anna Kuliscioff e l'età del riformismo. Atti del Convegno di Milano, dicembre 1976. Rome: Mondo Operaio, Edizioni Avanti!, 1978.

Anzi, Felice. *Il movimento operaio socialisto italiano (1882–1894)*. Milan: Edizioni Avanti!, 1946.

Arbizzani, Luigi. *Sguardi sull'ultimo secolo. Bologna e la sua provincia, 1859–1961*. Bologna: Galileo, 1961.

Balboni, Enzo. *Le origini della organizzazione amministrativa del lavoro*. Milan: Giuffrè, 1968.

Barbadoro, Idomeneo. *Storia del sindacalismo italiano dalla nascita al fascismo*, I, *La Federterra*, and II, *La CGdL*. Florence: La Nuova Italia, 1973.

Benería, Lourdes, ed. *Women and Development. The Sexual Division of Labor in Rural Societies*. New York: Praeger, 1982.

———, and Roldán, Marta. *The Crossroads of Class and Gender. Industrial Homework, Subcontracting, and Household Dynamics in Mexico City*. Chicago: University of Chicago Press, 1987.

Bodo, Paolo. *Le consuetudini, la legislazione, le istituzioni del vecchio Piemonte*. Turin: G. Giappichelli, 1950.

Bortolotti, Franca Pieroni. *Sul movimento politico delle donne. Scritti inediti*. Annarita Buttafuoco, ed. Rome: Utopia, 1987.

_____. *Socialismo e questione femminile in Italia, 1892–1922*. Milan: Mazzota, 1974.

_____, "Anna Kuliscioff e la questione femminile." *Anna Kuliscioff e l'età del riformismo. Atti del Convegno di Milano, dicembre 1976.* Rome: Mondo Operaio, Edizioni Avanti!, 1978.

Bozzini, Federico. *Il furto campestre: una forma di lotte di massa nel veronese e nel veneto durante la seconda metà del'800.* Bari: Dedalo, 1977.

Braudel, Fernand. *The Mediterranean and the Mediterranean World in the Age of Philip II.* Trans. Siân Reynolds. I. New York: Harper and Row, 1972.

Brianta, Donata. "Amministrazione e mediazione degli interessi: l'Ente nazionale risi." *L'amministrazione nella storia moderna.* New series, 3, vol. 2. Milan: Giuffrè, 1985.

Brithental, Renate, and Koonz, Claudia, eds. *Becoming Visible. Women in European History.* Boston: Houghton Mifflin, 1977.

Buffa, Eusebio. *Il Canale Cavour e il progresso economico e sociale del Novarese e della Lomellina.* Associazione irrigazione Est-Sesia, Banca Popolare di Novara, Camera di Commercio di Pavia, Ente Nazionale Risi. Pavia: Editrice Fusi, 1968.

Bulferetti, Luigi, and Luraghi, Raimondo. *Agricoltura, industria e commercio in Piemonte dal 1790 al 1814.* Pubblicazione del Comitato torinese dell'Istituto per la storia del Risorgimento, nuova serie, 4. Turin: Palazzo Carignano, 1966.

_____. *Agricoltura, industria e commercio in Piemonte dal 1814 al 1848.* Pubblicazione del Comitato torinese dell'Istituto per la storia del Risorgimento, nuova serie, 4. Turin: Palazzo Carignano, 1966.

Buttafuoco, Annarita. *Le Mariuccine. Storia di un'istituzione laica. L'Asilo Mariuccia.* Milan: Franco Angeli, 1985.

_____. *Cronache femminili. Temi e momenti della stampa emancipazionista in Italia dall'unità al fascismo.* Arezzo: Dipartimento di studi storico-sociali e filosofici dell'Università di Siena, 1988.

_____. and Zancan, Marina, eds. *Svelamento. Sibilla Aleramo: una biografia intelletuale.* Milan: Feltrinelli, 1988.

Cafagna, Luciano. "The Industrial Revolution in Italy, 1830–1914." *The Emergence of Industrial Societies. The Fontana Economic History of Europe.* Carlo Cipolla, ed. Vol. 4, part 1. Sussex, England: Harvester Press, 1976.

Cameron, Ardis. "Bread and Roses Revisited: Women's Culture and Working-Class Activism in the Lawrence Strike of 1912." Ruth Milkman, ed.

Women, Work and Protest. A Century of U.S. Women's Labor History. Boston: Routledge and Kegan Paul, 1985.

Camparini, Aurelia. "Lotte sociali e organizzazioni femminili. 1880–1926." Aldo Agosti and Gian Mario Bravo, eds. *Storia del movimento operaio, del socialismo e delle lotte sociali in Piemonte.* 2 vols. Bari: De Donato, 1979.

Caracciolo, Alberto. *L'Inchiesta Agraria Jacini.* Turin: Einaudi, 1958.

————. *Il movimento contadino del Lazio (1870–1922).* Rome: Edizioni Rinascita, 1952.

————. *Questione agraria e movimento socialista nella campagna.* Mario Spinella, Alberto Caracciolo, Ruggiero Amaduzzi, Giuseppe Petronio, eds. *Critica Sociale,* 2, 3 vols. Milan: Feltrinelli, 1959.

Cardoza, Anthony. *Agrarian Elites and Italian Fascism. The Province of Bologna, 1901–1926.* Princeton: Princeton University Press, 1982.

Carocci, Giampiero. *Agostino Depretis e la politica interna italiana dal 1876 al 1887.* Turin: Einaudi, 1961.

————. *Giolitti e l'età giolittiana.* Turin: Einaudi, 1961.

Casalini, Maria. *La signora del socialismo italiano. Vita di Anna Kuliscioff.* Rome: Editori Riuniti, 1987.

Castronovo, Valerio. *Cultura e sviluppo industriale. Storia d'Italia.* Annali 4, *Intellettuali e potere.* Corrado Vivanti, ed. Turin: Einaudi, 1981.

————. *La fase espansiva in età giolittiana. Storia d'Italia,* 4, part 1. Turin: Einaudi, 1975.

————. *Economia e società in Piemonte dall'Unità al 1914.* Milan: Banca Commerciale Italiana, 1969.

————. "Il potere economico e fascismo." *Fascismo e società italiana.* Guido Quazza, ed. Turin: Einaudi, 1973.

Cipolla, Carlo. "Per la storia delle terre della 'bassa' lombarda." *Studi in onore di Armando Sapori.* Milan: Istituto Editoriale Cisalpino, 1957.

————. "Four Centuries of Italian Demographic Development." *Population in History. Essays in Historical Demography.* D. V. Eversley, ed. Chicago: Aladine, 1965.

Clark, Colin. *The Conditions of Economic Progress.* 3rd ed. London: MacMillan, 1957.

Clark, Martin. *Modern Italy, 1871–1982.* New York: Longman, 1987.

Coppa, Frank J. *Planning, Protectionism, and Politics in Liberal Italy: Economics and Politics in the Giolittian Age.* Washington, D.C.: Catholic University of America Press, 1971.

Croce, Benedetto. *La letteratura della nuova Italia. Saggi critici.* 6 vols. 4th ed. Bari: Laterza, 1957.

Cuvià, Agata; Vettori, Giuseppe; and Vinci, Rosalba, eds. *Canti della protesta femminile.* Rome: Newton Crompton, 1977.

Dal Pane, Luigi. *Economia e società a Bologna nell'età del Risorgimento.* Bologna: Zanichelli, 1969.

Daneo, Camilo. *Breve storia dell'agricoltura italiana, 1860–1970.* Milan: Mondadori, 1980.

Decleva, Enrico. "Socialismo e etica del lavoro: La Società Umanitaria." Maurizio Degl'Innocenti, ed. *Filippo Turati e il socialismo europeo.* Naples: Guida, 1985.

Del Carrià, Renzo. *Proletari senza revoluzione.* 4 vols. Rome: Sanelli, 1975.

Degl'Innocenti, Maurizio. *Geografia e istituzioni del socialismo italiano, 1892–1914.* Naples: Guida, 1983.

————., ed. "Il comune nel socialismo italiano, 1892–1922." *Le sinistre e il governo locale in Europa.* Pisa: Nistri-Lischi, 1984.

Della Peruta, Franco. *Società e classi popolari nell'Italia dell'Ottocento.* Syracuse: Ediprint, 1985.

Detti, Tommaso. *Fabrizio Maffi. Vita di un medico socialista.* Milan: Franco Angeli, 1987.

Di Scala, Spencer. *Dilemmas of Italian Socialism: The Politics of Filippo Turati.* Amherst: University of Massachusetts Press, 1980.

Dovring, Folke. *Land and Labor in Europe in the Twentieth Century. A Comparative Survey of Recent Agrarian History.* The Hague: Martinus Nijhoff, 1965.

Facchinetti, Gabriella. "La lotta di classe nelle zone risicole del novarese e del vercellese." *Braccianti e contadini nella Valle Padana, 1880–1905.* Rome: Editori Riuniti, 1975.

Faccini, Luigi. *L'economia risicola lombarda dagli inizi del XVIII secolo all'Unità.* Milan: SugarCo, 1976.

Fedeli, Ugo. *Luigi Galleani. Quarant'anni di lotte rivoluzionarie (1891–1931).* Cesena: Edizione L'Antistato, 1956.

Fields, Valerie. *Wet Nursing. A History from Antiquity to the Present.* Oxford: Basil Blackwell, 1988.

Figurelli, Michela. "Il movimento contadino nel pavese dal 1894 al 1904." *Braccianti e contadini nella Valle Padana, 1880–1905.* Rome: Editori Riuniti, 1975.

Fiorani, Adolfo. *Se otto ore vi sembran poche.* Comune di Vercelli: Assesorato alla Coltura, 1976.

Gibson, Mary. *Prostitution and the State in Italy, 1860–1915.* New Brunswick: Rutgers University Press, 1986.

Ginsburg, Carlo. *Folklore, magia, religione. Storia d'Italia,* I. Turin: Einaudi, 1972.

Hartmann, Heidi. "Capitalism, Patriarchy, and Job Segregation by Sex." Martha Blaxall and Barbara Reagan, eds. *Women and the Workplace. The Implications of Occupational Segregation.* Chicago: University of Chicago Press, 1976.

Hilden, Patricia. *Working Women and Socialist Politics in France, 1880–1914.* New York: Oxford University Press, 1986.

Hobsbawm, E. J. *The Age of Revolution, 1789–1848.* New York: Mentor Books, 1962.

―――. *Workers: Worlds of Labor.* New York: Pantheon Books, 1985.

Horowitz, Daniel L. *The Italian Labor Movement.* Cambridge: Harvard University Press, 1963.

Howard, Judith Jeffrey. "The Civil Code of 1865 and the Origins of the Feminist Movement in Italy." Betty Boyd Caroli, Robert F. Harney, and Lydio F. Tomasi, eds. *The Italian Immigrant Woman in North America.* Toronto: Multicultural History Society of Ontario, 1978.

―――. "Patriot Mothers in the Post-Risorgimento: Women after the Italian Revolution." Carol R. Berkin and Clara M. Lovett, eds. *Women, War, and Revolution.* New York: Holmes and Meier, 1980.

Kaplan, Temma. *Anarchists of Andalusia, 1868–1903.* Princeton: Princeton University Press, 1977.

―――. "Other Scenarios: Women and Spanish Anarchism." Renate Brithental and Claudia Koonz, eds. *Becoming Visible. Women in European History.* Boston: Houghton Mifflin, 1977.

Kessler-Harris, Alice. *Out to Work. A History of Wage-Earning Women in the United States.* New York: Oxford University Press, 1982.

LaVigna, Claire. "The Marxist Ambivalence toward Women: Between Socialism and Feminism in the Italian Socialist Party." Marilyn J. Boxer and Jean H. Quataert, eds. *Socialist Women.* New York: Elsevier, 1978.

Leacock, Eleanor, and Safa, Helen, eds. *Women's Work. Development and the Division of Labor by Gender.* South Hadley, Mass.: Bergin and Garvey, 1986.

Lewis, Jane. *Women in England, 1870–1950: Sexual Division and Social Change.* Sussex: Wheatsheaf Books, 1984.

Livi-Bacci, Massimo. *A History of Italian Fertility During the Last Two Centuries.* Princeton: Princeton University Press, 1977.

Lloyd, Cynthia B., ed. *Sex, Discrimination, and the Division of Labor.* New York: Columbia University Press, 1975.

Mack Smith, Denis, ed. *The Making of Italy, 1796–1870.* New York: Harper and Row, 1968.

Maddalena, Aldo de. *Prezzi e aspetti di mercato in Milano durante il secolo XVII.* Università Commerciale "Luigi Bocconi," Istituto di storia economica diretto da Armando Sapori. Serei Studi, vol. 1. Milan: Malfasi, 1950.

Madden, Janice. "Discrimination and Male Market Power." *Sex, Discrimination, and the Division of Labor.* Cynthia Lloyd, ed. New York: Columbia University Press, 1975.

Magraw, Roger. "Popular Anticlericalism in Nineteenth Century Rural France." Jim Obelkevich, Lyndal Roper, and Raphael Samuels, eds. *Disciplines of Faith.* London: Routledge & Kegan Paul, 1987.

Manacorda, Gastone. *Il movimento operaio italiano attraverso i suoi congressi (1853–1892).* Rome: Editori Riuniti, 1963.

Manfredini, Maria Giuseppina. "Evoluzione della condizione giuridica della donna nel diritto pubblico." Società Umanitaria, *L'emancipazione femminile in Italia. Un secolo di discussioni, 1861–1961.* Florence: La Nuova Italia, 1962.

Michetti, Maria; Repetto, Margherita; and Viviani, Luciana. *Udi: laboratorio di politica delle donne.* Rome: Cooperativa Libera Stampa, 1984.

Moranino, Luigi. *Le donne socialiste nel biellese (1900–1918).* Vercelli: Istituto per la storia della resistenza in provincia di Vercelli "Cino Moscatelli," 1984.

Muttini Conti, Germana. *La popolazione del Piemonte nel secolo XIX.* 2 parts. Turin: ILTE, 1962.

Nardi, Sergio. "Bonifiche e risaie nel Ravennate (1800–1860)." *Atti del II Convegno di studi Gramsciani tenuto a Roma nei giorni 19–21 marzo 1960.* Rome: Editori Riuniti, 1960.

Nejrotti, Mariella. "Le prime esperienze politiche di Luigi Galleani (1861–1891)." *Anarchici e anarchia nel mondo contemporaneo. Atti del convegno*

promosso dalla Fondazione Luigi Einaudi (Torino, 5, 6 e 7 dicembre 1919).
Turin: Fondazione Luigi Einaudi, 1971.

Neppi Modona, Guido. *Sciopero, potere politico e magistratura, 1870–1922*. Bari:
Laterza, 1969.

_____. *Carcere e società civile. Storia d'Italia, 5*, part 2, *I documenti*. Turin:
Einaudi, 1973.

Nesti, Arnaldo. *"Gesù socialista." Una tradizione popolare italiana (1880–1920)*.
Turin: Editrice Claudiana, 1974.

Neufeld, Maurice F. *Italy: School of Awakening Countries*. Ithaca: Cayuga Press,
1961.

Pepe, Adolfo. *Storia della CGdL dalla fondazione alla guerra di Libia, 1905–1911*.
Bari: Laterza, 1971.

_____. *Storia della CGdL dalla guerra di Libia all'intervento, 1911–1915*. Bari:
Laterza, 1971.

Preti, Luigi. *Le lotte agrarie nella valle padana*. Turin: Einaudi, 1955.

Procacci, Giuliano. *The Italian Working Class from the Risorgimento to Fascism.
Three Lectures*. Monograph no. 1. Cambridge, Mass., 1979
(mimeographed).

_____. *La lotta di classe in Italia agli inizi del secolo XX*. Rome: Editori Riuniti,
1970.

Puccini, Sandra. "Alcune idee sul lavoro femminile: cultura egemonica e
ideologie progressiste." Giulietta Ascoli, ed. *La questione femminile in
Italia dal 1900 ad oggi*. Milan: Franco Angeli, 1979.

Quataert, Jean H. *Reluctant Feminists in German Social Democracy, 1885–1917*.
Princeton: Princeton University Press, 1979.

Quazza, Guido, ed. *Fascismo e società italiana*. Turin: Einaudi, 1973.

Ragionieri, Ernesto. *Storia di un comune socialista. Sesto Fiorentino*. Rome: Editori Riuniti, 1976.

Ragionieri, Ernesto. *La storia politica e sociale*. Vol. 1, part 3 of *Storia d'Italia*.
Turin: Einaudi, 1976.

Revelli, Nuto. *L'anello forte. La donna: storia di vita contadina*. Turin: Einaudi,
1985.

Rizzi, Amleto. *Aspetti economici e sociali di Novara e del Novarese, 1750–1870*.
Cronistoria Novarese no. 11. Novara: Stabilimento Tipografico E. Cattaneo, 1951.

Romeo, Rosario. *Cavour e il suo tempo (1810–1842)*. Bari: Laterza, 1969.

———. *Cavour e il suo tempo (1842–1854)*. Tome I. Bari: Laterza, 1977.

Rosselli, Nello. *Mazzini e Bakounine, 1860–1872*. Turin: Bocca, 1927.

Roveri, Alessandro. *Dal sindicalismo rivoluzionario al fascismo. Capitalimo agrario e socialismo nel ferrarese (1870–1920)*. Florence: La Nuova Italia, 1972.

Salvaco, Maria Adelaide. "Riflessi parlamentari delle lotte emiliane." Renato Zangheri, ed. *Le campagne emiliane nell'epoca moderna*. Milan: Feltrinelli, 1960.

Santarelli, Enzo. *Il socialismo anarchico in Italia*. Milan: Feltrinelli, 1973.

Schneider, Jane and Peter. *Culture and Political Economy in Western Sicily*. New York: Academic Press, 1976.

Scott, Joan Wallach. *Gender and the Politics of History*. New York: Columbia University Press, 1988.

Sereni, Emilio. *Il capitalismo nelle campagne (1860–1900)*. 2nd ed. Turin: Einaudi, 1968.

Snowden, Frank M. *Violence and Great Estates in the South of Italy. Apulia, 1900–1922*. Cambridge: Cambridge University Press, 1986.

Soave, Sergio. "Socialismo e socialiste nelle campagne dal 90 alla grande guerra." Aldo Agosti and Gian Maria Bravo, eds. *Storia del movimento operaio, del socialismo e delle lotte sociali in Piemonte*. 2 vols. Bari: De Donato, 1979.

Somogyi, Stefano. *L'alimentazione nell'Italia unita. Storia d'Italia*. 5, part 1, *I documenti*. Turin: Einaudi, 1973.

Sowerwine, Charles. "The Socialist Women's Movement from 1850 to 1940." Renate Brithental, Claudia Koonz, and Susan Stuard, eds. *Becoming Visible. Women in European History*. 2nd. ed. Boston: Houghton Mifflin, 1987.

Tax, Meredith. *The Rising of the Women. Feminist Solidarity and Class Conflict, 1880–1917*. New York: Monthly Review Press, 1980.

Tilly, Louise A., and Scott, Joan W. *Women, Work, and Family*. New York: Holt, Rinehart and Winston, 1978.

Tomasi, Tina. "Istruzione popolare e scuola laica nel socialismo riformista." *Scuola e società nel socialismo riformista (1891–1926). Battaglie per l'istruzione popolare e dibattito sulla "questione femminile."* Florence: Sansoni, 1982.

Tron, Emilio. "Canti di mondariso della valle padana." *Il mondo agrario tradizionale nella valle padana. Atti del convegno di studi sul folklore padano. Modena, 17–19 marzo 1962*. Florence: Olschki, 1963.

Villani, Pasquale. "Campagne." *La dimensione continentale*. Gian Carlo Jocteau and Nicola Tranfaglia, eds. *Storia d'Europa*, 4, Bruno Buongiovanni, ed. Florence: La Nuova Italia, 1980–81.

Webster, Richard. *The Cross and the Fasces. Christian Democracy and Fascism in Italy*. Stanford: Stanford University Press, 1960.

Young, Kate; Wolkowitz, Carol; and McCullagh, Rosalyn, eds. *Of Marriage and the Market*. London: CSE Books, 1982.

Zangheri, Renato. "I moti del macinato nel bolognese." Renato Zangheri, ed. *Le campagne emiliane nell'epoca moderna*. Milan: Feltrinelli, 1960.

Zappi, Elda Gentili. "'If Eight Hours Seem Few to You. . .'. Women Workers' Strikes in Italian Rice Fields, 1901–1906." Barbara J. Harris and JoAnn K. McNamara, eds. *Women and the Structure of Society*. Durham, N.C.: Duke University Press, 1984.

Zellner, Harriet. "Determinants of Occupational Segregation." Cynthia B. Lloyd, ed. *Sex, Discrimination, and the Division of Labor*. New York: Columbia University Press, 1975.

Dissertations

Aiazza, Wanda; Fontana, Francesca; and Gaia, Piera. "Vercelli e la Bassa: evoluzione storica, economica, sociale e culturale." Diploma thesis, Scuola per Assistenti Sociali del Comune di Casale Monferrato, 1978.

LaVigna, Claire. "Anna Kuliscioff: From Russian Populism to Italian Reformism, 1873–1913." Ph. D. dissertation, University of Rochester, 1971.

Articles

Are, Giuseppe. "Socialismo, liberismo e capitalismo industriale nell'età giolittiana." *Critica Storica*, 8, no. 4 (July-Aug. 1969).

Bandettini, Pierfrancesco. "The Employment of Women in Italy, 1881–1951." *Comparative Studies in Society and History*, 2 (1959–60).

Bucci, Susanna. "La guerra tra il pane e l'amore." *Nuova Donnawomanfrau*, no. 19–20 (Winter-Spring 1982).

Bullio, Pieraldo. "Problemi e geografia della risicoltura in Piemonte nei secoli XVII e XVIII." *Annali della Fondazione Luigi Einaudi*, 3 (1969).

Casalini, Maria. "Feminismo e socialismo in Anna Kuliscioff, 1890–1907." *Italia Contemporanea*, no. 143 (June 1981).

Della Peruta, Franco. "Infanzia e famiglia nella prima metà dell'ottocento." *Studi Storici*, 20 (July-Sept. 1979).

De Longis, Rosanna. "In difesa della donna e della razza." *Nuova Donnawomanfemme*, no. 19/20 (Winter-Spring 1982).

Detriagiache, Denise. "Un aspect de la politique démographique de l'Italie fasciste: la répression de l'avortement." *Mélanges de l'Ecole Française de Rome. Moyen Age. Temp Modernes*, 92 (1980–1982).

Detti, Tommaso. "Medicina, democrazia a socialismo in Italia tra '800 e '900." *Movimento operaio e socialista*, 2, new series (1979).

Faccini, Luigi. "I lavoratori della risaia fra '700 e '800. Condizioni di vita, alimentazione, malattie." *Studi Storici*, 15 (July-Sept. 1974).

Garin, Eugenio. "La questione femminile (Cento anni di discussione)." *Belfagor*, 17, no. 1 (1962).

Giovannini, Claudio. "L'emancipazione della donna nell'Italia postunitaria: una questione borghese?" *Studi Storici*, 23, no. 2 (April-June 1982).

Jocteau, Giancarlo. "Le origini della legislazione sociale in Italia. Problemi e prospettive di ricerca." *Movimento operaio e socialista*, 5, no. 2–3 (1982).

Kaplan, Temma. "Female Consciousness and Collective Action: The Case of Barcelona, 1910–1918." *Signs*, 7, no. 3 (Spring 1982).

Kessler-Harris, Alice. "Where Are the Organized Women Workers?" *Feminist Studies*, 3, no. 1/2 (Fall 1975).

Luraghi, Raimondo. "Sulle origini del movimento contadino nella pianura padana: il Vercellese." *Nuova rivista storica*, 40 (Sept.-Dec. 1956).

————. "Wage Labor in the Italian 'Rice Belt' of Northern Italy and Slave Labor in the American South—A First Approach." *Southern Studies*, 16, no. 2 (1977).

Masini, Pier Carlo. "La giovinezza di Luigi Galleani." *Movimento operaio*, new series, 6, no. 3 (May-June 1954).

Mazzoni, Gianna. "Molinella e Giuseppe Massarenti nell'età giolittiana." *Movimento operaio e socialista*, 20, no. 4 (1974).

Mattei, Rodolfo. "La prima coscienza in Italia d'una 'questione sociale.' " *Storia e politica internazionale. Rassegna trimestrale dell'Istituto per gli studi di politica internazionale*, 21 (March 1943).

Milkman, Ruth. "Organizing the Sexual Division of Labor: Historical Perspectives on 'Women Work' and the American Labor Movement." *Socialist Review*, 10 (Jan.-Feb. 1980).

Molyneaux, Maxine. "No God, No Boss, No Husband. Anarchist Feminism in Nineteenth Century Argentina." *Latin American Perspectives*, issue 48, 13, no. 1 (Winter 1986).

Offen, Karen. "Defining Feminism: A Comparative Historical Approach." *Signs*, 14, no. 11 (Autumn 1988).

Parr, Joy. "Disaggregating the Sexual Division of Labour: A Transatlantic Case Study." *Comparative Studies in Society and History*, 30, no. 3 (July 1988).

Passerini, "Donne operaie e aborto nella Torino Fascista." *Italia Contemporanea*, no. 151–52 (Sept. 1983).

Procacci, Giuliano. "Geografia e struttura del movimento contadino della Valle padana nel suo periodo formativo (1901–1906)." *Studi Storici*, 5, no. 1 (Jan.-March 1964).

Ragionieri, Ernesto. "La formazione del programma amministrativo socialista in Italia." *Movimento operaio*, 5, no. 5–6 (Sept.-Dec. 1953).

Sideri, Cristina. "Le origini delgi asili infantili e l'esperienza milanese." *Studi Bresciani*, 5, new series (May-Aug. 1984).

————. "Asili infantili di carità: aspetti della fondazione di un'opera pia milanese." *Il Risorgimento*, 34, no. 2 (June 1982).

Simpson-Hellert, Mayling. "Breastfeeding and Human Infertility." *Bibliography Series, Technical Information Services. Carolina Population Center*, no. 9 (March 1975).

Socrate, Francesca. "L'organizzazione padronale agraria nel periodo giolittiano." *Quaderni Storici*, 12, no. 3 (Sept.-Dec. 1977).

Tilly, Louise A. "Urban Growth, Industrialization, and Women's Employment in Milan, Italy, 1881–1911." *Journal of Urban History*, 3 (1977).

————. "Paths of Proletarianization: Organization of Production, Sexual Division of labor, and Collective Action." *Signs*, 7, no. 21 (Winter 1981).

Vigezzi, Brunello. "Le 'Radiose Giornate' del maggio 1915 nei rapporti dei Prefetti." *Nuova Rivista Storica*, 43, no. 3 (Sept.-Dec. 1959), and 54, no. 1 (Jan.-April 1960).

Villari, Luigi. "Il capitalismo della grande depressione. Crisi agraria e la nuova economia (1873–1900)." *Studi Storici*, 20, no. 1 (Jan.-March 1979).

Zangheri, Renato. "Andrea Costa e le lotte contadine del suo tempo." *Movimento operaio*, 1, no. 1 (Jan.-Feb. 1955).

————. "Un dibattito sulle risaie bolognesi agli inizi della Restaurazione." *Convegno di studi sul Risorgimento a Bologna e nell'Emilia (27–29 febbraio*

1960). *Communicazioni, Bollettino del Museo del Risorgimento, Bologna,* 5 (1966).

_____. "A trent'anni dalle leggi di riforma fondiaria. Un commento." *Studi Storici,* 20, no. 3 (July-Sept. 1979).

Newspapers and Periodicals

Annali della fondazione Luigi Einaudi.

Belfagor.

Bollettino del Museo del Risorgimento, Bologna.

Comparative Studies in Society and History.

Critica Storica.

Economica e storia.

Feminist Studies.

Italia Contemporanea.

Journal of Urban History.

Latin American Perspectives.

Movimento operaio e contadino.

Movimento operaio e socialista.

The New York Times.

Nuova Donnawomanfemme.

Nuova Rivista Storica.

Quaderni Storici.

Il Risorgimento.

Signs: Journal of Women in Culture and Society.

Socialist Review.

Southern Studies.

Storia e politica internazionale.

Studi Bresciani.

Studi Storici.

Index

A

Abbiate, Mario: and Constitutional Democratic Party, 196, 197
Abiategrasso, 274
Adua, 64
Affittuari. *See* Capitalist farmers
Agrarian classes. *See* Agriculturalists
Agrarian-industrial alliance: program of, 209–10
Agrarian question: anarchists' approach to, 57–58; economic depression (1873–96) and, 57; grist tax (*macinato*) uprisings and, 56–57, 63; *Inchiesta Jacini* on, 60; Mazzinians' approach to, 57; ruling classes on, 61; Socialist Party on, 57–58, 67; Renato Zangheri on, 56–57. *See also* Social question
Agricultural workers: and collective action, xii
Agriculturalists: antilabor militancy by, 281; and Giolittian system, 204–05, 209; and industrialists, 206–07, 208, 209; loss of political power by, 207; opposition of, to Socialist Party and labor movement, 209; and protective tariff, 205; role of, in national politics, 103–104. *See also* Rice farmers

Aiazza, Wanda and collaborators, 212, 272
Albano Vercelli: mobilization in, 90
Aldini, Antonio: defense of rice farming by, 28; on sexual division of labor, 13; on weeders, 28
Alghisi, Girolamo, 36; on weeders' diseases, 31
Altobelli, Argentina, 109, 199, 225; on Federterra program, 225; and migratory weeders, 190, 197–98, 211; on women's class consciousness, 260. *See also* Federterra
America, 271
Anarchist women: in Andalusia, 121; *La Voz de la Mujer* and, 269
Ancona, 275
Angeli, Luigi: on weeders, 28, 29
Anopheles mosquitoes: and malaria, 124
Anticlerical campaign: by Socialist Party, 261, 262, 265
Anticlerical ceremonies, 264, 265
Antifeminism: in Socialist Party, 70–71
Argentina, 269
Army: intervention of, in protests, 147, 158, 159, 160, 182, 183. *See also* Carabinieri; Labor struggle; Strikes
Artioli, Santè, 157

Jesus Christ: and socialism, 119
Judiciary system: support of, to rice
    farmers, 143, 144, 145

K

Kaplan, Temma: 121, on female
    consciousness, 164
Kessler-Harris Alice, 108, 163,
    164
Killing of workers: by police, 97
Kuliscioff, Anna: as author of "Il
    Monopolio del uomo," 74; femi-
    nism of, 76; law on woman and
    child labor and, 73, 125–26; on
    reformist socialist policies, 225–
    26; separation of feminism from
    socialism by, 251, 252; on social
    Darwinism, 75; on structure of
    family, 75, 252, 269; on woman's
    emancipation, 71; on woman's
    question, 74, 76; on women and
    Socialist Party, 263–64; on wom-
    en's suffrage, 253, 254, 255. See
    also Casalini, Maria; LaVigna,
    Claire; Mozzoni, Anna Maria;
    woman's emancipation

L

Labor bureau: and Giovanni Giolit-
    ti's policies, 171
Labor conflicts: in Bianzè, 93; in
    Crova, 94; government neutrality
    in, 80; in Latium, 162; in
    Lomellina, 96, 98, 148–49; in Ot-
    tobiano, 96; in Ronsecco, 94; in
    San Giorgio Lomellina, 96, 98,
    102; in Tronzano, 93–94. See also
    Strikes
Labor inspection, 126, 183, 189,
    227, 228–29

Labor setback: for harvesters and
    threshers, 211, 215–16; in 1914,
    212
Labor struggle: and army inter-
    vention, 101; in Po valley, 279,
    280. See also Army; Carabinieri;
    Strikes
Labor tribunals (collegi di probiviri):
    for farm workers, 152
Labriola, Teresa, 249
Lamporo, 157, 235
Lanza, Giovanni: legislation on rice
    farming and, 50
LaVigna, Claire: on Anna
    Kuliscioff's feminism, 76, 252,
    253. See also Kuliscioff, Anna
Il Lavoratore, 121, 217, 227, 254
Lavoratore novarese, 64
Law on rice farming, 51–52, 177,
    179–80, 272; amendment of, 186–
    87; and labor contracts, 275; mid-
    dlemen under, 190
Law on universal male suffrage,
    231–32
Law on woman and child labor,
    125–26, 231–32, 317n; and So-
    cialist Party, 253. See also Child
    labor; Legislation on rice farming
Lawrence (Massachusetts): strike in,
    108
Lazzari, Cosetta, 264, 276
League Federation of Farm Workers
    of Lomellina, 98
League Federation of Mortara: ne-
    gotiations with Comizio Agrario,
    95–96
Leagues: xiii, 67, 84, 85; constitu-
    tion of, 308n; mixed, in
    Lomellina, 102; neutrality of, in
    religious matters, 121; in Novara,
    101; organized by radical groups,
    85; strength of, in Vercelli and
    Lomellina, 104–105; in Vercelli,
    100
Leaseholders. See Capitalist farmers

Mazzini, Giuseppe: role of "patriot mothers" according to, 246; social question and, 53; worker societies and, 54

Mazzoni, Nino, 178, 180, 198

Mede, 20, 66

Medicina: weeders' strikes in, 58–59

Men: opposition to women's organization by, 108, 109, 110; women's political education by, 257, 258–59, 261, 263, 270

Merlino, Francesco Saverio, 266; editor of *Rivista critica del socialismo*, 71

Michels, Robert, 314n; on membership to Socialist Party, 111

Middlemen, 26; abuses by, 42–43, 140; during Spanish rule, 8; elimination of, 97, 144; food provided by, 35–36; recruitment of migratory weeders by, 113, 115; social legislation and, 8; tactics employed by, 82–83

Migration of agricultural workers, 187–88, 197; Renato Zangheri on, 188

Migratory squads: abuses of, by middlemen, 42, 94, 96; from Bobbio, 96; competition of, with local workers, 169; dependence on middlemen of, 94; housing for, 36–37; interception of, by striking weeders, 193; organized by Catholic priests, 175; places of origin of, 43, 139; as strikebreakers, 94 95, 101, 157, 159–60

Migratory weeders: cooperation of, with local weeders, 176; expectations of, 21; experience of, in labor protest, 139; morality of, 29, 112–13, 139–40; organization of, 199, 201, 203; relation between local and, 43, 96–97; solidarity of, with local weeders, 148, 149, 150, 182–83; strikes by, 158, 159, 160;

unorganized, 157. *See also* Organized migratory weeders

Milan: rice farming in, 1

Mirabelli, Roberto: women's suffrage and, 253, 255

Mirandola, 157

Mobilization: of agricultural workers, xi; impact of, on women's lives, xiv; of industrial workers, xi; of weeders, 100–01, 280, 281

Modena: strikes in, 58, 61

Modigliani, Giuseppe Emanuele, 103–104

Momo, Giovanni, 36

La Monda, 117, 136, 143, 146

Monda. See Weeding

Mondariso. See Weeders

Mondatura. See Weeding

Mondine. See Weeders

Monferrato, 43; migratory weeders from, 90

Il Monopolio del uomo, 252

Montemartini, Luigi, 89, 170, 202; farm workers' organization by, 218; on weeders' working conditions, 178, 180, 181

Mortara, 66, 82, 236, 265–66, 276; sanitary statistics of, 48; farm workers' congress in, 104–105; mayor of, and weeders, 176

Motherhood, 247, 249

Mothers, and child care, 37; subsidies for, 37

Mozzoni, Anna Maria, 109, 269; polemic between Anna Kuliscioff and, 74; on family and oppression of women, 72–73, 74, 75; and Italian Workers' Party, 71; law on woman's and child labor and, 73–74; role of, in Milanese Socialist League, 71–72; on Socialist Party and woman's question, 72–73, 74, 75; woman question and, 245, 246, 247, 248–49, 251; on woman's emancipation, 71; on

education and, 83. *See also* Rural
masses; Turati, Filippo
Socialist Party National Congress: of
Bologna (1904), 146; of Modena
(1911), 255; of Rome (1900), 79, 80
Socialist Party Provincial Congress
of Pavia: and weeders' organiza-
tion, 81–82
Socialist press: on weeders, 245,
256–58, 270
Socialist program: liberal policies
and, 279
Socialist propaganda: civil liberties
and, 88, 89; enforcement of legis-
lation and, 165
Socialist Provincial Federation of
Novara: agrarian program of, 66;
foundation of, 64
Società Umanitaria (or *Umanitaria*).
See Humanitarian Society
Somogyi, Stefano: on workers'
diets, 35. *See also* Weeders, di-
etary deficiencies
Sonnino, Sidney, 154, 156
Squad leader (*capo, capisquadra*). *See*
Middlemen
Spain: rice farming in, 207–08
Spectator, 168
Spolverini, Giovanni Battista: on
weeders' work, 24, 26, 28. *See also*
La coltivazione del riso
Statuto: reform of, 171
Strikebreakers: army protection of,
146; in Lomellina, 231; right to
work of, 147; unemployed work-
ers as, 129; use of, by rice farm-
ers, 146, 147, 150; in Vercelli, 235;
and weeders' unemployment,
147
Strikes, 26, 130, 182–83, 192, 197,
310n; in Albano Vercelli, 92–93;
by anarchists in Andalusia, 165;
in Bologna, 58–59; in
Borgolavezzaro, 148; in Con-

fienza, 162; in Crescentino, 93;
decrease in number of, 111–12;
in Formigliana, 93, 147; intervention of police, carabinieri
and army in, 98; in Italy, 150;
in Lawrence (Massachusetts),
163; in Lomellina, 161, 215,
230–31, 235–37; migratory
squads thwart, 175–76, 201; by
migratory weeders, 231; in
Milan, 58–59; in Mortara, 149;
in Novara, 95; in Olevano, 149;
in Po valley, 58, 67; results of,
147, 148; in Ronsecco, 211; in
Santhià, 147, 150, 159; statistics
for, 93, 126, 187; in Stroppiana, 93; in Tricerro, 211; in
Tronzano, 91; in Vercelli, 95,
146, 158, 159, 215, 235; in Vespolate, 148; by women textile
workers, 162, 163, 164; in
Zeme, 149, 159. *See also* Army;
Carabinieri; Labor struggle
Strikers: brought to trial, 161, 167;
prison terms for, 183. *See also*
Prison terms
Stroppiana, 54, 235
Sullerot, Evelyne, 252
Superior labor council, 119, 126,
134, 144, 170, 171
Supreme sanitary council: special
commission of, 144–45
Switzerland, 271

T

Tavallini, Vincenzo, 172
"Third" (*terzo*): abolition of, 142,
144, 155; extra weeding hours or,
91
Third international rice congress,
170, 172, 177